™

BESTSELLING
BOOK SERIES

CW00687141

References Rest of Us!®

Are you intimidated and confused by computers? Do you find that traditional manuals are overloaded with technical details you'll never use? Do your friends and family always call you to fix simple problems on their PCs? Then the For Dummies® computer book series from Hungry Minds, Inc. is for you.

For Dummies books are written for those frustrated computer users who know they aren't really dumb but find that PC hardware, software, and indeed the unique vocabulary of computing make them feel helpless. For Dummies books use a lighthearted approach, a down-to-earth style, and even cartoons and humorous icons to dispel computer novices' fears and build their confidence. Lighthearted but not lightweight, these books are a perfect survival guide for anyone forced to use a computer.

> *"I like my copy so much I told friends; now they bought copies."*
> — Irene C., Orwell, Ohio

> *"Quick, concise, nontechnical, and humorous."*
> — Jay A., Elburn, Illinois

> *"Thanks, I needed this book. Now I can sleep at night."*
> — Robin F., British Columbia, Canada

Already, millions of satisfied readers agree. They have made For Dummies books the #1 introductory level computer book series and have written asking for more. So, if you're looking for the most fun and easy way to learn about computers, look to For Dummies books to give you a helping hand.

Hungry Minds™

1/01

by Don Jones, Mark D. Scott, and Richard Villars

Foreword by John Gantz
Chief Research Officer, IDC's Global Research Corporation

Hungry Minds™

Best-Selling Books • Digital Downloads • e-Books • Answer Networks • e-Newsletters • Branded Web Sites • e-Learning

New York, NY ◆ Cleveland, OH ◆ Indianapolis, IN

E-Commerce For Dummies®

Published by
Hungry Minds, Inc.
909 Third Avenue
New York, NY 10022
www.hungryminds.com
www.dummies.com

Library of Congress Control Number: 2001091992

ISBN: 0-7645-0847-4

Printed in the United States of America

10 9 8 7 6 5 4 3 2 1

1O/QZ/QY/QR/IN

Distributed in the United States by Hungry Minds, Inc.

Distributed by CDG Books Canada Inc. for Canada; by Transworld Publishers Limited in the United Kingdom; by IDG Norge Books for Norway; by IDG Sweden Books for Sweden; by IDG Books Australia Publishing Corporation Pty. Ltd. for Australia and New Zealand; by TransQuest Publishers Pte Ltd. for Singapore, Malaysia, Thailand, Indonesia, and Hong Kong; by Gotop Information Inc. for Taiwan; by ICG Muse, Inc. for Japan; by Intersoft for South Africa; by Eyrolles for France; by International Thomson Publishing for Germany, Austria and Switzerland; by Distribuidora Cuspide for Argentina; by LR International for Brazil; by Galileo Libros for Chile; by Ediciones ZETA S.C.R. Ltda. for Peru; by WS Computer Publishing Corporation, Inc., for the Philippines; by Contemporanea de Ediciones for Venezuela; by Express Computer Distributors for the Caribbean and West Indies; by Micronesia Media Distributor, Inc. for Micronesia; by Chips Computadoras S.A. de C.V. for Mexico; by Editorial Norma de Panama S.A. for Panama; by American Bookshops for Finland.

For general information on Hungry Minds' products and services please contact our Customer Care Department within the U.S. at 800-762-2974, outside the U.S. at 317-572-3993 or fax 317-572-4002.

For sales inquiries and reseller information, including discounts, premium and bulk quantity sales, and foreign-language translations, please contact our Customer Care Department at 800-434-3422, fax 317-572-4002, or write to Hungry Minds, Inc., Attn: Customer Care Department, 10475 Crosspoint Boulevard, Indianapolis, IN 46256.

For information on licensing foreign or domestic rights, please contact our Sub-Rights Customer Care Department at 212-884-5000.

For information on using Hungry Minds' products and services in the classroom or for ordering examination copies, please contact our Educational Sales Department at 800-434-2086 or fax 317-572-4005.

For press review copies, author interviews, or other publicity information, please contact our Public Relations Department at 317-572-3168 or fax 317-572-4168.

For authorization to photocopy items for corporate, personal, or educational use, please contact Copyright Clearance Center, 222 Rosewood Drive, Danvers, MA 01923, or fax 978-750-4470.

Hungry Minds™ is a trademark of Hungry Minds, Inc.

About the Authors

Don Jones: Don Jones is the President of Iridis Consulting, LLC, an independent consulting firm specializing in Microsoft products and technologies. Don is an accomplished national speaker and author, holds several industry technical certifications from Microsoft and other vendors, and writes technical education courseware for high schools and colleges. Don lives and works in an RV with his partner and four ferrets. Don is also the author of the *Microsoft .NET E-Commerce Bible*.

Mark D. Scott: Starting when he was just 11 years old, Mark has been terrorizing computers for well over 25 years. From building computers from loose parts, to programming, to wiring together networks, to developing data-centric Web-enabled line-of-business applications, he has been there and back. He is a Microsoft Certified System Administrator, Solution Developer, Database Administrator, and Trainer. He is also Comptia A+ and Network+ certified. He even schnookered a college out of a BS in computer science. He currently works as a consultant for RDA, a provider of advanced technology consulting services.

When he is not writing, speaking at conferences, or billing clients, he helps pastor Faith Covenant Church in Quakertown, PA. You can find him up front on any given Sunday, playing his bass and singing off-key.

Richard Villars: Richard Villars is Vice President of Internet and E-Commerce Research at IDC, the world's leading provider of technology intelligence, industry analysis, market data, and strategic and tactical guidance for builders, providers, and users of information technology. Richard and his team are responsible for assessing worldwide Internet adoption and e-commerce implementation patterns across vertical industries. He is a frequent author and speaker at industry and Wall Street conferences on many issues including preparing enterprises for e-business and the future of small businesses in the world of e-commerce.

Before taking over IDC's Internet and e-commerce research, Richard spent 12 years tracking the network technologies and standards that are the foundation of the Internet. He has a bachelor of science in foreign service (B.S.F.S.) from Georgetown University with a concentration in science, technology, and international affairs.

Dedication

From Don: This book is dedicated to my parents, John and Rhonda. Thanks for your support, your love, and your belief that I could do anything I put my mind to.

From Mark: I dedicate this book to my wife, Sherry. Her tolerance of my forays into doing things I can't possibly find time to do is unbelievable. She is living proof there is a God who loves me.

From Richard: To my wife, Suzanne. Thanks for your love, support, patience, and insight into the differences between "grand visions" and the real world of running a business.

Authors' Acknowledgments

From Don: I'd like to acknowledge the invaluable e-commerce knowledge I learned from the folks at NotSoldSeparately.Com, and from a former boss, Nicole Valentine. I'd also like to thank my co-authors for their hard work and great attitude as this book was written. I'd also like to thank my keyboard for its ceaseless efforts, and I promise it a rest. Really.

From Mark: I'd like to acknowledge the folks from a former employer, Micro Endeavor. Ed and John gave me the opportunity to become all I could be. I also want to acknowledge the folks at RDA. Mark and Bryan gave me the support I needed to get this written. Also, I want to thank my co-authors, without whom this book would still be a collection of track-changes outlines that never got anywhere. And without Nicole, we would never have gotten anywhere.

From Richard: I'd like to acknowledge IDC's team of analysts who do the actual work of tracking Internet and e-commerce developments in Europe, Asia, Japan, Australia, Latin America, and Canada. I also want to acknowledge the hard work of IDC's global research organization that manages the global coordination of all these regional efforts. Finally, I want to thank Rob Rosenthal and Chris Silva for all their work supporting the creation of IDC's B2B research practice.

The authors would like to thank the editors at Hungry Minds, who dedicated countless hours to this book: Nancy Stevenson, Nicole Haims, Kim Darosett, and Teresa Artman.

Publisher's Acknowledgments

We're proud of this book; please send us your comments through our Hungry Minds Online Registration Form located at www.dummies.com.

Some of the people who helped bring this book to market include the following:

Acquisitions, Editorial, and Media Development

Senior Project Editor: Nicole Haims

Acquisitions Editors: Nancy Stevenson, Jill Byus Schorr

Senior Copy Editor: Kim Darosett

Copy Editor: Teresa Artman

Editorial Manager: Leah Cameron

Permissions Editors: Carmen Krikorian, Laura Moss

Media Development Manager: Laura Carpenter Van Winkle

Media Development Supervisor: Richard Graves

Editorial Assistant: Jean Rogers

Production

Project Coordinator: Nancee Reeves

Layout and Graphics: Karl Brandt, LeAndra Johnson, Gabriele McCann, Barry Offringa, Jacque Schneider, Betty Schulte, Jeremey Unger

Proofreaders: Laura Albert, David Faust, Angel Perez, Carl Pierce

Indexer: TECHBOOKS Production Services

Special Help

Steve Bush, LD, MA, Nicole Laux, Amy Pettinella, Christine Berman, Rebecca Senninger

---

General and Administrative

Hungry Minds, Inc.: John Kilcullen, CEO; Bill Barry, President and COO; John Ball, Executive VP, Operations & Administration; John Harris, Executive VP and CFO

Hungry Minds Technology Publishing Group: Richard Swadley, Senior Vice President and Publisher; Mary Bednarek, Vice President and Publisher, Networking; Walter R. Bruce III, Vice President and Publisher; Joseph Wikert, Vice President and Publisher, Web Development Group; Mary C. Corder, Editorial Director, Dummies Technology; Andy Cummings, Publishing Director, Dummies Technology; Barry Pruett, Publishing Director, Visual/Graphic Design

Hungry Minds Manufacturing: Ivor Parker, Vice President, Manufacturing

Hungry Minds Marketing: John Helmus, Assistant Vice President, Director of Marketing

Hungry Minds Production for Branded Press: Debbie Stailey, Production Director

Hungry Minds Sales: Michael Violano, Vice President, International Sales and Sub Rights

◆

The publisher would like to give special thanks to Patrick J. McGovern, without whom this book would not have been possible.

◆

Contents at a Glance

Cartoons at a Glance

By Rich Tennant

"I'm sorry, but 'Arf', 'Berk', and 'Woof' are already registered domain names. How about 'Oink', 'Quack', or 'Moo'?"

page 7

"So far our Web presence has been pretty good. We've gotten some orders, a few inquiries and nine guys who want to date our logo."

page 75

"Just how accurately should my Web site reflect my place of business?"

page 165

OK, one of you will stay in the field, but the other one will handle clients over the Internet.

But which one?! Brad or Igor?! Brad or Igor?!

page 283

"Is this really the best use of Flash 5 animation on our e-commerce Web site? A bad wheel on the shopping cart icon that squeaks, wobbles, and pulls to the left?"

page 371

Cartoon Information:
Fax: 978-546-7747
E-Mail: richtennant@the5thwave.com
World Wide Web: www.the5thwave.com

Table of Contents

Foreword

I've been a market analyst so long that I can remember when the Internet was called Arpanet and when a browser was someone leafing through a card catalog in a library. Some days when I contemplate the change wrought by the Internet, I feel like my grandmother must have when she took her first flight. Who'd've thunk it?

But my own astonishment at the changes the Internet has brought served me well when I had to build IDC's first forecast of worldwide Internet usage and Internet commerce. I'd seen enough bogus trends, busted technologies, and flattened growth curves in my career not to get carried away by what the sages were calling *a new paradigm*. I was a meat-and-potatoes analyst . . . kind of a Harry Truman, Show-Me, I'm-from-Missouri type. My forecast would be conservative.

Back in 1996 — just two years after the Web and browsers went big time — I conducted a two-day offsite meeting for my company with some of the leading corporate users of the Internet. These pioneers included Dell Computer, FedEx, Time Warner, Sandia Labs, and others.

That's when I became a believer. Here I was, for the first time, mingling with technology pioneers and not hearing war stories about disasters. All I heard were stories about amazing application rollouts — all of which were happening in incredibly short periods of time. These were pioneers without arrows in their backs! In fact, their experiences using the Internet had taken them to the point of no return — they were, and are, fanatical advocates for rapid change in their organizations.

My cynicism fell completely away when I conducted my first studies of return-on-investment (ROI) of successful Web-based applications — the numbers came back so positive that we couldn't publish them. No one would believe them!

These experiences led me to do a very careful job when I built IDC's Internet Commerce Market Model, now in its sixth year and seventh version. The pioneers were coming back with stories of Internet commerce gold in the hills, while our surveys of companies that had yet to implement Web sites were coming back with lukewarm statistics. We did extra surveys just to make sure I wasn't crazy looking for over $100 billion in Internet commerce by the year 2000. (It actually hit $300 billion.)

The number grows every day. Over 60 percent of small companies in the United States — and 90 percent of large companies — have Web sites. About

a third of these businesses can take orders through their sites. And almost all
the larger companies I work with have a corporate philosophy that selling (or
buying) through the Web has become a competitive necessity. E-commerce is
no longer an option; it's a core requirement.

The hard part is figuring out where to begin. Should you build a separate
online store? Maybe work through existing channels? How about finding a
partner, or going overseas? Perhaps you'd rather sell to new markets only, or
to existing customers. Should you use separate pricing and a separate sales
organization? What about joining an e-marketplace?

And then there are the technical issues, including security, uptime, reliability,
privacy, and connection to business systems. Pshew!

I wish I could tell you all the easy answers. You'll find as many leading-edge
commerce sites as there are ways to implement them. Charles Schwab did
it one way, Merrill Lynch another. Sears took a certain path; WalMart took
another. My best advice is just to begin. This book is a good start. Let the
authors and experts break it down for you in plain English so that you can
get a handle on where to begin.

After that, common sense coupled with the skills and people you apply to
the task will have to take over. Don't forget to listen to your customers.
Together you will find a way to progress on a journey from which, if you're
are successful, you will never look back.

I remember listening to the head of online operations of Mars' M&M division
talk about why he took that job rather than one as head of another business
unit. One job offered him a seat in the inner sanctum of the company's power
elite, from which he could help shape the destiny of the company by committee. The other offered him a chance to run a start-up company within a
company, and, if successful, shape the destiny of the company overnight.
He took the latter opportunity.

For you, e-commerce doesn't have to mean radical overnight change. But
when you've gone a few years down the path and look back, you're likely
to find yourself saying, as I do, "Who'd've thunk it?"

John Gantz

Chief Research Officer, IDC's Global Resource Corporation

Introduction

. . . .

E-commerce! E-business! E-partnerships! E-tailing! E-suppliers! E-procurement! You know from playing *Scrabble* that *e* is the most common letter in the alphabet, but who would have thought it would be this popular?

E-commerce is all the rage in the business world these days. With the dot-com gold rush of the late 1990s, it's easy to see why, but e-commerce seems to have some staying power beyond being the business fad of the moment. And with good reason. E-commerce has made a major impact on the way businesses all over the world operate — helping them cut costs, reach new customers, increase profits, and do amazing things.

So why did we write *E-Commerce For Dummies?* Well, in the process of becoming one of the most important boosts for businesses since the Industrial Revolution, e-commerce has built up a lot of mystery and mystique. The fact that computers are involved only makes matters worse, because technical folks (like us) tend to ramble on about network protocols and encryption sockets and all the other stuff that makes the whole topic seem more confusing. So in this book, we cut through the mystery and present e-commerce as what it *really* is: a new way of thinking about businesses and customers that use technology to give businesses an incredible number of growth options.

About This Book

This book isn't meant to be read front-to-back. You can read it back-to-front, middle-front-back, odd chapters first, even chapters last, sideways, or upside-down — anything goes. Of course, we're not going to stop you if you want to read from beginning to end. In fact, you may even find that the way we organized the book is the only way to go.

You may find that skimming through the Table of Contents leads you right to the chapters that interest you, and that our handy cross-references have you jumping throughout the book answering questions as they pop into your head. Great! Use this book in whatever way you want. We've tried to make the chapter titles and headings useful so that you can spot the material you want to read at a glance.

Don't feel that you have to memorize as you're reading. You'll always be able to find the information you're looking for if you forget what a particular term means, and we've included helpful definitions every time we introduce a new e-biz term or concept.

Conventions Used in This Book

Keeping things consistent makes them easier to understand. In this book, those consistent elements are *conventions*. Notice how the word *convention* is in italics? In this book, we put new terms in italics and then define them so that you know what they mean. If we introduce a new buzzword, we attach an icon to the paragraph so that you can see it if you're skimming. (See the section "Icons Used in This Book.") When we give you URLs (Web addresses) within a paragraph, they look like this: www.dummies.com.

Icons Used in This Book

To make your reading experience easier, we use various icons in the margins of the book to indicate particular points of interest.

 Sometimes you just can't talk about e-commerce without getting a little technical. To let you know when the tech stuff is coming, we mark it with this geekie fellow so that you recognize it for what it is. If you don't care or don't want the hassle of tech talk, just skip it. We don't mind.

 Ouch! We use this icon to mark paragraphs that explain how to keep yourself and your business out of trouble. Read these and take heed, as most of our warnings come from hard-earned experience.

 Anytime that we can give you a hint or a tip that makes a subject or task easier, we mark it with this little thingie for extra emphasis — just our way of showing you that we're on your side.

 This icon is a friendly reminder or a marker for something that you want to keep in mind for later use. We also use this icon to summarize the most important piece of information about a topic before you move on.

 E-commerce just wouldn't be the same without the technical jargon. We use this icon to help you not only identify technical terms, but also quickly locate the place in the book where we define those terms. That way, you can quickly flip back through the book to refresh your memory if you need to.

Whenever we talk about different ways of accomplishing something, we often include a hit list of pros and cons to help you decide which techniques are right for your business. And we use this icon to help you quickly find these helpful lists.

We tried to fill this book with as many real-life examples as possible. Case studies are usually separated into a box with a gray background and this handy icon attached, and they're a great way to see how real e-commerce companies use the concepts and techniques we talk about.

What You Don't Have to Read

Throughout the book you find a bunch of information in *sidebars*. These are the sections of text with a gray background. Don't feel that you have to read these sections to completely understand the topic being discussed — you don't! Some sidebars give you additional background information that we think you'll find interesting. Other times, we highlight case studies that show how what we're talking about is being used in the real (well, virtual) e-business community.

Foolish Assumptions

You know what people say about assuming, but we had to make a few assumptions when writing this book. First, we assume you're familiar with doing business in general, and how traditional businesses work. Although we don't assume that you're actually running a business (or helping to run one), we definitely approach certain topics from that viewpoint. Maybe you're a manager and you just want to be able to say, "Yes sir, Mr. Bigwig, I know about CRM, ERP, and e-marketplaces." Argh. Maybe you're a business owner and want to know how e-commerce can impact and improve the way you're already doing stuff. Whatever. We address this book to you, friendly reader. Just as long as you also know the *basics* of computing, like how to surf the Web, connect to the Internet, and so on. (Here we go again with the assumptions.) We assume you've participated in e-commerce yourself, perhaps by buying a product or service from a Web site.

How This Book Is Organized

We've divided this book into parts, organized by topic. The parts take you sequentially from e-commerce fundamentals through the snarl of legal, technical, and business jargon, to the final goal: A solid understanding of what e-commerce is and how it will help your company. If you're looking for information on a specific e-commerce topic, check the headings in the Table of Contents. By design, you'll find that you can use *E-Commerce For Dummies* as a reference that you reach for again and again.

Part 1: An E-Commerce Overview: You Will Be Graded on This

In this part, we introduce you to the mad, exciting world of e-commerce. We start by defining many of the terms used in the e-commerce world (which is ridiculously full of jargon) and outlining what e-commerce is and what parts of it you should care about. This part of the book touches lightly on just about everything you need to know about e-commerce, so make sure you read this even if you skip through the rest of the book. We also use this part to call your attention to things that you may not have thought of and to start you asking the questions that we spend the rest of the book answering.

Part 11: Making the Leap of Faith: Integrating Your Business

In this part, we talk about all the exciting things that you'll need to think about in order to make your traditional business into an e-commerce powerhouse. We give you lots of suggestions and recommendations, and we try to steer you away from the mistakes that other e-commerce companies have already made. This is all business-type stuff, designed to help you position your classic business for the brave new world of e-commerce.

Part 111: Setting Up the Front End of Your Business

After you decide what kind of e-commerce you want to do (and, as you'll discover, there are *lots* of ways to do e-commerce), and after you decide how e-commerce and your classic business operations will complement one another, you'll be wondering how to actually get things up and running. That's where this part comes in. Without getting into the gory technical details that would put Bill Gates to sleep, we walk you through an overview of designing and building your business' online storefront. You'll get lots of best-practices suggestions and tips for avoiding the pitfalls that cost many e-commerce companies bundles of money.

Part IV: Dealing with the Back Office

Setting up your online storefront will delight your customers, but what about your employees and internal business processes? In this part, we talk about how e-commerce works within your company, exploring topics such as Customer Relationship Management, handling the data your new e-commerce business will collect, and much more. And we talk about the back office processes — like fulfillment and supply chain management — that support your storefront, as well as how to integrate the computer systems you already have with your new e-commerce systems.

Part V: The Part of Tens

In true *For Dummies* style, this book includes The Part of Tens. These chapters introduce lists of ten items about a variety of informative topics. Here you find additional resources, hints, and tips, plus other gold nuggets of knowledge. The Part of Tens is a resource you can turn to again and again.

Where to Go from Here

Now you're ready to use this book. Take a look at the Table of Contents and find something that catches your attention or a topic that you think can help you solve a problem. If you're still not sure where to begin, we recommend starting with Chapter 1. It's a great introduction to e-commerce, and it will help orient you with the rest of the book.

Part I

An E-Commerce Overview: You Will Be Graded on This

The 5th Wave

By Rich Tennant

"I'm sorry, but 'Arf', 'Bark', and 'Woof' are already registered domain names. How about 'Oink', 'Quack', or 'Moo'?"

In this part . . .

Get ready for the ride of your life as we dive headlong into the wonderful world of e-commerce! We introduce you to the latest terms that the techno-geeks are hurling across the Internet, show you how bricks-and-mortar businesses are latching onto the Internet as a way to improve their revenue, and introduce you to the basics of formulating an e-commerce strategy. We also introduce you to all of the unique and bizarre relationships your business can get into. From B2B to B2C to e-marketplaces, to creating partnerships to improve the efficiency of your supply chain, this part is a great place to start your e-commerce adventure!

Chapter 1

E-Commerce: Beyond the Hype

In This Chapter

▶ Understanding how e-commerce works

▶ Finding out about e-commerce technologies

▶ Planning the right strategies and systems

▶ Building e-commerce business relationships

▶ Keeping the lawyers happy (or at least busy)

Congratulations! For one reason or another, you've decided to jump into the exciting world of e-commerce! You probably have at least a general idea of what e-commerce stuff you want to do, but trust us — there are a hundred little things you probably haven't even thought of yet that will become very important to your e-commerce plan. In this chapter, we introduce you to a few of those things. And don't worry — we also tell you where to find the answers!

You may hear people talk about *www* this and *.com* that, but there's a lot more to e-commerce than adding a few choice ws and cs to your company name. In fact, e-commerce encompasses several practices that your business may already be doing, such as automating order processes or helping your employees control shipping through the Internet. Also, plenty of companies work behind the scenes doing things that you're probably used to in the bricks-and-mortar world (the world outside the Internet), such as controlling inventory and processing payments. That's because the *e* in *e*-commerce stands for *electronic*. That's right, Edison — electronic.

We're not saying that just because something is as common as electricity that it's easy to use. We're just saying that if you're worried that life as you know it is going to change. . . .well, we can't help you with that. Knowing what you want to do is half the battle, and lucky for you — this chapter introduces you to the common e-commerce lingo so that you can start talking the talk. We also give you a sneak peek at how the various aspects of e-commerce work. When you have your sea legs (or is that e-legs?), you can move on to the important business of transitioning.

What Is E-Commerce?

Originally, the term *e-commerce* simply referred to the business of selling products and services online, and many people still think of e-commerce in that light. But the larger business community has started thinking of e-commerce in much broader terms. Today, e-commerce refers to the process of doing just about every aspect of business over the very public Internet. If you think about how complex businesses are, you'll start to understand why this e-commerce thing has turned the business world on its ear!

In the e-commerce world, people use code phrases to describe simple concepts. After you get a few of these under your belt, you'll keep up when talking to consultants, vendors, software firms, and business partners. Here are a few to get you started:

- ✔ **Business-to-consumer (B2C):** Selling to individuals in small quantities. It's equivalent to retail sales in the real world.

- ✔ **Business-to-business (B2B):** Selling to other businesses, usually more regularly and in higher quantities. You guessed it — this is the same as selling wholesale.

- ✔ **Business-to-employee (B2E):** Providing access to employee services through the Internet, 24 hours a day.

- ✔ **Supply chain:** Describes the businesses, from manufacturers to whole-salers to retailers to shippers, and even financial institutions, that get a product built and into the hands of the end user.

- ✔ **Online:** Using the Internet to browse and shop. Or to track orders. Or to offer customer service. You get the point.

- ✔ **Bricks-and-mortar:** Describes traditional stores, warehouses, and offices that live in buildings.

Even businesses that sell to other businesses have distinctive Web sites that provide information for customers, investors, suppliers, and the media (see Figure 1-1). These days, Web sites are like gigantic billboards — only these billboards are always changing.

E-commerce isn't just about selling products to consumers. It's about any business selling products and services to *somebody* — other businesses and consumers alike.

JARGON ALERT

A rose by any other name (Oh, you know the rest!)

Technically, *e-commerce* represents buying and selling goods and services electronically (electronic commerce, n'est-ce pas?) For example, order processing is a function of e-commerce. Others refer to *e-business* as using the Internet for any other business support functions that do not directly support sales, such as setting up travel arrangements for employees or transferring stock between warehouses. Because we don't like to split hairs, we're going to use the term *e-commerce* to include e-business functions. After all, everything your business does (such as customer service) should theoretically lead to more buying and selling.

E-business refers to computerized, Internetized business processes, such as customer relationship management, procurement, and so forth. Many businesses like to think of these processes as e-commerce because these processes directly impact a business' ability to buy and sell goods and services. Some businesses like to think of them as e-business because these processes don't directly impact the company's main operations.

The bottom line? Call it whatever you want to. E-commerce, e-business, or just "e-nnoying," these terms all mean basically the same thing: using the Internet and Internet-based technologies to make money. To keep things easy, we use the term *e-commerce* in this book to refer to all of these things.

Sowing the seeds for a more productive business

Businesses care about e-commerce for a lot of reasons — mostly because of increasing profits. Use your computers' work to increase revenue and reduce expenses, and you have a winner. Let your e-commerce effort

- ✔ **Reduce paperwork.** Everyone admits that paperwork is a pain in the neck; exchanging information between businesses electronically creates a paperless process.

- ✔ **Minimize mindless tasks and costs.** By eliminating the number of hours that your staff needs to enter data from a piece of paper into the business' computer system, you free them up to do something more productive.

- ✔ **Automate and control inventory.** E-commerce makes shipping faster and more efficient. Look for more about integrating into a supply chain in Chapter 16.

- ✔ **Enable competition and cooperation.** Look for more about using the Internet to purchase goods from partners in Chapter 17. Find info on being part of a trading community in Chapter 19.

Figure 1-1:
Lucent
Technol-
ogies uses
its Web
site to give
customers,
partners,
and
investors
information.

Harvesting the wheat: How e-commerce helps businesses

Very few people would argue that e-commerce offers no benefit to businesses. Just about every business can benefit in some way from implementing some kind of e-commerce. One of the greatest things about e-commerce is that it doesn't usually cost very much to do, especially when you compare it with the non-electronic way of doing the same thing.

For example, suppose that you run a small business that manufactures reproduction parts for classic cars. All the car buffs in your local area rely on you as a source of hard-to-find parts that they can use to restore old cars to their former glory. The problem is that you've pretty much saturated the market in your town. If you want your business to grow, you must find a way of attracting business from outside your town. Ideally, you want to sell your products to the entire country.

That can, of course, be a pretty expensive proposition if you only examine bricks-and-mortar options. Setting up those business relationships, hiring people to take orders, hiring more people to fill orders — all add up to a lot of investment.

Start looking at the ways e-commerce can make that process less expensive. You could put up a Web site that enables consumers from all over the country to place orders for your products. You could set up a separate Web site so that auto supply stores across the country can order your products at wholesale. Right there, you've made it easier for your business to grow.

Removing the chaff: How e-commerce can hurt businesses

Sadly, getting carried away with e-commerce and forgetting why you started looking at it in the first place is pretty easy. Although e-commerce does offer a truly enormous number of ways to help businesses, making changes to your business always offers the potential to hurt it as well.

Many businesses jump right into e-commerce without thinking it through carefully. You won't do that, of course, because you were smart enough to buy this book, in which we tell you what to avoid. Start by thinking about some of the following pitfalls:

- ✔ **No plan? No dice.** You should never take any major steps in your business without a plan that spells out exactly what you're going to do, and how this planned route is going to either save the company money or make the company filthy rich. E-commerce is no exception

- ✔ **Hungry? Don't gnaw on your arm.** Assess whether your e-commerce efforts cannibalize the rest of your business of profits and customers, and don't dump money and resources into a plan that will ultimately reduce profits — even if you think you can use it to increase revenue. E-commerce should enhance the other side of your existing business, not put it six feet under.

- ✔ **Growing pains? Think in terms of scalability.** If your business plan includes a course of action for handling an influx in sales, your e-commerce efforts pay off, you're already thinking. Classic stories of dot com businesses falling apart because they can't handle the sudden deluge of orders are classic for a reason.

- ✔ **Return on what? Decide if it's even worth it.** Will you spend more on e-commerce than you make from it? If you're planning to implement e-commerce technologies to increase your customer base, make sure that your business plan spells out how much the technology will cost you and how many new customers you're expecting. That should tell you how much each of those new customers is going to cost you — and whether the cost is worth the effort.

The considerations you make at the beginning of the process are the same considerations you should be making every step of the way — even after you roll out your initiative. See Chapter 3 for more on successfully figuring out your plan.

Getting Familiar with How E-Commerce Business Relationships Work

You probably understand a great deal about the business relationships your company already has. After all, those relationships — with suppliers, vendors, and customers — are the key to any successful business. Unfortunately, these relationships work much differently in the e-commerce world than in the traditional business world. Understanding those differences is critical to making your e-commerce venture a success.

The rigid supply chain, classic style

Most businesses work in pretty much the same way: no ifs, ands, or buts about it. If you're selling physical products, you participate in a fairly standard supply chain:

- The producer of the raw materials
- The suppliers that resell those materials
- The processors that make the raw materials suitable for use
- The manufacturers that combine the raw materials into useful products
- The distributors that wholesale the manufactured products from their warehouses
- The store that buys products from distributors and sells the products at retail
- The final consumer who buys the product from the store

Of course, other businesses, such as shippers, accounting firms, law firms, and so on, become involved with various portions of the supply chain as well. Your business probably falls into at least one of these positions in the supply chain, and your business may perform more than one of these functions. For example, you may buy products from a distributor and sell them not to a consumer but instead to another business, where your products become the raw materials in an even more complex product.

Each link of the chain has

- Something to buy
- Something to sell

- ✔ Some process that adds value to the product or service
- ✔ Some physical place of doing business, where people come to buy or return products or from which things are shipped
- ✔ Back-office folks, such as accountants, who keep track of the business' operations
- ✔ A catalog listing of products and services that are for sale
- ✔ Advertising and marketing campaigns used to bring in new business

Many companies operate on processes that depend entirely on their physical facilities to operate their enterprise. Can you imagine your grocery store without its building and shelves? To capitalize on the Internet, you need to think outside the box.

Flexibility e-commerce style

Although the process of getting raw materials moving through a series of processors, manufacturers, and distributors until they finally reach consumers is pretty much the same whether you're doing business online, offline, or on the moon, e-commerce business has its differences from traditional offline business. E-commerce enables businesses to create much more flexible business relationships, and to do business at almost any point in the supply chain without the use of

- ✔ A store or physical place of business
- ✔ Salespeople
- ✔ Back-office personnel
- ✔ Warehouses
- ✔ Products or services to sell (no kidding)
- ✔ A catalog
- ✔ Advertising or marketing
- ✔ Physical return counters

The best of all worlds is often a melding of the strengths of a bricks-and-mortar business with the potential and flexibility of e-commerce. By using the distinctiveness of an existing organization, you can market your value through the Internet and reach a larger, more diverse market.

Getting the Skinny on E-Commerce Markets

Adding e-commerce to your business mix offers you a great opportunity to consider your business market. Who is your customer? Who are your competitors? The great thing about e-commerce is that your customer base can potentially be much larger than in a traditional business.

The downside, of course, is that e-commerce gives you lots more competition, too. It really doesn't take much to participate in e-commerce (all you need is a Web site and something to sell), and you may sometimes feel like your business is floating in a sea of competing Web sites created by enterprising college students. Fear not, friend. Although you don't need much to do e-commerce, you do need real savvy to do e-commerce right — and successfully.

One of the most important things you need to examine about your potential e-commerce business model is how your marketplace will change. Most traditional businesses are limited to a geography supported by their real estate. The Internet levels the playing field, enabling you to expose your products and services to an international audience. It can make small fish big, and big fish even bigger. Check out Chapter 6 for strategies for developing a market in cyberspace.

Cyberspace is a term for the Internet or virtual reality created by computers.

Your marketplace also includes customers, and you should carefully think about how e-commerce will affect them. Will your current customers follow you to the Internet, or will they prefer to continue doing business with you the old way? What types of customers do you have? Will you be able to reach more of those customers online, or not? Think about the following cautionary examples:

- **Do teenagers want a subscription to the AARP newsletter?** Imagine that your business involves selling products mainly for senior citizens. You sell directly to the final consumer, and you've decided to add a Web site to your business so that you can sell nationally. Unfortunately, senior citizens represent a very small percentage of the Internet-connected population. You may have a hard time bringing your customers to your Web site because they're not connected to the Internet to begin with.

- **Can supersizing be a bad thing?** Imagine that your business sells office supplies. Most of your customers are smaller businesses that come to you because they prefer your personalized service to the faceless service they receive from major chains. Moving your business to a Web site can easily strip away that personal touch, putting you in direct competition with the other faceless megastores. In addition, you may find yourself competing on prices, an area in which the big boys can walk all over you.

All these nets and not a fish in sight

As you begin your exploration of the e-commerce world, you need to prepare yourself for terms such as *Internet, intranet,* and *extranet.* Techno-wizards like to use these terms to impress folks, but there really isn't that much of a difference between them. Here's what they mean:

✔ The *Internet* is a publicly-accessible network of computers located across the globe. Some of these computers are Web servers, and form the World Wide Web — the most popular use of the Internet. In addition to the Web, the Internet features a variety of other technologies for activities like transferring files, sending e-mail, and so forth.

Old-timers may also speak of the *ARPAnet,* which was what the Internet was called when it was still a research project jointly run by the U.S. government and major universities. Many of the Internet's key technologies were invented by government and university scientists, and made available to the public. Your tax dollars at work!

✔ An *intranet* is nothing more than your company's internal computer network souped up with Internet technologies. Maybe your company's network includes a Web server that has pages for job openings and information on the company picnic. Poof! You have an intranet. The difference between an *intranet* and the *Internet* (other than a few letters), is that the public doesn't have access to your intranet (at least, it shouldn't).

✔ An *extranet* is a little bit Internet, and a little bit intranet. An extranet is part of your company's network, which your company's employees can access. Select businesses that your company has relationships with can also access it. Extranets usually serve as a place for your company and its business partners to meet and exchange information. The general public doesn't have access to an extranet. Some companies may have several extranets, each allowing different business partners to perform different tasks.

Getting to Know E-Commerce Technology

The Internet is the worldwide network of all the world's networks — private and public — and all the computers that, through the miracle of Internet technologies, make up those networks. The Internet technologies — the stuff that enables all kinds of communication across the Internet — are what make e-commerce possible. Fortunately, software manufacturers have taken most of the key technologies and bundled them into convenient, easy-to-operate (well, most of the time) packages. Nevertheless, we would be remiss if we didn't introduce you to these technologies and explain what they're used for.

What makes the Internet (and e-commerce) work efficiently (and most importantly, securely) are hardware (the chips and wires and other stuff that create networks) and the software programs (which make the networks do what we want them to do).

Making sure that the technologies you're using are the fastest and most efficient is also important because every second that customers have to wait is another second closer to the time they click over to another site. Here's why Internet technology is so important:

- **Everyone's playing from the same sheet of music.** Without *protocols* (the rules every network needs to follow to communicate with other computers and other networks), computers wouldn't be able to talk to each other, and people couldn't communicate with computers. Protocols also provide ways to restrict who can access a company's information. These include basic technologies such as *TCP/IP* (Transmission Control Protocol/Internet Protocol), which is a basic communication program that sets the standard for connecting to the Internet, communicating in real time, and doing other Internet-type things, such as e-commerce, possible.

- **There's more than one way to skin a cat.** Network technologies, or communication technologies, connect the computers of the Internet together. Because the Internet is actually lots of people voluntarily connecting lots of computers made by different companies using software written by still other companies, there are lots and lots and lots of options. Mastering those technologies — or hiring people who have — can be the difference between killer sites that draw business and dull sites that send people away in despair. We clue you in on the people you need in Chapter 7 and the technologies in Chapter 13.

- **KISS: Keep it safe, silly!** Identity technologies take the place of driver's licenses and passports on the Internet, enabling businesses and individuals to verify the identity of the parties they do business with. Security technologies are meant to protect computers and the information they contain from unauthorized individuals, such as hackers. Whether they're doing it for their own sick pleasure or for industrial espionage, hackers specialize in crashing the computers your company depends on and stealing information from them. You need to understand the implications of putting sensitive data on the Internet, and implement security technologies to protect that data.

These technologies all play an important role in any e-commerce implementation, and although you don't have to know every detail about how all this technical stuff works, you do have to know how it all fits together. Fortunately, we dedicate Chapter 2 entirely to e-commerce technologies, how they work together, and which ones you need to concern yourself with.

Setting Up E-Commerce Strategies and Systems

E-commerce entails a lot more than just throwing up a Web site and taking orders online. E-commerce impacts your entire business, and you need a solid strategy in place before you actually begin doing anything. Developing your strategy is so important that we dedicate an entire chapter — Chapter 3, to be specific — to this topic.

For now, though, you should be thinking about what your business' goals are and developing the questions that you want this book to answer. Start by understanding the key players in your organization who will get your e-commerce project off the ground. You also need to understand how your competition is handling e-commerce — after all, you don't want to start a project that the competition will eventually manage to show up. Carefully reviewing your competition's e-commerce efforts will help you see what is and isn't successful, too.

Next, you have to put together a business plan. In Part I, we walk you through defining the business model that your company must adopt in an e-commerce environment, and help you identify the risks that can turn an e-commerce project into . . . well . . . if not a disaster, at least not a stunning success. We help you figure out how to analyze the costs of doing e-commerce, and help you define what will constitute success for your e-commerce efforts.

When your business plan starts to take shape, you need to plan to develop your relationships into e-relationships. In Chapter 11, we discuss serving your customers through the Internet. In Chapter 7, you can discover how to manage your virtual workforce. In Chapter 14, read how to work with providers to keep your e-commerce site running. Explore partnering with other businesses (Chapter 16) to help yours flourish and find tactics for working with business partners (Chapters 19 and 20).

With a complete e-commerce plan in hand, you must start thinking about implementing it, and about the impact this plan will have on your traditional business. The key is truly understanding the intimate details of how your business functions today so that your e-commerce plans complement that way of doing business rather than interfering with it.

E-commerce is supposed to help you save money and make money, not lose it! Always keep an eye on how e-commerce will affect your traditional business to make sure they complement one another.

One way to ensure that your company's traditional business dovetails nicely with your new e-commerce strategy is to examine the areas where e-commerce can provide an immediate benefit to your existing business. After you're sure that you know how your business works on a day-to-day basis, you'll probably start spotting areas for improvement — and we show you how e-commerce can be the tool for that improvement.

Finally, suppose that you have an e-commerce strategy worthy of a major military operation — in your head. The last step is to document that strategy so that everyone in your organization, as well as your business partners, investors, and other concerned parties, can understand it and are excited about it. We show you how to do that, too, in the form of a project vision, cost and risk assessment, and other important business documents: See Chapter 3.

Understanding E-Commerce Legal Issues (With Only a Few Lawyer Jokes Thrown in for Kicks)

If you think e-commerce has thrown the business world for a loop, you should talk to a lawyer! E-commerce not only enables businesses to quickly change to meet evolving market conditions, but it also allows them to come up with ideas that the legal system hasn't entirely caught up with, yet. (Probably because they're knee-deep in briefs.) Every country is trying to adapt its laws and regulations to this strange new world.

Lawyers will always find a way to muck up a good thing, adding tons of briefs and archaic terminology, such as *habeas corpus, ad damnum,* and *non compos mentis.* (Don't ask us what they have to do with e-commerce — we just picked them at random from a glossary of legal terms.) However, sometimes you need to take a few steps backward to take a step forward. Two recent landmark examples:

✔ **Auctions, bad taste, and the French. It figures.** Some folks decided to auction off some Nazi war memorabilia on Yahoo!, a popular Web site. Because the Web is international (it puts the world in World Wide Web), citizens of every country could participate in the online auction. Unfortunately, French law makes the sale or auction of Nazi memorabilia illegal. In a landmark court case against Yahoo!, the French government was able to force Yahoo! to prevent French citizens from accessing the auctions in question, even though the auction remained open to citizens of other countries. The bottom line? Even if something is legal in one country, you have to think about international law.

✔ **Hey, it beats taping songs off the radio.** Several major recording companies sued Napster, an Internet-based service used to exchange digital music, for enabling copyright infringement. Although Napster intended its services to provide a place for new and unsigned artists to share and promote their music, the recording companies alleged that Napster users were also using the service to illegally trade copyrighted music tracks. As this book goes to press, the U.S. courts still haven't come to a final decision on how to handle all of the nasty Internet-related copyright issues.

The Internet in general, and e-commerce in particular, open up a huge number of legal questions that hit closer to home, too. Consider some of the following questions, and think about how they apply to your business:

✔ If you have a B2C business, you'll be collecting information from your customers, including their names, addresses, e-mail addresses, credit card numbers, phone numbers, and so on. Even if you deal mainly with other businesses, you will exchange some pretty confidential information. How will you use this information? Will it be consistent with how your customers expect you to use their personal information?

✔ You have the potential to put a lot of your company's material and intellectual property online. For example, a product catalog may include written descriptions, product photos you paid for, and so on. These materials belong to your company, and placing them on the Internet makes them easy to obtain. Hooray! But placing them online makes them easy to copy. Boo! How will you protect your copyrighted material?

✔ Your e-commerce business may offer customers the ability to use services and resources that you sell them. For example, people have tried to sell their own organs (internal, not what they play in church) through eBay. One man even sold his soul, and then tried to sell it again. How will you govern your customers' use of these resources and services?

✔ Because the Internet is a global community, your e-commerce business is likely to participate in global e-commerce. In the larger global market, how do your trademarks and trade names stand up? The classic example is the McDonald's restaurant chain, which wound up in a bit of a legal battle when it opened a restaurant in Scotland. A local citizen named McDonald already ran a restaurant named McDonald's, and Scottish law gave the Scot priority over the use of his clan's name. Are your trade names and trademarks globally secured for your use?

You may want to secure your domain name as soon as you can. A domain name is used when people type your address on the Internet. For instance, cocacola.com is the domain name for (oddly enough), The Coca Cola Company. People have been buying domain names in hopes other people will buy them. One person made several million dollars by registering the domain name business.com. Get your name locked in before it's gone.

✔ When you begin selling things outside your local area (which is the whole point of e-commerce), all kinds of additional taxes and fees can apply to your business. If you ship internationally, you may have to deal with export fees, import tariffs, and international trade laws on top of taxes. Does your e-commerce business plan address these legal issues?

In Chapter 8, we discuss these and other legal issues, how other e-commerce companies have handled them, and how you can prepare a plan to deal with them in your e-commerce venture.

No book is a substitute for a competent attorney who is well versed in the particular legal issues (and mumbo jumbo) of your business' niche. This lawyer should know about the growing world of Internet and copyright law. Before embarking on any e-commerce venture, take your business plan to an attorney who understands the issues involved in interstate (and international, if appropriate) commerce and who can advise you accordingly.

CASE STUDY

Garnering trust with TRUSTe

eBay (www.ebay.com) has proven that auctions are a very successful way to do Internet business. The company realized early on that Web servers are its life. Hackers repeatedly attack eBay's site to try to crash those servers. With every attack, eBay improves its system. eBay also realizes that customers won't feel comfortable doing business unless they know that the venue is safe. By creating a comprehensive privacy policy and opening itself up to independent review by TRUSTe, shown in the following figure (www.truste.com), eBay has earned the loyalty of millions of auction-crazed customers. TRUSTe is a non-profit organization that seeks to educate Internet users and to encourage Internet sites to regulate themselves. eBay's diligent application of technology and good business sense have kept hackers and thieves away and kept customers coming back.

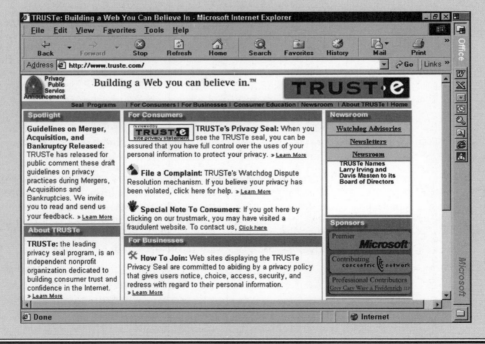

Deciding Where You Want Your Business to Go

You wouldn't have bought this book if you thought the whole e-commerce thing was all thorns and no roses. At its best, e-commerce can enable businesses to go in a completely different (and profitable) direction.

Although we can't help you decide the details of where your business needs to go, we can offer you the following options to get the ball rolling. You really should have an idea before you sit down to work out a business plan (which we cover in Chapter 3) and hammer out the details. Imagine the following scenarios:

- **The grass is always greener where you are. (Extending your market reach).** You're in the business of selling lawn and garden supplies to the happy homeowners of your community. You offer a wide selection of major outdoor appliances, such as mowers, seed distributors, and landscaping tools, but most of your customers never purchase those items. By adding a Web site to your business, you can extend your reach to include the entire nation, or even the world, making your product selection available to a wider range of consumers.

- **The check *isn't* in the mail. (Redefining your market reach).** You're a general contractor, and you hire a large number of subcontractors in various trades to help you build homes. Most of your business involves managing the contract, receiving invoices from subcontractors, and paying them. You decide to add a Web site to your business, on which subcontractors can submit invoices by filling out an online form. You interface the system to your accounting software, and suddenly your office becomes mysteriously paper-free. Subcontractors are paid on time, and you find you have better control of your cash flow. You didn't expand your market; you simply redefined it to be an online marketplace rather than a paper-based marketplace.

- **You can get paper paperlessly. (Consolidating your internal market to save cash).** Your company spends tens of thousands of dollars each year on office supplies, and much of this money is wasted because every department deals with a different supplier. You implement an intranet-based Web server that has an e-procurement application. E-procurement lets your employees order the supplies they need from their own computers without filling out endless requisitions (read all about it in Chapter 17). All your company's employees now send requisitions for office supplies through the Web site. The company can leverage its combined buying power to get better volume discounts from a consolidated list of suppliers. You consolidated an internal market — your company's employees — into a single buying group that saves the company time, effort, and money.

We talk more about e-commerce markets in Chapter 6 — and in Part IV of this book, we focus on ways to use e-commerce technologies to improve internal markets, such as your company's employees.

Because e-commerce is a set of technologies, you can add the technologies in pieces, and you can build the pieces in parallel or one at a time. In Chapter 3, we show you who you need to gather in your organization to put your plan together. See Chapter 5 for our discussion on how to integrate these new technologies into your current business.

Chapter 2

Welcome to the Age of E-Everything: Technology

In This Chapter

▶ Connecting with your customers through Internet technology

▶ Securing access so the good guys get in and the bad guys stay out

▶ Deciding how you want your Web site set up

▶ Finding the applications that give your business the killer edge

As you move your business into the digital world, you need the means to communicate safely and securely with partners and customers. You need to understand the building blocks on which your electronic business will be constructed. So in this chapter, we do a short overview of the pieces to the puzzle. Afterward, you'll be able to talk back to the cybergeeks when they launch into a tirade of technobabble, and ask intelligent questions. That will keep them off-balance and honest, and that's always a good thing.

We take a quick tour of the basic building blocks that form an electronic network, and move on to the locks and doors (network security) that keep everything safe. We also discuss locating a site for your electronic store. (Yes, we know the Internet is everywhere, but somewhere there is a computer that makes your site work.) When your tour is finished, you can concentrate on creating a site with killer apps that keeps folks coming back.

Understanding Internet Technology in Five Minutes or Your Money Back

The Internet got its name because it's made up of a bunch of independent networks (at its simplest level, a *network* consists of two or more computers hooked together to share resources) that are linked together. In other words, the Internet is a network of networks, which is both its strength and its weakness. As long as the owners of all those networks work and play well together, everyone can share information. Of course, to work together successfully, everyone needs to play by the same rules.

Fortunately, you don't need to know all the details to get your business' computers and networks connected to the Internet. You just have to buy the right software.

Joining the Internet Club

Of course, exactly how you connect to the Internet depends on what you want to do. Your business may already be linked to the Internet so that employees can surf the Web and send e-mail. This isn't quite enough oomph to do e-commerce, though. The most significant aspect of Internet technology is how easy it makes communicating and transferring information. You've got real time, baby. You can have that information anywhere in the world as fast as you can click the mouse.

What you can do with your business network depends on how you decide to structure the Internet connection. You can

- **Exchange data with the world:** If you're like most managers, you want the whole world to click to your company Web site, look around, get information, and buy stuff. You can set up a network on the Internet that links your company with the whole world. You can think of this technology as the window into the cleanest, shiniest, and most efficient room in your organization. It's also the kind of network connection you're used to seeing when you go online.

- **Exchange data with your employees — and no one else:** An _intranet_ is a private computer network that is not accessible to the vast herds of individuals roaming the Internet. In other words, it stays private. Intranets usually use the same protocols that the Internet uses, but only company employees can access them. Intranets are often connected to the Internet (although they don't have to be), and employees can use them to surf the Web and send e-mail over the Internet.

Internet technology enables you to exchange classified information that's for your employees' eyes only. Using intranets, you can create internal Web pages devoted to human resources, stock purchasing, strategic plans, and more. Now employees can't say, "I never got the memo."

- **Exchange data with partners:** An _extranet_ is a cross between a private network (or intranet) and the Internet, which is as public as can be. Extranets are private computer networks that are neither totally private nor completely open to the public; instead, they are accessible to specific companies and individuals to which you grant access. With this controlled access, extranets become a great way for your business partners to obtain and provide information that you may not want to make available to the general public.

✔ **Exchange some data within your organization, other data between your organization and its partners, and some data with the rest of the world:** You can set up intranets and extranets that coexist peacefully with each other, and enable employees in your organization to share information with each other, with partners, and with the world. For example, you can extend your extranet to let your suppliers find out how many screws you have and when you will need more. They can proactively ship those screws to you, or ask when you want them. Think of the paperwork and errors you could eliminate! (We tell you how to do this in Chapter 16.)

Extranets, intranets, and the Internet all share the same technologies — the real difference among them is who has access to the resources on the network. If you're a complete geek, you can find out more about Internet technologies in *Networking For Dummies,* by Doug Lowe (published by Hungry Minds, Inc.).

Net What? Deciding How Far to Go with Your Network Strategy

Networks aren't cheap. Extranets cost a bundle. Connecting to the rest of the world can cost a small fortune — every month.

You need to prioritize your needs. Internet connectivity can be bought based on usage. The amount of Internet you buy is called *bandwidth*. Bandwidth is a measurement of how much and how fast you actually send and retrieve data through the Internet. You need to buy just what you need.

Then you need to protect your assets. By using software and hardware, you let people see some of your corporate data — just the bits you want them to see. You need to protect the rest from prying eyes. We talk about the parts and systems that help you do this in Chapters 10 and 13. Before you can figure out the parts you need, however, you need to discover what you will do with your Internet connection.

Instantly Understanding Real-Time Communication (Just Add Water)

Every computer on the Internet communicates with a protocol, or computer language, called *TCP/IP* (Transmission Control Protocol/Internet Protocol).

TCP/IP actually started out as a very low-level protocol that controlled how computers sent data to each other. As the Internet became more popular, its users needed to send specialized data to one another, such as Web pages, e-mail, discussion groups, and so forth. The Internet currently uses a variety of TCP/IP protocols, including

- ✔ **HTTP (HyperText Transfer Protocol):** This protocol is used to transmit requests for Web pages from a Web browser to a Web server, and to transmit the actual Web page from the server to the browser.

- ✔ **SMTP (Simple Mail Transport Protocol):** This protocol is used to send e-mail from one computer to another across the Internet.

- ✔ **NNTP (Network News Transfer Protocol):** This protocol is used to send discussion articles across the Internet to news servers. News servers also use this protocol to keep each server's copy of the news synchronized with other servers.

- ✔ **FTP (File Transfer Protocol):** This protocol is used to transmit files — such as programs, documents, and graphics — across the Internet.

Web sites are a way of transferring data from one computer to another. By using HyperText Transfer Protocol (HTTP), you can send files, such as HTML pages, GIFs, and JPEGs to people on demand. All the user needs to do is type in the address of the file or page into his browser. You can build Web sites inside your intranet or just for the people connected to you through extranets. A *public site* is available on the Internet for anyone who can find the address.

Check Your Pocket Protector at the Door: How ISPs Move Packets of Information

The closer you are to a Tier 1 ISP, the closer you are to fast, reliable Internet because your data passes through fewer connections to get to the Internet's backbone. Many Tier 1 ISPs maintain direct connections with other major Tier 1 ISPs, allowing them to transfer data without routing it to the backbone, for even better performance. It pays to find out how your ISP connects to the Internet.

Networks are connected to the Internet through an *Internet service provider,* or ISP. That ISP may, in turn, connect to its own ISP, which may connect to one of the major ISPs, such as MCI/WorldNet, that provide the major Internet connectivity in the world — the so-called *backbone* providers. Your customers are connected through a similar tiered setup. With all these different connections, shown in Figure 2-1, you'd be surprised that customers' computers can find their way to yours.

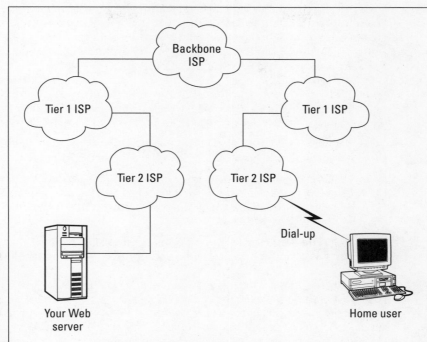

Figure 2-1:
Tiered
Internet
connec-
tions.

Backbone ISPs form, well, the backbone of the Internet. Their customers are *Tier 1* ISPs, such as PSINet and UUNET. Tier 1 ISPs serve major corporate customers, and also serve *Tier 2* ISPs. Tier 2 ISPs generally serve smaller businesses and dial-up customers. *Tier 3* ISPs chain off of a Tier 2 ISP to serve small or specialty customers.

The Internet transfers information in *packets*. Packets are just tiny units of data. They have to be small so that *routers* (which carry data packets) can transfer the data efficiently. In fact, a single e-mail message travels the Internet several tiny packets and several routers so that they can be reassembled into a single file at the destination. In Figure 2-2, you can see how routers interact with each other. The process works like this:

1. **The packets leave the Web server and are directed by your network router to your ISP's router.**

   Your ISP's router receives the packets. Because they're not destined for a computer connected to this ISP, the packets are routed to the next-higher tier.

2. **The Tier 1 ISP sees that the packets aren't intended for any computers on *its* network, so the packets are forwarded to the next tier.**

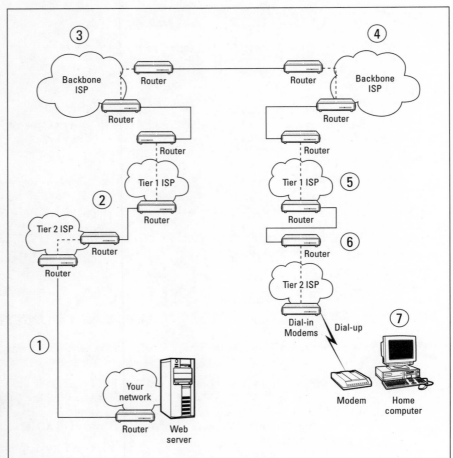

Figure 2-2:
Routers at
work.

3. **The backbone ISP sees that the packet is destined for a computer on another backbone.**

   Because all backbone ISPs are connected, the packets can be forwarded.

4. **The backbone ISP sees that the destination is located on one of its customers' networks, a Tier 1 ISP.**

5. **And so the process continues.**

6. **And so on, and so forth, yadda yadda yadda.**

7. **Finally, the packets are delivered to your computer.**

Being a Pied Piper: Attracting Customers to Your Site

To help people find you on the Internet, you need a *domain name* (which we discuss in more detail in Chapters 8 and 13) so that customers can find you. Your domain name becomes part of the worldwide domain name system, or *DNS*. DNS is your business' online address. One of the services that your ISP provides is a *DNS server,* which enables other computers to locate your computers.

Your domain name helps other computers find your Web servers (so they can get your HTML pages), your mail servers (so they can reach you through e-mail), your File Transfer Protocol (FTP) servers (so they can trade files with you), and other services. You can have multiple sites with your domain name as well. For example, Dell has its main sales site, `www.dell.com`, but it also has a Web site just for support, `support.dell.com`. Both are part of the `dell.com` domain.

Building digital crossroads with portals

A B2C *portal* is a Web site that enables customers to find information and provides a gateway for users to a cornucopia of additional Web sites. Some B2B portals bring individual businesses in the same industry together so that they can do business. Most B2C portals make money by selling advertising space on their sites in the form of banner ads. B2B portals often take a percentage of business' profits.

Technically, any Internet search engine — such as Google (`www.google.com`) — is a B2C portal because search engines crank out a list of sites on the Web that match search criteria. But the real portals are sites such as AOL, Yahoo!, MSN, and Excite, which offer search engines, Internet directories, news, lifestyle articles, weather information, traffic reports, and many other features. By offering these extra features, portals give users additional reasons to visit, increasing traffic and therefore advertising revenue.

Portals are part of a system of *e-marketplaces,* which are venues where businesses congregate and let the e-commerce magic happen. We discuss these communities in Chapter 19.

Embracing friends and customers with virtual private networks

What if you want certain people — such as employees or certain business partners — to be able to access the resources on your private intranet from across the Internet? More importantly, how can you ensure that the data they access — which must be transmitted across the public Internet — remains confidential?

The answer is a *virtual private network,* or VPN. A VPN enables select individuals or organizations to access the resources on your company's intranet. Outsiders usually must log in with a username and password. The upshot is that you can protect your assets (wouldn't want to let strangers in now, would you?) from outsiders without sacrificing the flexibility and efficiency of sharing data with partners. We discuss VPNs in a bit more detail in Chapter 13, but if you want even more info, you closet geek, pick up a copy of *Virtual Private Networks For Dummies,* by Mark S. Merkow (published by Hungry Minds, Inc.).

Securing Your Network

Any business that opens its network to the outside world runs the risk of letting bad people in. The media are full of stories about hackers who steal credit card numbers and other confidential information — something you certainly don't want to experience firsthand.

You need digital sentries that can protect your data and keep your systems from being attacked. You also need to know who is accessing your network and what they're doing. And, hackers aside, you need protection from computer failures so your business doesn't grind to a halt when a computer dies or the power goes out. (We have a saying: "It's not *if* your hard drive fails, it's *when* your hard drive fails.")

Determining how you stack up with backups

If a disaster occurred at your office and all your files were lost, how would your business fare? Could you recover? More than 67 percent of businesses that suffer a catastrophic loss of business records fail within one year. Ouch. How's that for bad luck?

That means you want a back-up and recovery system that can quickly restore your information. You can run a fairly low-cost, manual system, or you can use the Internet to move copies of your data to safe locations. You can even keep systems in multiple offices (even in different countries) that work together and appear to be one single system to your customers, vendors, and employees. We address disaster recovery strategies in Chapter 13.

Getting up close and personal with firewalls

One thing you can do to protect your network is install a *firewall.* A firewall prevents outsiders from accessing your intranet from the Internet. Actually, a firewall can also prevent your intranet from accessing the Internet — that's how good it is at stopping traffic. With a firewall outsiders can see the information you want them to see and protect everything else. Firewalls are standard-issue for e-commerce sites.

Discovering the proxy server

You can also use a proxy server on your network. Many firewalls, in fact, can double as proxy servers and vice versa. A *proxy server* is designed to improve the speed with which your network's users can access the Internet, and to help hide your network's structure from the Internet.

Methods of authentication

You need some way to verify users' identities — whether they are users attempting to access your intranet or customers who want to use your Web site. Internet technologies offer several authentication methods, and you can mix and match as necessary to meet your company's needs. See Chapter 13 for more info.

Web Site Hosting Options

To put your e-commerce site into production and get customers to use it, you need a publicly-accessible Web server. But just as you don't need to own a building to have an office (because you can rent), you don't need to own any servers to have an Internet site. Of course, just as when you lease office space, you can't do just anything you want on someone else's property. In this section, we introduce some of the options you have for hosting your Web site, and list some pros and cons for each option. For more detail on this options and the benefits and disadvantages, turn to Chapter 10.

Self-hosting: Not for beginners

The good old do-it-yourself method, self-hosting is a big step to take. You'll be responsible for *everything*.

When you do it yourself, you're on your own. You have to purchase and maintain every aspect of your site yourself, including power, network connections, servers software, climate control, and fire suppression.

We haven't even scratched the surface of items that you need to deal with. Of course, as the owner of all your resources, you have full control over them. You decide when to upgrade things, when to leave them alone, when to purchase new servers — everything.

Co-locating: Make the host partially responsible

In a co-location arrangement, you own all your servers and equipment, but you rent space in a hosting facility to house them. This arrangement takes some of the more mundane burdens off of your staff and enables you to focus on your business. But don't expect to do things exactly the way you want in someone else's house.

Co-locating enables you to focus on your equipment and software, and not worry about physical factors like electricity, climate control, and network connectivity. Some co-location facilities even monitor your servers for you, notifying you of any major problems with your hardware or software.

The downside to a co-location agreement is that you give up some control. In order to make their services easier to manage, co-location facilities often impose restrictions, including

- ✔ Limitations on how your servers can be configured.

- ✔ Limited access to your servers, usually during business hours (unless an emergency occurs).

- ✔ Limitations on your network bandwidth, primarily based on how much you're paying. All the co-location facility's customers share the network, so you're not allowed to hog it.

Leasing server space: Good for starters

A step beyond co-locating, leasing server space enables you to run your site on someone else's servers, at its facility, using its network connections. The only thing you own is some of the software running on the servers. All the pros and cons of co-location apply (see the preceding section). You also get better monitoring of the servers because the hosting company owns them. But you have more restrictions on what you can do with the servers because the hosting company owns them.

A big advantage of leased space is that smaller companies can be hosted on the same server as other smaller companies, allowing them to split the cost for expensive hardware and network connections. Shared server space is generally sold based on the amount of traffic coming to your site and the amount of hard drive space you use on the server.

The downside to shared server space is that more than one company relies on the server. If one company starts to really take off, the server will devote most of its resources to that company. If the hosting company doesn't notice and fix the situation, your customers may start noticing the slowdown. Keep an eye on your shared server's performance to make sure your site is getting its fair share of the server's resources.

Pieces, pieces everywhere! Spreading service around

You can always spread your content around a little. For example, the main text of your Web site can come from your servers (which may be self-hosted, co-located, or on leased server space), but the graphic images on your site may come from a completely different location. The Web not only makes this possible, but actually makes the process completely invisible to your customers, who think all the information is coming from your site.

Some companies specialize in helping you distribute your content. One such company is Akamai (www.akamai.com). Using proprietary routing algorithms, its systems deliver your site's graphics, audio, and video content to your customers faster than you probably could on your own.

Chapter 3

Before You Do an E-Thing, Get a Plan Together

In This Chapter
▶ Devising plans for a successful e-commerce rollout
▶ Identifying the people and processes you need to succeed
▶ Leveraging your strengths to make the leap into e-commerce
▶ Making your e-commerce venture profitable

To make an e-commerce initiative work, you need a well-crafted plan that enables your business to match its strengths against the challenges of doing business on the Web. The trick is that every business does its e-commerce dance its own way. Some businesses attempt to be the next big thing (and end up as one-hit wonders) whereas others prefer something a little more classic. Say a little Billie Holiday? Not your taste? Whatever mix of rhythm and soul you add to the mix, you need to have a plan.

In this chapter, we show you the elements that businesses use to move successfully to the Internet. Then we pick up the pace a bit so that you can join in on the jam session. Find out how to synthesize everything you've heard into a clear thread of musical perfection that represents the direction in which you want your business to go.

Gathering the Key Players

In order to put together an e-commerce initiative, you need to enlist the help of key players within your organization. These folks can answer your questions and support the e-commerce effort. Without the aid of your key players, the project is doomed to fail before it starts. Table 3-1 is a summary of the people you need to make this work.

When you create a team, make sure its membership represents your entire company if you can. You should do your very best to make sure that someone from every department has a voice.

Table 3-1	Roles for Developing an E-Commerce Plan
Role	**Responsibilities**
Facilitator	Neutral party who keeps the plan on track and acts as a mediator between disparate points of view
Project manager	Person who will manage the project going forward
Line-of-business managers and senior executives	Decision-makers who need to understand and approve the project; often includes department managers, vice-presidents, and presidents
Project champion	Someone from the business side (not IT) who feels strongly about the project and gets buy-in from non-tech employees
Subject matter experts (SMEs)	People with expertise in the existing business; includes people who know how things are currently done, product experts, and IT experts
Executive sponsor	Key executive who allocates the budget to pay for the project

These roles can be difficult to isolate, so a single person might fulfill multiple roles (an executive sponsor may also be the project champion, for instance). You may also find several people who, together, fill one role.

Because the project team tends to consist of programming geeks and nerds (whose unique world and expertise we discuss in Chapter 7), the project champion's important role is to act as a bridge between the project team and the rest of the business. Project champions are discovered rather than appointed. They often serve some other role in the planning stages and emerge as the project unfolds. Watch for tell-tale signs (pom-poms, spontaneous cheering) and then assign that person more and more tasks to act as a liaison.

Navigating stormy seas with a facilitator

You bring together the corporate brain trust — but how can you get them to pull together to develop the solution you need? The facilitator

✔ Combines strong leadership skills with his or her negotiation skills. The facilitator has business analysis acumen. This person knows just how long to let discussions go, how to keep them on track, how to think out of the box, and how to cut to the chase on an issue or argument.

Previous experience facilitating big corporate changes is a definite plus.

✔ Has an agenda for initial planning meetings and understands what needs to be accomplished.

✔ Needs to be a neutral party.

✔ Is usually needed only for the initial planning stages of the project.

Of all the roles filled in planning, the role of facilitator is filled most appropriately by an outside consultant.

Producing project managers

The project manager drives the project to completion. He or she guides the troops, manages the milestones, keeps the project on track, and keeps everyone informed on the project's status. He or she is the first full-time member of the project development team. We discuss the project manager's role in detail in Chapter 7.

Settling issues with senior management

For your business to invest the time and money required for a successful e-commerce project, you need senior management support. You need buy-in from finance, operations, sales — well, everyone. More specially, you need the support of departmental and division managers, vice-presidents, presidents, and chief executive officers.

You may find that there is little unity among the top brass. (Insert management joke of your choice here.) If that is the case, your project is in trouble before you start, and you need to know that from the start. A good facilitator can help draw consensus from the group, but ultimately these executives have to agree to work together to make your project successful.

Dealing with the subject matter experts conundrum

You need to dedicate employees to the project who know your firm and how you do business today and who can interface between departments. These *subject matter experts* (SME) bridge the gap between your existing business and the new e-commerce systems. They work side by side with your Web designers and programmers to translate your business into an automated e-commerce experience.

SMEs need not be technology-savvy — but they should not be afraid of technology either. A good SME can help your techno-geeks get up to speed on your existing business and systems, often saving them weeks or months in the process.

The best SME candidates are usually those indispensable folks who are responsible for the day-to-day operations of your business, so you must decide where they are most beneficial to the company. You may need to split their efforts, or let them help the project team for a short period of time and then go back to business as usual.

Defining the bottom line: The executive sponsor

Someone within the organization ends up with bottom line responsibility for the project. This person allocates the budget and is held accountable for the project's completion. This is your executive sponsor.

The executive sponsor is a member of the senior management team — the head of IT, the vice-president of sales, or even the president. The project manager reports to this individual. The executive sponsor must have authority to make decisions and direct the team to a successful conclusion.

Seeing Is Believing: Developing a Project Vision

If you don't have a target, you are not likely to ever hit it. The project vision outlines the objectives of your e-commerce initiative. This is where you tell everyone what you want to do and why you want to do it. Because it seems to be how these things go, there are parts to developing a project vision:

- ✔ Define the business problem
- ✔ Propose a solution
- ✔ Build a business justification for the project

Brainstorming the problem and creating a problem statement

You wouldn't be starting an e-commerce initiative unless you had a business problem to solve. Maybe you think of it as an opportunity or goal, but we refer to it as the *business problem* (we don't invent the terms, we just share 'em). Create a clear statement explaining how you want to use e-commerce to improve your business. Work with the entire team to state this problem.

The problem statement doesn't need to include any technology. It should be written in plain English in terms anyone can understand:

✔ **Good (if extremely brief):** "We want to increase our customer base by expanding into areas where we have no stores." This statement clearly defines the task.

✔ **Not so good:** "We want to put up a Web store using IBM Websphere on a Compaq Proliant server." This statement is too shortsighted because it doesn't explain the technological babble or explain the problem.

Don't worry about offering a solution until everyone agrees on what the problem is. As a matter of fact, posing a solution too early can interfere with the creative process (what you've no doubt heard referred to as *thinking outside the box*) of defining the problem. Even if you think you already know how you want to solve the problem, hold back. If you have the right solution, the other members of your group will see it and reach the same conclusion.

Use the following steps to help define the problem you want e-commerce technologies to solve. The facilitator schedules the first meeting. All the key players should attend the first meeting.

1. **The attendees go around the room suggesting problems, relationships between problems, and effects of problems.**

   For example, someone may start by saying, "We're not making enough money." Another member may say, "Returns on our widgets are high and sales are slowing down."

   The facilitator writes suggestions on a whiteboard (or easel or overhead — whatever you have) so everyone can see them. Another individual may also want to take notes so that you have a record of decisions and so that action items can be followed up on.

2. **The facilitator encourages everyone to listen to one another. People tend to develop tunnel vision and consider things only from their individual perspectives. Cross-pollination of ideas can be eye opening.**

   The facilitator has to be in control of the meeting, and may need to politely remind the CFO to wait his turn and keep an open mind so that another key player can speak her turn.

3. **Organize the comments into ordered groups. Use this outline to define the business problem statement.**

   Following the example in Step 1, you may create a "sales channels group," " a "supply chain group," and a "customer service group."

4. **The facilitator selects a key player to create an outline or first draft of the statement, incorporating all of the comments and notes from the initial brainstorming session.**

5. **At the next meeting, the team reviews the statement draft.**

   Team members provide suggestions, feedback, and any new ideas that are generated by seeing the problem in writing.

6. **The facilitator selects a volunteer to incorporate the comments into a final statement, which is then distributed to the entire team.**

The facilitator should drive this process, but your team members must do the work. This is your problem, and only your people can define it.

Understanding *all* the potential benefits of e-commerce is just as important as understanding *all* the risks, so be exhaustive, completely honest, and make sure you cover both.

Brainstorming solutions

Like the problem statement, the solution statement should be described in plain English that everyone in the company can understand. You still shouldn't address the technology to solve the problem, except in the broadest terms:

✔ **Good:** "Use Internet technologies to extend our reach to areas where we have no stores."

✔ **Not so good:** "Implement an international Web portal that uses dynamic ASP pages, video conferencing, and e-mail blasts to contact customers."

Anyone can tell you what's wrong. You need to help key players figure out creative solutions. Here are some tips for soliciting solutions from your e-commerce team when they work out a solution:

✔ **Mix things up.** Break into small groups. Mix the groups with people from different departments. Have each group develop a proposal for solving the business problem.

✔ **Make sure the facilitator keeps things on track.** If the meeting becomes a forum for solving every gripe from every department in the company, nothing will be accomplished. You have a specific problem to solve, and the solution needs to address that problem directly.

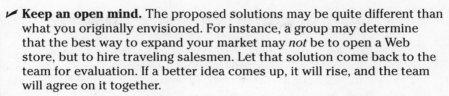

✔ **Keep an open mind.** The proposed solutions may be quite different than what you originally envisioned. For instance, a group may determine that the best way to expand your market may *not* be to open a Web store, but to hire traveling salesmen. Let that solution come back to the team for evaluation. If a better idea comes up, it will rise, and the team will agree on it together.

You may find that combining ideas from several solutions provides the optimal plan. Doing so enables you to address the broadest base of concerns throughout all departments in your organization.

What's in it for me? Building business justification

Part and parcel with defining solutions is determining how the business will benefit from the effort required to implement the solutions. After you choose a solution, have the team come together and list the reasons this solution is best and what your organization can expect to get back from its investment. Have someone take notes so that the team's rationale is documented along with the problem and suggested solution.

Here are some common problems and how an e-commerce initiative can help solve them:

✔ Improve customer service without increasing staff. (See Chapter 11.)

✔ Work more closely, smoothly, and efficiently with business partners to save money. (See Part III.)

✔ Get the systems in your sales, accounting, and other departments to work together (at last!) to reduce paperwork and costs. (See Chapters 5, 15, and 16. Ah, heck, this solution is covered throughout the whole dang book — we firmly believe that the only solution is an integrated solution.)

✔ Stave off the competition that is rapidly consuming your market share. (See Chapters 6 and 19.)

✔ Support your remote locations and employees everywhere in the world. (See Chapter 5.)

✔ Save money on supplies and operating expenses. (See Chapter 17.)

You can use Internet technologies to support your business in innumerable ways. You can also spend a ton of money and never see a dime in return. No new venture is worth doing if it doesn't improve your bottom line.

Setting enabling goals and terminal goals

Before you get too far into creating a plan to solve the business problem, you have to define expectations for your online business. The reason you jumped into this e-commerce project was to achieve your *terminal goals* — the major goals you want to accomplish — for example, increasing the company's net income by $1 million.

But how are you going to get there? Not without taking some baby steps, we can assure you. You should set several *enabling goals* — the small goals that enable you to meet the bigger goals — before you think any further about what domain name you want to use or what color logo will look best on customers' Web browsers.

For example, your terminal goal may be to increase sales in a specific area or demographic. An enabling goal may be to increase the number of visitors that come to the site or to increase the number of products offered on the site.

As you can see in Table 3-2, which shows how your enabling goals should lead directly to your terminal goals, even a small choice in wording can affect your processes.

Table 3-2	Mapping Enabling Goals to Terminal Goals		
Enabling Goal	*Terminal Goal*	*Aligning Enabling Goal and Terminal Goal*	*Strategy*
Increase the number of visitors to the site to increase sales.	Increase company profits.	This particular enabling goal doesn't map very well to the terminal goal. Of course, increasing traffic *should* increase sales. But more traffic in the store doesn't always mean more paying customers, and an increase in sales doesn't always mean an increase in profits.	In achieving the terminal goal, traffic to the site may incidentally increase, but not necessarily. A better way to state the enabling goal may be, "Increase sales volume on the site."

Enabling Goal	Terminal Goal	Aligning Enabling Goal and Terminal Goal	Strategy
Perform targeted direct e-mail marketing to increase repeat sales to customers.	Increase overall sales volume.	This enabling goal is probably one of several enabling goals for this terminal goal. By stating a method that will be used (direct e-mail marketing to increase repeat sales), this enabling goal clearly leads directly to the terminal goal.	This type of enabling goal not only offers a measure of success, but also shows a solution-based approach to fixing performance issues. By looking at how well repeat sales are doing in comparison to overall sales, you can analyze how well the direct e-mail marketing campaign to past customers is working.

Developing (Or Refreshing) Your Business Model

If you're going to get your e-commerce venture off the ground, you need to take a hard look at how you do business today. If you're an executive in your company, you may think you know exactly how your business works. And, at a high level, you probably do. But do you know the details? Of course not! That's why you hired all those people who work for you — to manage the details. But now you need to know who handles orders, who approves purchasing parts, what work is done on paper, and what is done on computers. How many times does the same information get re-typed? Your SMEs will fill in the blanks as you develop your business model.

Turn your project manager and business analyst loose (yup, the very project manager and business analyst we describe in Chapter 7). They will capture your business processes in graphs and charts — *lots* of them. You need a diagram for every major business process that goes on in your company and you need graphs that show how these processes interact with one another. You need to clearly define how the different departments within your company interact.

Figure 3-1 shows a sample interaction of various departments to complete a transaction. Yes, we know the stick figure looks a lot like something a kindergartner would draw, but bear with us — we're going somewhere with this. The flow of business (called a *use case* when it's represented in a diagram) and the individual steps that need to be taken to close that sale are clear — crystal clear, in fact. (We suppose we really did learn everything we really needed to know in kindergarten.)

Obviously, there's no one way to take on the task of creating or updating a business model because every business is different. However, here is a general plan to get things rolling:

1. **The business analyst and project manager gather information.**

   They go from department to department to find out how each department works. As a matter of fact, they will probably create a catalog of processes and take them on one at a time.

2. **The business analyst and project manager summarize the information they gather and run those summaries past the department heads.**

   They need to make certain they got the story straight.

3. **The business analyst and project manager break down the processes into *use cases*.**

   Use cases are graphical representations of business processes (refer to Figure 3-1). They include text that describes each step of the process in the diagram.

4. **The business model is distributed to SMEs.**

   SMEs and department heads are forced to look at the silly ways processes are performed and systems and people interact. Reactions range from belly laughs to deep clinical depression. Some SMEs and department heads notice errors and return corrections. See the section earlier in this chapter "Gathering the Key Players."

5. **The business analyst and project manager correct the model and *baseline* the document.**

   Baselining is a formal process in which all key players sign off on the document. The document doesn't have to be perfect, but everyone who has looked at it and try as they might, no one can find anything else left to fix.

6. **The key players gather together, drink coffee, and review the report, incorporating their decisions about philosophy, identity, goals, influences, and market position.**

   If all goes well, the goals and influences match up with the actual business practices, and the business practices *make sense*.

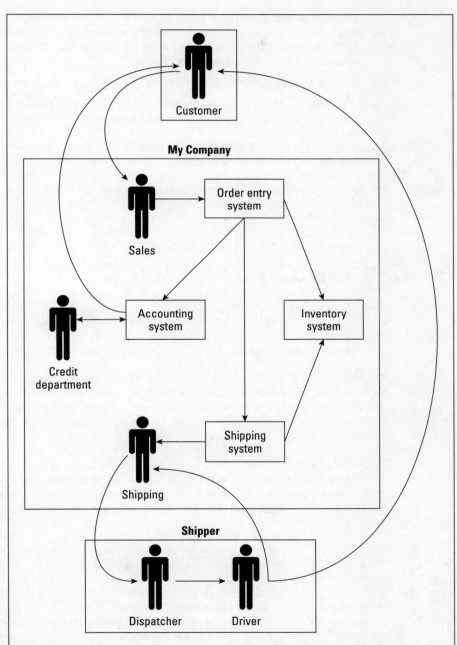

My Company

Customer

Sales

Order entry system

Credit department

Accounting system

Inventory system

Shipping system

Shipping

Shipper

Dispatcher

Driver

Figure 3-1:
This use case demonstrates how a simple sales system works.

7. **The key players heartily thank the business analyst, project manager, department managers, and SMEs for a job well done. Then they start working on creating a business plan that integrates their e-commerce vision into the whole business picture.**

   Relevant areas of the model are distributed to staff for their edification.

   If all doesn't go well, anyone will be able to see pretty clearly where things need to be fixed before moving forward.

Make sure every department in the business contributes, and make sure everyone is being perfectly frank about what works and what doesn't work in your processes; this is not the time to fake it. Don't draw diagrams that reflect how everyone *thinks* the process works, or how they know it *should* work — stick with reality. Draw things the way they are, and you'll get a clear picture of how your company operates on a day-to-day, nitty-gritty level.

Finding the Solution (Model)

The process we describe in the previous section "Developing (Or Refreshing) Your Business Model" shows exactly how your company really works (or doesn't work) so that you can immediately spot the areas where your new e-commerce business needs to tie in to your existing business processes.

The result should be a completely new set of business process charts based on your business problem and proposed solution (see the section earlier in this chapter called "Brainstorming solutions"). The whole big ugly mess is called a *solution* model. The solution model re-draws your processes, showing where and how you can improve.

Figure 3-2 is a revised use case of the original use case represented in Figure 3-1. The diagram shows how the solution model should decrease manpower and move faster. Even in the simplest business processes, it surprises us how often a diagram will uncover a misconception about how orders are processed or business is done.

Try identifying where employees are doing repetitive tasks by looking through your e-commerce business model — these are perfect opportunities to implement automation. Automations should become part of your *solution* model, too. For example, if you create software to automate the exchanging and processing of order information, that same software should also be able to process orders for every other part of your business. Continually examining your business to find out where traditional and e-commerce methods can complement one another will streamline both sides of your business and reduce expenses for everyone.

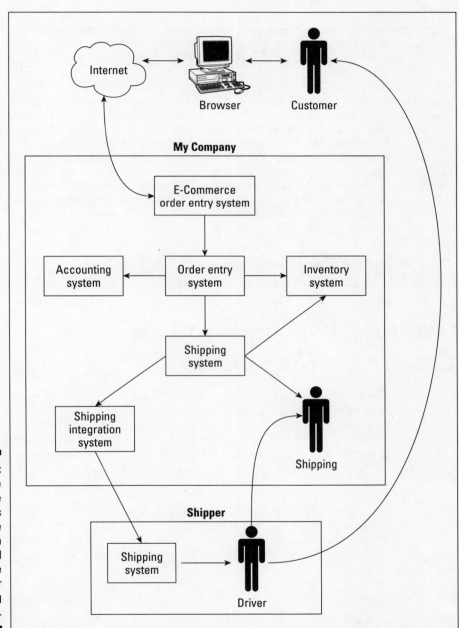

My Company

Internet

Browser

Customer

E-Commerce
order entry system

Accounting
system

Order entry
system

Inventory
system

Shipping
system

Shipping
integration
system

Shipping

Shipper

Shipping
system

Driver

Figure 3-2:
This use
case
represents
how the
solution
model will
improve
your
existing
systems.

Integrating books and clicks

Barnes & Noble knows how to integrate bricks and mortar with the World Wide Web. After being challenged by the meteoric success of Amazon.com, the book superstore chain countered with an e-commerce site of its own, Barnes & Noble.com (www.bn.com). In 1999, Barnes & Noble added Internet kiosks to its retail stores to enable customers to access the Barnes & Noble Web site. The company also made the forward-thinking decision to purchase iUniverse.com, which distributes e-books.

Of course, this two-fold strategy begs the question "How does one compete against oneself?"

In the case of Barnes & Noble, the stores and Web site have complemented, rather than competed against, one another. For example, in 2000, the Barnes & Noble stores continued to grow and revenue continued to rise. During the same year, sales at Barnes & Noble.com increased by 65 percent. By working with an integrated business plan, the book superstore is able to compete in both real space and cyberspace — profitably.

What Do You Have to Lose? Creating a Risk List

The most important thing you can do to evaluate your e-commerce plan is to take a close, realistic, even pessimistic view of it. Have the team look at the plan and point out the places where disaster is most likely to fall and compile the list — you end up with your very own risk list. If you know where the dangers lurk, you can safely navigate the rapids and enjoy the benefits listed in the previous section. So get your key players together, and let them have at it!

When you're putting together a risk list, be sure to review the list of benefits to see if some of the benefits of the plan also come with great risk. For example, you may find that some of the benefits require the use of new and unproven technologies, therefore making them risks themselves.

Here's a sample risk list to get you started. (Try to be realistic; "The world might end tomorrow" is a little off target for this particular exercise.)

✔ This project could distract key resources within the company, causing the rest of the business to suffer.

✔ We will be placed on the same level as our major competitor, a company that already does most of its business online. (Yes, this is a risk as well as a benefit!)

✔ Our customers may not want to change the way they do business with us, so the cost of an e-commerce project may not generate profits.

✔ Increasing the number of products we offer by using a Web site will create warehousing and distribution issues.

✔ If we decide to use alternative warehousing options, we have to create partnerships that make us vulnerable — we have to count on those partners to ship products on time.

✔ Our employees may feel threatened by the project and refuse to use it or recommend it to customers.

Prioritizing potential risks

After you get all your risks in a row, have a volunteer from the e-commerce team enter it into the formal record. Make sure that the list is available to members of the team at each team meeting — you can compare the list to the benefits you expect to realize from your e-commerce venture.

Sit down with your project's key players and start prioritizing the risks. Rank them in order of how likely they are to occur. Assign two numbers, ranging from 1 to 3, to each risk (the lower the numbers you assign, the higher the likelihood the risk will become a disastrous reality):

✔ The first number indicates how likely the risk will become a reality.

✔ The second number indicates how devastating you think the risk will be if it occurs.

For example, one risk is that your Web server could crash, preventing customers from accessing your online business. How likely is that? Very — it *will* happen, sooner or later. So give that risk a likelihood of 1, for "will definitely happen at some point." How devastating will it be? Pretty much totally devastating. So give it a 1 for "this will kill us if it happens."

Try to keep your likelihood/potential for devastation numbers on a scale of 1 to 3 (high, medium, and low). This scale will make the list easier to work with and keep you from splitting hairs when assigning priorities to your risks.

After you assign numbers to all the risks, arrange the list in order of likelihood and rank each item by how bad things would be if and when a disaster occurs. Then move on to less-likely risks, and so on.

Plan to revisit the risk list regularly — at each status meeting — and revise it periodically as risks arise and are mitigated. Use the risk list to prioritize your efforts — doing so will keep the project on track.

Mitigating possible risks

After ranking the risks for your e-commerce strategy (see the preceding section), you can start looking at how to *handle* those risks should they occur. Your plan shouldn't go any further until you at least come up with a scheme to handle the risks rated as "likely to occur."

Ideally, you should have a plan to mitigate every risk on your list. Each risk carries a potential financial loss, and each mitigation strategy carries a financial cost. Does the risk justify the cost?

> **The scenario:** Death of a Web server.
>
> **The risk:** Loss of dinero (bummer), potential to lose customers (ouch), damage to the 'rep (gasp — not the 'rep).
>
> **The conundrum:** How much are you willing to risk?
>
> **Mitigation scenario number one:** You have only one Web server. If it dies you could lose as many as three days' business while you purchase and set up a replacement server. If you generate $10,000 per day in revenue, your risk is $30,000 — plus the cost of a new server, plus the damage done to your reputation and the loss of customers who may never come back.
>
> **Mitigation scenario number two:** You opt to purchase a second backup $50,000 server now.
>
> **Burning question:** Is plunking down a *real* $50,000 for a server now a justifiable risk when compared to the *potential* loss of $30,000 (not to mention your reputation)?

If you thought we were going to answer this question, you've got another thing coming. For one thing, we over-simplified this example. The server could drop once a month, costing you $30,000 *per month* in lost revenue. A second server could reduce your company's response time to your users and prove a beneficial investment as your company grows. Or it could sit in a corner gathering dust.

As you develop mitigation strategies, evaluate them in terms of the entire project — the overall cost, ongoing maintenance costs, profits you expect to receive, costs of missed opportunities, and a host of other factors. You hired smart people — let them hash out a solution that produces the greatest increase in profits. When they give you their opinion, move on to the following section to determine the return on investment.

Determining your return on investment

You need to calculate your expected *return on investment*. You estimate the cost of the project and then divide it by the estimated savings per year.

Determine how long it will be until you have recouped your investment and you have your return on investment. If you invest $250,000 to get your site running and it increases corporate profits by $150,000 per year, your ROI is 1.67 years.

As you create a realistic business plan, start looking at the real costs associated with doing business on the Web, and see how those costs stack up against the income you expect to generate.

Forecasting expenses

Most of the costs of doing business on the Web seem fairly straightforward and include the following:

- ✔ The salaries for new employees who will build and operate the online business
- ✔ The cost of the products that the online business will sell
- ✔ The cost of the Internet connections the business will require
- ✔ The cost of the physical hardware — servers and other computers — that the business will run on
- ✔ The fees paid to contractors and consultants you hire to help build the site

You usually have a huge initial cost before any new revenue rolls in. After the business is up, running, and profitable, costs fall off significantly. Make sure that your business plan includes sufficient capital to make it through this start-up phase and carry the business until it begins to generate income.

The biggest variable in calculating your costs is the amount of time it will take to build the business and how long the business will have to operate before it begins generating income and then turning a profit.

Staying on Track and Measuring Success

The bottom line is that your e-commerce business plan has to have a bottom line. You can estimate your total costs and you can examine all the risks, but you need to be able to measure your progress and success. Many businesses forget this very important step, allowing themselves to be caught up in the general excitement that goes along with a new e-commerce project. Drawing a line in the sand is an important step — this is where the rubber really meets the road.

What do we mean by *success*? Whatever you mean by success. Only you can define the word as it applies to your e-commerce venture. However, if you ask us, we'll tell you that Rome wasn't built in a day. Success is a process.

Your definition of success may not have as much to do with your business' overall fiscal goals as you may think. In fact, we think your definition should be incremental and based on a timeline. (Check out the section "Setting enabling goals and terminal goals" earlier in this chapter if you need a refresher on enabling goals.) Set calendar-based goals — possibly several of them — that define specific performance measurements that are important to you. Here's an example:

- **First Quarter Goal:** To have at least 1,000 visitors a day after one fiscal quarter of operation. **Enabling goals:** To get products and brand names to more customers; to meet marketing's goal of using the site as a way to increase awareness of the offline business.

- **Second Quarter:** To make enough income to cover the salaries of the employees hired specifically to run the site after two fiscal quarters of operation. **Enabling goals:** To meet finance's goal of making the site self-supporting; to meet customer service's goal to channel 50 percent of customer service traffic to the Web site; to meet inventory control's goal to fulfill orders in two days instead of four (whether they are placed over the Internet or by phone).

- **Third Quarter:** To establish a minimum growth rate of 1,000 additional visitors per month, 100 additional orders per month, and $5,000 additional gross revenue per month after nine months of operation. **Enabling goals:** To meet operations' goal of making the online store perform like one of your bricks-and-mortar stores; to meet sales' goal to penetrate market regions where you have no bricks-and-mortar outlets; to get twenty-five percent of new customers to encounter the business for the first time through the Internet.

- **Fourth Quarter:** After one fiscal year of operation, the online store will begin generating a net profit. **Enabling goals:** Bricks-and-mortar stores report an improving level of profitability, so the success of your e-commerce efforts is the result of real growth and market share improvement, not just moving bricks-and-mortar clients to your Web site; inventory turns will have doubled while returns are stable; increased sales volume enables you to negotiate lower prices from vendors, also increasing your bottom line.

- **Third Year:** After three years of operation, the online store's profits have paid for the initial hardware and development costs. You have been given a promotion and sent to a company paid e-commerce conference — in Hawaii.

Get every one of the key players to sign off on the calendar-based set of goals. The goals should be specific and quantifiable. As you meet the goals, you will know that your site is successful.

If you fail to meet a goal, you need to decide if the goal was unrealistic or overly ambitious. Either way, you need to get to the bottom of the problem and turn things around — immediately — even if coming up with the best solution means finding and fixing a flaw in your original business plan.

Chapter 4

Understanding and Transitioning into E-Commerce Business Models

- -

In This Chapter

▶ Understanding and overcoming e-commerce obstacles

▶ Getting to know e-commerce business scenarios

▶ Getting to know e-tail details

▶ Opening markets by selling to (or through) other businesses

▶ Partnering up with other businesses online

- -

*L*ots of people can describe how traditional businesses work. Lots of people think that if they had enough money, they could start and run their own business. Lots of people thought that they could start an e-commerce business and make money. And lots of people were wrong.

E-commerce doesn't follow the same predetermined models traditional businesses use. Buying from your computer screen may be the next step in the evolution of catalog sales, but unlike people, catalogs (and Web sites) can't anticipate customers' desires based on recent purchases or suggest additional, better, or higher-priced items when customers make selections. And catalogs never e-mail customers to update them on the shipping status of their purchases.

Your business can increase its customer base and open doors to new revenue streams and markets by creating a Web site that plays up the versatility and convenience of the Internet, and by playing down the fact that customers won't receive the warmth that only a human interaction can provide. This chapter shows you the many e-business relationships out there, how they work, and what you have to do to make your business fit in, stand out, and make money.

Selling Retail Products Anywhere and Everywhere

Here's the deal: No venue is perfect. For example, some of the downsides to retail stores — the cost of storing inventory, the limitations of shelf space, and the tyranny of business hours — are greatly alleviated on the Internet. The Internet has no hours, and Web sites have no space limits.

The big revolution of the Internet, of course, is the ability to sell practically anything to practically anyone, regardless of where the company or customer is located. And we say *revolution* rather than *advantage* because how well you perform will determine whether it's an advantage or a disadvantage to your company. Use the following sections to adjust your eyes to the way things look, feel, and act online. Then absorb all of these details so that you can make the most of what you know.

Emphasize the strengths of doing business on the Internet, and you gain new customers and new markets. By working around the disadvantages of online shopping, you keep customers coming back — and you build customer loyalty.

Accentuating the positive and eliminating the negative on your site

If you want people to visit your online store, you need to exploit your advantages over your bricks-and-mortar competitors. Well, good thing you've got a permanent billboard that broadcasts to the world exactly what you sell and how you work.

You should make your goal to make your Web site as gooey and sticky as possible. No kidding. A *sticky* site, in Web terms, is a site that keeps users clicking, and clicking, and clicking. You lure customers to your site with first impressions — if customers like what they see, they'll *stick* around. So, what do you do? For starters

 ✔ **Convince customers that your site is safe.** Buying over the Internet is scary to many consumers and businesses. Customers are terrified by stories of stolen credit cards and identity theft. Credit card companies even run ads to capitalize on this fear. You must convince customers that your site is safe and secure.

 ✔ **Make your site simple.** Customers may have trouble making buying decisions based solely on Web site descriptions. Shopping online isn't really different than shopping from a catalog, but many customers feel like they've entered the *Twilight Zone*. Their initial apprehension is natural, but you need to make your site simple and easy to navigate so customers feel at home on your home page without any effort or wasted time.

✔ **Provide a myriad of entry points to help customers get to your site.** Finding anything on the Internet is a challenge (what with so many *things* to wade through). Unfortunately, your site is no exception. Getting banner ads on partners' Web sites, encouraging business partners to add links to your home page, getting good press that highlights your Web address, and amplifying your conventional advertising to get the word out, are all ways to help people find you in cyberspace.

✔ **Provide extensive product information.** Humans learn a lot about things through senses other than their eyes. Although you obviously can't let customers touch or handle your products before they buy, your Web site enables you to provide a great deal more information about the product that a bricks-and-mortar store can.

Using location, convenience, and savvy selling to your advantage

At first glance, using a computer network and a fancy Web site to get around that old-school retail scene seems pretty difficult. How can the e-tail end of your business compete with the instant delivery your retail business offers? And how can slick graphics compete with the friendly smile of Zelda, who has been your customer service rep for eons? You can't really compete directly, but you have to remember that many customers regard the advantages of face-to-face transactions as a double-edged sword. That's why the fact that every Web site is accessible from anywhere in the world — as long as there's an Internet connection — is so revolutionary. Here's the sweet and lowdown on doing business online:

✔ **E-commerce coup: Location means nothing.** When was the last time you even noticed where an online company was actually headquartered? Customers buy stuff, and they either get the stuff right away (when they shop offline) or expect their purchases to be delivered to them fairly soon after they purchase them. One small problem, though — a customer doesn't care if your business is in Mazatlan, Mexico, and he's in Caribou, Maine. He still wants the fresh taco sauce you sold him yesterday — yesterday.

✔ **E-commerce challenge: Location means everything.** Well, maybe the nothingness of location makes it *everything*, at least when it comes to determining the target audience of your site. But we don't mean to get Zen on you. Some efforts don't offer a return on investment. Unless your site is specifically designed for international commerce and your company is already doing business internationally (or has specific plans to do so), stick with what you know when you start out. If you like to throw caution to the wind, get a good lawyer (or an army of them) together with your technological staff so that you can deal with the use of language and graphics on your site, legal issues, tax issues, currency issues, and lots more stuff that gives us headaches to even think about.

You can always internationalize your site in a future phase of development.

But before you throw your computer out the window and consider door-to-door sales, we're going to turn those frowns upside down. Here are some pros to using the Internet to sell goods and services:

- ✔ **E-commerce coup: Retail isn't all that.** Retail doesn't translate only into dollar signs. It also can mean, "I have to go out in my car on this rainy day, stand in line at the store, and deal with salespeople." The Internet doesn't offer instant delivery, but it does offer pain-free *instant gratification*. You can shop anytime — online stores don't have to close. Ever. And purchases are delivered directly to you. Some sites allow you to ship gifts directly to their recipients — talk about convenience — and will even gift-wrap them for you and print a personal message on the packing slip. We talk more about shipping in Chapter 18.

- ✔ **E-commerce coup: Humans sometimes aren't very nice.** The human touch can often mean, "Eww, ol' Zelda's toothless grin is kind of creepy," or "The shopping mall is crowded, the salespeople don't know what they're talking about, and the cashier doesn't know how to process my credit card." You can compete with advantages like that!

- ✔ **E-commerce coup: Commerce internationale.** The advantages of international commerce are obvious. It's a great big world out there, and most of the folks in it have money to spend. That doesn't mean that international e-commerce is especially easy. If you really want to try it, then you have to put everything into successfully pulling international e-commerce off. That means dealing with the headaches — and quit that annoying whining, Mr. Millionaire.

Opening the floodgates

Gateway (www.gateway.com) expanded its mail order, telemarketing business to both the Web and bricks-and-mortar stores. Gateway's Web site enables people to build custom computers and have them delivered right to their homes. And through stores across the United States, Gateway has gained access to markets that telemarketing and the World Wide Web could never reach.

Gateway's annual report tells a powerful tale. It doesn't report on the channels Gateway uses to sell its products; instead, it reports on the customer demographics of who bought Gateway products. By integrating its business, Gateway grew to a $9.6 billion enterprise as of fiscal year 2000. Moral: You can have your bricks-and-mortar, and sell on the Web, too.

Airborne Express earns its wings

Airborne Express (www.airborne.com) uses the Web to help you ship your packages quickly. You can use its Web site to schedule pick up, calculate shipping rates, and even track packages while they're en route to their destinations.

You can use the services of Airborne Express to get your packages out the door, and use its Internet services to help your customers track packages, whether they're being sent by air or ground.

E-Commerce: Selling without . . .

So how does e-commerce change the way you work? Surely e-commerce can't somehow magically prevent a distributor from having to maintain a warehouse — warehouses are the whole point of being a distributor!

E-commerce doesn't really eliminate any steps in the distribution chain; it just eliminates *redundancy* in the distribution chain. If you take a good, hard look at some of the traditional business models you're already accustomed to, it seems that every link in the supply chain (the businesses that work together to get products to customers as we discuss in Chapter 16) buys products, stores them in warehouses, pays taxes on them, sells them to someone, receives returns, and so on.

Although you can eliminate salespeople, warehouses, storefronts, and many other overhead costs in an e-commerce business, carefully consider whether you should. A wise man once said, "Just because you *can* do a thing, does not necessarily mean you *should* do that thing." He may not have been talking about e-commerce, but that wisdom definitely applies to e-commerce!

Selling without a physical storefront

Selling without a physical storefront means that you're open for business 24 hours a day, seven days a week. People from anywhere in the world can reach you day and night.

Of course with a virtual store, you don't have to find clerks who will man the store at 3 a.m. No commercial lease, no water bill, no property tax. But now you have a computer infrastructure to deal with. You have a room full of strange boxes, and you have no idea what they do. You depend upon arcane wizards — network engineers, Webmasters, and Web designers — to keep you up and running. And although you don't need as many employees, they sure cost more!

CASE STUDY

For Chrysler's sake — that's a great site!

Ever been hassled by car salesmen when you're shopping for a vehicle? Avoid the noise by going online to any of the major U.S. automobile manufacturers to interactively build a vehicle with the exact features and options you want. At Chrysler's Web site, for example, you can see the additional cost for each choice (option) you select. It's amazing how simple it is for a customer to talk himself into a much more expensive vehicle just by giving him choices and leaving the decision to himself.

With e-commerce, you still have the same basic process of presenting your offering to customers and overcoming their objections. You need to replace a salesperson who can look customers in the eye, with a compelling story that answers customers' questions and helps overcome their objections.

TIP

Many of the techniques used in catalog sales work well for Web sites. But you have a whole slew of tricks that catalogs lack:

- ✔ You can monitor your customers' online activity and interactively *upsell* (sell better, more expensive models) or suggest appropriate (more expensive) accessories and add-ons.

- ✔ You don't need to wait for the next printing of the catalog or flyer to sell new products; you can change your site everyday, if you want.

- ✔ You can program your site to adapt to the individual needs and interests of each customer.

- ✔ You can build customer profiles that remember what people like, what they have ordered in the past, and how they tend to use the site. Then your servers can deliver a customized site that organizes services and products in a manner that is most likely to attract the attention of that customer.

PROS AND CONS

One downside to not having salespeople is that you miss out on the benefits of the really good ones who earn their keep. Although you can add interactivity, information, slick graphics, and bells and whistles to your Web site, you can't replace a good salesperson's ability to read customers, make them feel at ease, overcome their real objections, and close the deal. (If we could write software that did all that, we would have cashed in and bought an island).

Selling without warehouses

Virtual warehousing is one of the most exciting aspects of e-commerce, and one that many businesses have been able to benefit from. The idea is that when you take orders from your customers, you don't actually have any inventory on hand. Instead, you transmit the orders to your distributors and suppliers. They, in turn, ship the products to your customers directly — you never actually see the products.

Making a virtual warehouse work requires solid business relationships with your distributors and suppliers, and good contractual agreements. However, not all distributors and suppliers are willing to act as virtual warehouses.

Getting supplies and distributing goods

Online, you don't need to distribute goods to each physical bricks-and-mortar store you have, so you can keep inventory and costs low. And by partnering with suppliers, you can automate the ordering process and keep the pipeline of goods flowing without errors and delays.

People who make purchases on the Web don't expect to be able to touch or hold products. They make decisions based on the information you provide (unless they have touched and felt the product elsewhere). That opens the door for *preselling*. From books and CDs to movies and new technology items, many products are presold on the Web. If you capture the customer before a product hits the store shelves, you can beat out your competition without even being first to market. Cool, huh?

Retail stores have a long and relatively slow *supply chain* (the process of getting stuff from the manufacturer to the customer). A manufacturer makes something, physically ships it to a distributor, and the distributor ships the product to the store; the store places the product on display and sells it to Johnny Q. Public.

Businesses can take advantage of the Internet to speed up the supply chain in one of two ways:

- ✔ As soon as a product is available, you can start selling it, even if you don't have it in stock.

- ✔ Or, customers can preorder products that haven't even been released yet.

Speeding up the supply chain requires serious cooperation between your business and its suppliers, vendors, shippers, and systems. Systems? Yeah, you need to integrate your technology (and data) with partners to pull off quick deliveries. See Chapter 16.

Auto sales the Autobytel way

Autobytel.com (www.autobytel.com) combines the strength of the Web with the power of salespeople. You can go to its site and browse through a large selection of used cars. Tell the site what you're looking for, what you're willing to pay, and how far you're willing to drive, and it generates a list of vehicles, complete with photos. After you choose the vehicles you're interested in, the site passes your name onto a salesperson at the car dealership.

Selling without advertising and offering incentives

Many Web sites enable users to compare the prices of your products with the prices your competitors' products. If you all sell gizmos but you charge 20 percent more for the exact same gizmo than your competition does, you really need to offer some sort of incentive for customers to want to buy it from you. It's not like customers have driven to your store from across town and will buy the item just because they happen to see it. The bottom line: You must add value to your products and services — real value that you can sell though the Web.

Advertising via e-mail can be more annoying to customers than sending junk snail mail, but if you do it right, it can be a very effective sales tool. See Chapter 6 for more on marketing.

On the Web, you can get your catalog, brochures, flyers, and ads out there just as soon as you approve them, in Internet speed. As soon as you can conceive something, you can get it out there and try it. Post it on your Web server. Get your business partners to put it on their sites, too.

Go to Dell, dang it!

Dell Computer (www.dell.com), one of the largest suppliers of PCs in the United States, builds computers to order. Dell has found that online orders have a 20 percent lower return rate than orders that are placed over the phone. Customers who design their own PCs on the Web tend to get exactly what they want, without other people confusing the issue or misinterpreting the results.

It's common for one business to place ads for another business on its site. Organizations can trade links or charge for them. Ads can build your site and also serve as a source of income to fund your e-commerce endeavors.

Banner advertising enables you to place ads in high-traffic sites such as Yahoo!, MSN, or AOL. A simple click on the ad takes the customer right to your store — try to do that with a billboard! Even better yet, you can place your ads on the Web sites of companies that sell complementary products. For example, companies such as AOL can get links on Gateway's and Dell's Web sites.

Selling without return counters

Do you have fond memories of trying to return an unwanted purchase to your local Mega Mart? Return counters are a retailer's greatest nightmare. Retailers are caught between wanting to increase sales and wanting to maintain good customer relationships. Retailers would *love* to do away with return counters, if only they could.

Sorry, e-commerce can make *counter* go away, but it can't get rid of the *returns*. There is a bright side, though: By using the impersonal abstraction of the Web to handle returns, you remove much of the stress and potential abuse that return counters have come to embody.

You have to make sure that your online store clearly states your return policies. Set clear, easy-to-understand policies, indicating a maximum length of time for returns, who will pay for return shipping charges, whether original shipping charges are refundable, what types of merchandise can and cannot be returned, and so forth.

Now for the return process itself. When a customer wants to return merchandise, have your online store issue a return authorization number of some kind, along with directions for the customer to return his or her purchase. Then after you receive the returned merchandise, you can credit the customer's credit card account or ship exchange merchandise, as directed. No muss, no fuss. And by conducting the return through your computer system, returning that merchandise to your distributor is much easier, too. Your computers can immediately obtain a return authorization from the distributor, if necessary, and print the necessary paperwork for the item to be shipped back so that you can receive credit for it.

Many customers want to return purchases they make through the Web to bricks-and-mortar stores. This type of arrangement can be an accounting nightmare, trying to balance the profit of the sale (made in one account) against the return charge (made to a different account). However, it can also help elevate your level of customer service to a notch above the competition, winning you a gold star and plenty of loyal customers.

B2C, B2B, and C3PO: Alphabet Soup That Spells Payola

So what will your take on e-commerce be? How will it fit within your existing business? Technology can make a lot of wonderful things happen for your business, but it can also make some especially horrible things happen to your business. Rather than focusing on what e-commerce technologies can do for your business, focus on what your business _needs_ e-commerce to do.

Never let technology be your guide! E-commerce is merely a set of technologies and techniques designed to help you build business. Your business has to be your guide on what you will do with e-commerce.

To help get your imagination flowing, in the next few sections we take a look at some common e-commerce business models. We discuss the pros and cons of the different models to help you decide whether your business can benefit from any of them.

The main difference between online B2B and bricks-and-mortar business relationships is that online business customers aren't looking for your company to become a _vendor_ (the business that sells widgets, and nothing but widgets, at a decent price); they're looking for you to become a _partner_.

E-tailer business models

E-tailing is the electronic version of retailing. (Remember, we have to put an _e-_ at the beginning of any term to make it new and exciting.) E-tailing is perhaps the most visible and, until recently, the most common form of e-commerce. It's the easiest to conceptualize because it deals with a form of commerce that everyone is familiar with. Here are some variations of e-tailing that are worth looking at:

✔ **Adding e-tailing to an existing retailer:** Taking an existing retail business online — becoming a _bricks-and-clicks_ retailer — gives you the greatest chance for success in the e-commerce world. Existing bricks-and-mortar organizations have an established business model and customer base. They have already developed vendor relationships and built a supply chain. All they are really adding is a new means of grabbing sales.

Of course, existing retail businesses also face considerable challenges when going online. Shipping individual products instead of cases of goods worldwide is not a trivial undertaking. Building a staff to handle the e-commerce side of the business and keeping those folks integrated with your existing business can be taxing. And your new, exciting e-commerce endeavor may threaten existing employees. If you can integrate e-commerce with your existing business, you offer your customers the widest range of options.

✔ **E-tailing from scratch:** Starting an e-tail business from scratch is one of the most complicated ways to get into e-commerce. You have all the usual hassles of starting a new business on top of the challenges of starting an e-commerce business. On the other hand, you have the flexibility to do things any way you want. If start-up costs are an issue, focus on virtual warehousing and other techniques to reduce or eliminate the need to carry inventory. This strategy requires a heavier up-front investment in software development because your e-commerce systems have to be able to communicate with your distributors to exchange order and catalog information.

Many *dot coms* (businesses that sell solely through the Web) have funded their efforts by selling stock and using the money to build their sites and advertise their operations. The fourth quarter of 2000 proved that this philosophy is flawed. You need a solid business model that will yield a profit within a reasonable amount of time. But getting partners to help fund your effort can get you over the hump and keep your effort moving forward.

✔ **Keeping e-tail and retail separate:** If you're not ready to put the reputation of your existing business on the line, consider forming an independent Internet business. By defining clear lines of distinction between your traditional business and your online business, you can keep your online business at arm's length. If it succeeds, you win. If not, you can cut it loose, without affecting your existing business.

Keeping your e-business a distinct and separate business entity often results in failure if you're just trying it to test the waters. Learning to sell a new way with new tools takes a lot of time and energy. Of course, you can hire an experienced e-business manager who is highly motivated to make the venture succeed (it's that or get in line at the unemployment office). But unless you're ready to commit the time, effort, and funds to make this venture work, you should not expect to succeed.

Selling products to other businesses

Study after study confirms that the largest potential for e-commerce lies in business-to-business (B2B) transactions. Building partnerships and relationships with other organizations can save time and money, and reduce frustration by minimizing errors, paperwork, and overhead costs.

The heart of B2B is getting partners onboard. After all, it takes two (or a dozen, if you're ambitious and ambidextrous) to tango. You need to find common ground for sharing information and determining how you can equitably help each other save money by reducing time and paperwork for one another. The bottom line is the improvement in your company's bottom line. Read through Chapter 17 for more on saving through *e-procurement*.

Another advantage of B2B is the integration of systems. By establishing long-term relationships with your business customers and automating processes, you save yourself and your business customers a lot of paperwork, overhead, and errors. Offering automated supply-chain services to business customers can win you new clients and open new markets. This value-added method of delivering goods can make you the preferred supplier for your business clients.

Adding e-commerce to a B2B scenario requires a lot more creativity than simply installing a Web server with an online storefront. Here are some examples:

- ✔ **Helping smaller customers:** If you distribute products to smaller retail stores, you can, as the middleman, help them do a better job and be more competitive by creating an online portal storefront, called an *e-marketplace*, which other businesses put their brand name on. You develop a complete catalog and ordering system, and partner with your customers to create branded versions of the online store with their names on it. This technique enables smaller retail businesses to offer everything you carry, without requiring them to make the investment required to actually stock it all.

  You may charge a small additional percentage for products sold through the Web site to cover your additional costs. You still have the benefit of being able to deal with the retailer, who will deal with the final consumer for product returns, customer service problems, and so on.

- ✔ **Webifying special orders:** If you produce specialty items, you may have trouble building a retail-to-distributor network — in other words, getting retailers to stock those items. These items are likely low-volume, high-cost items that help round out retailer offerings but don't justify the cost of maintaining inventory. By offering these specialty items through Web retailers, the retailers don't have to stock the products; all they need are the product specifications to post on their Web sites. They carry a full product line, and you open many more doors of opportunity, at little or no cost to yourself.

- ✔ **Getting standardized:** The e-commerce world continues to grow and evolve. Exciting technologies are being developed to create standards for common business information such as invoices and purchase orders. Investigate these technologies and start developing the e-commerce software that you need to take advantage of. These standards will make it easier for your customers to place orders, pay you, and manage their relationship with you — all electronically.

When more customers start dealing with you online, your salespeople will have time to focus on finding new customers rather than worrying about keeping old ones in the family.

Middleman feeling the squeeze? Not V-SPAN

V-SPAN (www.vspan.com) offers video- and audioconferencing services to its B2B clients. The company developed a self-service conferencing system that can be branded for its client resellers. Now resellers can offer a full range of broadband Internet services to their customers, including videoconferencing, without building a videoconferencing infrastructure and directing their clients to other vendors. V-SPAN gets the additional business and keeps others from building competitive businesses.

Developing partnerships

Be sure you understand the important distinction between being a vendor and being a partner because this difference is one of the biggest challenges to online B2B — and it's a pretty radical shift from the way businesses typically interact offline. If, as a vendor, you cannot deliver, your customer just gets on the phone and calls someone else. As a business partner, you have rendered ineffective the planning systems of your partners and violated trusts on which they plan their enterprise.

E-commerce business partnerships require a greater investment of time, technology, and funds when the relationship begins. That investment is repaid when the process of placing orders and scheduling shipments is automated. You invest more for a larger return in ongoing business that helps everyone involved operate more efficiently and profitably.

You need to do a lot of work when you establish an online B2B relationship that you've never experienced offline. Some of these activities may seem like a big pain, but they all reap benefits as well:

- ✔ **E-commerce challenge: You have to establish how data will be exchanged.** The offline world's methods of phone, fax, and mail aren't sufficient. You need to agree on file formats, delivery methods, processing deadlines, and performance guarantees.

- ✔ **E-commerce coup: After you can exchange data, things run wickedly fast:** Systems can trade data with one another. No paperwork, no human error — and your people are free for more important tasks than shuffling paper.

- ✔ **E-commerce challenge: You have to agree on a contract.** Agreeing on terms can be tough because everyone wants to get the most protection and benefit. Be prepared to live up to your salespeople's promises in writing.

✔ **E-commerce coup: Contract in hand, you can count on the business.** Integrating business systems between companies is no small task, so when it's done, you have some serious commitment from your customers. It's a great way to solidify business relationships.

✔ **E-commerce challenge: You have to spend some face time with customers.** Although your electronic relationships may start online, you'll want to establish some kind of personal contact with your customers to close the relationship. That personal contact gives your customers a sense that a real person in your company cares about them, and can help to smooth out the bumps in a new relationship.

✔ **E-commerce coup: You're not just another dot com to your customers.** It profits your customer to see you do well. Your fates are tied, and you can help one another succeed.

Setting up contracts and sharing data

Always create a schedule for the establishment of your relationship, and ensure that the schedule includes a period for testing the relationship — check that data is being exchanged correctly, that both sides are happy with the process, and so forth.

A key component of B2B is exchanging data, whether it's information being purchased outright or simply information being exchanged to facilitate the business, such as purchase orders and invoices. You can share business data a billion ways with a million variations, but you'll probably want to focus on the popular ways of sharing business data.

Business agreements can be complex documents. They must be, in order to protect the interests of everyone involved. Never enter into a business agreement without a written agreement that has been reviewed by your attorney. Make sure your attorney is aware of your business concerns, such as customer ownership, and that he or she reviews the business agreement to ensure it addresses and protects your concerns.

Building e-marketplaces

Some online companies are simply too small or specialized to successfully run their own online businesses. One of the great advantages of the Internet is that many different companies can come together in one venue to complement one another, providing a more complete shopping experience for their shared customers. This arrangement is called an *e-marketplace*.

E-marketplaces are the electronic equivalent of shopping malls. They can be organized horizontally, providing a common set of products to different

Sam Walton became a multimillionaire: You may want to take note

Wal-Mart is the leading retailer in the world (as of this writing) because of a number of innovations, including sharing information. In addition to orders, Wal-Mart lets vendors know how their products are selling throughout Wal-Mart stores. By providing analytical sales data, the vendors can better tailor their advertising, product offerings, packaging, and other factors to keep sales humming. And Wal-Mart benefits because the vendors work to find ways to sell more of their products through Wal-Mart's bricks-and-mortar locations.

industries (such as PaperExchange, at `www.paperexchange.com`) or vertically to support the needs of a specific market (Ventro, at `www.chemdex.com`). Read more about e-marketplaces in Chapter 19.

Here are some e-marketplace advantages and disadvantages:

- ✔ **E-commerce coup: Happy customers = increased profits.** When a wide breadth of products and services are available and consumers can find everything they need (or want) in one stop, they tend to spend more and to come back for seconds.

- ✔ **E-commerce challenge: If one vendor ticks off a customer, customers stop using the site.** If customers go to an e-marketplace and one of the vendors disappoints them, those customers are likely to abandon the site. And even though *you* would never let them down, you become guilty by association.

- ✔ **E-commerce coup: Share and share alike.** E-marketplaces enable small online businesses to coexist and prosper together, just like a shopping mall does. Like shopping malls, online marketplaces allow the participating businesses to share some costs, making it more feasible for them to have an online business.

- ✔ **E-commerce challenge: All the businesses suffer if business is bad.** If an e-marketplace fails, everyone loses the investment they placed in it. The community has to decide what it is willing to invest to get the site to succeed. Insufficient investment is a guarantee of failure.

Well-managed e-marketplaces, like well-managed shopping malls, provide a balance of participating businesses that sell a variety of products and services. Ideally, each business in the marketplace should have a monopoly on the products or services it offers so that the businesses within the marketplace can complement one another. You never want to have to compete with six other online haberdashers.

CASE STUDY

Your prayers are answered — finding property *and* casualty insurance info at one site

Property and Casualty.com (www.property andcasualty.com) allows over 350 different vendors to work together to provide products and services aimed at property and casualty insurance agents and companies. From communications and account management software to insurance products, this site provides a great place to start looking for answers. And each participating company has little investment risk in participating in the project.

Selling products through other businesses

If you make and sell products, or you provide services, that complement the products and services of other businesses, why not join forces and help one another profit? E-commerce enables you to do business through, with, over, and under other businesses. What's more, e-commerce makes it easy and reliable to play Twister with your partners.

Just be sure that the trading you do with partners (of products, services, and information) is on the level and that your business doesn't get locked into an unfavorable situation. Call in legal backup! (Yes, that is an order.)

An E-Commerce Twist: Selling Service with a Cyber-Smile

Here's a fact: If the Internet isn't the perfect medium for selling and disseminating information, it's a close second. By nature, the Internet allows instant delivery of electronic goods (such as downloadable software and documents) and helps people work together across the world more easily than they otherwise could.

Fact number two: Much of the overhead costs for consulting organizations, service organizations, and other companies that sell so-called *soft goods* (useful stuff that you can't put in a box and ship to customers but that travels quite well electronically) comes from maintaining offices and physical locations.

One hand washing the other: Referral partners

One way to sell through other companies is to ask for referrals, also referred to as *cross-referencing*. Cross-referencing allows customers to find out about products and services that complement the ones they're looking at or purchasing online. Here's how the process works.

✔ You distribute widgets to Partner A. You can ask Partner A to suggest that customers purchase your size-four widget holder, complete with cleaning kit, whenever the customer purchases a size-four widget.

✔ Perhaps Partner B sells widget-tracking software that you distribute. Partner B can recommend that customers check out your widget software training classes.

Whatever the arrangement, referrals can be a great way to boost business — for both businesses. Of course, you have to cut your partners in on the action, but the upside is that if you refer customers, you can get a little slice, as well.

Remember, your partners may not want to sell your complementary products and services alongside their own wares because you might cut into their action and distract customers from their core business. After all, your partners are in this to make money, too. Try explaining the upside of making a referral arrangement with your partners: Internet shoppers are a tough demographic — they want the complete package. As long as partners offer referrals to *their* partners — who, in turn, offer the complementary products or services — they build their core demographics and increase the possibility that customers will come back. Tell your partners, "I know this sounds like a pyramid scheme, but I promise you that if we do this right the bottom line will increase across the board." (Then tell them you were just kidding about the pyramid scheme reference.)

Here's what these two facts have to do with each other. The Internet enables businesses that sell soft goods to offer improved service to their customers and save money on annoying costs such as rent and operating expenses.

Selling information

Companies have long sold marketing information, such as mailing lists, research results, and demographic information, to other businesses.

The Internet makes it possible for these companies to do business faster, more efficiently, and more frequently than ever before. In fact, information of every kind is easy to sell across the Internet in ways you may not have imagined. Watch out for privacy issues when it comes to selling data — change is always a-brewing where the Internet is concerned, and laws (like the Graham-Leach-Bliley Act) that aim to protect consumers' privacy rights are being passed all the time.

Consulting at a cut rate

talenthill (www.talenthill.com) has taken the Internet to heart. Staffed with consultants who have worked with other top-notch consulting firms such as Andersen (www.andersen.com), which you may know by its former name, Arthur Andersen, and Deloitte and Touche (www.dttus.com), talenthill now plies its services through the Internet. Fees are greatly reduced (as little as $80 per contact), and folks with Internet access can get high-level guidance for their business.

Consulting: It's not just for bricks-and-mortar businesses anymore

One of the most common services sold in the business world today is consulting. When a company provides *consulting* services, it's in the business of renting the knowledge of a person or a group to another person or group. The Internet stands ready to change these transactions.

In addition to the traditional Internet technologies you may think of that enable you to market products nationally and around the world — for example, e-mail and Web sites — other technologies make bringing consulting services online a no-brainer. For example, many consulting firms use a combination of video-conferencing, online information sharing, and online collaboration. Consultants don't have to get together in a physical location to share their thoughts and discoveries, and they don't have to be in the customer's facility while they work. They can deliver work the minute it's complete through Internet-based communications to minimize delays.

Many of these technologies are the same ones that make it possible for company employees to work from home more easily than ever before; we discuss these technologies in Chapter 7.

Part II

Making the Leap of Faith: Integrating Your Business

The 5th Wave   By Rich Tennant

"So far our Web presence has been pretty good.
We've gotten some orders, a few inquiries and
nine guys who want to date our logo."

In this part . . .

How do you go about making your traditional business an e-commerce business? All of the business rules are the same (except for the ones that aren't), and the business models are the same (except for how they're different), so how hard can it be? In this part of the book, we take a look at how you can actually get to work integrating your existing business so that it can compete in this new-fangled, fancy, real-time, ultra-modern thing called the Internet. Get ready to start making up new rules for making your e-business as successful as your traditional business.

Chapter 5

Integrating Your Business

*Y*our decision to move to e-commerce affects every aspect of your business. You will create new departments and positions. You will build new systems and develop new ways for measuring success. You will automate parts of your existing processes and find new ways of doing things. You will leverage the strengths of your business partners to improve how you do business.

This chapter shows you how to take on the new issues and opportunities that you face and how to fully utilize your greatest assets — your employees — to successfully and profitably move your business forward.

As you integrate e-commerce into your organization, you create new positions, as well as add new responsibilities, to existing job descriptions. We humans do not like change, so the manner in which you present the transition to your staff could easily determine its success or failure. You must get the key players in your organization to buy into these staffing changes.

These new positions often command high salaries and tend to attract many applicants, particularly within your own staff. Make the job requirements and the risks clear so that your staff members can make good decisions on whether to pursue these roles. Check out Chapter 7 for more about the new work force.

Understanding the Challenges Your Existing Processes and Systems Face

The best thing about your new e-commerce venture is also your biggest challenge. Business is going to come pouring in from new avenues, increasing your staff's workload *and* adding new duties. Too much business may be a great problem to have, but if you are unprepared for it, it can be a disaster. Here's what you have to watch out for:

- ✔ **Inefficient order-processing systems:** You need to make certain that you are processing orders efficiently. (We talk about automating these systems in the section "Updating, Automating, and Integrating Systems" later in this chapter.)

- ✔ **Shipping and fulfillment issues:** You need to handle the new requirements of shipping. If you're not accustomed to doing a lot of shipping as a part of your existing business, you have to really beef up your shipping staff (read how to put out these fires in Chapter 6).

- ✔ **Customer service overload:** Customer service is different over the Web than it is offline. You get new problems, such as, "I can't find what I'm looking for on your Web site" and "But I didn't mean to place that order when I clicked the Buy button." You have new remedies, such as sending an e-mail response, speaking to customers in chat rooms, or canceling an order through a new computer program. Your customer service personnel need to be trained, and, at least at the beginning, you'll likely need more staff. See Chapter 11 for more on customer service in the e-commerce world. If you implement customer relationship management to keep up-to-date on your customers, your staff will need training to learn to use it effectively. We tell you more about CRM systems in Chapter 15.

- ✔ **Management debacles:** The methods and metrics you currently use to track success will get a facelift while you use them to assess your e-commerce efforts and the development of successful e-marketplace strategies. Although you started in the right place buying and reading this book, you are only at the beginning of your journey.

Updating, Automating, and Integrating Systems

Your business has already achieved a measure of success. Moving to e-commerce should enhance that success and allow you to grow into new markets and new levels of profitability. As you clearly define your existing business processes, it won't take you long to discover ways that e-commerce technology can make those processes better. You can automate systems and empower disparate parts of your business to communicate with each other (and the virtual world outside your business' servers) more quickly and more clearly. But no matter what you do, you need to integrate at least a couple of your systems so that they can share important data in real time.

Many processes must cross process boundaries. For example, shipping products requires you to decrease inventory and update accounting so that an invoice is generated. This is a *transaction*. You're only asking for trouble if the inventory gets updated and the accounting system doesn't (or vice versa).

When integrating systems, you need to conduct transactions across systems. Because you use different applications, you need an external process to make certain that both systems update. If one fails, it must *rollback,* or undo, the update on the other systems so everything stays in sync.

Preening your processes

The process of developing e-commerce often benefits your entire organization by forcing you to improve and automate existing systems (maybe systems you've had no reason to look at all these years). And, of course, you need to build new systems to accommodate the changes of selling on the Web. Start by evaluating your existing processes. Look at the processes in order of importance to your business.

Try to be as fair as possible (no grade inflation, now) when you ask the following questions:

✔ **How automated (or manual) is the process?**

If Mabel has to take the orders entered in the sales system and type them into the accounting system, you are wasting time and money, and you introduce the potential for errors.

✔ **What ideas do you have for accelerating the process?**

If Mabel holds orders for 30 or 40 minutes, you miss shipping the last four orders that day. What happens on the days when she is off sick or on vacation? You need to keep your orders moving full speed, all the time.

✔ **Will the process hold up if (when, we hope!) the volume from new channels increases?**

What happens when Mabel types all day, and the orders haven't been re-typed? You have to hire another Mabel, buy another computer, and endure the costs and hassles that come with both.

Call in your business analyst to determine which systems need help, and where you get the best return from your investment. This analyst can grade your systems, let you know where you stand, and also show you ways to save, just as we describe in Chapter 7.

If you find that your processes are receiving poor grades, you don't have to take steps to solve the problems all at once. You can improve and automate systems incrementally. You can pay the salaries of a lot of data-entry clerks before you can justify a $750,000 automation project.

Improving your existing systems

You can derive the greatest benefit from your systems through integration of as many systems as possible. For example, if your customers can find out which products you have on hand and when you can deliver them, they have no other reason to go to a competitor's Web site. That means you need to make sure that your order-entry system and your accounting system can talk to each other — and to your inventory and manufacturing systems.

Don't fall victim to the mañana complex. Some things just have to be taken care of as soon as possible. If you reserve a product for a customer that is on credit hold and turn away a new client because you have nothing to deliver, you've missed a golden opportunity — and lost money. Figure 5-1 gives you a better idea of what we mean.

In Figure 5-1, you can see that the Web server needs to ask a database server for product catalog information. The server needs to talk to the minicomputer to check inventory; it needs to talk to the accounting mainframe to check credit balances and insert sales orders; and it needs to update the CRM system whenever customers place orders. This common scenario highlights the need to get the computer systems in your organization to work with one another.

Your Web site needs access to information from all these different systems. You need to replace the daily inventory printout and projected delivery schedule and manufacturing report with electronic equivalents that provide up-to-the-minute data. Your Web site is not the only thing that will enjoy the change. Your staff needs all this data as well. Integrating systems can improve productivity and reduce costs throughout your organization.

Application integration is a major undertaking. Carefully plan an enterprise-application strategy and framework that will support your organization's current needs and future growth.

Adding new systems to provide new opportunities

Some of your existing processes are most likely manual, which means that they'll probably need to be replaced with automated systems that provide accurate, timely data to your Web site. To find out about evaluating the systems you already have in place, see the section "Preening your processes" earlier in this chapter.

Carefully plan what systems will be replaced. Compare the costs with the benefits. You do not need to automate anything until the return on investment justifies the costs. It makes no sense to develop a $250,000 system to replace two $30,000/year employees.

Office Depot plays the integration game

Office Depot (www.officedepot.com) has knit systems and people together through its IT systems. Customers can purchase computers from Office Depot through its Web site, by phone, or at one of its bricks-and-mortar locations. The company's internal systems integrate all sales, regardless of channel. Office Depot can service its customers regardless of how and where they made a purchase, and its systems can combine resources to provide the highest level of service.

Parlez-vous français? Getting systems to talk

The term *enterprise* comprises the people, locations, and systems that make up your business. Most enterprises have different kinds of computers and different kinds of *applications*, or programs. And, for the most part, they don't share information easily with one another.

You can more rapidly integrate your applications by establishing an enterprise frame for sharing data across systems. Most Enterprise Resource Planning (ERP) systems provide an architecture and framework for sharing data. This means they have defined a common way that programs can share information. With one common communication method, you can find programs that help the systems communicate. They also enable processes to interact with one another transactionally.

ERP systems can be quite costly. Although they create a means of getting disparate applications to cooperate, they require customizations. But don't let cost or difficulty prevent you from rolling out an ERP system. Although it's a massive effort, ERP affords some of the greatest advantages in terms of costs savings.

To be successful, your e-commerce system needs to be based on a system of integrated communications. Choosing the right approach to actually make this integration a reality depends on a variety of factors:

- ✔ What common language or communication devices will cross systems most effectively?
- ✔ What software do you need to buy or write to handle these translations?
- ✔ What systems have the capacity to do the extra work of translating data to get the systems to talk?
- ✔ What do your existing systems already have to facilitate this communication?

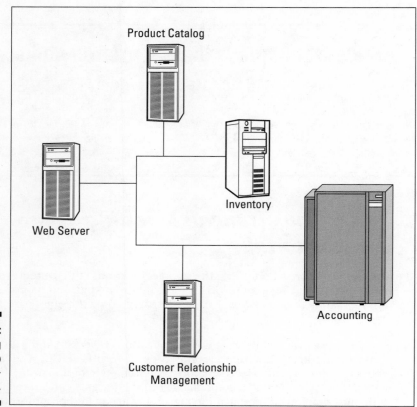

Figure 5-1:
Integrating
systems to
support e-
commerce.

Many systems are designed to speak in common protocols, such as EDI, XML, and other standards. You can use these standard mechanisms to keep systems talking to one another. You can also purchase commercial off-the-shelf software, such as NonStop Tuxedo software, available from Compaq (www.compaq.com) middleware, which helps facilitate translating business information from one format to another. Tuxedo, for example, controls transactions across systems, which keeps your systems working together without incident. *Middleware* is a program that helps systems communicate and work together.

Keeping Your Systems Safe

In the age of the Internet, protecting the flow of data in your systems is essential. As you integrate your internal systems with public Internet systems, you need to protect your business from hackers and intruders. You need to implement protection on several levels:

✔ **Keep the boogeyman out.** Protect your network from unauthorized access through the public Internet. You can use firewalls, proxy servers, and other physical network devices to keep intruders out.

✔ **Make sure that you're dealing with the *real* John Doe.** Most software includes authentication to keep unwanted intruders out. Make certain that those systems are implemented and that you have a password policy that makes it difficult to get into the software illegitimately.

✔ **Keep your competition from getting too much information.** Set policies that limit the amount of information that the Internet systems can access. Isolate as much of the public information on your site — such as product prices or descriptions — from the private business information you want to keep from your competitors, such as sales totals or customer lists.

You can create a *demilitarized zone (DMZ)* that separates your internal systems from the public Internet. You connect your Web server to the public Internet with one connection and to your intranet with the other. Figure 5-2 illustrates how a DMZ is wired. For more on securing your network, see Chapter 20.

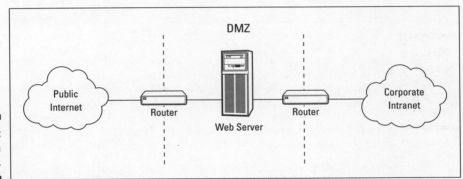

Figure 5-2:
Creating a
DMZ.

Finding the New Balance: Integrating Accounting for E-Commerce

Integration of e-commerce systems often changes the processes you use for accounting. Much of the business acceleration and cost savings that you gain through e-commerce systems come from automating paperwork and approval processes.

Your accounting system needs to share data with your e-commerce system. You need to check credit on the fly, enter orders and generate invoices automatically, and process credit cards online while customers wait.

Accelerating to keep up

The famous greeting card manufacturer Hallmark learned a stern lesson in application integration. Offering flower delivery through its Web site (www.hallmark.com), the company uses a different model than its major competitors, 1-800-FLOWERS (www.1800flowers.com) and FTD (www.ftd.com). Unlike its competitors, which provide flowers from hundreds of florists located throughout the nation, Hallmark prepares its flowers in a central facility and ships them overnight throughout the nation. One Mother's Day, Hallmark's CEO placed an order for his mother near the end of the day. There was a last-minute, mad dash to get that order out the door.

To keep up with the demand, particularly during peak times such as Mother's Day, Hallmark implemented order, inventory, and warehouse management systems that integrate with its online storefront. Orders received by 9 p.m. must be completed and shipped by midnight in order to arrive in the hands of customers in time. Automation is what enables Hallmark to attempt to compete in this market. Using automation to accelerate business processes and handle real-time data allow Hallmark to use a distinct business model to compete.

Many accounting systems have updates and modules that facilitate e-commerce integration. Accounting software from Great Plains (www.greatplains.com), Solomon (www.solomon.com), and others can easily handle the additional requirements your e-commerce system adds to the accounting system.

So what do the bean counters need to watch in your e-commerce business? A lot. Look for the following capabilities in accounting application software:

- **Count every penny.** Track direct costs for e-commerce deployment. These costs include employee salaries, software and hardware expenses, and costs for Internet access.

- **Count the indirect costs.** Capture indirect costs, such as training costs and expenses relating to system design and deployment. Many existing employees will be affected, directly or indirectly, by the e-commerce rollout.

- **Assess new revenue streams.** Don't associate many traditional sales costs (such as commissions) to new sales channels, and don't associate new expenses (such as single-item delivery costs) to traditional streams. New categories and processes for tracking need to be integrated into the system.

Most e-commerce efforts run at a loss in the initial year or two. The initial costs of setting up the system take some time to amortize. Although you should have forecasted this, keep track of your progress so that you achieve profitability on schedule.

One person, one customer

One of the hardest things to do is identify the same customers across systems. For example, we worked with a customer that opened a store on Yahoo! Customers who frequented its bricks-and-mortar stores would also buy from the Internet. This made it difficult to know which customers were counted twice — once on the Internet and once at the physical store. This parallel purchasing can alter demographics and other metrics. We solved the issue by writing custom software that used common data, such as a mailing address, to combine the Web store customers with the bricks-and-mortar customers.

Delivering accounting data to Web systems

You have to let your Web software know some things about your business in order to function. From credit data to information about your customers to order history, you must expose some of the data to your e-commerce site. The art is protecting that data from unauthorized access.

Getting the lowdown on customers

Many e-commerce systems keep their own customer profile data. But for most enterprises, the accounting system maintains order history and credit status. That means that you need to connect your accounting data to your Web customer data. You need to choose how you get this data from your accounting system:

- ✔ **Periodically.** You can periodically export customer data from accounting into the Web system. Periodically exporting duplicates data, but it takes pressure off the accounting system to deliver data on demand to the e-commerce software. It also protects the rest of your customer information because the Web servers have no direct access to your accounting data. If you have mainframes, this data can be exported in text files and easily imported into your customer database.

- ✔ **Interactively.** You can interactively draw data from the accounting system when your Web system needs it. This process consumes resources from your accounting system but provides the most up-to-date information. And you do not duplicate data. Interactive connections with your accounting software can facilitate automating order entry and interactive processing of payments.

Show me the money: Handling payments

Interactive e-payments from customers can accelerate cash flow. Of course, your accounting system needs to handle *e-payments* online to get the full benefit from this. E-payments include credit cards or checks. You can find out more about accepting payments over the Web in Chapter 12.

Many sites allow payment though alternate means. If you allow customers to pay by paper checks, money orders, or other methods that your business doesn't immediately receive, you must hold onto the order until payment clears. For many firms, this is business as usual. The hard part is connecting the Web order to the payment prior to release.

If you establish a B2B site, you may need to handle automated payments. Your accounting system has to validate those payments. You may also need to synchronize the purchase of goods and placing orders with customer requests. By acting as a member within a supply chain, your system coordinates with your business partners to automate order delivery. And your accounting system lives at the heart of this transfer. You can discover more about supply chains in Chapter 16.

Revisiting your reports

With all the accounts and new things to track, you need to come up with some new reports, and you need to revise some old favorites. Because tracking e-commerce revenues and expenses differs widely from tracking your existing sales figures, you need to work with your staff to find the right measures. Things you want to watch include

- ✔ **Cost-of-sales.** On the Internet, you can often track sales specifically to advertising that got people to buy — this is a great resource with very detailed information on what works and what doesn't. (Look at Chapter 6 for more details.)

- ✔ **Systems charges.** Many of the systems will be specific to your e-commerce project, such as software development and Web server expenses. Other costs are shared with your other systems, such as costs for ERP systems that improve business processes throughout your organization.

- ✔ **Revenue reporting.** If you integrate sales through the Internet and bricks-and-mortar stores, it is difficult to tell how one is doing compared with the other. If you completely isolate them, you limit customer options (such as where they can return goods). Your paradigm for analyzing revenue will alter the way you report.

You can also deliver reports using your e-commerce technology. Web-based reports can be kept up-to-date automatically, using color and graphics to display data in ways that make figures easy to understand . . . and save a rain forest or two along the way.

Many organizations need a quick daily read on critical indicators, such as daily production and revenue. Web reports are a simple, direct means of communicating this information.

Finding the bottom line

Many e-commerce sites enjoy meteoric growth. They enjoy triple-digit sales-growth figures and often show little signs of slowing. They also require an enormous initial investment to get off the ground. Generating $200 million in sales isn't that great if you spend $300 million to earn it.

Your initial business plan should provide guidelines for measuring success. The bottom line is not always the profitability of the Internet site. If your Web presence helps increase market share or prevents a competitor from stealing customers, it may earn its keep without earning sky-high profits. You can also *cannibalize* your bricks-and-mortar customer base and turn e-profits at the expense of your other revenue chains.

You need to measure the effect of your e-commerce effort as it integrates with your entire organization. Correlate your e-commerce activities with the other activities of your organization to see the overall picture.

Integrating Sales

Moving into the World Wide Web opens the door to new markets and new customers. Your sales force must learn to woo and coo customers in a completely new manner. Customer relationships through the Web are different, a blend of technology and personality.

Bulking up for e-commerce

When computer retailer CompUSA first rolled out an e-commerce presence, it expected to succeed on price alone. It created a distinct business, Cozone.com, that did not build on the name or bricks-and-mortar locations that CompUSA has throughout the United States. Cozone.com attempted to cash in on the Internet explosion, but failed.

What succeeded was CompUSA's business-to-business efforts. By deploying a reliable, high-speed network to connect its stores, CompUSA stores throughout the country can share data on pricing and inventory. Although this backbone currently supports offline sales, it forms a foundation for future ventures in online sales. The rollout of a SAP R/3 ERP system to integrate store sales helps unify the company and prepare it for more automated sales efforts.

Sales and product information

In most organizations, sales professionals spend a great deal of time answering simple, redundant questions about product features and capabilities. You can post much of this information on the Web, which helps everyone involved in the process:

- ✔ **Sales people can access the site** (either the public site or a private site for employees) to get to the most current sales and technical information. This is one of the fastest ways to disseminate data on product changes, price updates, promotions, and competitive analysis.

- ✔ **Third-party sales channels can get up-to-date information** from the Web site. They can also leverage your site to improve their sales. Providing this support to your third-party sales channels can add a great deal of value to your business partnerships and provide a distinct competitive edge.

- ✔ **Customers can get information** that helps them make decisions. The site can provide extended technical data, product comparisons, answers to frequently asked questions, case studies, and a variety of other support information. Because this is self-serve, they can read only the information they need to make their decision or answer their question. And the data is available 24 hours a day without tying up your sales staff.

Product configuration

People like to create things. By providing customers with the ability to design and configure the custom options on products, you help them convince themselves to buy it. See the case study on Chrysler in Chapter 4 for an example.

Allowing customers to configure their own products also reduces errors and returns. Dell and others have found that having customers choose their own options reduces mistakes and communication errors. Also, customers take more responsibility for the configuration if they enter the order data themselves. And they are more likely to keep the product they specified.

Pricing and proposal systems

Pricing can be quite complex. Calculating product discounts, sales commissions, and costs for adding options and accessories can be a nightmare. Software systems can provide consistency to determining price. You can support your sales force in a variety of ways:

✔ **Standardized quotes:** Help salespeople organize quotations and proposals for customers and prospects by storing that data within your database. Having access to the history of the contact and previous proposals can help salespeople address the current needs and objections of these prospects. Proposals can be generated automatically and delivered more quickly, which reduces administrative overhead and provides a more consistent image.

✔ **Checklist verification:** Provide an interactive checklist to ensure that all product features and accessories have been addressed. This checklist helps keep salespeople honest and can get new people up-to-speed much more quickly. It also reduces errors.

✔ **Consistent pricing:** Automatically determine prices to keep pricing consistent. Doing so also enables you to apply promotions and complex pricing schemes with mechanical efficiency.

Salespeople do not always sit behind their desks. Providing access to pricing and proposal systems through the Internet keeps these powerful sales tools as close as the nearest Internet connection.

Order entry and fulfillment

Throughout much of this book, we discuss the construction of Web storefronts. You can provide customers with a catalog of products and services, enabling them to use the Web to place their orders. Integration of enterprise applications enables you to deliver those orders to customers with a minimum of paperwork or bureaucracy.

You can also build systems that receive orders from your business partners. Those orders can be automated to help accelerate business and reduce costs for both you and your customers.

The Kroger Co. is the nation's largest grocery store chain. It has examined the Internet as an outlet for selling groceries, but has yet to find a model that fits its business. But it has put the Internet to work in another way. It uses GlobalNetXchange (GNX) auctions to procure supplies for its stores. Kroger needs to get provisions to over 2,300 stores in 31 states. By automating order entry and fulfillment, GNX helps Kroger contain costs and deliver goods to its network of bricks-and-mortar locations.

Relationship management

As you open more sales channels to your customers, data about your customers' activities becomes scattered across a variety of systems. But whether customers buy on the Web, in a store, or over the phone, they have a relationship with a single company. You need to pull together the information from all your systems to provide a unified view of all the activities of that customer in a single place.

Customer Relationship Management (CRM) software helps coalesce this information and organize it. Salespeople can use it keep track of all the contacts your organization has with its customers. Your Web systems can also use it to analyze customer activity and react to patterns that indicate relationships or waning. You can find out more about CRM systems in Chapter 15.

Easing Your Staff into the E-World

When you start new initiatives, people feel threatened. They worry that they won't catch on to the new skills they have to learn. Fearing change, they wonder whether they will lose their jobs, have new stress in the workplace, or discover that nothing about the changes will benefit them. And these are the people you need in order to make everything work.

Your Web projects are top secret. Make certain that you remind your employees that your progress reports are for their eyes only. Most people enjoy being trusted with confidences, and you can use this trust to improve camaraderie.

You're not going to develop your system in one day. Most systems roll out incrementally in phases. Here's what you should do to involve employees involved:

- **Tell your staff what's up.** After months of watching you plan, employees surely know that their world is changing — the wait is a little less excruciating if you let them know what to expect.

    - Use e-mail to circulate news on the progress of the system.

    - Use a simple Web site, published on your company's intranet (your company's private, internal Internet), to provide an overview of the initiative and your progress to date.

    - Deploy discussion groups for employees to try. This not only allows you to test the systems you will deploy for your customers but also keeps your employees involved in the process.

- **Turn employees loose on the system.** Provide regular demos and let the employees test the system. Enabling your employees — the people who know your business best — to become familiar with the system you're implementing solicits not just their support and enthusiasm, but also their invaluable expertise.

IDC has forecast that e-learning will continue to help companies solve their employee training for some time to come. Table 5-1 shows the revenue in millions of dollars.

Table 5-1   Worldwide Corporate E-Learning Review by Region

Region	1999	2000	2001	2002	2003	2004
North America	1,176	2,320	4,213	7,372	11,816	15,072
Japan	270	556	1,014	1,625	1,840	2,213
Western Europe	147	352	789	1,474	2,632	4,387
Latin America	69	139	264	489	789	1,023
Asia/Pacific	26	48	84	150	251	418

One timesaving solution to the training problem is to provide online training. Using computers to deliver training can really help in a number of ways:

✔ Online training can be delivered on demand rather than in pre-scheduled classes that you cannot afford to cancel.

✔ Online training forces employees to use their computers and their browsers. If you have a staff that is uncomfortable using computers, you can help those individuals overcome their fears.

✔ Each employee can move at his or her own pace, repeating lessons as required to ensure that he or she understands how to use the new systems.

✔ E-learning systems can easily record employees' training progress and provide their managers with clear, timely assessments.

Chapter 6

Marketing and Competing in Cyberspace

In This Chapter

▶ Developing brand recognition in cyberspace

▶ Carving out an e-commerce niche

▶ Identifying and understanding e-customers

▶ Making your mark on the Internet

The fundamental principles that make marketing important are the same whether you're in cyberspace or the so-called real world. You need to find the people who need or want the gadget you have to offer; convince them to purchase the gadget from you; and then offer them such good service that they not only tell all their friends but also come back again (frequently, you hope) for more gadgets. So much for Marketing 101.

Here's the catch: The methods and techniques you use to reach customers in cyberspace are very different than in the traditional business world. Where they go in cyberspace, how they get there, why they stay, and why they leave are all different. Vive la difference!

In this chapter, we explore proven methods for developing brand recognition among Web customers. You use these techniques for building and keeping an online customer base.

John Doe™: Developing Brand Recognition

If someone asks you whether you want a Coke or Pepsi, you immediately know you're being asked about a carbonated cola beverage — with distinct yet subtle differences between the two. Both these major cola bottlers spend millions of dollars trying to coerce you into having a definite opinion about which one you prefer.

How do you accomplish this same brand recognition in cyberspace? Why do so many people buy books from Amazon when Borders or Barnes & Noble both have excellent Web sites, backed with bricks-and-mortar locations? You need to build a site that flaunts your organization's uniqueness, advertising that draws customers, and highways on the Internet to get people the·e.

Defining your brand distinction

Every organization has a value proposition that defines why people should do business with that organization. You may never have clearly defined yours, but it exists nonetheless. You may have the lowest prices or the widest selection. You may have unique products not available anywhere else. You may offer services, individually or in interesting packages, that help people in a special way. Perhaps you offer the best customer support and service in the industry.

You have to capture this value proposition in Web graphics and your Web site. Traditional advertising concepts must evolve to use the revolutionary changes offered by the World Wide Web. You need to maintain the image of your existing business and find ways to extend that brand distinction to the Internet.

Ziff Davis provides a wide variety of magazines to the computer industry, making money by selling advertising. Its Web site is positioned as a key provider of information for the computer industry. By providing simple, easy-to-use sites — and providing simple access through links, portals and email (we discuss all this later in the chapter) — Ziff Davis is the first stop for thousands of computer professionals looking for critical information.

In e-commerce, even more so than in traditional commerce, you can't just open a store and cry out, "Come buy it from me; I have it, too!" Most bricks-and-mortar companies use geographical convenience as a major competitive advantage — an advantage completely lost for Internet competitors. You have to give customers a reason to do business with you instead of your competition. You have to find out what makes your business better and then play those advantages to their fullest in the Internet marketplace. You have to communicate those advantages to online shoppers, as well as earn their trust and respect.

Building e-presence

Sites that people recognize and talk about on the Web have what's called *e-presence*. E-presence is about more than just looking good (although that's a big part of it). These businesses are almost household (or office-hold) words. You build this kind of presence, or brand recognition, in the Internet world by using the same principles (if different media) as in the traditional business world: marketing and advertising.

So how do you build your e-presence? Surf the Internet for a while and see how the other guys do it. You'll find that most major Internet commerce sites have a few things in common:

- ✔ **Great design:** The site has a professional-looking design, including a carefully planned layout, well-designed graphics, and a consistent look across the site. Your site should also reflect your traditional corporate image — logos, colors, advertising campaign themes, and so forth.

- ✔ **Memorable logos:** The site prominently uses branding tools (such as logos) and proprietary features (such as Amazon's one-click shopping).

- ✔ **Navigability:** Customers have easy access to the various portions of the site. The customer should be able to get to what she wants in four clicks or less. Use menus, site maps, and shortcuts to help achieve this goal.

- ✔ **Recognizability:** The site is advertised on other sites in the form of banner ads that reflect the brand. Even when surfing elsewhere, Web users recognize the logo, tag line, and familiar colors that represent your site and your business.

- ✔ **Incentives for customers to stick around:** The main page of the site showcases special promotions of featured products and services and changes those promotions frequently. For B2B sites, highlight your newest products and services.

- ✔ **Current information:** Publish news that means something to your customers, such as how your products and services make their lives easier. Case studies and examples of how to use products give existing customers cause to return and potential customers reasons to be interested in your site.

- ✔ **Up-to-date appearance:** The site often has special graphics for holiday seasons, keeping the site's appearance fresh and up-to-date.

These are the features of an impressive Web site that customers believe is successful and worthy of their business.

You can't substitute image for substance. Flashy graphics and a slick appearance may get you started, but it won't keep you going. You need a real competitive edge to your site to build a sustained customer base.

Just like in traditional business, competitive advantages on the Internet are what you make of them. So be sure to play up your advantages and get the most mileage from them that you can.

Building credibility and trust

The only way to win lifelong customers who sing your praises across the rooftops and the chat rooms of the world is to make good on your promises.

Delivering the goods efficiently, politely, and with as little intrusion on the customer's life as possible will make your customers love you, and they'll tell their friends about how great you are. Failing to deliver can destroy your online business faster than you can imagine.

Industrial Espionage: Carving Out an E-Commerce Niche by Spying on the Competition

Your success depends largely on building a base of Internet customers. Your organization's distinctions must be tailored to match the character of the Web. Your success may come down to finding the way to meld your special approach to business with the Web.

Evaluating your competitors' strengths and weaknesses

You cannot stand apart from the crowd unless you are distinctive. Three sites cannot all offer the lowest price. You need to know what your competitors are doing, and what they declare as their added value.

Have your marketing department or your business analyst (see Chapter 7 for the low-down on business analysts) investigate your competitors' sites. You need a comprehensive picture of what your enemies say about themselves before you start. And remember to anticipate a reaction from them after you start to play your hand. Keep checking their sites regularly, at least on a quarterly basis, depending on how volatile your market space is.

Digging up the dirt behind the home page: Who are your competitors' partners?

You need to find out which of your competitors' strengths are internal and which result from partnerships that they maintain with *other* businesses. Finding out this information may require some careful detective work and a few well-placed phone calls, but your efforts are likely to be rewarded with invaluable information.

CASE STUDY

Disasters "R" Us

Toys "R" Us created an online store in time for the 1999 holiday shopping season. The site offered a tremendous number of advantages over its major competitors — Amazon.com and eToys.com — including an established retail brand name with enormous recognition and popularity. Toys "R" Us also offered the same perks as its competition, such as gift-wrapping, order-status tracking, an easy-to-use Web site, and a great selection. The advantage paid off — the Toys "R" Us Web site was an enormously popular virtual destination for parents taking care of their holiday shopping online.

And then the other shoe dropped. Products didn't ship in time for holiday gift-giving. Orders were filled with the wrong products. The gift-wrapping was sloppy. Toysrus.com was so overwhelmed with the consumer response that it couldn't keep up. The business lost thousands of dollars in sales and untold thousands in customer trust and loyalty. Disgruntled customers filed lawsuits. Many people undoubtedly thought twice about returning to the Web site the following holiday season and may have been tempted to check out online competitors such as Amazon.com, which had experienced relatively few troubles (and certainly less negative media coverage) during the same holiday season.

Toys "R" Us managed to make lemonade out of its lemons and worked out a partnership with Amazon.com. Toys "R" Us supplies its name brand and inventory; Amazon provides its Internet technologies and delivery organization to get the toys delivered on time and in good order. Whether you partner or develop the strengths you need to compete, you cannot afford to go out into the e-wilderness ill-prepared.

JARGON ALERT

For example, you may discover a competitor that offers a staggering variety of products. You have no idea where your competitor found all those products, and you know you couldn't possibly match its selection. Some digging may reveal that your competitor is simply using *virtual warehousing* (selling products from someone else's warehouse and shipping only the products that sell) and has a relationship with a better distributor than you have. Now that you have this information, you can establish a relationship with the same distributor and get the same great prices and selection your competitor has! Read more about establishing e-business partnerships in Chapter 16.

Lying down with the enemy: Partnering

As you examine your online competition, think carefully: Are they *all* competitors? For example, suppose you're in the business of selling materials to general contractors who use those materials to build houses. Your product line includes widgets of various sizes. After searching the Internet, you find several other widget suppliers. All carry a wider selection of widgets than you do, but none of them caters to general contractors specifically. Are they competition?

Maybe — or maybe not. One of the advantages that you recognize in your business is that you offer credit terms to your contractors, which enables them to buy your products and pay for them after they receive payment from *their* customers. Those competitors you found on the Internet might make better *partners,* allowing you to offer a wider selection of widgets to your customers, while maintaining your niche in the Internet marketplace.

 When you examine a competitor's strengths and weaknesses, try to think of ways that your two businesses might work together to increase business for both of you. But also be careful about going into business with a new partner, taking care to establish a business relationship that protects you from losing your customers to your new partner.

Finally, a Place Where Size Doesn't Matter

How can you possibly compete with those major Internet megasites? Why would customers buy things from little ol' you when they can deal with the mighty competition? Because on the Internet, size really doesn't matter (well, sort of). You can be a big dog, too, if you adopt the right mindset.

If you can deliver value, you can compete. If you try to sell the products like IBM does at a 20 percent higher cost, you'll likely fail. Conversely, if you have a value proposition that is better than what the big boys offer, then you have equal footing in the Web to exploit it.

So how can you tell the difference between large, well-funded companies and their smaller competitors on the Web? Most Internet customers ask themselves the following questions:

- ✔ Does the site have a professional appearance? Are the graphics neat and attractive, and are they used consistently throughout the site?
- ✔ Does the site respond quickly, delivering pages after only a couple seconds' delay?
- ✔ Does the site offer features expected on a major site, like a wish list, a shopping cart, various shipping options, and so forth?
- ✔ Do the products on the site include photos with well-written descriptions?

If the answers to these questions are "yes," then customers will probably believe the site is a well-funded, successful business. In short, if it *looks* like a big dog, then it must *be* a big dog. We show you the ropes of designing this type of site in Chapter 10.

Not having a physical address can play to your advantage. None of the previously mentioned factors is especially expensive to produce, so a small company can look like a big company just as easily as the big company can! The fact is that most Internet businesses operate with relatively few employees. You just have to make sure your site *looks* like a big, successful company, and everyone will assume it is.

Looking like a big, successful company has far greater benefits than just making you look good. It also makes customers more willing to trust you, select you over the competition, and remain loyal to you. Looking good pays off in increased customer loyalty and makes it easier for you to fight off your competition.

Getting Into Customers' Heads: Surveys

You can conduct several different kinds of customer surveys, including: *demographic surveys,* which help you determine which age groups, genders, races, and socioeconomic groups tend to use your business; and *satisfaction and exit surveys,* which help you refine and customize your business so that you can retain loyal customers and attract new ones.

Companies spend millions of dollars each year conducting surveys by using a variety of methods you're probably *waaay* too familiar with. Whether a company mails out questionnaires to randomly-selected households, hires professional survey-takers to accost people at local shopping malls, or uses telemarketers to call customers during dinnertime, most people have a fairly basic attitude about surveys:

- ✔ They hate them.
- ✔ They hate businesses that use them.

Internet shoppers are even touchier about surveys than the average Joe. After all, two of the big reasons they shop on the Internet are to save time and to remain somewhat anonymous. That's hard to do that when somebody keeps asking personal questions.

Nonetheless, customer surveys provide enough benefits — such as demographic information or feedback on a new site design — that businesses keep conducting them. Fortunately, the Web makes it possible to conduct surveys a bit less ruthlessly and much more efficiently. Here are some ideas:

- ✔ **Don't hit your customers with more than a couple questions at a time.** You may have 50 questions you want to ask — ranging from customers' annual household salaries to the number of dogs they have — but only ask customers two or three questions per visit to the site. Eventually, you'll have a full set of answers.

✔ **Work with outside surveying companies.** These companies offer customers incentives to complete online surveys (prizes, product coupons, and so forth) and can help you get more demographic information more quickly than you could on your own. (See the sidebar elsewhere in this chapter, "BizRate asks the questions.") Firms such as Jupiter Research (www.jupiterresearch.com) and DoubleClick (www.doubleclick.com) can help you learn about your market.

✔ **Offer incentives for answering questions.** Make sure that customers see the personal value of participating in a survey. Let them know you'll use the information to improve your product mix to cater to their interests, or that you'll be able to reduce the amount of advertising you send out by targeting it to their lifestyles.

Of course, money talks. You can take money off (discount) a purchase or drop shipping charges for anyone who answers your questions. Immediate aggrandizement offers are strong inducements.

Know thy customer: Demographic surveys

The customer base that you develop as a bricks-and-mortar organization is often quite different than your online customer base. To succeed at reaching new markets, you must determine who your Internet customers are and what attracts them to your business. And, although you can open new markets through e-commerce, you may cannibalize your existing customer base. You need to understand who your customers are, what they want, and how your online business can meet their needs.

Demographic data also tells you whether you're dealing with individuals or businesses. You can also track the area of the country (or world) that customers live in, how much money they make, how many kids they have, and what kinds of hobbies they tend to have.

This information can be a gold mine to all aspects of business, online and offline. Of course, demographics are *more* important for the online end of the business because they enable you to understand who your customers are.

Don't assume that just because you have a good idea of your bricks-and-mortar demographics that you automatically know your online demographics. Some groups of people are more likely to shop online, for example, than others.

Know what attracts thy customers: Satisfaction surveys

A key to maintaining a successful business, of course, is understanding what attracts your customers. Is it that you simply have the best prices available?

Or is it your superior customer service? What about the fantastic Web site design you created? Understanding what attracts customers to your online business enables you to keep the most popular items you sell in stock and thus retain loyal customers. You also can bring in new customers by understanding what's working on your site and expanding on those successes.

One way to find out what's working on your site is simply to ask your customers what they like about it! You can do this by conducting *customer satisfaction surveys*. You can conduct these surveys on your Web site immediately after a customer checks out, or conduct them via e-mail.

You should also consider hiring an outside firm to help you conduct satisfaction surveys. An outside firm helps ensure that your survey is conducted in the same, impartial way with each customer, and that the results are quickly compiled into useful information. These companies may conduct their surveys over the telephone, via e-mail, or in the case of industry leader BizRate, on its own Web sites (see the sidebar "BizRate asks the questions").

No matter how you choose to do them, customer satisfaction surveys play two very important roles:

✔ First (and most obviously), they provide you with feedback on what your customers think of you.

✔ Second, they let your customers know that you care enough to solicit their opinions (and on the Internet, *everyone* has an opinion).

BizRate asks the questions

BizRate.com (www.bizrate.com) is one of the Internet's most successful and visible market-research firms. The main focus of the company's business is to conduct surveys of customers' online shopping experiences. Merchants sign a contract and pay a fee to sign up with BizRate. The merchants then modify their online checkout to display a BizRate pop-up window after customers finish checking out. The banner ad offers customers the opportunity to rate their experience with the merchant, and the chance to win a cash prize in the process.

Customers complete a brief online survey, which includes standard BizRate questions as well as merchant-defined questions. BizRate shares this information with the merchant, who can use it to gauge its level of customer satisfaction in a variety of areas. BizRate also creates aggregate (summarized and combined) information about customers, such as the average number of online purchases made per month by all BizRate users.

BizRate is the de facto leader in its industry. Customers trust the BizRate brand, which leads to a higher ratio of completed surveys, making BizRate — and its customers — more successful.

An online complaint box

In the traditional business world, satisfied customers tell one or two friends about their wonderful consumer experience, but unhappy customers tell ten. The e-commerce world is about moving information. News spreads like wildfire, and crosses a large number of geographic and market barriers. People e-mail, visit chat rooms, and discussion boards. They feel free to talk to strangers. You don't your business to turn up in a Web site dedicated to exposing bad sites. You're better off meeting customer complaints head-on and correcting them quickly.

Make sure that a customer service professional (or a staff of them, if necessary) reviews customer feedback and that your customer service staff is empowered to address customer complaints. Whenever possible, follow up negative feedback with a phone call to add a personal touch. Be sure that customers know that you want to address their concerns, and then make sure you understand those concerns completely. Find more ideas on keeping customers happy in Chapter 11.

In the faceless world of the Internet, with no store manager to complain to, customers often view satisfaction surveys as evidence that you care about them and their business, and they appreciate your concern. A few simple questions can give the information to customize your site and personalize your customers' experience.

- Did they find what they were looking for?
- Why did they come to your site (price, selection, reputation, warranty, financing, and so forth)?
- What did they like the most about your site?
- What do the like the least?
- What would most improve your site?

Determining why people don't buy: Exit surveys

What if you build it and nobody comes? Finding out why shoppers visit your site without purchasing anything can be tremendously difficult. You often have no contact information, so you can't reach those shoppers to do a follow-up survey, which is certainly the most obvious way to find out what the problem is. So what can you do?

One trick that's been gaining popularity is to program your Web pages to present an *exit survey* to shoppers who leave the Web site without completing a purchase, or even more importantly, shoppers who abandon a shopping cart full of items. The exit survey should

✔ Appear on customers' computers as a small pop-up window with a couple of short questions asking the customer why he or she chose not to purchase anything and whether he or she plans to return.

✔ Offer to save customers' shopping carts so that when they return to the site, the carts will still contain the items they originally placed in them.

✔ Contain a link to a more comprehensive questionnaire that tries to get more detail from customers regarding their decision not to purchase. You can also offer additional incentives to encourage them to buy.

Don't make the exit survey too long or intrusive. Remember, you've already lost the customers at this point — don't risk annoying them, or they may never return!

Understanding E-Profiling

Profiling is the activity of tracking customers' activities. The pages they visit, the way they navigate the site, and the product they purchase (and the ones they skip) all paint a picture of how your site operates and what your customer is looking for. You can use that picture to customize product offerings, specials, and advertising, and to boost sales.

Actually, profiling isn't a concept new to e-commerce. Businesses have been doing it for years. American Express, for example, tracks what types of credit card purchases you make and then sends the information to you for your records. You probably find this information helpful when you categorize your tax deductions; it's also a gold mine for American Express. Knowing the products that customers like to buy, and when they like to buy them, enables businesses to set up advertising for the goods that customers are already in the mood to buy (which is why your get all those flyers with your bill).

The kind of profiling that credit card companies do in the bricks-and-mortar world is peanuts compared with what businesses can do on the Web. On the Internet, profiling enables Web surfers to customize their browsing experience while also enabling Web sites to get a sense of the users' activities, interests, and habits. The reason you can track and profile customers online is because every action an online customer takes involves a computer under your control (usually your company's Web server).

Web sites can literally track enough information to completely recreate a customer's entire experience on the site. Here's some of the stuff you can track from an e-commerce site:

✔ Products that shoppers place in their shopping carts and services that customers request. You can learn which of your organization's offerings interest shoppers.

✔ Items in a shopping cart that are actually purchased, and items that are discarded or abandoned. You can use this information to learn which products need help getting out the door.

✔ The promotions that customers click. You can even track which links result in a customer placing the product in a shopping cart or purchasing the product.

✔ Every single click that customers make on your site, allowing you to trace their paths through the site as if they had left a trail of bread crumbs.

✔ Who refers customers to your site.

✔ Which page customers spend the most time at when they visit the site and which page they visit least often.

✔ Which page is the most frequent *exit page,* or the page that customers see right before they leave your site.

Combined with demographic information obtained in surveys, profiling can be an extremely powerful tool. You can determine what pages on your site are popular, how customers are getting to them, how customers are using the rest of your site, how well your advertising is working, and much more. See Chapter 15 for more on mining this data.

All this profiling doesn't come without a cost. The process of profiling your customers can generate a tremendous amount of data, and storing and analyzing that data can require a lot of database horsepower. Make sure you understand the technical and performance implications of any profiling you choose to do, and be prepared to spend money — *horse power* translates into *moolah* in 58 languages. We talk more about these systems in Chapter 13.

Using profiling technology respectfully

Although profiling is a very useful way of getting important data that forms a demographic profile of your customers, you have to understand how profiling works and why customers are leery of this type of data-gathering. HyperText Transfer Protocol (HTTP), the way data goes from your server to the user's computer, records every user action independent from every other action. In other words, Web pages have no memory. To enable customers to have continued customized experiences, the important information is saved in files called cookies, which are actually stored on customers' hard drives. Here's how cookies work:

1. **Wendy the Web browser visits a site like Yahoo! and customizes her very own Web page by entering personal data, such as her name, account information, and password.**

   The customized page enables Wendy to see news stories that interest her and find out what movies are playing in her city.

2. **Yahoo! saves this information on Wendy's hard drive in files called cookies.**

3. **Wendy is greeted by name the next time she logs on to the Internet and clicks her way to her very own personalized Yahoo! page.**

4. **Meanwhile, Yahoo! takes the information Wendy has provided and uses it to customize its advertising.**

How does all this profiling work? Primarily through the magic of *cookies*, which are small pieces of information passed back and forth between Web browsers and servers. When users conduct a search, the search engine may pass a small cookie with an identification number to them. The users' Web browsers store this information on their computers. When they visit your site, you can read that ID number and ask the search engine for any information associated with it. Of course, this information exchange requires that you and the search engine have a business and technical relationship, and presumes that the search engine is letting its customers know that this sort of thing is going on.

The benefit of cookies is that customers get the convenience of customized features. The downside is that consumers feel uneasy about the potential for a business (or anyone else, for that matter) to track every little thing they do on a Web site. Individual-privacy advocates are shocked at the potential for abuse that Web-based profiling presents. Profiling has earned a bad rep as being too Big-Brotherish, invading privacy and stealing people's constitutional rights. You can allay your customers' fears if you

✔ **Make *conservative* your watchword.** Start by implementing only the level of profiling you absolutely need to accomplish your business goals. Technically savvy consumers can tell when Web-based profiling is in use, and they may not appreciate it.

✔ **Shout your policies from the cyber-rooftops.** Be explicit about the profiling you conduct on your site and how you use the information you collect. For example, by posting a privacy policy on your Web site, you can explain that you keep a database of customers' purchases from your site, and that you use that information to target banner ads on the site so that customers see ads for products similar to those they've purchased in the past.

We talk more about protecting your customer's privacy in Chapter 11.

Profiling with partners

Profiling on the Web isn't limited to the data that you collect on your own Web site. Far from it! Web-based profiling technologies make it possible for businesses to find out about their customers' activities on other Web sites, too. For example, imagine that one of your customers goes to an Internet search engine, such as Excite, and searches for information on blueberries. After surfing for a few minutes (okay, hours), the customer surfs over to your online store. Although you don't sell blueberries, you do sell some great jars and canning supplies that customers can use to make blueberry jam. So the technical geniuses in your organization make sure that the first few banner ads the potential customer sees feature those canning products, increasing the likelihood of a sale.

 Although useful to businesses, this is the type of profiling that really gets people scared. After all, if you can turn their interest in blueberries into a customized, mini ad campaign, what's to stop the government (Big Brother) from tracking their movements on the Internet? Allay fear and suspicion by being honest and upfront with your customers. Let them know where you get your information, how you use it, and who else you give it to.

 You will end up aggregating most of your data, and it's not like you're sending out individual customer names and addresses. You're simply sharing demographic statistics — for example, that 27 percent of customers who buy widgets are females 20–25 years old. You are not part of a conspiracy. You're just doing business. Still, the laws are changing; only gather information if you really think it will help you help customers without being invasive. Also, keep up to speed with your lawyer.

Expanding Your Market and Reaching New Customers

The great lure of e-commerce, of course, is that all online businesses are, by definition, worldwide. The products and services you want to sell become instantly available to anyone with an Internet connection, no matter where he or she is on the planet. This enables you to reach new customers who simply may not have been aware of your company's existence before.

Obviously, some of your traditional business' customers will take advantage of your new online business. But how can you attract totally new customers to expand your market?

Unfortunately, no simple solution exists, but here are some basic things you should consider:

✔ **Location, location, location.** Most businesses find that the biggest obstacle to attracting new offline business is geography. "Hey," you think, "Location is not a problem for the online end of my business. I can extend to new markets just by getting my online store up and running and extending my existing marketing and advertising efforts to include the entire nation — or the world." Think again. This simple thinking could lead your company headfirst into disaster.

Language, currency, and most importantly, delivery are key considerations. In Asia, most people take delivery at convenience stores. IDC research shows that any site can attract lots of global browsers, but only sites with local functions get global buyers.

✔ **Being (or at least having) all things for all customers.** If, in your traditional business, clients have to go elsewhere for some necessary goods (the online end of your business), using techniques such as virtual warehousing may enable you to add new products and services without a lot of overhead.

✔ **Being an online one-stop shop.** E-commerce businesses often succeed by becoming one-stop shops for their customers. Amazon.com and buy.com are excellent examples of this tactic. By expanding their product lines to include more and more selection, they become a good single source for Internet shopping. Although you may not need to create an entire online department store that appeals to everyone, you can certainly offer a wider selection of products and services to the market niche that your traditional business serves.

Spreading the word

Reaching new customers is also a matter of marketing and advertising. Simply launching an online business doesn't guarantee that customers will come; you need to advertise and market your online business to bring in new customers.

Online marketing and advertising aren't especially different from traditional marketing and advertising, so the skills and tactics that you use in your traditional business carry over quite well. What's different is the cost of marketing and advertising — which is often much lower than traditional techniques — and the medium used.

Just about every traditional advertising medium — from print and radio to television — has a counterpart on the Internet:

✔ Banner ads — those small, sometimes-animated graphics that appear almost everywhere on the Internet — are the print and television advertising of the Internet. They offer short, concise messages and encourage users to click the ad to be whisked away to the advertiser's site for more information.

✔ Direct-mail pieces are replaced on the Internet by direct e-mail, and many consumers have the same reaction to junk e-mail, or *spam*, that they do to junk mail delivered to the homes.

✔ Press releases and product reviews by independent reviewers exist on the Internet, too, in the form of online magazines and consumer information sites.

And lest you think the Internet is a world wholly unto itself, the traditional advertising media — billboards, direct-mail pieces, print ads, and television ads (including mega-expensive Super Bowl halftime ads) — are being used every day to draw customers to online stores.

Waving your banner with banner ads

If you've been on the Internet for more than 30 seconds, you've probably seen a banner ad or two. Or ten. They're easily the most popular form of Internet-based advertising, and they do seem to work. But how?

You need to become familiar with common banner-ad techniques that are used across the Web (although the ad salespeople would be delighted to explain this to you over and over again if you want):

✔ **Impressions:** Some companies charge you for advertising based on the number of impressions your ad gets. An *impression* is simply the act of displaying your ad to a user. Often, you pay a fixed amount for a specific number of impressions, to be delivered within a specific period of time.

✔ **Clickthroughs:** Some companies charge for *clickthroughs,* and may even add clickthrough charges on top of a basic fee for a number of impressions. A clickthrough occurs when a user clicks your ad and is taken to your site. This is the best the ad can do for you — from there, it's up to your site to convert the shopper into a paying customer.

✔ **Targeted ads:** Some advertising companies offer *targeted ads.* One great example of a Web site that provides targeted banner ads is Yahoo!. If users visit Yahoo! and perform a search for automobiles, they mysteriously see banner ads for — can you guess? — cars. Yahoo! charges extra for this service, and the fee may be warranted because it helps ensure that the ad is at least of passing interest to the user.

A million other schemes and techniques can make banner ads more effective. The trick is simply to partner with advertising companies you trust and feel comfortable with, and let them explain the various options to you. In the end, make sure you understand how much it's going to cost you to get a new customer on your Web site, and use that figure to do some comparison shopping among different types of advertising.

Penetrating the Global Market

The World Wide Web is just that — *worldwide*. As a result, your online business has the immediate opportunity to become global, simply by being online. Are you prepared?

Doing business internationally is a far cry from doing business at home. If your traditional business is strictly domestic, all the language, legal, and other issues that go along with being an international business may completely distract you.

Consider the following:

- ✔ Are you prepared to fulfill international orders? This may involve tariffs, export laws, strange shipping charges, and more.
- ✔ Can you accept foreign funds as payment?
- ✔ Although English is an internationally understand language in business, American customs, idioms, symbols, and gestures are not. Is your Web site designed for a global audience?
- ✔ Do you understand the legal issues of doing business abroad, including taxes, liability, copyright, and so on?

Chapter 8 provides a good overview of the legal issues involved with doing business internationally, but it is no substitute for experience. Setting up an online business is complicated enough without dragging international issues into the picture, so you may want to consider restricting your online business to domestic customers until you're firmly established. Then you can start expanding to serve other markets.

Eating Yourself Alive? Avoiding the Risks of Online Business

How could being online possibly hurt your business? That depends on how you define your success and how well you plan your online business. Your online business presents two main dangers to your traditional business: cannibalization and distractions.

Cannibalization

Cannibalization occurs when one side of the business — sometimes an online store — damages another side — such as its retail stores — by drawing business away from it. You can cannibalize from your own bricks-and-mortar stores or you can steal from your partners. The key is to keep increasing revenue and lowering costs, regardless of where your customers buy.

Cannibalization has always existed in the traditional business world, of course. Pepsi was concerned when it introduced Pepsi ONE — a new diet soft drink — that it would draw sales away from Diet Pepsi, but it was hoping that it would draw *more* sales away from its competitor Diet Coke. On the surface, e-commerce cannibalization doesn't seem so bad because you're not really *losing* customers, you're just shifting them around . . . right?

That's where e-commerce cannibalization can sneak up and surprise you. After you've converted some (or all) of your customers to online shopping, you're playing in the much larger and much more competitive e-commerce arena where it's possible to lose a customer in seconds simply because the competition's Web site has prettier colors. So although the prospect of losing traditional customers to your online business may not seem so bad, remember that it's *very* difficult to retain online customers after they see what else e-commerce has to offer them.

Distractions that steer firms off-course

Another big danger of adding e-commerce to your business is that doing so will simply distract you from the traditional way of earning money. Although e-commerce has a lot of advantages and potential, the old, boring way of doing business has a lot going for it, including the fact that it has worked pretty well for the past few hundred years. Ignoring the traditional side of your business to concentrate on your e-commerce business can be a costly mistake.

E-commerce can be very distracting. You have to make a million decisions every day, and your online business will change and grow at a speed you never expected and in ways you probably can't even imagine. Reacting to these changes requires quick decision-making, which can often have the effect of shifting your attention away from your traditional business.

So what can you do? Make e-commerce a part of your total business plan. Make sure you have managers who understand e-commerce, and who are empowered to make decisions and devote their entire attention to the online business. Manage the online business as you would any other part of your business, and apportion your time appropriately.

Got them online denim blues

Consider this saga about Levi Strauss & Co. (www.levi.com). This venerable American business opened an online store for its denim jeans. Although the site posted poor numbers, opening this site infuriated the bricks-and-mortar stores in Levi's sales channel. The traditional stores that carried these products were so incensed that they diverted their advertising and marketing dollars elsewhere, and jeans sales suffered. By trying to sell directly, Levi Strauss was in danger of cannibalizing the sales of its bricks-and-mortar business partners.

Just like a traditional business, a new online business may take a while to become self-sufficient and profitable. Many e-commerce ventures have to be supported by a profitable traditional business to get them on their feet. Don't bet the bank and risk damaging your existing business through neglect!

Reaching Out and Zapping Your Market: Taking Communication to the Next Level

Without the benefit of face-to-face contact, you need to find other ways of getting — and keeping — in touch with your customers. Fortunately, the Internet is an interactive medium, and you can leverage Internet technologies, such as discussion groups, electronic mailings, streaming video, and other technologies to replace the lack of face-to-face contact and keep your customer's experience at your Web site fresh.

Online discussion groups

Discussion groups, also referred to as *newsgroups* or *bulletin boards*, are the Internet's most common form of public discussion. The Internet features discussion groups for almost every topic imaginable, allowing users to freely post comments, questions, replies, opinions, and general information. Many Internet users spend *hours* each day keeping up with the discussion groups that interest them — which makes discussion groups a powerful tool for promoting your business, if used properly.

Keeping people informed through newsgroups

Newsgroups are a great way to post information about your business — new products or services, new Web site features, answers to product-support questions, and so forth.

Many of the folks who participate in newsgroups have a strong belief that the Internet in general, and newsgroups in particular, should be commercial-free. They won't take kindly to your using public newsgroups to promote your business, so tread carefully. Be careful not to cross the fine line between providing useful information and marketing your business.

Building customer communities

Customer communities offer a great way to promote your business. Basically, a community is a set of private newsgroups that you run for the benefit of your customers. Because the newsgroups belong to you, you can feel free to do as much promoting as you want. Many online merchants have made excellent use of customer communities to build their brands and their businesses. Communities also enable customers to help one another use the products you sell. You can leverage your customers' expertise — all for the price of a little drive space and some Internet bandwidth.

Red Hat (www.redhat.com), a seller of Linux-based operating systems, effectively uses discussion groups. Users ask questions about how to use Red Hat Linux. Other users and support engineers provide answers to those questions. By sharing experience and know-how, new users can get the answers they need, and experienced users can share what they have mastered — everybody wins.

Spam, spam spam spam, spam spam spam spam

Did you ever see the Spam sketch from the television show *Monty Python's Flying Circus*? A group of Vikings in the background of the scene periodically start chanting, "Spam, Spam Spam Spam, Spam Spam Spam Spam," drowning out all the other characters' dialogue. The term *spam* has since become a generic reference to all the junk e-mail that Internet users receive by the virtual bucketful, which can often threaten to drown out the legitimate, important e-mail you receive every day.

The official definition for spam is *unsolicited e-mail,* meaning the recipient never asked to receive e-mail from the sender. For example, if your online store's checkout process asks shoppers for their e-mail addresses, and you then use those e-mail addresses to send out promotional e-mail messages (without informing your customers in advance that you plan to use their e-mail addresses in that fashion), you're guilty of *spamming*.

Many Internet service providers (ISPs) have rules about sending unsolicited e-mail. If you ignore those rules and an annoyed recipient reports you to your ISP, you could easily be charged a fine or even lose your Internet connection altogether. Carefully review your ISP's terms of service and make sure you follow its rules.

In addition to upsetting your ISP, spam also upsets the recipients — your customers. Few people enjoy receiving junk mail, and even fewer enjoy receiving junk e-mail. Customers have been known to simply stop doing business with online merchants who send spam.

So how can you avoid raising your customers' ire? Simple — don't spam them! If you intend to collect e-mail addresses on your site for the purpose of sending promotional messages or e-mail newsletters, make sure you clearly state your intentions when you ask for the information. Give customers a chance to *opt out,* or state that they do not want to receive e-mail from you. Ideally, you should only send online mailings, such as newsletters, to customers who specifically *opt in,* or request such mailings. And make sure your e-mail messages include information about how recipients can easily remove themselves from your list and avoid future mailings, if they desire.

Using streaming media

Streaming media enables you to provide rich, interesting audio and video content to customers and, at the same time, add value to your online business.

In the bad old days of the Internet, users had to *download* audio and video files — transfer the files to their computers — before they could play them. Because audio and video files can be so large in size, and thus take a long time to download, very few users bothered. *Streaming* media allows customers to begin viewing (or listening to) the content almost immediately. The content continues to download as the customer watches (or listens), staying just ahead of the customer. This technique — embodied in technologies like Real Networks' RealPlayer (www.real.com) and Microsoft's Windows Media Player (windowsmedia.com) — has made Internet-based audio and video an exciting reality.

In your face with videoconferencing

One great way to reach out and touch your customers is *videoconferencing*. Videoconferencing enables you to talk face to face with your customers by using low-cost video cameras and computer speakers and microphones. Your customers can see you (or your designated representative) and talk and respond to you in real time. Videoconferencing puts a face on the otherwise anonymous world of the Internet, and brings a much-needed human element to the world of online commerce.

You can use videoconferencing to hold one-on-one virtual meetings with individual customers. And by combining videoconferencing technologies with chat technologies, you can spice up chat rooms and increase traffic by creating a more personal experience.

Freely available videoconferencing products like Microsoft's NetMeeting (`www.microsoft.com/netmeeting`) put videoconferencing in the hands of your customers for free. Other technologies are available for different types of videoconferencing, from one-on-one meetings to mega-events with thousands of virtual attendees.

Chapter 7

Getting Virtual: Adding Geeks to Your Existing Workforce

In This Chapter
▶ Deciding which staff your business really needs
▶ Determining how many employees you need
▶ Bringing in reinforcements, renting reinforcements, and training from within
▶ Finding the right employees — and keeping them

Getting your business online means getting a new breed of workers in your organization. Whether you plan to hire them, borrow them, or rent them, your employees act together as the bridge between your carefully crafted plans and a real, operating e-commerce venture. In this chapter, we show you which positions you need to fill to get your project off the ground and how to figure out the right level of staffing. Good employees with the right skills may be elusive, so we also tell you where to find the right talent to hire. And for the beatniks in the reading audience, we also talk about alternative staffing solutions that can prove handy in today's understaffed technical world.

Defining the Cast

E-commerce ventures involve a staggering number of complex, interrelated technologies, especially if you're tying the Web side of your business into an existing business model. And Web sites and other technical aspects of e-commerce businesses just don't build themselves — talented people build them. What you're after is a specific set of skills. Often, employers need to hire (or rent, as we discuss in the section "Bringing in hired guns," later in this chapter) several people because finding one or two people who have all the skills you need may be next to impossible. However, you could get lucky and find that gem of a person who can fill several roles in your project. Understanding those roles is extremely important so that when the time comes to wade through the resumes, you can decide which players are right for your team.

For managers, you want individuals who have proven track records in managing and completing projects. Programmers and Web designers need to have done more than read a book or be able to spell HTML. Look for people who can point to real projects and clearly define what they did on those projects. Also, discover if they can work in a team environment. References will tell the tale, so take time to check them. And if you have technical people you already trust, ask them to test the knowledge of your candidates as part of the interview process.

Another unique theme in geeks is that they tend to flock. If you hire Joe Smith as a project manager, he may know people he has managed before. These little groups already have relationships and often work well as a team.

Table 7-1 describes the different positions in your organization.

Table 7-1	Web Rollout Staff		
Job Title	**Primary Responsibility**	**Manages**	**Reports To**
Business analyst	Models business processes and finds improvements	No one (this person tries to direct others, but no one listens)	Business manager
Project manager	Has overall responsibility for keeping project on track	Programmers and Web designers	Business management
Software architect	Creates the overall design for the Web site and chooses the primary technologies	No one (but may assist the project manager in directing the programmers)	Project manager
Web designer	Designs graphics and the user interface for the site	No one (with luck)	Project manager
Programmers	Writes the code that enables the site to function	No one (hopefully)	Project manager or (possibly) senior programmer
Quality assurance	Ensures that the proper processes have been used and that the site delivers as promised	No one (but may try to manage the programmers)	Project manager

Job Title	Primary Responsibility	Manages	Reports To
Network engineer	Keeps the servers and network gear running	No one (has preciouslittle time for managing others)	Manager of information technology
Business manager	Keeps e-commerce initiative on track	All team members	Senior corporate management

Analyze this: Why a business analyst is key

Technical folks are great with technology, but they sometimes aren't so good with pure business. Businesses pay tech geeks tons of money every year to develop custom computer software, and a lot of that money is wasted because the finished software doesn't do what the business needs. That's where the *business analyst* comes in. The business analyst's job is to make sure that all the rules you set up in your existing business are consistently followed and reflected in your Web site.

The business analyst figures out the rules you already have in place for doing business and writes them down, clearly and concisely. For example, you have rules for checking payments before shipping. Whether the rule applies to the way your company processes credit cards or verifies personal check information, the analyst writes a formal procedure for determining whether the order can ship — a procedure that can be converted into a program.

The following list highlights just a few of the good business analyst's many hats:

- **Customer advocate:** Another important aspect of the business analyst's job is to stick up for customers in the Web development process. The business analyst must understand your customer demographics, and make sure that the techies are developing the site in a way that suits your customers' needs and preferences. This role is critical if your site will deal with customers who aren't technical experts and who have a different perspective from the people actually developing your site.

- **Taskmaster and critic (in a nice way):** A business analyst makes sure that the front end and the back end of your site work consistently with your traditional business — and that the new techies follow the rules of the game.

Never underestimate the ability of technical folks to ignore business rules when it's convenient. Creating software that authorizes a credit card at one point in time and applies a charge to the card later is much more difficult than creating software that closes transactions when the customer places the order. Left on their own, many technical people would make your Web site work the way that's easiest for *them*, not for your customers.

✔ **Devoted loyalist to the minute details:** The business analyst needs to be completely dedicated to your project and should have the authorization to make decisions about how certain business rules should be implemented. This means knowing how things already run.

Don't think for a moment that your project can scrape by with you, or another existing employee, acting as a business analyst. Big mistake! With one person focused entirely on this stuff, you can prevent the project from either becoming a distraction to your main business or being held up while a part-time business analyst tries to play catchup dealing with questions.

A business analyst should have

✔ **A thorough understanding of how your business operates.** If this person hasn't been working with you for very long, he needs time to learn how you do business before recommending improvements.

✔ **Experience in business management.** Require a minimum of two years in a position where the candidate used and improved business processes. It's a real plus if she has used technology to improve and automate those processes.

✔ **Preferably, a business degree or other formal business education.** Can you spell MBA?

Five or more years of experience may well be the equivalent of an MBA, but a business analyst also needs to prove he has the skills to communicate your processes to others.

✔ **A working knowledge of how business processes are automated (that is the point, after all).** A business analyst doesn't need to know how to do it, just be able to explain what needs to be done.

✔ **Extraordinary communications skills.** A business analyst has to speak to techies and businesspeople and be clear to both. He or she needs to understand the technology well enough to perceive the difference between real technology problems and geek double-talk.

✔ **Great interpersonal skills.** This person will have to get along with technical folks in some stressful situations.

Look for candidates who have a strong background in finance. Return on investment (ROI) and forecasting are a big part of the e-commerce rollout process these days, so being on top of how financial issues affect implementation of rules is very important.

Keeping on top of things with a project manager

The slave driver, the old ball and chain, the whip cracker! Some say the hub of the wheel. Whatever you call the poor sucker, the *project manager* is the guy or gal responsible for getting your Web development project underway, keeping it on time, and finishing it on budget. Although this person should have strong technical skills that enable him or her to keep up with the technical folks on the project, the project manager focuses on managing deadlines and goals. This person makes sure that everyone else on the team is on schedule and that the project comes to a successful (and timely) conclusion.

The project manager is the ringleader for your project — the one person whose job is completely focused on making all the different pieces of your Web development machine work smoothly together to finish your project on time.

You have plans. You have deadlines. You have goals and expectations. The project manager's job is to take all the plans, goals, deadlines, and expectations (and more) and produce a Web site. Here's a list of the project manager's job responsibilities:

✔ **Getting the show (and all the itty-bitty individual shows) on the road.** The project manager maps out an initial project plan, assigns resources, and manages those resources so that the project's important milestones are completed on time.

Web development projects often have several phases of development, many of which happen in parallel time frames. These smaller projects depend on other projects to stay on track so that the whole thing comes together seamlessly (the key words: *no glitches*).

✔ **Policing (in a nice way) the key players.** Watch out, partner, there's a new sheriff in town. The project manager makes sure that everyone on the staff is fully and efficiently utilized at all times. If the project manager sees that one employee is slaving away trying to keep up while another one is taking three-hour lunches because he's so bored, then the project manager may shift responsibilities around to even the load.

E-commerce projects draw on an enormous number of different skills and disciplines, many of them in their infancy. The development staff often has to work with outside resources such as graphic designers or marketing professionals (not to mention outside partners that are hosting your business' Web site or linking your site to their own site). They have to work well with one another, too. The project manager has to help facilitate this complex, fast-moving interaction between people by making sure everyone has the necessary resources, that everyone is finishing assigned tasks on time, and that tasks are being smoothly handed off from one discipline to another in a planned, efficient manner.

When the time comes to hire a project manager, look for these characteristics:

- ✔ Well-organized and detail-oriented. The project manager needs to know everything that needs to be done, who is supposed to do it, and when it will be done.

- ✔ Project management experience is a huge plus — there's just no substitute for having actually done it before! If the project manager doesn't already have e-commerce experience, he needs to be familiar with the technologies in order to guide the staff.

- ✔ A technical background, preferably in software development. Two years of experience in keeping everyone on track will help keep your project on track.

- ✔ Formal education is a plus, but experience is more important. Schooling can help in communication skills and knowledge of the technology, but it seldom prepares a person to run a team.

- ✔ Great interpersonal skills. The project manager is the bridge between the business and the techies, which is no small task. She also needs to know when to be tough and when to help people out.

- ✔ The ability to multitask and keep track of several different things going on at once. Most programmers are very task focused, which is a good trait, but not in a project manager; project managers live to be interrupted.

- ✔ The ability to delegate and hand off assignments. Project managers should not make a habit of being a direct contributor to the project.

Programmers often become project managers because it is the next logical step on their career ladder. The skills of a programmer are very different than those of a project manager. A project manager's organizational and communication skills are much more important than his or her code-crunching power.

If you find a candidate with business analysis skills and project management qualifications (yes, the perfect employee), this person can be a project manager who doubles as a business analyst. But beware! The job of project manager (to keep things on time and on budget) can easily conflict with the job of business analyst (to make sure the Web site works for the business). Having two different people in these roles creates a desirable point of interaction — these two pivotal point people can play off each other and make compromises that achieve *both* goals.

The Project Management Institute (www.pmi.org) is a non-profit organization that provides certification, education, and standards for project management. With over 75,000 members, the institute provides a wide range of services and help for project management professionals. The site lists qualifications for project managers, seminars, training and development classes, and awards that recognize excellence in project management.

Making the blueprint: What architects do

A Web development project isn't unlike a construction project — everything starts with the *architect,* who has the job of creating the technical blueprint for your Web site. Unlike building architects, who translate people's desires into concrete and siding, the technical architect looks at all the hopes and dreams (and business requirements) laid out in a business plan and translates them into technical specifications that the development staff can easily understand. Architects usually are the highest-paid technical staff members and must have the broadest technical backgrounds. They work for the project manager and produce a specific plan for implementing the technologies required by the site.

Here's what an architect does:

- ✔ **Gets the show together so that the project manager can take the show on the road:** It's all well and good for your technical staff to deal with the business requirements and goals in the business plan (after all, that's what you hired them to do), but the techies really need to know which technologies to use and how to use them. They also need to have a sense of how all the different technologies work together. Architects provide this *technical blueprint,* a solid, clear look at the picture, complete with technology selections, diagrams, flowcharts, and much more. No construction project has ever succeeded without a solid plan, and an e-commerce development project is no different.

  The architect is also responsible for the technical orchestration of the project. He or she must ensure that all the pieces work together in harmony. When questions come up in the middle of the project, or when a change to the blueprint has to be made, the architect provides a coordinating presence to make sure that everything is integrated according to the original vision. You see, many members of the project team may work on little pieces of the project without ever working on the whole thing. Seeing the big picture enables the team members to identify and avoid bugs, or even to find flaws in the plan. When everyone is on the same page (or blueprint), the result is a completed Web site that has a consistent technical background, is *scalable,* and is easy to maintain. Scalable sites can easily grow as the business grows without having to re-create the site to enable it to handle more customers and traffic.

✔ **Be a know it all:** Web sites use a wide variety of technologies — Java, VBScript, databases, Web servers, CGI scripts, HTML, XML, DHTML (and a dozen other acronyms), not to mention graphics, and more. The architect is the one person on the development staff who must be familiar (at the least) or well-versed (preferably) with all of them. The architect is responsible for selecting the technologies that are used to implement various portions of your site's functionality, and is responsible for developing the technical methodologies used to put the site together.

Technical methodologies are common practices used by all developers. If everyone writes programs the same way, you can maintain them much more easily, and the pieces of the site are likely to work together better.

The very worst thing you can do is to turn programmers loose on a project without giving them a blueprint that includes technical methodologies. Face it, programmers (at least good programmers) are very smart. All smart programmers (and you hired the best, right?) can think of at least two ways to do any task, and you'd better be sure that they'll try all of them. Why do programmers do things like this to make your business site a hopeless mishmash that's impossible to fix or maintain? Because they can. The architect should keep the programmers informed and on a short leash.

What should you look for in a qualified architect? Start with the following short list of qualifications:

✔ A good technical background. The architect needs to understand how the various technologies associated with the Web work, but doesn't necessarily need to know the commands off the top of his or her head. Here are some of those technologies:

  • HTML and dynamic HTML

  • XML and related technologies

  • Database design and development

  • Programming (generally in Java or C++ and in Visual Basic)

  • Middleware (COM+, CORBA, MQ Series, Tuxedo, and so on)

  • Commercial off-the-shelf software (SAP R/3, BEA WebLogic, Lotus Domino, and so on)

  • Server hardware and operating systems

  • Application server products (database servers, application servers, Web servers, and so on)

  • General Web development

- ✔ Excellent communication and technical writing skills.

- ✔ The ability to grasp the big picture and break it down into smaller components.

- ✔ Previous experience successfully choosing technologies for e-commerce sites. It's best if the architect has implemented sites with several different technologies (such as Microsoft ASP pages and Unix-based Java) so he or she has experience comparing technologies. Check references.

- ✔ Formal education is a definite plus, but many skilled coders and architects don't have college degrees. The technologies are often too new for colleges to keep up.

Architects, with their broad technical background and highly marketable skills, can be among the most difficult staff members to hire. This is a good role to consider outsourcing (see "Insourcing and Outsourcing," later in the chapter). You don't need the architect on a daily basis. After the architecture is documented, you just ask questions when they arise and have the architect inspect construction as it occurs.

Creating art: A good Web designer is a good thing

The *Web designer* — the Picasso of your Web project — has the role of designing every aspect of the site's appearance, usually by using HTML (HyperText Markup Language). Obviously, this is an important job!

How architects keep it real — and consistent

Technical methodologies are an incredibly important — and often overlooked — aspect of an e-commerce project. Here are some of the questions these methodologies address:

- ✔ How do customers fill out forms on the Web site?

- ✔ How does the company want navigation elements to work?

- ✔ How do customers and employees access the database across Web servers?

- ✔ How do you save the shopping cart or other tools for customers to use on a follow-up visit?

By having a single architect design important processes using one consistent methodology, every piece of the Web site works in the same way, even though each piece may have actually been programmed by a different person. In the long run, businesses save money because maintaining and modifying the site in the future will be much easier.

The Web designer is responsible for the *look* and *feel* of your Web site, with the *look* being the visuals — graphics and layout — and the *feel* being the customer experience:

✔ **The visuals, man:** The Web designer is responsible for the visual appeal of the site. This person handles the graphics and layout that make up a site's visual component. He or she works with marketing to maintain consistent branding and a consistent corporate image throughout the site. (See Chapter 6 for more on marketing in cyberspace.)

✔ **The experience, dude:** Although this is a less obvious aspect of the design, the Web designer creates and implements the features that define the *customer experience*. A good designer can bring out subtle nuances that affect how customers interact with the Web site — and, ultimately, how they feel about this interaction.

If the site designer does a brilliant job, customers will become interactively involved in the site. It will stimulate their senses and draw their interest. Just as a bricks-and-mortar store designer creates displays that attract and engage shoppers, the Web designer creates a site that helps draw products and services to the attention of your site visitors.

✔ **The connection, man:** The Web designer is also responsible for making your site easy to use. How will customers get from your site's main page to a product detail page? How will they remove items from their shopping cart? How will the checkout work? If the site is confusing or difficult to use, you'll lose customers.

Don't overlook the importance of creating the perfect customer experience when you're in the market for a designer. Ask to see the sites that potential candidates have created. Play around to see how well those sites work. Look out for sites that don't seem very *intuitive*. An intuitive design anticipates how most users would do something or use a tool. No confusion? No problem. Look in Chapter 9 for ideas on well-designed Web pages.

Web designers aren't necessarily graphic designers. The ability to create engaging graphics is different from using those graphics to engage people in using your site. Do store designers build the displays or place them in the store to get the best use from them? Your Web designer can work with the artists from marketing or your advertising agency to get killer graphics and them place them in the site to make them shine.

What do you look for when filling the important role of Web designer? Start with the following characteristics:

✔ **A good sense of design and layout.** Ideally, you want a person who has designed several sites. This person needs to have experience in helping people navigate programs and have a good sense of graphical layout.

✔ **Hands-on experience.** Individuals can get hands-on experience two different ways. Your Web designer may have experience in graphic design (print or media advertising) and have learned the tools of Web design. Or he or she may have experience in designing program interfaces and have mastered graphical design and layout. Either way, you want someone with at least a year of experience and proven success.

✔ **Tools of the trade.** Although you can create HTML with any text editor (Microsoft Word, Notepad, EMACS, and so on), most Web designers use tools specifically designed for Web layout (Macromedia Dreamweaver, Microsoft FrontPage, Adobe PageMill or SiteMill, Allaire HomeSite or ColdFusion, and so on). Because graphic design experience is a major plus, knowledge of graphics programs — such as Adobe Photoshop, Macromedia Flash and Shockwave, CorelDRAW, and others — is also quite useful.

✔ **A thorough understanding of HTML.** You're not out of order in asking someone on your staff who understands HTML to conduct a technical interview, and you should ask to see some samples of the candidate's HTML work.

Ask for a portfolio from potential candidates. Look for portfolios containing attractive, easy-to-understand Web sites (or brochures, or articles, or whatever) that are well laid out.

Beware of candidates who say they work primarily with a *What You See Is What You Get* (WYSIWYG) Web design tool, such as Microsoft FrontPage. A good Web designer may use a WYSIWYG tool to do an initial page layout, but he or she should readily move on directly to the real deal — HTML code is the only way to go to tweak Web pages for a perfect finish.

I write the code that does the whole Web thing: Programmers

The very first programmer may not have been Barry Manilow (and certainly wasn't Al Gore, no matter what he says), but *programmers* (also called developers) are the foot soldiers in the war to complete an e-commerce site. Programmers *write* (or create from scratch) the code that makes your Web site more than just a big electronic billboard.

Programming can actually be broken down into several major areas, each with its own specialist programmers. Most Web sites need to make use of more than one type of programmer. Here's what programmers do:

✔ **Build the darn thing:** So your business analyst and architect have come up with all the rules that govern how your site will operate and how technology will be used to implement those rules. The time has come for your programmers to pick up hammers and nails and start building a Web site!

A programmer's basic job is to teach a computer how a business operates. He or she does this by using a programming language — such as Java or Visual Basic — to write the complex instructions that the computer understands. The end result is a program (also called an *application*) that does whatever you want it to.

✔ **Create interactions where none previously existed:** In a Web project, programmers may create dynamic Web pages that interact with your customers. They may also create standalone software applications that run on your servers to accomplish specific back-end tasks, such as authorizing credit cards or updating inventory levels. Programmers may also create programs on your database server in order to automate certain tasks, such as order processing, catalog maintenance, and so forth.

Programmers come in all different skill levels, with expertise in many different programming technologies. The architect and project manager can tell you what technologies your project will require and the skill levels the programmers should possess.

From a skill-level standpoint, programmers are generally divided into three rough groups:

✔ **Junior programmers** are usually new to the field (or to the technology they'll be working with) and require the supervision and assistance of more-skilled developers to guide them. Expect junior programmers to complete about 25 useful hours of work in a 40-hour week. They're great for the mundane programming tasks that bore more senior programmers.

✔ **Mid-level programmers** are the mainstay of any development team and can generally put in a solid 35 hours or so of productive work in a 40-hour week. They're experts in their chosen technology and probably have some familiarity with other related technologies, too.

✔ **Senior programmers** are the stars of the show, with expertise in more than one development technology. Although they can put in as much productive time every week as a mid-level programmer, their real value comes in their ability to guide and mentor junior and mid-level employees and to help keep the project flowing smoothly. A solid senior programmer with good experience can often double as a project manager.

How can you tell if a programmer is worth his or her salt? Consider the following qualifications:

✔ **Speak the language.** You need programmers who can write code and configure software for your project. Your project manager should choose programmers with necessary skills in the following areas:

- Designing and implementing databases, usually in some form of Structured Query Language (SQL).

- Writing code components in C++, Java, or Visual Basic, and scripting in JavaScript, VBScript, Perl, Python, or some other language.

- Connecting components with middleware like Microsoft's COM+, IBM MQ Series, or CORBA.

- If you purchase a commercial off-the-shelf package, like Microsoft Commerce Server, or IBM WebSphere, programmers need to know how to configure the software.

Not every programmer will know every language you need. Build a team, with each member contributing some vital skill to the project.

✔ **Experience, experience.** There is just no substitute for experience in these projects. Although many of the best coders have little or no formal education, they can always point to a number of projects they have completed. You can verify that experience through:

- Industry certifications

- Code samples

- Technical interviews

- References

Beware! The Web development industry is positively loaded with programmers whose experience consists solely of the project they did in their college programming course, or of the time they spent messing with Java at home. Look for programmers with actual business-related experience. Ask for references — and check them!

Programming is a solitary endeavor, so don't worry if a candidate has the social skills of a rock. You're not hiring a receptionist; you're hiring a technical wizard. And don't freak out about hair or clothing — heck, you may as well make every day casual dress day — because programmers may not see daylight often.

Finding the bugs: Your quality assurance cop

Okay, the work is done! Or is it? Finishing the work is one thing and discovering whether the site works correctly is quite another. Does it work like you intended it to? *Quality assurance* is one team role that most business executives are sure they can do without — until they actually try to do without.

Most managers ask, "What's the matter? Can't your high-priced programmers do it right the first time?" This question comes up most often when money is an issue. Can't you hold programmers responsible for testing their own code? Can't programmers at least test each other's code? The answers are "Yes," "No," and "It's not that simple."

Here's what QA team members do:

- ✔ **Develop a test plan.** Your business analyst and project manager develop business requirements, but someone needs to assure those requirements are fulfilled by your site. QA develops a series of tests that prove that each and every business requirement is satisfied.

- ✔ **Be the customer from Hades, and love every minute of it.** The QA person's job is to be the worst customer possible, pushing the wrong buttons and leaving things blank, to make sure your Web site gracefully handles these errors and guides customers in fixing them.

- ✔ **Write up a report.** When they find errors, QA specialists don't just send a note to the programmers that says, "These are broken." They send back a detailed report, describing exactly what they did, what they expected to happen, and what happened instead.

- ✔ **Verify best practices.** QA specialists also ensure that the entire project follows good processes. They use the technical methodologies provided by your architect and make certain they are baked into the mix. Well-constructed projects tend to deliver as promised and are much easier to maintain going forward.

QA specialists save you time and money because they can quickly find errors that would otherwise be left for your customers to uncover. And, unlike your customers — who will give your programmers absolutely no useful information to work with — a QA specialist can provide programmers with the information they need to quickly eliminate the errors.

What goes into making a good QA specialist? Look for the following characteristics:

- ✔ **Familiarity with the QA process:** QA specialists should be knowledgeable in creating use cases and test plans, maintaining standards, and overseeing quality in construction. Knowledge of automated testing tools is very important as well. RadView's WebLOAD and Mercury Interactive's Astra LoadTest are just a few of the many tools available.

- ✔ **Methodological approach to the QA process:** This is an essential quality to look for because QA specialists need to reliably and systematically repeat set after set of actions to arrive at a result. (Can you say anal retentive?)

- ✔ **Experience:** So what position doesn't require previous experience? QA specialists need to have spent time in a formal QA process and have experience developing and implementing test plans and verifying project success.

✔ **Good communication and interpersonal skills:** QA specialists need to convey to programmers exactly what they did to produce an error, and must clearly document the tests they conduct. Because they are often telling the programmers they are wrong, and can throw off the project schedule when things aren't right, QA specialists need to have patience and a thick skin.

A good QA leader can enlist the services of non-technical staff to test the site. This extends your capabilities without incurring additional overhead.

Do not look for technical expertise in a QA specialist. They need to know and care about what your site is supposed to do, not how it does it.

The problem is that QA specialists tend to uh, *annoy* everybody else. Without the right attitude, QA is just another word for delay and pickiness. Everybody needs to be clear that QA is a key part of making your site right.

RDA (www.rda.com/consulting) provides technical consulting on large software projects and Web sites. It has developed a methodology that includes building a team of teams. It clearly defines the responsibilities and communication flows between team members.

RDA allows many people to work together and keep the project on track. It can integrate its consultants with other technical personnel, including its client's workers. This team approach helps consultants and in-house IT professionals work together in harmony and allows RDA to supplement the client's staff with just the skills it needs.

Need network engineers? All aboard

The information technology world divides itself firmly into two camps, and so far we've only dealt with the so-called software side. The other side — the hardware or systems side — deals with your servers, your network, your client computers, and more.

The *network engineer* is, in many respects, a jack of all trades, but we've tried to narrow down some characteristics:

✔ **God-like knowledge of networks:** A network engineer should be familiar with server hardware, server operating systems, and networks, connections to other networks (such as the Internet), e-commerce software, database software, and any other software purchased to run your business' site.

Network engineers install, configure, maintain, repair, and operate the servers that make your online business exist. They have to literally assemble servers from boxes of components, install software, troubleshoot and resolve problems, and make use of a bewildering array of industry reference materials to get everything to work together.

✔ **24-7 availability and extensive knowledge of first aid:** Network administrators carry pagers and cell phones because they know about Murphy's Law: Software rarely breaks down in the middle of the day. Like all hardware — including your network, desktop computers, backup tape drive, and so on — your servers will eventually break down. Your network engineer does the fixing — no matter what time of day or night the breakdown occurs.

Plan to equip your network engineer (or engineers, if you need more than one) with a pager or cell phone. Also add lots of late-night pizzas to your budget, and lavishly compensate those network engineers for their diligence.

Network engineers also perform maintenance when things are quiet and the systems aren't real busy — nights and weekends. Network engineers keep very flexible schedules. You must understand that if they run server maintenance from 1 a.m. to 3 a.m., they aren't likely to come in at 8 a.m. the next day.

What makes a good network engineer? Start with this list of qualities:

✔ An ability to learn quickly, and apply what's learned

✔ A solid understanding of server hardware and operating systems (see Chapter 14 for more on servers and operating systems)

✔ A solid understanding of Internet networking

✔ A proven track record in setting up servers with public Internet access of six months or more. Formal education in systems engineering (tech schools often provide these, as well as four-year schools) is a definite plus.

✔ An industry certification, such as the Microsoft Certified Systems Engineer (MCSE) certification or the Sun Certified System Administrator for Solaris certification

✔ A willingness to go the extra mile and be on call when necessary

Beware! A great many network administrators pass themselves off as network engineers. An administrator is great at helping resolve network problems or creating new user accounts on an existing server, but you need the higher-powered engineer to build and maintain those precious servers and networks.

Demand experience and have a knowledge expert (on your staff or hired for the purpose) to test their actual knowledge. It takes an engineer to know an engineer.

Want a Webmaster?

After your site has been designed and developed, the *Webmaster* takes over day-to-day operations. A mix of Web designer, programmer, and network engineer, a Webmaster is responsible for making sure a Web site maintains an even keel and is responsive to your customers. The Webmaster's job involves

✔ **Keeping it real:** The Webmaster is responsible for making sure the site runs smoothly. Because modern Web sites can involve dozens of servers and hundreds (or thousands) of Web pages, this is no easy task! Anytime that your Web site needs updating or remodeling or anytime any changes are going to occur, your Webmaster should coordinate those changes. Think of your Webmaster as a server cowboy, responsible for keeping servers in line and functioning smoothly, keeping your Web pages error-free, and ensuring that everything's quiet on the Web frontier.

✔ **Responding to customers:** When customers run into a technical problem on your site, they should have the option of e-mailing your Webmaster, who should respond — promptly and courteously — with assistance. The Webmaster is the first line of defense for many Web sites' customer complaints, and you may want to have this person report jointly to your chief information officer and customer service director.

Here's a list of qualifications to look for in a good Webmaster:

✔ **A smattering of skills common to Web designers, programmers, and network engineers.** For example, a candidate with base-level knowledge of Visual Basic, C++, or Java programming, some graphic design experience, and a good understanding of network hardware and software is worth an interview. Look for proficiency in at least one of these three areas.

✔ **Good customer interaction skills.** Webmasters often are the first line of defense when customers need placating because the site has suffered a technical problem. Candidates for this job should have good communication skills, and, ideally, should carry an industry certification, such as Certified Internet Webmaster.

You may find that an existing technical employee (such as a network engineer or Web designer) is flexible enough — and has the appropriate skills — to be your Webmaster. When you're hiring technical staff, think about what interview candidates might fill this important role.

Estimating Your Project Size and Time Frame

After you determine which positions are created by your e-commerce plan, you need to determine how many people you need to fill each type of position. You also need to figure out when you need them to start work. (There's nothing worse than a bored programmer.)

Your project will have a definite life cycle associated with it, based on your business needs. Not every technical professional can be useful in every phase of the project, so it makes sense to conduct a kind of just-in-time staffing effort, where you bring staff members on board exactly when the project demands their skills.

Estimating the size of your project requires that you already have a solid plan for it in place. (Check out Chapter 3 for everything you need to know about putting together an e-commerce plan.) It also usually requires that an architect create a basic blueprint for the project, just so you can get an idea of how many different technical pieces are involved in the project. Working together, an architect and business analyst can come up with a solid plan for your site; the architect and a project manager can then work out a timeline for the project and estimate the number of staff hours that are needed, as well as the number of programmers, Web designers, network engineers, QA specialists, and other professionals that are needed.

A major factor in determining how many people you need is determining how much time you have. A project on a slow timeline can get by with fewer people for a longer stretch; a project that has to be done tomorrow needs a lot more people working with each other at the same time.

The gestation period for an elephant is 24 months, no exceptions. Twenty-four elephants cannot make a baby elephant come out in one month. Some parts of a project can and should be done on the same schedule as others. Other things are sequential, no matter what you do.

Understanding Your Staffing Options

As you deploy your new e-commerce initiative, your existing staff members may have a lot of interest (and apprehension) about the transition. You can capitalize on your employees' proven loyalty and knowledge of the business by encouraging them to apply for and move into the new positions that have been created as a result of your e-commerce strategies. You can also find creative ways of flexibly bringing in employees with the skills your new business direct requires.

Estimating your staffing needs: Don't do everything at the same time

You need to know whom you need and when you need them. When you build a house, you don't ask the builder to live with you, and you certainly don't expect every type of professional that we discuss in this chapter to show up on day one of the XYZ Corporation's e-commerce transition and start working. You need to ramp up to get online while developing a staff that can keep the site humming after you get rolling.

The first three positions to fill are the business analyst, architect, and project manager. These individuals define the project, create a formal plan for it, and spell out exactly which bits of the project have to be completed when. The project manager should then be able to tell you which skill sets you need to start the project's development. (Read the previous section, "Defining the Cast," to get the who's who on staff positions.)

The basic approaches are insourcing and outsourcing. *Insourcing* takes people who already know your business and trains them on computer systems and technology. *Outsourcing* brings in computer experts that you teach your business to.

Outsourcing is a common enough business concept — if you can't do a job yourself, hire someone else to do it for you. Outsourcing is an especially valid alternative to hiring a permanent employee when what needs to be done is relatively short-term. (Unless you're the kind of manager who likes to hire permanent employees only to fire them after they've done a good job. Yuck.) On the other hand, insourcing enables businesses to take advantage of the employees they already have.

In the IT world, your permanent staff may fear outsourcing — and often with cause. When companies outsource IT functions, there are often layoffs and massive asset transfers. You don't have to outsource everything — just the temporary functions that have a definitive end.

Insourcing is a relatively new concept and is currently unique to the information technology industry. Insourcing focuses on the untapped potential of your existing non-technical employees.

Finding strength in your own staff

When it comes to e-commerce, what good are existing, non-technical employees? The answer is plenty good. After all, they know your business — how it runs, what works, what doesn't work, what makes money, what loses money, and so on. Your existing employees can be even more valuable to your company if you can turn them into technical professionals. Here are a few reasons why:

- ✔ **Pro: Existing employees can maintain the company's vision.** Because existing staff members already know how your business works, you don't have to worry about them doing things that work counter to your business' goals.

- ✔ **Pro: Adding to your employees' skill sets will increase their value and loyalty to your business.** Turning existing staff members into technical professionals increases their value to your business and improves their loyalty to the business — all while filling much-needed technical positions on your staff.

- ✔ **Pro: Working with known commodities.** When you insource, you already know the employees. You know whether they show up to work, they work well with others, and they understand and support your business values.

- ✔ **Con: You don't know how they will do on computers.** Loyal, hard-working employees don't always do well on computers or work well with geeks. You can mitigate these risks by using aptitude testing (available from most training companies) and just by common sense. If they can't get their e-mail or put someone on hold on the phone system, they may not have demonstrated aptitude for technology.

Micro Endeavors, Inc. (www.microendeavors.com) specializes in turning business-savvy professionals into technical wizards with its I.T.SkillsPlus courseware (www.itskillsplus.com), which is available at many community colleges in the United States.

Many technical training companies, such as ExecuTrain (www.executrain.com), and many local colleges and technical schools, can help you develop custom programs to train employees in computer technology. They can help identify employees with computer aptitude for computers and design a course of study to help provide the skills you require.

Bringing in hired guns

If you can't spare anyone on your existing staff, you may have to bring in some outside professionals to fill your technical needs. *Contractors* are often the best way to get an e-commerce project off the ground and onto the 'net.

One advantage that contractors have is experience on a wide variety of projects — experience that they can bring to your project. A good consulting firm provides skilled programmers, architects, Web designers, and network engineers. Small, yet well-equipped firms — such as notsoldseparately (`www.notsoldseparately.com`) — provide a complete set of services for e-commerce projects, including graphic designers and QA specialists. Larger contracting firms — such as the Accenture, PricewaterhouseCoopers, KPMG, and others — provide a greater range of experience and vast technical resources that can prove useful to your project (albeit at a higher price).

A good consulting firm can also help you search for permanent staff members by providing references, conducting technical screenings, and more.

Here are a list of benefits and possible risks to calling in outside help:

- **Pro: Getting the best.** People with proven track records in e-commerce are scarce and difficult to hire. Consulting firms provide an environment these experts enjoy, so they often attract the best. You can rent the best from them, and then stop paying for them when the task is done.

- **Cons: You don't own them.** Consultants often serve more than one customer. You may need to share their time and attention. And they don't come cheap. You often pay more for each consultant than the vice president who oversees them.

Integrating and cross-training staff

Many organizations cross-train information technology (IT) personnel, allowing them to work with or shadow employees in other departments. Cross-training helps the IT personnel understand the tasks of people in other departments, and thus design systems that make those employees' jobs easier and more efficient.

For instance, Kraft Foods sends top executives to Northwestern University for formal training in computer technology. The company also matches IT professionals with business managers to help them understand the business. The synergy created by partnering technical staff with business managers helps the managers understand the systems that the IT department has created, and also helps the IT department understand business processes well enough to deliver systems that are catered to processes.

American Airlines works with BroadVision, the company that provides Web technologies for the American Airlines Web site. American Airline employees observe BroadVision employees doing their jobs, and BroadVision employees listen and learn while watching American Airline employees perform their job functions. Getting employees from both companies to work in the same room side-by-side helps overcome difficulties such as the terminology barrier (most disciplines have their own vocabularies, which is why we define so many terms in this book) and helps both sides communicate and support one another.

What do you need to maintain? Re-evaluating staffing needs down the line

All businesses — especially e-commerce businesses — are in a constant state of change. What differs — especially with online businesses — is the rate of change. Online staffing needs may undergo a complete revision every 18 months, or even more frequently.

Determining how many staff members to maintain requires that you first determine what rate of change your online business will maintain. If its cycle will be fairly short, then you can always have a business analyst and an architect work on a new phase of development while programmers and Web designers finish up the previous phase and your Webmaster finishes implementing the phase before that.

On a longer cycle, you may prefer to bring in consultants as architects and project managers, and to supplement a relatively small programming staff with contractors. The consultants and contractors leave after a development phase is complete, and, until the next development cycle begins, your smaller staff handles day-to-day maintenance issues.

In the best of worlds, you occasionally will find yourself working with an absolutely brilliant staff member. Perhaps she'll be a programmer who's simply faster than anyone you've ever seen, or an architect who excels at creating clear, concise blueprints for programmers to follow, or a Webmaster who can program in his spare time and play network engineer on the weekends.

Do whatever you have to do to keep these gems on staff. Offer a bit of extra salary, a kind word, a flexible work schedule — whatever. Truly bright technical people are rare, and you should do everything you can to hang on to the ones that you're lucky enough to find.

Calling All Geeks: Nabbing the Best Nerds Around

The experts and specialists you need to build your site are hard to come by — already over a quarter-million other positions like yours are sitting empty. You need to seek out the right people and draw them in. You have to separate the pros from the posers and hire your staff; then you need to find the right incentives to keep them both active and happy.

Finding out where the techies roost

Part of the problem in hiring technical people is simply finding technical people. The fact is, more technical jobs are available than there are people to fill them. That means you can assume that all the technical people already have jobs. And although some of them are unhappy with those jobs and looking for new ones, most of them aren't actively looking for a job. That's not to say you can't hire them — you just have to reach them and let them know you're looking.

Many of the usual hiring tactics work fine for hiring technical professionals — job fairs, classified ads, and so on. But those methods are geared to finding people who are *looking* for a job. How can you make contact with qualified professionals who aren't necessarily looking, but who could still be lured to your team by a good offer?

When in Rome . . . networking through the Internet

Most technical professionals have more than a casual relationship with the Internet, so it stands to reason that surfing the Web is a good place to find new employees. Don't just post ads on the job-search sites, though — *hunt* on the Internet. Frequent newsgroups and discussion boards, such as those maintained by Microsoft, Sun, Oracle, and others, to find well-written, intelligent professionals who may just be waiting for the right offer from you to join the team.

That said, Internet-based job-search sites aren't a bad place to look, either. But beware: Most responses you get from job postings on these sites will be from technical recruiters, not from prospective employees. If you prefer not to work through recruiters, clearly state "principals only" on your job posting.

Following success: Sometimes stealing is okay

If you can't find the technical professionals you need, you may start coveting the ones working for other successful organizations. Why not lure them away? If your competition has the technical folks you need, surely some of them aren't completely happy with their pay, their benefits, or their working environment. And you're just the one to offer them a better deal! Discreetly contact them and find out what it would take to move them.

Be aware that most technical professionals are under legal agreements not to work for their companies' competitors when they leave. Some states have found these contracts to be unenforceable, so you may have some leeway for stealing employees directly from your competition. As always, consult a business attorney for the latest, most accurate advice in these sticky situations.

Your competitors aren't the only ones with technical professionals — practically every company has a few. Find some successful companies and see what you can do to dislodge a few valuable human resources, or find a not-so-successful company and offer a life preserver to the worried employees. All's fair in love, war, and e-commerce — but remember, other businesses can do the same thing to your people if you're not careful.

Off with their heads: Considering headhunters

As if e-commerce wasn't bad enough with the potential of cannibalization (see Chapter 6), you may have to deal with headhunters, too, although they prefer to be called *recruiters*. Finding qualified technical professionals is so difficult that some companies find people for you. A recruiting firm sends you reams of resumes to peruse and arranges interviews, all while charging a hefty fee for the service.

Are recruiters worth it? Sometimes. Good ones can save you a bundle by producing the perfect resume right off the bat. Bad ones send you everything in their databases, hoping one will catch your eye, which basically saves you no time at all. Cultivate relationships with good recruiters and cut off the ones who aren't earning their fees.

Building a nest where the techies will flock

If you've seen a few technical professionals' resumes, you know that techies don't all spend years and years at a single job. Technical professionals can become easily bored and demand a quality working environment; subsequently, they're easily lured by a better offer from another company. That's a trick you can use to hire some technical employees. But you need to know how to keep other companies from using the same trick against you.

Salaries that sell

Technical professionals can be expensive. And you'll need to pay to get the very best (sometimes, you even need to pay to get less-than-best). Of course, not every staff member has to be the very best — the whole point of junior programmers, for example, is that they're entry-level and can't command a premium salary. But senior programmers and architects, in particular, will need top dollar. Read the trade publications, such as Computerworld (www.computerworld.com), InternetWeek (www.internetweek.com), eWEEK (www.zdnet.com/eweek), and Microsoft Certified Professional Magazine (www.mcpmag.com), to get a picture of the latest (and ever-changing) salaries.

Providing a piece of the pie

One way to cut back on your salary expenses, and still offer a great package to your technical employees, is to offer them stock options. That makes a portion of their compensation tied to the success of the company, which they have a good amount of control over. The better job they do, the more those options are worth, and the more money they'll make.

You don't have to hand out all those options at once. Encourage employees to remain with the company for longer by spreading options out over a few years.

Going beyond money

Today's competitive job market requires employers to pony up more than just salaries and stock options. Consider some of the standard benefits offered to every employee at high-tech companies, such as Microsoft (who's definitely interested in retaining technical employees):

- Company-paid relocation packages
- Fully-paid health and dental insurance
- Company-paid health club memberships
- Flexible working hours
- The ability to work from home when appropriate
- Casual dress environment (sometimes this can mean khakis and polo shirts; sometimes shorts, t-shirts, and sandals)
- Three or more weeks of paid vacation (usually increasing with seniority)
- Spousal job-search support when relocating
- Domestic partner benefits
- Free soft drinks, juice, and coffee
- Credit union membership
- Substantial signing bonuses
- Annual performance-based bonuses and raises up to 10 percent or more
- Private offices for nearly every employee (and every office has a window, too, even if it only looks out on the hallway)

Creating a competitive benefits package is an excellent way to complement a competitive salary and stock option offer, and is an excellent way to retain employees, too.

Chapter 8

Handling Legal Issues

*I*n the grand scheme of things, the Internet is quite new, and the lawyers and politicians haven't quite figured out how to sink their hooks too deeply into it — yet. The Supreme Court and Congress have not yet worked out where the lines cross between First Amendment free speech guarantees and congressional control of interstate commerce. But even if the Internet had been around for generations, like everything Internet-related, Internet legal issues would be in a state of rapid change — you'd still have to keep an eye on them. Make sure that your business attorney keeps an eye on the latest legal cases and advises your senior management about the best way to respond and react to changes!

The Internet puts an interesting new twist on legal issues that traditional business are familiar with. Protecting your brand and your business' intellectual property becomes a more difficult task, and protecting the rights and privacy of your customers becomes a more important priority than ever before. You also have to face new legal ramifications of collecting and paying taxes and of doing business across national borders. In this chapter, we cut through the confusing legal jargon and spell out the issues you need to start thinking about as your online business becomes a reality.

The purpose of this chapter is not to give you legal advice. This chapter is intended to help you understand some of the specific legal issues that e-commerce businesses face so that your business (and its attorney) can more easily make decisions that will best suit your needs. Although some great books and Web sites offer free legal advice, the *best* legal advice you can get comes from a competent attorney who has a good understanding of your business and the complex legal issues surrounding e-commerce.

If you don't have legal representation yet, you can seek aid from many sources. The Small Business Administration (SBA) has excellent resources to help smaller businesses locate resources like this. Also, many states provide help. For example, California has a business portal (`www.ss.ca.gov`) where you can find references to a wealth of useful information. Such resources won't replace a good lawyer but do give you a place to start.

Understanding and Managing Intellectual Property

The United States has several laws specifically designed to help corporations and individuals protect their intellectual property — including the intangible components that help create a brand image. Most other countries have similar laws, although they differ in important details from the laws in the United States.

The term *intellectual property* is used to describe one person's or business's ownership of creative work and innovations, such as Amazon's one-click shopping feature. Use of another person's or business's intellectual property may require permission or the payment of royalties — interested parties should always query the originator of such material before use.

Identifying and protecting your brands

A *brand* is a combination of product names, logos, slogans, and other intangible materials that make your business uniquely identifiable from your competitors. You may already have created a unique look and feel that makes your products and services stand apart in traditional business.

Brands are much more than logos and graphics. They become the communication of your value proposition — those things that make your organization unique from your competition. For example, Wal-Mart uses a little smiley face in its commercials to portray its friendly, down-home atmosphere and low prices. This image wouldn't work as well for Macy's, but it's fine for Wal-Mart.

The key to your success lies in building a clear, recognizable online brand that draws people back to your Web site again and again. Unfortunately, if you're successful at creating a brand, you become a target of less-scrupulous businesses that would rather borrow your company's ideas and benefit from your accomplishments.

What makes an online brand an online brand? Good question. An online brand image contains the following characteristics:

- ✔ **A domain name (or several):** Macy's, which has an online presence with the registered domain name `www.macys.com`, would be in a world of hurt if the domain `macys.com` were owned by an offshore retailer of merchandise seconds.

- ✔ **A logo (at least one):** When you see that big white-and-blue-striped ball logo online and click it, you expect to turn up at AT&T rather than at McDonald's. This logo gives AT&T instant recognition without saying a word.

- ✔ **A tag line or slogan:** These are short reminders of your value proposition. Whether you wear makeup or not, you may recognize "Easy, Breezy" as a slogan for makeup manufacturer Cover Girl. If you're daring enough to visit `www.covergirl.com` you will be reminded of the ease and breeze of Cover Girl's online beauty guide. Just in case you forgot.

- ✔ **A consistent look and feel:** When you visit the Creative Labs site, you know it by the consistently applied navigation aids, page footers, color scheme, and logos of each page. That familiarity makes it easier to get around the site.

- ✔ **Special features:** Some sites are well known for a special feature, such as a unique checkout process.

You may have different lines of business, each with its own unique identity. Develop a distinct brand for each line of business by relating the brands through common graphical devices and ubiquitous links from one brand to the other.

Getting to know trade names, trademarks, and service marks

To build an online brand, you must design your Web storefront, online services, product descriptions, and other content to complement (and in the best case) expand your company's offline image. Protecting your image online is not negotiable; with so many ways to transport content electronically, you need to ensure that everything that remotely resembles intellectual property (including your company's name, products, and services) is *trademarked,* meaning that your company has exclusive ownership of it.

You can use legal means to protect your company's name, products, and services, and of course, you can plaster symbols all over your site that say, "Don't *go* there" to people thinking about tweaking something of yours and repackaging it as theirs. Here's a list of common trademarks and what they mean:

✔ **Trade name:** A *trade name* — also called a *brand name* — is the name that a company commonly uses to describe itself in the marketplace. A trade name offers the lowest grade of legal protection because it doesn't necessarily have a mark associated with it. Although your use of a trade name can be defended in court, U.S. law provides no specific protections.

✔ **Trademark:** A *trademark* (™) is a specific mark that is attached to a name, logo, slogan, or some combination of these that distinguishes an organization's products from the products of others. For example, trade-marked property, such as Google.com's logo, is usually accompanied by a ™ symbol. In this case, the tiny trademark indicates that Google claims exclusive rights to the color, size, shape, and appearance of the logo (not to mention the funny name). This mark isn't a laughing matter; Google, and any other company with trademarked properties, is saying with this little symbol that it is willing to defend (in court if necessary) its claim to use the trademark.

✔ **Service mark:** Somewhat related to the trademark is the *service mark,* which often appears next to the name of a slogan or the name of a ser-vice identifying it as a service. Service marks carry the ˢᴹ symbol. For example, "You've Got Pictures" is a service from AOL and accordingly carries a service mark. This symbol serves as a warning to others not to develop an Internet picture-sharing service and call it *You've Got Pictures.*

✔ **Registered trademark:** The granddaddy of trademarks is the registered trademark (®). Intellectual property is associated with a registered trademark that been registered with the U.S. government. The govern-ment researches the piece of property in question and awards the mark if it discovers that no other company claims exclusive use of it. The fed-eral government also recognizes that the company that has registered the property (called the *registrant*) maintains exclusive use of the prop-erty. Registering trademarks provides the best protection because U.S. law protects them. You want to register your trademark before you make significant investments in developing it as a brand.

U.S. law protects registered trademarks that are used online exactly as it protects them when used in traditional businesses. Your attorney can help you decide which marks should be registered with the U.S. govern-ment to best protect your online brand.

Some countries have wildly different trademark laws than the United States. Some countries have no trademark laws at all, requiring companies to defend their property in court if they are challenged. If you do business internation-ally, be sure that you and your attorney decide on the best way to protect your business' property abroad.

Understanding and Protecting Your Domain Name

Domain names help people find things on the Internet. Computers connect to each other based on Internet provider (IP) addresses, which are like phone numbers. To make it easier, the Internet community devised the *Domain Name System (DNS)* to automatically convert the domain name (such as www.dummies.com) to an IP address (192.168.0.1). Because you want your customers to find you easily, you want a domain name that links to your company.

Internet con artists will use any component of your company that they possibly can to make your customers think they're doing business with you. Check out Table 8-1 for an at-a-glance look at some infringements that others may intentionally try to perpetrate against your business. Keep reading the following sections for more detailed information about how these scams work and how you can avoid them.

Table 8-1	Protecting Your Domain from Intentional Infringement		
Scam	*The Lowdown*	*Example*	*How to Beat the Scam*
Domain-name rip-off is the practice of setting up fake Web sites using common misspellings of more-popular URLs. Usually, an attempt is also made to mimic the original site's look and feel, logos, and brands.	No-good-niks may be stealing your traffic to do business with your customers, or they may be after your customer's ID and credit cards. Or, scamsters may just want to extort money from you.	Perpetrators may register similarly spelled domain names, such as mycopany.com or mycompny.com, to draw customers from your name mycompany.com.	Your best protection is to watch for scams, and to make sure your site is professional looking and complex enough that it's difficult to duplicate easily. Also use techniques such as e-mail confirmations to let your customers know who they're doing business with.

(Continued)

Table 8-1 *(continued)*

Scam	The Lowdown	Example	How to Beat the Scam
Domain-name hijacking is the practice of sneaking in and purchasing a domain name the instant it comes up for renewal — beating out the company that originally registered the name for its legitimate business venture.	The idea is to hold this very important piece of intellectual property hostage and force the business to buy it for an exorbitant amount of money.	Two days after `mycompany.com` registration expires, Dave Dastardly pays the fee and takes control of the name.	Keep your registration paid up. The burden falls on you.
Unscrupulous folks will use deceptive links and redirection tactics to accomplish the same goal as domain-name rip-off: To get customers from a legitimate business site to a fraudulent site.	The goal is to obtain personal and financial information from customers.	The scam is completed by linking your logo to a site with pages that look like yours, collecting payment information, and stealing your customers' credit card information (and their trust in you).	Quickly report abuses to Fraud Watch International (`www.fraudwatch.com`).The thief won't have profile information on your customer, so showing that you know your customers assures them that they have clicked to the right place.
Scamsters use similar names from another domains to attract browsers.	The goal is to use your name to gain traffic. They may also try to deal fraudulently with your customers.	The ploy is to register `mycompany.com.cz` to steal customers from `mycompany.com`.	Particularly if you do business internationally, register your domain in international domains.

Scam	The Lowdown	Example	How to Beat the Scam
Evil-doers use variations on a name or trade product to attract customers from your business.	The goal is either to steal your customers or to hold the domain name for ransom, with the intent that you will buy it from them.	MyCompany manufactures the one and only Widget, which may be trademarked or protected by patent. Dave Dastardly registers `widgets.com`.	Register the name of your company, common variations of name, and your leading products.

Make sure you own not only your domain name, but also all the major variations, misspellings, and abbreviations of it! (See the upcoming section "Understanding and protecting international domains" for more information.) And don't forget to register domains for your most popular brands. Not only can you prevent infringement, but you can also offer customers as many points of entry to your business as possible.

What's in a (domain) name?

Internet names are broken into *domains*, or general groups of names. One of these top-level domain names is placed at the end of your domain name, after the last period of your URL address. The domain name database, administered by InterNIC (`www.internic.org`), originally identified seven domains:

`com` for *com*mercial ventures; `.org` for nonprofit *org*anizations; `.net` for providers of Inter*net* services; `.edu` for *edu*cational institutions; `.mil` for United States *mil*itary installations; `.gov` for United States *gov*ernmental

institutions; `.us` for the *U*nited *S*tates (each country has its own two-letter abbreviation)

A domain name has to be unique within its domain. For example, you won't find more than one `MyCompany.com`. The tricky part is that you can find a `MyCompany.com`, a `MyCompany.org`, and a `MyCompany.net`. Who knows? When you register your domain name, you may have even more choices for consider the alternate domains.

A common way bad people try to steal online brands — at least briefly — is to hijack business' domain names. Here's what you should do to avoid this problem:

✔ **Register your domain name — fast!** Try InterNIC (`www.internic.com`) for info about domain registrars. Always keep the registration fees paid up!

✔ **Pay your fees — immediately!** Make sure the registrar receives your payment quickly. Also, get a confirmation that your registration has been renewed.

Internet links can point people anywhere. You can place text, graphics, buttons — almost anything visitors can click — to send them anywhere. If your logo, trademark, or slogan is used on a site as a link to a bogus destination, your customers can be stolen. Because this diversion happens without your knowledge or permission, this is difficult to protect against.

Understanding and Protecting International Domains

Every country has its own top-level domain (see the sidebar elsewhere in this chapter, "What's in a (domain) name?"). Each country has a two-letter extension appended to the end of the domain. Thus, `assus.com.tw` is a different domain name than `asus.com`. Asus, a manufacturer of computer components, wisely registered both names because it commonly does business in both domains.

Controlling Your Name and Trademarks

Many companies use common nicknames or abbreviations for their organizations. Many people think that Coca-Cola and Coke are synonymous. When customers look for Coke on the Internet, they may search for `coke.com` or `cocacola.com`. Because Coca-Cola registered both names, either will result in a hit.

The New York Times was not so lucky when it registered `nytimes.com`, hoping to save its browsers a few keystrokes. Someone noticed that `newyorktimes.com` was not registered and nabbed it. *The New York Times* ended up taking this person to court to get use of the trade name it had already wielded in the market place for over 100 years. The newspaper won, but who wants the hassle of a court case?

The bottom line is to think out name variations and then register the common ones. If you want to investigate who has what names, go to InterNIC (www.internic.org) and use its WHOIS system to see who owns every registered domain name. If you believe someone has your trade name, you can register a complaint with the Internet Committee for Assigning Names and Numbers (ICANN) (www.icann.org).

Safely Swapping Brand Names with Other Businesses

Just as you have concerns about people properly using your online brand, they have concerns about your using theirs. You may think that because you're not doing any harm, you can casually use another company's trade name or logo on your site — if you carry that company's products, for example. But your best bet is to always get written permission to use another company's brand name, logo, or another portion of their brand. And because you likely use images of their products, you should secure permissions.

Many companies grant you this permission when you become a distributor or reseller of their products. Other companies may require you to specifically request permission. Make sure that you draw up a permissions agreement that details exactly how you plan to use the other company's brand components. You can get standing agreements to cover you in long-term relationships, such as distributorships.

In bricks-and-mortar stores, the packaging that acts as the primary advertising medium was created by, and controlled by, the trademark holder. On your Web site, you choose how to portray the product. Companies can become very testy when they don't like the way you present their products.

Handling legal requests to use your brands and logos

You need to make sure that your company's brands, logos, and Web design are protected from upstanding businesses that want to promote themselves by using your business' good name and reputation. For example, some retailers may request permission to use portions of your brand — such as the logo — to advertise your products to their customers. By using your logo as part of the product's information on their sites, those businesses gain legitimacy. And of course, your business gets some free advertising. Not bad, eh? Well, not quite. You may face pitfalls. Always make sure you give this permission in writing and specify exactly how the other company may use elements of your branding (such as a logo, slogans, and other copyrighted materials).

Handling contracts and permissions

You can work with your attorneys to create boilerplate contracts that help others understand how you want them to treat your branding elements. The contracts can be flexible without giving away the farm. Businesses have done this for years and years; cooperative advertising has been key to getting advertising for years immemorial. Working with your customers (or your vendors) cooperatively can easily produce a win-win scenario. Just make certain you have legal recourse for prosecuting abuse of your branding information.

You should use every means at your disposal, including trademark, copyright, and patent laws, as well as legal action, to protect your online image.

Protecting Software Patents, and Copyrights

Two important aspects of U.S. law that protect intellectual property are patents and copyrights. You may feel fairly comfortable in your knowledge of *patents*, which for a set period of time protect your original inventions from being copied by some competitor without giving you credit; and *copyrights*, which protect original content from being distributed by anyone other than the content's creator. However, patents and copyrights don't work exactly the same way online as they do in the traditional business world.

U.S. law says that the creator of any original work — a written work, a piece of art, an audio recording, and so forth — has the exclusive right to determine how that work may be used. In practice, you have to *register* an original work to be copyrighted if you want U.S. law to fully protect you.

Other countries' copyright laws differ from U.S. law. Make sure you understand another country's laws in order to fully protect your property. Also, many countries have signed treaties with the United States, promising to honor U.S. copyright law if the U.S. honors *their* copyright laws. Your attorney can help you understand the implications of these laws on your business' intellectual property. You can get the lay of the land at www.uspto.gov (United States Patent and Trademark Office).

If you do business internationally, you should secure international copyrights to protect your work abroad. You can go to the World Intellectual Property Organization (www.wipo.org) for more information.

Copyrights only protect the actual work, not the idea of the work. For example, if you were to paint a picture of a house, you would have a copyright over your picture, not over the idea of painting pictures of houses.

One-click, two-click, three-click, four

One of the most famous examples of online patent and copyright law in action is Amazon.com's 1-Click ordering process. In this process, registered Amazon customers provide their shipping, billing, and payment information to the Web site. Amazon stores this information on its computers and gives those customers the option to enable 1-Click checkout (which, you may have guessed by the name, is a speedy checkout process).

Several other Web sites took this idea and began implementing variations of the 1-Click process. But Amazon had secured a U.S. patent on the new process and immediately filed for patent infringement. In the end, U.S. courts upheld Amazon's position and patent, and the other sites had to stop using their versions of the 1-Click process unless they had an agreement with Amazon to license the process. By choosing to patent (not copyright) the process Amazon protected its source code, *and* the *idea* of 1-Click.

Have the members of your legal team review your Web site before it goes live so that they can make suggestions for securing patents, copyrights, and trademarks as appropriate.

The concept that you can't own an idea may seem fairly obvious. However, it has become an important concept in the world of online commerce because it applies to computer software — and with all the talk you're already hearing about intellectual property, you can see how easily things get murky.

Imagine that you create a new catalog system that makes it easier than ever for customers to find and purchase products online. By U.S. law, you automatically own a copyright on the program code that makes your catalog system work. For better protection, you can register your copyright, and no one else will be able to use your program code without your permission. However, this protection may not stop your competition from using the *idea* of your new catalog system. Nothing prevents competitors from observing how your system works and writing their own software to mimic yours — it's perfectly legal to do so. What you need to protect the new process is a *patent*.

In the online world, you can use a patent to protect either a specific process or a specific design. For example, many online businesses have filed for design patents on specific elements of their Web sites, such as fonts that they specially created.

When you contract consultants, pay careful attention to the wording of the contract. Many consultants will use a boilerplate contract that gives them ownership of the code they create and gives you license to use it. If a contractor develops it on your dime, you should own it.

In order to obtain a patent, you must clearly document the process or design being patented, and you must demonstrate how the design or process is unique, and not merely derived from an earlier design or process. Although the patent makes your design or process easily accessible to the general public (all patent documents are considered public property), U.S. law protects your exclusive right — for about 20 years — to use the protected material. But securing a U.S. patent does not guarantee protection in any other country, and other countries have vastly different patent laws. If you need to protect your design or process internationally, you need to secure patents from the countries you do business in.

Protecting Your Customers' Privacy

Information about your customers is a gold mine of marketing information. Not only can you use that information to market products and services to your customers, you can also sell that information to other businesses. Of course, your customers have invested their faith in you to protect their personal information. If you violate that trust, they may sue or protest loud enough that politicians get involved. You need to understand and balance the rights of your organization with the rights of your customers.

Basically, customers don't want you to sell their names, addresses, e-mail addresses, phone number, or other personal information — in some cases even credit card number and bank account numbers — to other companies. What you can do is *aggregate* customer information. Aggregate information anonymously adds the demographics of your customer (age, location, education level, interests, magazines they read — any personal information you collect) into totals. So although no one discovers that Milton Milktoast bought jeans from your Web site, you can state that 38 percent of your sales of jeans were made to males aged 25-32 with an education level of a bachelor degree. Milton is part of that 38 percent. Aggregate data helps companies measure the effectiveness of their advertising within the marketplace. This information is quite valuable — and marketable.

Any time you plan to share information, you should have a written contract. That contract should specify

   ✔ How the information can be used

   ✔ How it must be stored

   ✔ Who owns the shared information

   ✔ That the contract protects your customers' rights as they are spelled out in your privacy policy

Finally, an Act with an easy-to-remember name: Graham-Leach-Bliley

The Graham-Leach-Bliley Act, which went into effect on July 1, 2001, requires financial institutions to adopt policies and procedures to protect consumers' "nonpublic personal information." The law, which is the first of its kind, requires financial institutions to provide notice to customers about the kind of information they intend to share — and with whom they intend to share it. Banks must gain consent and offer consumers a choice about whether they want this information shared; they must also enable consumers to access and correct personal information. *And,* banks are obligated to provide customers with a means of correcting errors. Financial institutions must prevent the loss, theft or misuse of the personal information they collect from individuals.

Although financial institutions are the only businesses affected by the new law, you should talk to your legal counsel about its implications where your business is concerned.

Your privacy policy is a legal contract between your business and your customers. Like any other contract, your attorney should review it before you begin using it on your site.

Setting up privacy policies

Few Web sites these days lack a published privacy policy, even if the only way to find it is to read the small print at the bottom of every page. But everyone has a privacy policy for a reason, and your site should have one, too. You will be asking your customers for personal information — names, addresses, e-mail addresses, and payment and account information — and your privacy policy is a contract between you and your customers about how you plan to use that information.

Although a few laws are already on the books regarding how online businesses can collect and use customers' personal information, you can bet that any serious problems resulting from a business' use of private information will quickly result in laws being passed. Protect yourself by being up front and honest with your customers. Don't hide your privacy policy or make it difficult for customers to find; practice full disclosure and let customers know how you plan to use their information. If you're hesitant to disclose the details of your plans for using their information, perhaps you should think about changing your plans to something you are comfortable sharing.

The World Wide Web Consortium (www.w3.org), a non-profit organization that develops standards and common protocols for use on the Internet, has established the Platform for Privacy Preferences Project (P3P). This project allows a Web browser to automatically query Web sites for their published privacy policies. If the privacy policy violates the personal privacy preferences of users, a warning lets them know that any information that they offer this Web site can and will be used against them in the marketplace. Microsoft's Internet Explorer will support P3P to help individuals protect their identity information. If you want to set people at ease, you will want your Web site to provide P3P data to user browsers.

Selling, renting, and sharing customer information

Before you can begin to draft your privacy policy, you need to decide exactly what you want to do with the private information your customers give you. Your business may have no choice but to use information internally in various ways — to process orders, to create targeted advertising or other personalized features, and so forth. (After all, that's why you asked for the information in the first place.) However, you may also want the opportunity to share your customers' information with other companies. Be clear in your mind exactly how — and with whom — you will share customers' information (names, addresses, e-mail addresses, phone numbers, and so forth). Look for more detail in the earlier section "Setting up privacy policies."

- ✔ *Renting* means you may allow another company to use your customers' information one time only for a fee. The other company does not maintain a copy of the information; if the company wants to use that information again, it must come back to you and pay for a second turn.

- ✔ *Selling* means that you provide a copy of your customers' information to another company, who becomes the owner of that copy. That company can resell (or rent) the information and use it in any way it sees fit, unless your agreement specifies otherwise.

- ✔ *Sharing* can be the same thing as renting *or* selling, without the fee. The distinction is whether you retain ownership of your customers' information, or whether the other company now owns a copy of that information that it can use as it sees fit.

Customers generally are more opposed to having their information sold than to having it rented. Because you will ultimately be disclosing — in your privacy policy — exactly what you will do with customers' personal information, try to stick with uses that your customers won't mind.

Decide whether you want to give your customers a way to restrict your use of their information. For example, if you plan to rent e-mail addresses to other companies, you may want to offer your customers the option to specify that their e-mail address not be rented. Offering this option can go a long way toward making a lenient privacy policy more palatable for your customers.

 Whatever your privacy policy says, make sure that your programmers create the necessary tools and programs to actually implement those details. For example, if you want to give customers the option to specify that you cannot share their e-mail address, you need to create a special Web page on the site that enables customers to specifically choose this option.

Deciding what to include in your privacy policy

After you know what you want to do with your customers' information, you need to write it up into a privacy policy. The policy must detail exactly what information you will ask your customers to give you, what you will do with that information, and which pieces of information may be provided to other companies or individuals. You should also outline the process you will use to determine who you will share information with.

Your policy might include the following basic information:

✔ **What information is collected and how it is used.** Your customers are asked for their names and addresses for shipping and billing purposes only, and are asked for payment information in order to process their orders only. Customers are asked for e-mail addresses in order to process their orders and facilitate communications with your company.

✔ **How information is stored, where it is stored, and for which purposes the information is kept.** You store all customer information on your servers. You send e-mail to customers regarding orders that they have placed, and offer your customers the opportunity to receive promotional e-mail from you and will send those e-mails only to the customers who request them. You will stop sending these e-mails to customers who request that you do so.

✔ **How information that's gathered is combined with existing data to provide extra benefit to customers.** You keep a record of all customer purchases and activity on your site. This information is attached to your customers' other personal information and may be used to target advertising or promotional e-mails so that you can provide personalized information to your customers.

> ✔ **How the businesses you share information with plan to handle the data you send.** You may share customers' names, addresses, and e-mail addresses with other organizations that offer products or services your customers may be interested in. These organizations agree in writing to treat your customers' information in substantially the same way that you do.
>
> ✔ **An assurance that information is used responsibly.** You do not share customers' payment information, order history, or site activity history.

Provide a link to your privacy policy on every page of your site, perhaps in the footer at the bottom of each page. You should also provide a link to the policy in a more prominent location whenever you ask customers for personal information so that they can easily see how you plan to use this information.

Changing your privacy policy

A time may come when you need to change your privacy policy. In fact, you should constantly evaluate the policy to ensure that you haven't left anything out. But certainly when you change your policy, you need to make customers aware of the change. Perhaps you want to make your customers' e-mail addresses more widely available for rental, and you want to give your customers the opportunity to request that you never share their information with other companies.

Your original privacy policy should include a paragraph that describes how you will communicate any changes to the policy, such as sending an e-mail notifying your customers of the change. Make sure you follow this procedure to implement a revised privacy policy.

If you change your policy — suppose that you decide to start renting out your customer list — you cannot apply the new policy retroactively. You cannot promise people you will protect their personal data and then, after you collect it, decide to sell it.

Sharing customer information with partners

After you decide with whom to share your customers' information and reach that an agreement, you need to decide how you will share the information.

If you're selling the information, this decision is easy. Just come to a mutual agreement on a file format to use and send the information on its way. If you're renting the information, things can get more complicated.

You could just send the information and trust the other party to use it as you have agreed upon and then discard it. But the best way to ensure that the data is only used once is for you and the other party to agree to have a bonded third party handle the information. Many companies, such as MessageREACH (www.messagereach.com), provide information-handling services, which serve a similar purpose as bonded mailing houses in the traditional business world. You provide the third-party company with your customers' information; the other party in your information-sharing agreement provides the third party with a template e-mail message, for example. The third-party company joins the two to create a promotional e-mailing and then discards your customers' data so it can't be reused. By posting a bond, these third-party companies provide you with monetary insurance against your customers' information being misused or used more than once.

As with any legal contract, have your attorney review any information-sharing contracts before signing them. You should also provide a reference copy of your privacy policy to the companies you share information with so that they understand what your customers' expectations are.

Indemnifying your organization

You can get into hot water if the company you share information with isn't prudent. For example, suppose you sell your customers' mailing addresses to a company that wants to send promotional mailings to those customers. But the other company isn't careful, and your customers' names and addresses wind up posted all over the Internet. Who's to blame? You need to *indemnify* your business — protect it from legal responsibility.

Your customers will definitely blame you because they entrusted their information to you. Make sure that the contracts you create for sharing information make it possible for you, in turn, to blame the other company. You can do so by specifying financial damages that the other company will have to pay if it fails to protect your customers' information according to the terms of the agreement. You'll need that money to recover the goodwill of your customers.

Anytime when you share your customers' information, you open yourself up to liability. Make sure your privacy policy and your information-sharing contracts work together to protect you as much as possible. Your attorney, of course, should help you write both documents to best achieve this protection.

Understanding Licensing and Other Restrictions

Your site is built on several companies' products: Web server software, e-mail software, database software, server hardware, e-commerce software, and much more. All those companies expect to receive some compensation for their efforts — generally in the form of money. Furthermore, you will spend large sums of money to get developers, consultants, and vendors to create and customize your site. You need to protect your investment so that those individuals don't just slide out the door and sell your custom software to your competitors — at half the price you paid to develop it.

Licensing commercial off-the-shelf software

To get your online business up and running, you'll probably purchase *off-the-shelf* software rather than have software written from scratch just for your business. Off-the-shelf software brings with it the issue of *software licensing* — an issue that has gotten more than one online company into deep trouble.

Modern commercial computer software isn't actually sold; it's licensed, much like you might license the right to use a popular cartoon character on a piece of merchandise. You pay a fee, and in turn, you gain the right to use the software according to the terms of the license. And the terms of the license dictate how many license fees you need to pay — and trust us, *one of each* is almost never the right amount! Fortunately, most software purveyors have significant discounts for larger numbers of licenses.

Desktop software — such as Microsoft Office — is usually licensed on a one-copy-per-computer basis, meaning you have to buy one copy of Office for every computer that will run it. Some server software is sold that way, too. Other server software is licensed per-processor, meaning you have to pay a licensing fee for each microprocessor the software will run on. So, for a server with four processors, you have to pay four times the fee to run on a single processor server.

Actually, you rarely buy four actual copies of the software. You usually buy one copy, which includes a manual and CD-ROM, and then you buy additional licenses, which gives you the right to run your one copy on additional servers or processors.

So who's forcing you to buy all these copies? Well, some software licenses come with special keys, which are like secret codes that the software requires to run. If the software finds itself running on a four-processor server, it will refuse to work unless you've given it the secret code for a four-processor license.

Other software is less strict, but this is federal law you're dealing with, and you'll have to pay some stiff fines if you're caught running software without a license. Software manufacturers make their money by selling those licenses, and they're quick to prosecute if they catch you cheating.

The United States Department of Justice has a task force investigating computer crime and intellectual property theft. You can find out more about the latest events at www.cybercrime.gov.

Managing and accounting for software licenses

The key to complying with your software license agreements is careful management of your licenses. Most software licenses are physical pieces of paper, and you should protect them as carefully as you would protect your stock certificates. Store them in a fireproof safe or, better yet, in a bank's safe deposit vault. These licenses are your proof that you paid enough to legally operate your software, and they'll be your backup if anyone challenges your compliance with your software licenses.

If you've ever wondered why companies bother having a chief information officer, or CIO (sometimes called a chief technology officer, or CTO), software licensing is one reason why. Make it your CIO's responsibility to understand and keep up with these requirements.

Make sure that you — or someone in your company — clearly understands those software licenses and their requirements. Unfortunately, every software manufacturer has a different license and different requirements. One software package might include a so-called site-wide license, which allow you to run the software on every computer in your site. Other software might be licensed by the number of processors in the computer it runs on, or by the number of users who connect to the server to use the software. Some software has special licensing requirements when used on the Internet. Many companies, such as Microsoft and IBM, have special Internet connection license fees for using their software products with Internet applications. Be certain you ask the rules for using a vendor's software on the Internet before you license it.

Most major software vendors offer software solutions to help you manage your software licenses. Many of them are free with the products. Microsoft, for example, offers a licensing service on its servers that can help track and prevent illegal use of licenses.

Looking at open-source software

The e-commerce gold rush was accompanied by a renewed interest in so-called *open source* software, notably the UNIX-compatible operating system known as Linux. Open-source software gets its name from its unique software license, which makes the source code — as well as a compiled, usable version of the software — freely available to just about anyone. You can purchase operating systems such as Linux, and Web servers such as Apache, for little or no money, and modify them to suit your specific needs, if necessary.

The downside to free software, of course, is that fewer people are around to help troubleshoot problems. Although paying thousands of dollars for traditional commercial software isn't ideal, knowing that the company can provide technical support if you need it is comforting.

Some popular open-source software (such as Linux) is compiled and redistributed by commercial companies (such as Red Hat) that also provide support for it.

Intellectual Property and the Rights of Your Developers: NDAs

By the time your online business is up and running, your developers will have invested thousands of hours in creating and debugging customized software to make it work just the way you want it to. And you will have invested potentially hundreds of thousands of dollars in those developers' salaries, tools, and computers. So who owns this stuff?

Owning what you buy

U.S. copyright law generally holds that any work created for a company that pays you a salary belongs to the company and is categorized as work-for-hire. Thus your developers — including consultants — are legally constrained from slipping out the door with your code and taking it to the competition.

Your developers are not legally constrained from taking the knowledge in their heads to your competition, and doing the same work all over again faster and cheaper, thanks to the knowledge they gained when they did it the first time for you. A current common practice to have developers and contractors sign *non-disclosure agreements* (NDAs) and other contracts to prevent them from disclosing the knowledge they gain at your company to your competition. Some companies even go so far as to prevent their employees from working for a competitor for a period of time after they leave the company.

Various U.S. courts have differed about the legality of non-disclosure agreements. Be sure to consult your attorney for advice on the best way to protect your company's assets. Work with an attorney to develop a non-disclosure agreement that can be enforced in your locale.

Whatever you do, make sure that you and your attorney take measures to protect the software and knowledge that is created while your site is being developed. You want to make it as difficult as possible for your competition to gain and use that software or knowledge.

Owning a contractor's work

Complicating the software-ownership issue is software produced by contractors. Although the software is generally considered a work-for-hire product, and therefore owned by the company that paid for it, contractors are in the habit of speeding up their work by using blocks of code (modules) that they developed on their own or that they developed for other companies. Make sure your contracting agreement addresses these issues:

- ✔ **Ownership:** Ideally, you should have exclusive rights to all the software created for your company.

- ✔ **Code origin:** If the contractor use modules of code not created specifically for your company, require the contractor to warrant that it has the right to distribute the code to you and that you have the right to use it in your business.

- ✔ **Intellectual property:** The contractor may have intellectual property he has developed and is willing to license to you. You will not own exclusive use, but you should get a perpetual license to use the code. This gives you the advantages of faster development and proven code.

- ✔ **Indemnification:** Have the contractor indemnify you if he is sued for copyright or patent infringement based on the code delivered to you. You want to be protected if the contractor steals code and you are unaware of the theft.

Your attorney should be familiar with these types of agreements and should review them before you sign them. Most contractors' agreements are designed to protect their interests and not yours, so be sure to modify the agreement until it's mutually acceptable to you both.

Sharing new technologies through licensing (Hey, if you can't beat 'em, join 'em)

If your project does include some great new technologies — such as a faster way to process credit cards online — you may find yourself with an unexpected cash cow. By ensuring that you have exclusive rights to the software, you open up the possibility of licensing the software to other companies that may find it useful.

Don't get too caught up in software licensing. Remember, distractions from your core business can create problems. If you find yourself with a really marketable piece of software, consider setting up a separate company to focus on licensing it.

Death and Taxes

One of the intriguing things about the Internet, in the United States at least, is its apparent freedom from state sales taxes. This freedom from tax can often compensate for shipping charges in your customers' minds, enabling you to compete with their local businesses. Of course, there is no true freedom from taxes. You need to understand when you need to collect those taxes and how you account for them.

With taxes in particular, everything you read — in this book, online, or in another book — should be considered a guideline only. Only a competent tax attorney can provide legal, accurate advice.

U.S. taxes

Currently, the U.S. government only requires you to collect taxes on purchases that are shipped to a state where your business maintains a physical location. But this has been an on-again, off-again topic of hot debate in Congress and will no doubt come up again from time to time.

For example, if your company has its headquarters in New York and has only one other physical location — a warehouse in California — you only have to collect and report sales tax on orders shipped to either of those two states.

You don't usually collect taxes on orders shipped to other states because you're not officially doing business in those states. Don't ask us; we didn't write the tax laws. We're just reporting what we know.

Just because you may not have to pay state taxes doesn't mean you shouldn't be aware of any local taxes you may be liable for. If you have a physical business location in a locality that imposes its own sales tax, you may have to collect that tax on some orders, as well.

International taxes

If you're doing business outside the United States, all bets are off. Some countries impose a national sales tax, such as Canada's GST, in addition to state- and local-level taxes. Even though you are a U.S. business, you may be liable for collecting some or all of these taxes, not to mention tariffs, export taxes, import taxes, and a host of other fees.

If you import to the United States, you may or may not need to pay excise taxes and tariffs. This varies from country to country, so you need to seek expert advice on the taxes and fees you will be required to pay.

Being an international business isn't just about having a Web site accessible from anywhere in the world. Taxes are one of the most important — and difficult — topics that you will have to grapple with. Make sure that you have an experienced attorney to help.

Also consider taxes from the aspect of foreign investors. If you company has investors who live and pay taxes outside the country where your headquarters operates, you need to learn the tax laws for those countries — likely with the help of an international tax lawyer. International shipping companies also often provide services to help customers ship their wares across national boundaries.

What gets taxed?

Within the United States, state tax laws vary widely. Outside the U.S., of course, tax laws are all over the map — literally. Within the U.S., you may or may not be required to collect sales tax on any number of types of products, including food, clothes, computers, computer software, certain services, and more. Some states require you to collect sales tax on shipping charges or handling charges, or both, or neither.

Because we haven't yet used up our quota of the word *attorney* in this chapter, we'll say it again: Make sure that you have a competent attorney to help you determine your tax liability.

Import/Export in International Marketplaces

One of the promises of the Internet is instant international sales presence. Of course, you can't sell just anything to anyone — the government keeps an eye on these things and wants to get its piece of the pie. It wants to control what people buy from whom, and even what is available. Before you start taking orders from international customers, you need to understand the restrictions and costs of selling to people in other lands.

Growing up in the U.S., we have a hard time imagining restrictions on the products we buy. Sure, you generally have to be 21 to buy alcohol, 18 to buy tobacco products, and of a minimum age to see certain movies. But that's pretty much the limit on the day-to-day product restrictions Americans face.

It's *really, really* different overseas.

Restricted countries

American companies aren't allowed to do business in some countries unless they have special permission. These countries are generally considered unfriendly, but then again, they may be just fine — the list changes constantly.

Nothing is stopping the citizens of restricted countries from shopping on your site and placing orders, though, so you bear the responsibility to make sure you don't try to ship something to someplace it's not allowed to go.

Restricted products

The U.S. government doesn't want you to ship some products past our borders without special permission from the U.S. State Department. These products may include animal or agricultural products, computer software with powerful encryption capabilities, and so forth.

Other countries have outlawed certain products that the U.S. doesn't mind your selling. These products may include animal or agricultural products, or certain other everyday products or services that violate the country's laws or customs.

Part III
Setting Up the Front End of Your Business

The 5th Wave   By Rich Tennant

"Just how accurately should my Web site reflect my place of business?"

In this part . . .

You've got the terminology, you've got the e-plan, now it's time to put everything in action and build your online business! We'll spare you the gory technical details (well, most of them anyway) and stick to the important stuff: Designing an online business your customers will love, keeping your technical people under control, and staying on top of the latest techniques and technologies to keep your online business distinct and competitive. Have a geek nearby to receive marching orders, 'cause here we go.

Chapter 9

Planning Your Storefront

. . . .

In This Chapter

▶ Designing your customers' online experience

▶ Wading through your online options

▶ Planning for that personal touch

. . . .

With your e-commerce strategy complete, and your plan of action in hand, get ready to jump right in and start building your online store.

Hold on a minute. Don't build a thing until you have a plan. Sure, the project architect will be the one building the blueprint for your online store, but you have to make sure that he or she knows which features you want and need — and which features you can live without.

The features and design of your online storefront should be every bit as strategic as your decision to go online. In this chapter, we walk you through designing your online storefront using the myriad of options available to you to make the most of your business.

 Roughly a billion e-commerce technologies are available. Your project architect needs to know what you want your business to do before he or she can select the technologies that are the most useful. Tell your architect exactly what you need — let him or her worry about how to get it done!

Designing Your Site with the Customer Experience in Mind

Too many businesses create online stores that work the way *they* think they should work, not the way customers think they should work. And sometimes, businesses create online stores that obviously weren't designed to begin with — they just sort of happened as the site's programmers made ad-hoc decisions about how things would work.

Why thou shalt design first, and build second

In the old testament days of the Internet, the online arts and crafts retailer Craftopia (www.craftopia.com) focused on getting online quickly. And Craftopia did get its site up quickly, but it didn't run as well as the company had hoped.

For example, Craftopia had a valid business reason to create a checkout process that required customers to sign in with an e-mail address and password before making a purchase. After all, Craftopia wanted to know who its customers were. Craftopia didn't consider the frustration that customers feel when asked to sign in. This type of registration is akin to telling shoppers in a retail store that they have to complete a survey before cashiers will take

their money. Responding to customer complaints, Craftopia decided to enable customers to check out without registering. Unfortunately, Craftopia couldn't do much to redesign the site, so the company had to settle for jury-rigging instead. Now customers can make purchases without registering, but they don't have *any* option to become registered users. Craftopia was left with an anonymous clientele.

Craftopia could have started out by planning its checkout process so that it offered the best of all worlds: enable new customers to check out quickly and then have them register as users after completing the transaction. The company could then have had everything it wanted — registered users and their money.

The benefit of a good design is that your customers have engaging, stress-free experiences every time they visit the site. Emphasis on *every time* — a good design and an enjoyable online experience say to customers, "Glad to see you! Come on back and see us again real soon!" Design the customers' experience as carefully as a Broadway choreographer might design her Tony-award-winning dance numbers.

Designing Catalogs

Don't make the mistake of purchasing e-commerce catalog software and then adapting the way you organize your products and present your wares to fit the catalog's style. What you'll end up with is a big ugly catalog mess. Instead, design the catalog that you think best suits your business and customer needs, and find a product that either accommodates your design or can be customized to do so.

Of course, organization is a necessity, but some forms of organization are more useful than others. After all, why would customers look for widgets in an area that quite clearly displays your inventory of doodads? You need an idea of where readers might look first for products — and why they would look there.

That's taxonomy, not taxidermy: Finding the right organization for your catalog

Your catalog's taxonomy is more than its organization. Taxonomy is a classification system. A good taxonomy enables customers to find products where they would intuitively look for them, and it gives your staff a road map of where to place new products so that customers can intuitively find them.

The easiest classification-system setup is a *parent-child* relationship. In these relationships, each category is associated with a parent, that can be linked to one or more other *parent* categories, and which also can have one or more *child* categories. For example, an small online bookstore might use departments, such as Fiction and Biography, as the parent categories in its catalog. Larger sites, such as Borders.com, may add additional layers of parent categories, such as Books" and Music." Figure 9-1 shows you how a sample catalog taxonomy might look. So how does the taxonomy help customers? If they are looking for a work of fiction to read on a trip, you can ask what they like (mysteries, romances, science fiction) and then give them a list tailored to their desires.

You can also use the taxonomy for alternative classification systems. Isaac Asimov wrote a great deal of fiction and non-fiction. Instead of searching by the kind of book Asimov wrote, you can allow people to search by his name. These alternative organizations enable you to help more people find what they want, quickly and easily.

Here are some benefits of parent-child taxonomies:

- **The Zen factor (Simplicity):** You don't have to worry about departments, subdepartments, or anything else. You have all the flexibility you need to expand and contract the taxonomy depending on your inventory.

- **The *It Takes a Village* factor (Cross-links):** A child category can have many parent categories. For example, suppose that you run an online clothier. If you have a fairly small selection of polo shirts for men, women, and kids, you can link the polo shirts category to all three parents: Men, Women, and Kids. Shoppers can easily find polo shirts of all sizes, colors, and styles in one place — whether they are browsing for men's, women's, or kids' clothing.

- **The *Sybil* factor (Same name, different stuff):** Some categories may have the same name but unique contents depending on which parent they are linked to. Say you sell men's, women's, and kids' clothes, and you specialize in casual wear. It makes sense to have unique Jeans categories under each parent category, each with contents that pertain *only* to the parent. Here are a couple of good reasons to do this:

- Women's jeans and kids' jeans are different, and a shopper browsing for kids' clothing would not expect to come across women's jeans.

- Also, if you specialize in casual wear, having a single category that contains jeans for men, women, and kids could be very cumbersome for customers to wade through. You could also add a new parent, Jeans, that enables customers to link to men's jeans, women's jeans, and kids' jeans.

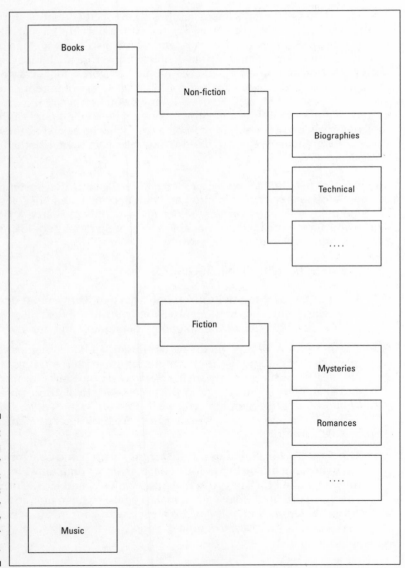

Figure 9-1:
This catalog taxonomy enables customers to intuitively narrow down their searches.

A business that cares about its user-friendly site as much as it cares about its sensible slacks

L.L. Bean (www.11bean.com) does a great job with its online catalog. The first page is broken down clearly by categories — men, women, and children. But that is not the only way people look for goods. The catalog also has seasonal sections, such as gifts for mom on Mother's Day or graduates in June. Customers can find these products in the special sections and the regular spots under men, women, and children. The alternate organization helps customers find what they're looking for more quickly — which makes them happy shoppers.

Keep your catalog hierarchy as simple as possible. Doing so allows you to create cross-links that make your catalog flexible and easy to use, and allows you to rearrange your catalog structure much more easily as your business grows.

Organize your catalog in ways that *customers* think of your products, not the ways your business does. Many vendors organize products based on their suppliers, but your customers couldn't care less where you bought your products. You want to make the organization easier for your customers, not you.

More than just flipping pages: Considerations for making products easy to find

Customers want to be able to get in, find what they want as quickly as possible, and get out. After you've figured out how you want to organize your online catalog, consider which features you want to incorporate. We recommend that you add both *searching* and *browsing* features — just make sure that your catalog design, including the taxonomy, lends itself well to both of these functions (see the preceding section, "That's taxonomy, not taxidermy: Finding the right organization for your catalog.") You also need to keep in mind some fairly simple rules that can make creating a catalog either a job from hell or a very rewarding experience.

If your customers can't find a particular product on your Web site — and find it fast — they assume you don't have it. They won't ask for help; they will just go on to another site until they find it.

The most common way of building browsing features into a storefront design is to have a *navigation bar* (shown in Figure 9-2) along the top or left sides of each page. The navigation bar is a graphical device that helps people find whatever they are looking for. It may take them directly to a new page, or it may give them additional choices. Each click gets them closer to their goal.

You can also use a *drop-down list* of the top-level categories in your catalog. When the customer clicks the drop-down button (or *select* control, in HTML terms), a list of choices appears. Customers can click any of the items in the list to drill for the gold that lays hidden in the subcategories you created.

Figure 9-2:
Design your site to draw viewers' eyes to the navigation bar. Also make sure those buttons are easy to read.

Make sure that the browse options you provide for customers are easy to understand, easy to use, and attractive.

Searching — the great e-revolution

The big advantage of shopping online over shopping in a store is the ability to conduct a targeted, specific search. *Searching* enables customers to type a word or two into a text box and be rewarded with a list of products that match. Imagine if you had this feature in your local Mega-Mart — no more hours spent wandering around looking for just the right birthday gift! Usually, search products enable users to use keywords in a product's name, description, or both, to yield results.

Make sure that your catalog function is designed to work with your search feature. If you want search results to reveal a small picture (called a *thumbnail*) of the products, you have to make sure that every product in the catalog includes a thumbnail and a larger photo.

Carefully plan how your site's search capabilities should work. Draw some sample pages on paper to illustrate what you think is the best way to design the search feature. Hand the plan and sketches over to your project architect, who will build them into the blueprint for your site. In Figure 9-3, you can see a site that uses search, catalog, and thumbnail features.

Figure 9-3: Plan your site so that customers can find whatever they desire as quickly and easily as possible.

Retaining customers with first-class service

Your site represents your organization. Whether you build a retail storefront or a B2B support site, you need the site to provide service to your customers. The best philosophy is customers first, commerce second.

That means taking care of things you may not have thought of, such as providing order tracking, return information, service information, product-use sheets, customer forums, and other mechanisms designed to help customers understand the products and services they buy from you. We talk more about providing customers with the best levels of service in Chapter 11. And we cover how to go beyond selling on your site in "Using the Storefront to Encourage Customer Action, Satisfaction, and Return Visits," later in this chapter.

Designing Shopping Carts

Shopping cart technology enables customers to wheel around your virtual store, plucking wares off virtual shelves and placing those wares into a virtual basket. But because you have no wheels, wares, or shelves online, it's just as easy to say that a shopping cart is a glorified order form, a tally of the goodies customers intend to purchase from you. No big whoop. In fact, most shopping carts on the Internet enable customers to do pretty much what you'd expect them to do:

- ✔ See the name and price of the products they have added

- ✔ See (and change) the number of doohickies they want to buy

- ✔ Remove products that they've decided against and then continue shopping or proceed to the checkout

Boring! Shopping carts are overlooked as storefront tools. Make your shopping cart design a little more like the real thing. Here are some ideas to help you improve your shopping cart technology:

- ✔ **If you're going to have features, make them do something:** Add cool-looking, fast-reacting buttons that enable customers to quickly add and remove items and change the number of whazzoos they want purchase. Don't add bells and whistles just for the sake of adding bells and whistles.

- ✔ **Cross-sell and upsell:** If customers put the Widget 500 in their shopping carts, you know that they're interested in that widget. So consider adding this text on the Widget 500 Web page, "If you like the Widget 500, you'll love the Widget 650 Gold. Click here to learn more." You can also make suggestions, such as "Click here for batteries for your Widget 500." Make it easy for customers to get to those items and add them to their shopping carts.

- ✔ **Advertise special promotional items:** Bricks-and-mortar stores put the impulse stuff — such as candy, magazines, and so on — right by the cash register. So on your Web site, why not add a small clickable banner that hawks your online specials? Add some impulse cash to that sale while customers are in the mood to buy.

- ✔ **Find out if customers want it supersonic fast or reasonably priced:** The first thing that most sites ask customers when they're ready to check out is, "How would you like your order shipped?" Why not include that option right on the shopping cart screen? A drop-down list that enables customers to select the type of shipping they want to use and to change the shipping (and automatically recalculating the total shown in the cart) is a dream come true. Check out Chapter 12 for considerations in calculating shipping.

Another option on the shipping calculation is to let customers see an itemized list of prices and the subtotal. Customers feel better when they know how much they're paying (before it's too late to turn back) so that they can decide whether getting that marble statuette tomorrow is worth the shipping cost. And businesses benefit from giving shipping costs and subtotals because doing so speeds up the checkout process.

Don't put so much stuff on the shopping cart screen that customers can't find what they're buying. Use these features in combination to get the best bang for the buck. But remember, form follows function.

On B2B sites, you may not have a shopping cart at all. Or the shopping cart may act as a purchase requisition. Purchase requisitions require different information, such as authorization codes and charge codes. You need to add those features. You can find out more about B2B e-procurement in Chapter 17.

Designing Checkouts

The most important part of the customer experience — getting customers to cough up the dough — is the part customers like the least. When you plan and design your checkout process, keep in mind the worst checkout experience that you've ever had to ensure that such an experience will never happen to your customers.

The benefits of checkout design: Breaking things down

When you ask customers to use your Web site, there is always the risk that they will mess something up or provide inaccurate information. Your programmers can write code that makes sure that all the blanks are filled in, but programmers don't always have the greatest level of tact (not to mention ordinary communication skills). Simply telling customers that they did something wrong, without telling them specifically what they did wrong, is more likely to lead to frustration — and an abandoned order — than a completed transaction.

Design your checkout system with a minimal number of easy-to-understand steps, each of which appears on a separate screen. Ideally, new customers should be able to complete the checkout process in three screens: shipping info, billing info, and order review. Repeat customers should be able to complete the checkout process in even fewer steps — such as a single order-review screen — unless the information you have on file has changed since their last purchase.

The checkout process should be an exciting time for your customers, so don't lose them with a poorly designed checkout system that confuses them, slows them down, or puts obstacles in their way.

Checkout systems should be easy for customers to understand and should give customers some idea of how much further they have to go to complete an order. Figure 9-4 shows the Southwest Airlines site (www.southwest.com), which includes an online booking process that is easy to understand.

Figure 9-4:
Southwest
Airlines
uses
graphic
indicators
to guide
customers.

Defining your checkout

To design a great checkout, you must first decide on the information you absolutely *need* to get from your customers in order to complete their purchase. This information must include

- Billing information, including the customer's address and e-mail address.

- Delivery address.

- Shipping method, if this information hasn't already been provided. (See "Designing Shopping Carts," earlier in this chapter, for more information about the cool ways you can use shopping carts.)

- Payment information, such as a credit card, credit card number, and credit card expiration date.

Now make a list of all the information you would *like* to get from your customer:

- ✔ A user name and password so that you can track future orders.

- ✔ Permission to add the customer to an e-mail newsletter, which you send out periodically to entice customers to return to your site. The folks in your marketing department will berate you if you miss the opportunity to feed them names and addresses.

- ✔ Demographic information, such as the customer's household income and hobbies.

Finally, make a list of convenience features you would like to offer your customers. Here are a few examples:

- ✔ For returning customers, automatically filling in their address (and even payment) information, which you collected from a previous order.

- ✔ For new customers, enabling them to choose whether they want your site to store their personal information.

- ✔ Keeping the checkout process as convenient, pain-free, and quick as possible, by limiting the number of screens customers see and the number of mouse clicks they make.

Working out a design

After you put together the requirements for your checkout process, start building *use cases*. A use case defines what each part of the checkout will do. On a piece of paper, draw a Web page and list the steps that the end user will perform while working on this page. The use case lets you think out and imagine the process. It also clearly conveys what you expect to happen to your executive management and software development team.

You don't need to get technical with the use case; everyone should be able to understand it. It provides an excellent means for mapping out what you expect to see as the checkout experience.

Most experienced project managers and software architects (discussed in Chapter 7) are familiar with use cases and can help you. You can work together to get just the right user experience before anyone writes a single line of code.

Make absolutely certain that you protect customers' payment information with your life. Encrypt the information; keep it on a secure, protected database server; and do anything else that you and your technical team can think of to ensure it never gets into the wrong hands. Because if it does, you'll lose customers, gain unwanted media attention, possibly find yourself in an untenable legal situation, and be generally unhappy. We talk more about collecting payments and securing payment information in Chapter 12.

Using the Storefront to Encourage Customer Action, Satisfaction, and Return Visits

When you think about speed, real time, efficiency, and commerce, you probably say, "I just need to get the customer to the product, and I need to get the product sold." In a way, that's what we tell you in a hundred different ways in this book. But you've learned from business experience that you can snare customers in a zillion different ways. Here's a short list of things you may want to add to your storefront to ensnare them:

- Sign-up pages that allow customers to subscribe to (and unsubscribe from) e-mail communications, such as newsletters.

- Wish lists ("It would be great if you had this . . ."), suggestion boxes ("It would be great if you did this . . ."), and complaint forums ("It would have been great if you hadn't . . ."), and other site tools that let customers tell you what they think of you and your site. If they feel like you are listening, they will want to return.

- Self-service components, such as order tracking, customer service, and so forth.

- Gift-reminder calendars to remind customers of important personal dates that may require some gift shopping on your site.

Each of these features can be valuable to your online business if they are designed so that customers can easily take advantage of them. Make sure that you present your project architect with well-thought-out designs for how each of these features should operate.

TIP

Tips from the design gurus

No matter which portion of your Web site you are designing, use the following tips to make things go as smoothly as possible for customers. Keep these tips in mind when designing your checkout, catalog, shopping cart, or other site features:

✔ Never ask for more than ten pieces of information on a screen. This allows you to ask customers for their billing name, address, city, state, zip code, phone number, and credit card number and expiration date on one screen. It does not allow you to collect shipping information on the same screen. Asking for too much information on one screen is overwhelming, especially for customers with small computer monitors.

✔ Always make sure that customers know what will happen when they click something.

For example, a checkout process with buttons labeled Next or Continue doesn't provide any clue as to what will happen when those buttons are clicked. Instead, use meaningful labels like "Click here to enter your shipping information," or "Click here to finalize your order and send it to us."

✔ Make sure that you provide a confirmation screen for every major action that customers take to let them know whether or not it was completed successfully.

✔ Use colors and graphics to clearly indicate what customers should do. When a new screen appears, customers should be able to immediately figure out what they're supposed to do on that screen and how to do it.

Design Considerations for the Subversive B2C Pro

Your online storefront has to do more than attract shoppers and convert them to paying customers. It also has to collect a good deal of information for your business, and your design determines how well it is able to do so. In this section, we discuss some of the information-gathering options available and how you can take advantage of these options to create a storefront that your business will love as much as your customers.

You need to make some important design decisions about how you will identify your shoppers, what information you want to gather about them, and how you want to monitor their use of your site for marketing purposes.

Identifying anonymous shoppers

The Web is completely anonymous by nature. When customers perform a search on Yahoo! or browse for books on Amazon.com, those companies have no idea who those customers are. This is a bad thing (at least, marketing and sales say so). Businesses want to know who their customers are, which is why they all offer customers the opportunity to sign up, register, or identify themselves. Registration usually involves filling out a short form, picking a password, and providing some personal information, such as their name and address.

By having your customers register with your site, you can build relationships with them. You can e-mail them, snail-mail them, fax them, or call them. You can explain to them why they need to buy from you and only you. Of course, they know that's what you're going to do. Sometimes they don't mind, and sometimes the threat of the upcoming promotional onslaught is enough to send them scurrying.

Registering users tells you exactly who they are. You can use the information to make your site better, emphasizing what sells and eliminating what doesn't. Determine the demographics of your clientele so that you know to whom you should target your marketing efforts.

Anonymous shoppers can drift in and out without threat. Some people will let you know who they are after they find out who *you* are. Bricks-and-mortar stores don't ask customers to identify who they are before letting them shop there. By not asking customers to register, you pose less of a threat and retain more traffic. But you also don't get marketing information.

You may want to find a middle ground. Let everyone browse anonymously. Make people register in order to start a shopping cart. Collect some of the information you need for checkout when customers register to simplify the checkout process.

Tracking shoppers' movements

Most Web servers and e-commerce software packages have the capability to create *log files* that help you track customers' movements through your site. A log file is a record of every page and graphics file that the users ask the server to deliver. By analyzing the log files (as discussed in Chapter 15), you find out which pages on your site are most popular, which paths through your site most often result in a sale, and other important information.

You have a variety of methods for tracking customers, depending on how they are using your site. For example, if customers log in, you can easily track them as they move through the site. From a business standpoint, tracking customers from the moment they enter the site is highly desirable because it generates the maximum amount of information about your customers' shopping habits on your site. You can find out what pages they visit, how they get from one page to another, and what they were looking at when they added the item to the shopping cart.

If your customers don't log in right away, you can still track them, although not as reliably (you won't know it was Susie Smith at 45 Park Avenue, Bethesda, Md). Web servers can track customers by the address of their computers, which is provided with every page request a customer makes of your server. For example, Susie Smith is IP address 192.168.0.1 (we talk more about Internet address in Chapter 2). Unfortunately, large Internet service providers (ISPs) like America Online make identifying customers even more difficult. Every time Susie logs on to AOL, she gets a different address. And when she disconnects, Billy Bob Anderson gets to use the address she just surrendered. Figuring out who is who gets difficult.

You can give everyone who logs in a *cookie* — not an Oreo, a small text file that gives them a temporary ID number. You can use the cookie to track customers as they move from one page to another, without knowing who those individuals are. You still find out how they move from page to page.

Cookies got a bad rap. Many people believe that because cookies identify people, they violate their constitutional right to anonymity (as if there were such as thing). Although most browsers work with cookies, they give users the ability to turn cookies off. Your site can make good use of cookies, but it shouldn't depend on them.

You can add up the movement of your customers to discover how they move through your site; this is called *aggregation*. If 75 percent of the people who visit your site go from the widgets page to the doohickeys page, you may want to see what is on that page that draws so many users. If 80 percent of the people who go to the thingamagig page leave your Web site without buying, you may want to change that page to encourage customers to stay.

Also make sure that your project architect understands how you intend to use the tracking information after it has been collected. Your project blueprint needs to include the necessary reports to compile and display the tracking information in a useful way.

Designing a Personalized Site

To make customers feel valued, salespeople call customers by name, remember their birthdays and anniversaries, and show an interest in them. This personal attention is even more important in online commerce, which is faceless and anonymous. Adding personalization helps customers feel more at home and, hopefully, makes them more likely to buy from you in the future.

A variety of tools are available to help you manage site personalization. Microsoft's Site Server, BEA WebLogic Server, and iPlanet e-commerce servers all include personalization features. These features enable you to store customer information — such as favorite brand, last product purchased, last time of visit, and so on — in a database and retrieve that data when the user returns. Your staff can then program the site to use that data as a salesperson would — making suggestions and showing options that the customer would be interested in.

Planning personalized catalogs

A personalized catalog should offer more than just a rundown of your available products. It should offer the products that a customer is most interested in, based on past purchases and any demographic information that he or she provided.

In the world of B2B, personalized catalogs enable customers to take advantage of lower list prices for products based on historical volume of purchases or pre-determined volume discounts.

Any demographic information you collect needs to relate to your catalog so that your Web site software can select products and product categories most likely to interest your customer. Most high-end e-commerce packages, such as Microsoft's Commerce Server 2000, include tools for creating these data relationships, but you still have to define exactly how you want your site to present this personalized experience in order for your programmers to use the tools.

You can leverage personalized catalogs by taking customers to the main page of their favorite catalog product category instead of taking them to your home page when they visit your site. You can also arrange product category listings by the customer's preference, as indicated by past shopping and buying patterns. Anything you can do to quickly get customers to the products they will most likely be interested in will be beneficial to your business.

For example, a site like Sephora.com (`www.sephora.com`) can send you an e-mail that seemingly reflects your personal preferences in makeup, based on your previous purchasing habits. You are just a click away from your next purchase.

If you decide to enable customers to personalize catalogs, remember that you have to build this feature into your overall design plan — not just for catalogs, but also for the checkout process and for collecting demographic information. Make sure the project architect knows what you want, and be sure to check out "Tell me more about these shoppers: Dealing with demographics" for more on about collecting demographic information. See "Designing Catalogs" for more info on catalogs, and take a look at "Designing Shopping Carts" for more on checkout processes. All of these sections are located earlier in this chapter.

Planning personalized self-service

The most common self-service feature of any Web-based business is order tracking. Customers expect this feature. If you don't have it, they'll think your site (and business) is second-rate.

In addition to having order tracking in your arsenal of self-service features, how else can you create a more personalized self-service area on your site? Here are some thoughts:

- Offer a way for customers to look up helpful tips, product documentation, or software downloads that relate to the products they've purchased. By personalizing this feature and displaying information related to their purchases, customers won't need to waste time searching for items.

- If customers need to return an item, let them use your Web site to generate the return authorization forms, including packing slips and mailing labels.

- Order tracking can be personalized to a degree. Rather than requiring customers to go to your Web site to look up an order's status, inform them by e-mail when their order ships and send them another e-mail to confirm when their order should arrive. Customers will appreciate this extra step and will feel more comfortable relying on you to handle their future purchases just as competently.

The cost of creating these personalized features will be repaid through increased sales. Customers will prefer to shop with you if they know they have so many customized, easy-to-use tools to manage their orders and find support information after their purchase is complete.

Your Best Sales Weapon: Using E-Content in Your Design

E-commerce is the buying and selling of stuff across the Internet, but your e-commerce venture won't be successful if you're not making your e-commerce venture a *business*, as well. What we mean is that getting customers to find and buy stuff is okay, but if making purchases is your customers' only interaction with your online business, you need to branch out.

Take advantage of the opportunity to include online promotions, newsletters and fliers, press releases, and all the other things you want to share with your customers. Of course, you can't just tack these things on to a completed site — they have to be built to be a part of the site. It's time to think about how to flesh out your site by using e-content.

Drawing them in with promotions

Promotions are a tried-and-true way of enticing customers to do business with you in the traditional way, and they're just as valid for getting them to do business with you online. The problem with online promotions, though, is that they are not tangible (the way coupons in the Sunday paper are) and therefore are harder to regulate.

Coping with coupons

The traditional retail world has two types of coupons: those that can be used for a discount off of a specific product (or group of products), and those that can be used for a discount off an entire purchase.

Online coupons are intangible and come in three flavors:

- **Coupons that consist of a code, which can be given to anyone and used by anyone.** These are usually good for a discount off an entire purchase, free shipping, or something similar, although they can also be used to give discounts for a specific product or group of products. This type of coupon is most often given as an enticement to attract new customers, and most often is included in an e-mail sent to a rented address list.

  The problem with coupon codes is that anyone can use them, making it difficult to judge their impact. Friends can pass the coupon code back and forth, and unless you program your Web site to prevent it, a single customer can reuse a coupon code on multiple purchases.

- **Coupons that are tied to a specific shopper.** This may be a reward discount off a future purchase, or a targeted marketing coupon good for a specific product. The advantage of these coupons is that they can be used only once by a specific shopper.

  The problem is that you can only issue these coupons to shoppers who have registered on your site. This means you can't issue them to potential shoppers, making these types of coupons best suited as rewards or as targeted marketing promotions.

- **Coupons that are tied to a specific e-mail address.** Although subject to the problems of bad e-mail addresses that plague every e-commerce site, these coupons can be issued to potential shoppers (assuming you have their e-mail address). These coupons usually consist of a code that the shopper types in, which your Web site matches to an e-mail address. You have more control with these coupons because they can't be easily shared or reused.

Be especially careful with coupons that can be shared or reused. Every coupon hits your bottom line directly, and so-called anonymous coupons can have a devastating effect if they reach a wider audience than you intended.

Gaining another sales opportunity with gift certificates

Online gift certificates are a form of tender, just like cash or credit cards, accepted only at your store. Gift certificates are a great way to lock customers into doing business with you. You can also take advantage of the time lag between the purchase of a gift certificate and its redemption to earn some money, by keeping the gift certificate funds in an interest-bearing savings account.

 Make sure that you have an e-mail address for each gift certificate — either the sender's or the recipient's. That way you can send a reminder e-mail if the gift certificate isn't used after a specified period of time.

 Some businesses have a policy that unused gift certificates expire after a certain amount of time. Although this can be a great way to boost your profit margins, it's also illegal in some states. Because your Web site can do business in any state or country, you may find yourself subject to laws that don't exist in your home state. Check with your attorney before you establish any policies regarding online gift certificates.

Extra! Extra! Online newsletters!

Online newsletters are a great way to provide extra value to your customers, keep your business' name in their minds (as we discuss in Chapter 6), and push a marketing message at the same time.

Believe it or not, many customers *enjoy* receiving well-written, informative e-mail newsletters and don't mind if they contain a marketing angle. What irritates customers is blatantly self-serving junk e-mail that has no purpose other than to part them with their money. If you have an online newsletter, make sure it contains something that your customers will appreciate.

 Send your newsletters only to customers who ask for them (see Figure 9-5). And provide a way for customers to sign up without making a purchase and a way for customers to take themselves off of your mailing list.

 Make sure your posted privacy policy explains what you will do with a customer's e-mail address. It's perfectly okay to share, rent, or sell customers' e-mail addresses if you've given them fair warning that you may do so. On the other hand, if you tell them you're going to do that, many customers will not give you their e-mail address (or their business).

 Your ISP probably has rules against sending e-mail to people who haven't asked for it. Carefully review your terms of service with an attorney to make sure you're not violating any contractual obligations.

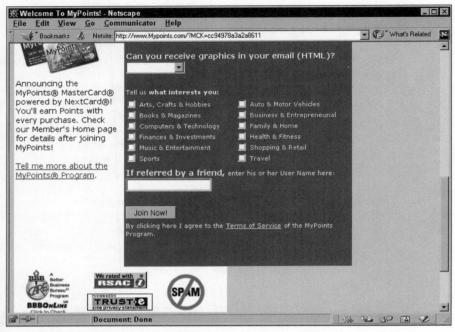

Figure 9-5:
Give
customers
as many
options as
possible,
including
whether
they want a
text-only
version
of the
newsletter
or one that
has all the
glitz of your
Web page.

Patting yourself on the back: News, press releases, awards, and honors

You should always be excited about the opportunity to let your customers know what's going on within your company. By treating them as part of your corporate family, they'll be excited to hear about the good things that are happening and will reward you with more business.

Make sure your site includes a place for online versions of press releases, any news regarding your company, and information about awards and honors you've won, charitable contributions you've made, and so on. Customers like to know they're doing business with a winner, and this is a great way to share the love with them.

You may also want to offer customers the opportunity to subscribe to an e-mail list specifically for news about your company, especially if you deal primarily with other businesses as a supplier or distributor. They'll appreciate hearing about new distribution arrangements you've made, new product lines you'll be carrying, or new markets that you'll be entering. Periodically send out something just to keep your business' name in their minds.

Inviting Your Customers to Make Themselves at Home

One great use for e-content on your site is giving your customers the ability to make your site their *home page* — the page their browser automatically loads up whenever they go online. Some browsers refer to this page as the *start page*.

The advantages of being someone's home page are pretty obvious. Your page is the first thing they see when they go online, giving you the opportunity to throw a promotional message at them and keep them on your site. Of course, to make your site compelling enough to be a home page, you also have to provide some things your customers will find valuable. Here are some suggestions:

✔ Offer your customers the day's headlines. Form an agreement to pull content from news sources, such as Reuters or the Associated Press.

✔ Create an online community, including discussion boards, chat rooms, and other features (which we discuss in Chapter 6), and feature them prominently on the page that customers can designate as their home page. The community should relate to the products or services that you sell, giving interested customers a reason to check in every day — which is, in turn, a reason for them to make that page their home page.

✔ The first thing most people do when they go online is perform a search. Accommodate them by providing a pass-through to a major search engine, such as Yahoo! or Excite. Customers should have the option to search for keywords on your site, or to have their search processed by the search engine. They may stay on your site only long enough to type in a few keywords and hit Enter, but that's long enough for a couple of advertisements or other promotional messages to sink in.

✔ Allow customers to customize their home page to display specials about products that they're interested in, a weather report for their town, or even local headlines. Several online services can provide local-interest information, which is a compelling reason for customers to make your page their home page.

Very few online businesses bother making their sites compelling enough for customers to make them their home page. The exceptions, of course, are online portals, such as Yahoo! or Excite, that are in the business of serving up customized information. By expending the time and resources to make your site a valid starting point for your customers, you gain a tremendous marketing opportunity by being the first thing customers see every time they go online.

iWon, uWon, we're all winners at the home page

iWon (www.iwon.com) has a compelling reason to make its home page everyone's home page. It continually runs games that allow people to win prizes. To be eligible for prizes, users must go to the iWon page each day and complete a certain number of activities. Every day, someone wins a prize. Many users set iWon as their home page to remind themselves to complete the activities and remain in the running. Techniques such as these will keep customers coming to your home page and exposed to your advertising and specials.

Chapter 10

The Least You Need to Know about Building Your Storefront

In This Chapter

▶ Deciding how to build your store

▶ Developing sites that sell

▶ Testing your developed site

▶ Getting your site set before going live

*Y*ou've planned, you've designed, and now you're ready to build your electronic storefront! Well, not you, perhaps, but definitely your Web designers and developers. However, in its quest to develop the site that perfectly matches your business needs, your technical team will undoubtedly come to you with a lot of questions as your project progresses.

To help you make these decisions and effectively collaborate with your techno-buddies, here we tell you about some of the technologies that go into building your site. Although you may not need to know exactly how e-commerce sites are developed, you do need to have a rough idea of the basics so that you can understand your technical team's lingo, answer queries regarding site development, and make smart decisions to help your site become the best it can be.

Finding the Right Site Development Solution for Your Business

If all these setup choices and options overwhelm you, try to keep your fruit straight — you know, compare apples with apples. To help with that, look over Table 10-1 for a one-stop comparison of your store building options.

Table 10-1   Options for Building Your Store

Option	Customization	Features	Price	Start-up Time	Responsibility
Do-It-Yourself	Maximum flexibility	Anything you want	$$$$	Generally the slowest option	You, Da Man! — with complete responsibility
Outsourcing	Maximum flexibility	Anything you want	$$$$$	Faster than doing it yourself	Plenty of overall responsibility; fewer day-to-day worries
Low-end ASP	Often very little	Minimal common features	$	Who has time? Get up and running now!	Virtually none
High-end ASP	Usually a lot of options — the more you pay, the more options!	The more you pay, the more features you can have	$$$$$$	Pretty fast	Very little
Low-end off-the-shelf software	Little or none	Minimal common features	$	Who has time? Get up and running now!	Very little
High-end off-the-shelf software	Usually a lot of options	Usually feature-rich; can require extensive custom programming	$$$	Depends on how much custom programming is required	Depends on how much custom programming is required

Feeling overwhelmed? Consult a professional

Feeling groggy with all the choices, jargon, and pros and cons you face when you're trying to build a storefront? Join the crowd. Your best bet is to select a consultant who is familiar with the variety of e-commerce products in the marketplace. Let a professional analyze your needs to help you select a product that best suits your business. Although consultants commonly charge a hefty sum for this service, we consider that their fees are money and time well spent. Ask your business colleagues for references to reliable consultants in you area. You can also ask software publishers, such as Sun, Microsoft, or IBM, for referrals to dependable partners. You may well save more money in the long run when you calculate your time's worth and possible wasted dollars on inefficient or incompatible software.

Obviously, the choice of what to do depends a great deal on the feature set you want, the responsibility you're able to take on, and the money you have to spend. Here's some more information:

- **Commercial Off-the-Shelf Solutions:** Plenty of software manufacturers make off-the-shelf solutions designed to quickly launch you right into the e-commerce world. These products range in complexity and capabilities, as well as price. At the bottom end of the scale are products such INEX Commerce Court Lite (www.inex.net), which sells for about $600. At the top end of the food chain are products such as Commerce Server 2000 from Microsoft (www.microsoft.com/commerce) and Net Commerce from IBM (www.ibm.com), both starting at around $6,000.

  You can also find high-end e-commerce products that also handle a great deal of back-end business functions (starting at $25,000), such as the products offered by Baan (www.baan.com). Don't faint: You can easily spend upwards of $100,000 for other e-commerce packages. You Scrooges can just drive to your local computer store and pick up *turnkey* (pre-written software that requires little customization or configuration) e-commerce software for under $100. Here's what to look for in any product, no matter what it costs:

  - **Platform:** If you're committed to a certain platform, you need to select an e-commerce package that can runs on it. Think of it this way: It's kinda hard to drive a train on a gravel road.

  - **Features:** Simply put, different e-commerce packages do different things, depending on price and the potential purchaser. The $100 product you pick up at your local computer store probably has a minimum amount of functionality — it's probably limited to a simple, fixed catalog; credit card payments, and some simple layout options. Products such as Commerce Server 2000 are more of an e-commerce toolkit that developers can use to build a site, rather than a completely turnkey solution.

- **Integration:** Software that comes ready to talk to your accounting, customer relationship management, and enterprise resource planning systems can save a bundle in writing custom integration software.

- **Flexibility:** Weigh whether you'll need to customize it, and determine whether you even can. Less expensive products offer little or no customization capabilities, and high-end products may need considerable customization before you can begin to use them.

- **Scalability and availability:** As the demands on the software grow and as you get to the point where you cannot afford to have your Web site down, the need the Web site software to run simultaneously on multiple servers grows. That means the need for enterprise grade software and additional servers for handling data, transactions, and security. And none of this comes free. Ah, the price of success.

✔ **Outsourcing Store Design:** After you choose your software, you may opt to hire (or outsource) another company do the site development for you. *Outsourcing* is the contracting out to another business any work that you could do in-house. You can outsource Web design and hosting services, or application applications — enabling another business to build and run your site for you. See Chapter 7 for more information on outsourcing. Here's a sneak peek:

- **Look for a business that's been around the block (a few times).** As part of your pre-hiring detective work, check out the work of different firms. Lean toward selecting a firm that has past experience in developing sites like what you want your site to become.

  You can also choose to go with a less experienced firm . . . perhaps a startup or a spinoff of a successful firm. Realize that you're taking a risk on unproven experience.

- **Look for the whole enchilada.** Look for firms that offer all the necessary services in house, including graphic design, programming, Web design, hardware installation, and any other skills that you don't have on your staff.

- **Look for a one-track mind.** Look for firms that specialize in using only a few e-commerce products, such as Commerce Server or Net Commerce. Firms that claim to work with everything often haven't worked with anything — they lack focus and experience.

✔ **Using an ASP:** ASPs provide a full range of services to develop and run your Web site for you. These providers can develop your Web store, put it on their servers, and keep the whole thing running. For a fee, you get an instant online store — and never break a sweat. ASPs can be a great way, though, to get a small business up and running while concurrently developing a bigger, more customized site. We clue you in on the details in Chapter 14. Advantages of going to an ASP include:

- Quick roll out

- Reduced risk (You're not buying hardware and software)

- Borrowed expertise (You're not hiring techies)

The downsides of using ASPs include:

- Fewer customization options and less control

- Higher costs

✔ **Rolling Your Own:** You can design your own e-commerce software, design your own site, and host and maintain it yourself. (Pshew!) If you go this route, regardless whether you use your own technical staff or hire outside contractors to supplement your in-house skill set, the distinction is that you're the one in charge of your site's development.

The e-commerce slang for such a venture is *Rolling your own*, meaning that you start with a basic e-commerce product such as Commerce Server or Lotus Domino, and then program the features your business needs. You're responsible for finding the right graphics, designing the Web pages, programming the necessary interaction between servers and customers, creating the databases, and so forth.

This option does give you an awesome amount of control over your site, but generally takes longer than outsourcing the development of your site unless you're lucky enough to lure some very experienced programmers to your staff. Doing it yourself also gives you the confidence that your staff has the skills to support and grow your site, which can be more difficult if someone else developed your site to start with.

Developing a Usable Site

Sometimes the best-designed site can be unusable for reasons that weren't apparent when it was originally designed. For example, you can write great software that uses the latest Extensible Markup Language (XML) technology and looks great on Microsoft Internet Explorer when the computer screen is set to 1280 x 1024 resolution at true color. But contrary to popular belief, some customers *do* use Netscape Navigator — and many Web pages are best viewed at a 800-x-600 resolution.

Setting some ground rules of speed

Your Web designers and programmers have a lot of flexibility in how they implement your designs. Setting some ground rules for the site's overall performance and usability will help them select the methods that best meet the needs of your business and your customers. Feel free to add your own rules as you see fit, but we strongly recommend that you include these basics.

✔ **The four-click rule:** Essentially, a customer must be able to access any portion of the site from any other portion of the site in four steps. A customer viewing a product detail page in one product category must be able to browse to a different product in a different category in four clicks or less.

By sticking with the four-click rule, you'll ensure that your customers aren't far away from anything they may want to access on your site.

✔ **The ten-second rule:** This rules dictates that each page must load and display in a customer's Web browser, using a connection speed that is common across your customer demographic, in ten seconds or less.

If your site will mainly do business with other businesses, a common connection speed might be high-speed lines like a T1 (high-bandwidth dedicated line) or digital subscriber line (DSL) connection. That means you can make pages larger and more complex and still load within ten seconds. If you do business primarily with families or individuals, you should expect the slower connection speeds of conventional PC modems — you'll have to make your pages less complex to get them to display within this optimal ten-second window.

✔ **Least-common-denominator rule:** Different computers use different browser software. Developers like to use high resolution, and high color screens on large monitors. You customers usually don't. Set standards for browser software, screen resolution, and color use.

Many of the common page design tools — such as HomeSite by Allaire, FrontPage by Microsoft, and Dreamweaver by Macromedia — give your designers an estimate on download time for the page while they design it. Companies like Mercury Interactive offer per-use services that run download-time stress tests on your site from multiple locations across the real Web. A little upfront testing can go a long way.

Going with the flow

After you set your rules, consider other factors that make customers want to stay and browse and easily make purchases. You can have the coolest site in the world, but if your users can't navigate it with ease or have trouble at checkout time, you're doomed.

Set specific navigation goals with your technical staff that your site must meet. These goals should all be related to making the site easier for your customers to use, and help make your basic ground rules more specific. Here are some reasonable goals that the customer should be able to easily do.

✔ Use search to locate a specific product on the site within one minute

✔ Browse to a desired product, without searching, within two minutes

- ✔ Surf the site for five minutes and be able to describe the daily special offer

- ✔ Surf the site for ten minutes and be able to name at least two featured products

- ✔ Add an item to the shopping cart in one second (ching!)

- ✔ Remove an item from the shopping cart in one second (rats!)

- ✔ Check out in five minutes or less using a credit card (new customer)

- ✔ Check out in three minutes or less using a credit card (return customer)

- ✔ Sign up for an e-mail newsletter in two minutes

- ✔ Register for a user account in five minutes

After you establish your navigation goals and the site development progresses, you may want to tweak these goals to allow a little more leeway, or to make them tighter, if necessary. You may have a product picture that you allow customers to choose. Although you can't control how fast that picture will appear on the customer browser through a typical 28.8 Kbps modem connection, you can make looking at the picture optional.

Finding an Effective Page Design

From the Office of Really Obvious Statements comes this gem: Not every Web site uses effective page design techniques. C'mon, you know it's true. We won't name names (even if inquiring minds *do* want to know), but you've seen them with their garish colors, multiple fonts, and information crammed so tightly together it's all but illegible. Kind of like Mardi Gras gone bad.

Some basic design elements to consider and look for when you're surfing for the good, the bad, and the ugly include using white space to your advantage, reducing clutter, effectively using of banner ads, and maintaining consistency in the content, look, and feel of your site.

Using white (or some other color) space effectively

One of the most important aspects of Web page design is careful use of white space. Look at this page that you're reading. Everywhere you see chunks with nothing in them (the top, the bottom, the margins, between the paragraphs) is white space. You could also call it red space, black space, or whatever other color you choose for your Web pages' background — the important concept is that it's *blank* space.

Better than lines or other elements, the judicious use of white space helps break a page into distinct visual areas, allowing the eye to draw its own invisible lines. For example, look at your daily newspaper and notice the lack of lines between the columns. Now find some old vintage newspapers from the early 20th century or before, when lines were used to break up articles and columns. Notice how much more cluttered the page appears?

White space can also be used to draw the viewer's eye toward a specific element. Consider the Web page shown in Figure 10-1.

A clear area of space separates the menu items from the main text. A band of white space along the top draws the eye both to the logo and to the banner ad in the upper-right corner of the page. A wideband on the right helps keep the block of text narrow enough for comfortable reading, and white space along the top of the block makes the Welcome headline stand out without the use of bright colors or a huge font size.

Every Web page should have a certain amount of white space on it. If you find that you can't include all the content you wanted and keep ample white space, cut down on the content and keep the white space. Your graphics designer has the best feel for this — when he or she screams that you cannot fit any more on the page, listen!

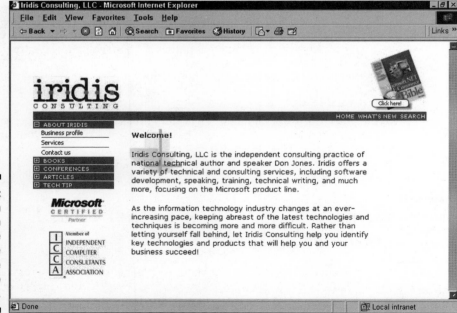

Figure 10-1:
A clean
design with
great use
of white
space, if we
do say so
ourselves.

Cutting down the clutter

Just like those coat hangers in your closet, clutter can multiply at a furious rate. Resist those urges to cram everything onto a single page or you'll end up with a visual mess. More importantly, you risk losing sales because your information becomes diluted, lost, or too difficult for your customer to find.

Don't overstuff your pages. You can always move information to other pages, providing links to them. For a before-and-after example of pre- and de-clutter, take a look at the Web page in Figures 10-2 and 10-3. The left-hand menu of the page (Figure 10-2) presents an awful lot of options in the left-hand menu, and this design flaw competes with the otherwise good use of white space. By redesigning the page to use collapsible menus, as shown in Figure 10-3, the amount of information presented is reduced, even though the user still has all the original options available.

Reducing clutter doesn't happen by accident — it's an important design decision that you and your Web designer make up front. Your pages have to include just the right amount of information, as well as easy-to-find links to any additional information your customers may need.

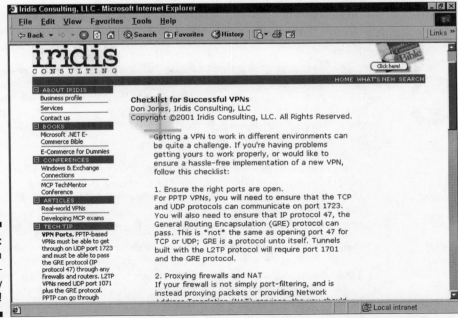

Figure 10-2: Information overload — too many options!

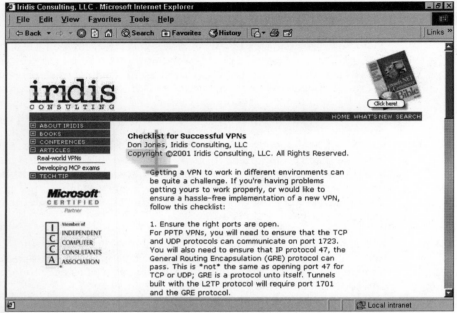

Figure 10-3:
A cleaner
look by
reducing
clutter.

Being consistent

When people see your graphics and layout, they decide the type of company you are. Just as you can feel the difference between Macy's and Wal-Mart just from the layout and design of the store, your Web pages convey a sense of the type of company you are. The biggest thing you can do for your site design to add professionalism is to ensure a consistent look and feel throughout the entire site. Here are some tips:

✔ **Use colors and graphics consistently.** If you choose to use different colors for each department or product category on your site, make sure these colors are used consistently in each department, and that each department has an otherwise similar look to the others. Such a design scheme reinforces your overall online store.

✔ **Require that your writers and copy editors maintain the same voice.** You want your site to seem as if it were all written by a single person. This uniform editorial tone will improve the consistency and professional image of the text on your site, making your customers more comfortable. Have someone with editorial experience and training keep your site descriptions consistent.

✔ **Adopt a master template for every page in your site.** Again, using a basic repeating design creates a professional-looking, continuous aspect to your site's design. These elements should be a part of your site's overall consistency so that the same colors and graphic elements are always used to indicate the current department. This template should include common elements that will appear on every page of your site, including

- Background graphics
- Banner ads
- Logos
- Menu bars
- Page headers and footers

Don't make every page so consistently alike, however, that customers can't figure out where they are on your site. Use colors and graphics as a tool to help customers know what product category they're browsing, what portion of the checkout process they're in, and so forth.

The lifeblood of many Web sites, banner ads enable you to not only advertise other companies, but also to feature your own products and services on your site. As with any form of advertising, though, ad design and placement are key to the ad's success. Use banner ads strategically throughout your site, and choose different sizes to make them fit in best. You can include a banner ad in the margin of a page, at the bottom of a menu bar, or even in a footer at the bottom of a page. Again, the watchword is moderation. A bevy of banner ads distracts from the actual content of your site and makes it seem like a giant electronic billboard.

Adding Pizzazz with Dynamic Page Elements

Because the dynamic, exciting aspects of the Web make online shopping so compelling for many consumers, Web pages should be more exciting than their printed cousins. (Face it: We've got better toys.) After you get the nuts and bolts determined for your site (as we detail in the earlier section "Finding an Effective Page Design"), jazz up your pages with dynamic elements:

✔ **Jack-in-the-box windows:** A great tool to grab your customers' attention while spotlighting something special is a pop-up window. For example, you can use a pop-up to remind your customers of a special limited-time sale or offer. Pop-up windows are critters that appear on their own, as if by magic, when your customers visit key pages on your Web site.

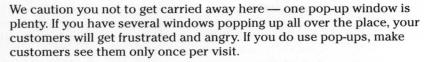

We caution you not to get carried away here — one pop-up window is plenty. If you have several windows popping up all over the place, your customers will get frustrated and angry. If you do use pop-ups, make customers see them only once per visit.

✔ **Animation:** Consider adding a dynamic feature like animated GIF files (one of the many graphic formats common on the Web), or more complex animation using products such as Flash (from Macromedia; www.macromedia.com). Most site designers use animated banner ads to attract attention, and you can use animation in other key elements of your site to add a dynamic look.

Although animated graphics take longer — sometimes *much* longer — for a customer to download, these tools are great for catching and maintain a customer's attention. Call it the Magpie Syndrome: Most people like bright, shiny things.

✔ **Using dynamic style:** Your Web designer can use other dynamic styles to make your site more interactive. Using these styles also helps give customers visual cues when they do certain things, such as move their mouse pointers over buttons that can be clicked. Common dynamic techniques include

- **Menus** that the customer can open or close at will.

- **Buttons** that highlight or change colors when the customer points at them, encouraging the customer to click them.

- Helpful **pop-up tips** that let customers know what will happen if they click on a particular button or graphic.

- **On-screen information** that dynamically changes depending on what the customer does. For example, a shopping cart screen might recalculate the customer's order total instantly when the customer selects a new shipping method.

Using Browser Technology to Catch a Majority of Online Consumers

At least a dozen different Web browsers are on the market, each with varying degrees of popularity. On the Windows platform, Microsoft Internet Explorer is currently the reigning king, with Communicator from Netscape coming in a distant second. America Online has a special version of Internet Explorer bundled with its software. Some folks use the inexpensive browser, Opera. On the UNIX platform, Communicator holds a compelling lead, along with the open-source Mozilla browser and several others.

In short, this glut of variety makes Web development as interesting as possible (slight sarcasm) because every Web browser implements the so-called Web standards slightly differently. Communicator displays tables a bit differently than Internet Explorer, and Opera supports a slightly different scripting language than Mozilla. Your customers, of course, will use some version of all these browsers, making it very difficult to create a Web site that looks and behaves the same for everyone.

You may never get your site to look and behave exactly the same for everyone. Just try to get as close as possible.

Accounting for browser functionality

With all the variety on the Web, design professionals need to keep track of which browser can do what, and make decisions about what features should and should not be used. Start with features that are common to a wide variety of browsers. After your site has been up and running for a while, your servers' logs can give you some information about what browsers are being used to visit your site the most. You can then start improving your content to use features supported by those browsers, ignoring the capabilities — or lack thereof — of other browsers.

A good Web designer can find a common ground for most of the features you want to implement on your site, creating pages that look and behave pretty much the same on any major Web browser running on any major computer platform.

Catering to the masses means making compromises, though. You simply can't do some things effectively if your goal is to support a wide range of browsers and platforms. Don't drive your Web designers crazy trying to accomplish the impossible — let them help you set reasonable goals for what can be accomplished, and let them suggest workarounds when important features simply can't be accomplished on a particular browser you want to support.

Rather than providing cross-browser content, you can also choose to provide alternative content for different browsers. For example, if you decide that you need to support every single Web browser in use on the planet, you have a tough job ahead of you. After you tranquilize your Web designers and strap them in their seats, tell them you're willing to accomplish your goal with browser-specific content.

With this technique, your designers create a set of pages that support a set of browsers that share common functionality. They then create a similar set of pages geared to browsers with different features and functionality. Your programmers create one master page that detects which browser a customer is using and sends them to the set of pages specifically designed for their browser.

This technique provides flexibility at a high price — your Web designers and programmers will have to spend 50 to 75 percent more time per additional set of pages they have to create. This technique is best used only for critical pages in your site, such as a shopping cart page or a set of checkout pages.

The good, the bad, and the ugly of interactivity

If you're used to programs that retrieve data from databases when you click a control, Web browser-based programs can be a bit of a shock. Traditional Windows applications keep connections to the database and talk to the database server at 10 million to 100 million bits per second.

On the Web, you have to go back to the server from your browser to get more data. If you use a 56K-modem connection, you are communicating with the server, which is 175 times slower than connecting through a local area network (LAN). The bottom line is that your Web applications need to work different than traditional applications. You need to think carefully about when and how you get information from your server.

Fortunately, new technologies, such as XML, can make Web applications appear as interactive as typical Web applications. This makes much richer applications possible.

Putting Your Design to the Test

After you build your site, you have to make certain that it works. This process encompasses much more than the mechanics of moving between pages and submitting orders (although that's important, too) — your site must sell. It must project the image of your brand and draw customers back, again and again. Establish a clear set of measurements that rate your level of success and point the way toward future growth and development. In Chapter 3, we discuss creating your initial e-commerce initiative plan. Measure your product against the standards set in that plan.

When you conduct some testing on your site, you'll find additional things that you need to add to improve how it works. We guide you through some of the common ones, and you can decide where they fit in to your overall plan.

Never, ever, ever, ever, *ever, ever,* EVER put your site, or any new piece online until all have been thoroughly tested. Sound the horn and bring in the QA specialists — this is their chance to shine. (For more on quality assurance, read through Chapter 7.) Resist this temptation even if your programmers assure you, "It's perfect . . . you don't even need to test it." They're lying. We know — we're programmers and we do it all the time.

The first part of your testing process is, of course, to make sure everything actually works. To make that sure everything looks and behaves just as it should, your QA specialists need to perform their tests using every type of browser and computer platform that your customers might use. Your QA specialists should look for

- **Layout:** Does everything look like it should? QA specialists should be given some of your original design documents with sample pages to compare with the finished product.

- **Functionality:** Do all the dynamic features work? Again, your design plan should indicate what specific features do what, so that your QA folks know what to test.

- **Navigation:** Are all the pages there? Any broken links? Do the links all go to the right places? Your design document and some common sense will help your QA specialists understand what's supposed to happen.

- **Behind-the-scenes functionality:** Do orders work? Credit card payments? The whole back-end system? Make sure these systems work as designed.

Check out the handy, inexpensive utility VMware (`www.vmware.com`). This utility enables multiple *virtual computers* (so named by VMWare) on a single computer. Your QA testers can simultaneously test on Windows 95, Windows 2000, Linux, and so forth, all on a single machine and all at the same time.

Gathering Customer Feedback with Usability Testing

After you know that your page is viable and widely accessible despite browser and platform variables, it's time to see how well your customers like it. Because you want customers to like your site and because you want them to become return visitors, find out what they think about your site. You don't even have to be intrusive or blatant, which is sometimes the end result of soliciting feedback from surveys or filling out a feedback form. Find out what your customers really think by including them in a usability test of the site.

A *usability test* sets specific goals that you want your customers to be able to accomplish. Your goals should cover flow, navigational ease, and the amount of time it takes your customer to compete a transaction. These goals test your customers' ability to perform key tasks, and also test the effectiveness of your site's navigation, advertising, shopping cart, checkout, and other features. After you establish the test, you need to actually carry one out.

Nobody on your technical staff, including your QA specialists, should do your usability testing. Your co-workers are too familiar with the site, and they also may not fit your target customer demographic. You need to determine whether a new customer, who fits your target demographic, can reach your goals on the usability test.

Round up some folks in your target demographic — ideally, some of your current offline customers. You have the option of just giving them the URL for the test version of your site, but this presents the disadvantage that you can't time them. Better yet, have them go into your office for the test so that your QA folks can hover nearby with stopwatches to take accurate timings (plus you get the opportunity to schmooze them with lunch or something).

If you can wrangle an in-house test, ask the testers to sit down at computers and give them the list of goals without the time limits. Have someone discreetly time your testers and keep an eye on what they're doing. If your testers can't meet your time goals, you want to know what they got hung up on. One way to do this is to hook a separate monitor up to the test computer and let one of your QA specialists follow along as the tester completes the goals on the test.

Chapter 11

Giving Customers What They Want: Service!

In This Chapter

▶ Building customer relations and loyalty through e-relationships

▶ Informing customers about your products and services

▶ Helping customers use what they buy

▶ Listening to customers and using their feedback to improve your business

*E*veryone has favorite stores and vendors. People trust companies when they can find the right combination of price, service, and selection. The principle is the same in the e-marketplace, but how you gain a customer's trust is quite different.

In this chapter, we show you how to build relationships with customers through the Internet, how to put that loyalty to use to increase sales and your customer base, and how to develop mechanisms to help customers make purchasing decisions and use the products they buy.

You find out how to utilize your suppliers' and manufacturers' technologies to make your customers feel loved, and how to provide mechanisms for customer feedback so your customers feel important — and so your site can continually improve.

Knowing the Goals of Effective Customer Service

In the rush to get your site up and running, some of the special touches that make a site warm and inviting are often lost in the shuffle. But like any store, your site needs to make shoppers feel that they are welcome and appreciated. You need to give customers a reason to return, and your site has to provide something that your competitors' sites lack.

The easiest thing to do is let your programmers develop your site as they see fit. They are usually eager and willing to do this. The problem is that they are not typically sales-oriented or customer-service-oriented people. Many of the programmers we know can't even claim English as their second language (or their third). And they are Americans!

Your subject matter experts (SMEs) can be invaluable here. (See Chapter 3.) They can help provide the process and wording that explains to your customers, in terms to which they are accustomed, what you are doing and why. Their input helps keep your site on target.

Using a friendly face

Most companies have a certain image that they want to project when dealing with clients. Whether your company's image is serious or lighthearted, button-down pinstripes or baggies and sandals, you should maintain that image throughout your site. The style in which your Web site presents information and instructions, and your choice of graphics and layout, should project that image.

Frequently using *error messages* (those annoying boxes or screens that pop up when a customer enters information incorrectly) doesn't improve your company's image — those codes are annoying for a reason. Instead, error messages turn customers off. Your customers are computer-literate enough to know that computers freeze up, act funny, or spit back cryptic messages when they don't know what to do with the information users supply. (What the heck does `-21928374 ADO Error: Cannot access data source` mean anyway?)

When they're familiar with a program, most users are able to get around error codes; however, customers visiting your site are unfamiliar with its inner workings. When these error messages appear onscreen, they're usually quite cryptic (remember, writing clear English is not a skill that's common to programmers), and customers are left with no clue what they should do next. Even though they don't like to, your programmers can create clear, friendly error messages. The tone of an error message is important because it is a reflection of your company. It's also important that your QA (Quality Assurance) team tests those error messages and minimize the necessity of using them at all by providing clear, concise, and complete instructions that don't leave customers feeling like Dummies.

You need to communicate your image — your customer experience — to your design and programming staff. You should also make your expectations known to QA. If you think out what you want your customers to experience before you design, you can factor these elements into the mix at every level. At your weekly project meetings, find out how things are going. Give your team members enough latitude to vent without letting things get out of hand. Help your team members step back from their part of the technology to see the project, as your customers will.

Responding to the preferences of customers through profiles

Another way to build customer relationships is to create and maintain customer profiles, which provide clues to customers' wants and needs. You can store information such as customers' expressed preferences, their last purchase, and their current model of widget, and use that information to make customers feel unique, special, and valued. You can find more detail on customer profiling in Chapter 9.

Increasing Loyalty Electronically

A purchase is a matter of small decisions that add up to a decision to buy. To build loyalty and customer commitment, you can ask small questions that get customers in the habit of saying *yes*. "Yes, I like this color." "Yes, your product helped me." "Yes, this site is easier to use than others I have seen." "Yes, I want to save the shipping charge on this order." Each *yes* you receive from the customer builds trust and acceptance. They learn to trust you and your suggestions, which keeps them coming back.

Making your Web site sticky (It's a good thing, we promise)

MSN (www.msn.com) is the portal site for Microsoft that enables users to customize their individual MSN home pages by adding and removing features. Microsoft encourages users to use its MSN page as their browser's home page. It also conditions customers to clicking links on the Web page, saying *yes* and making MSN part of their daily lives.

You want to encourage your customers to come back — to make you their home page. iWon.com (www.iwon.com) does it by offering daily contests. To enter, you need to show up at this site every day. Stock brokerages such as Ameritrade (you need to have an active account) use news and financial information. eBay, one of the stickiest sites on the Web, helps you personalize your visits via its My eBay feature. Finding an irresistible hook to keep your customers coming back will make you site very sticky.

In the e-commerce world, you want to condition customers to click the Yes button often. You want to reward them with small surprises and gifts, such as free shipping, price discounts, or an extra product. Is it Machiavellian? Yes. Are we taking a Pavlovian approach to customer relations? Yes. Does it work? Yes!

Remember, loyal customers can make your site into a hot location — the power of e-mail, message boards, newsgroups, and chat enable customers to sing your praises (or rue the day they ever clicked into your domain) to more people much faster than ever before. Here's a list of things you can do to increase the number of loyal customers that return do more business with you:

- **Give people options.** By offering customers simple choices, you have more power to produce these choices than you may realize. Let customers customize their shopping page, putting their preferences on top. By configuring that page, customers take ownership of how your site works for them — and feel more like a partner than a customer. For example, Earthlink enables each customer to configure a personal home page.

- **Feel customers' pain.** You need to listen carefully to your customers and listen to their opinions regardless of whether they are complaints or compliments. Each time you communicate with customers — whether by e-mail, phone, or snail mail — invite them back and offer them incentives to see what is new and different about your site.

- **Provide feedback links.** Put a link on the site that helps customers let you know what's wrong. Then make darn sure they get a prompt response. Don't send an auto-response and ignore the request. Handle feedback with the same respect you would show customers if they turned up in person at your office.

- **Keep 'em coming back.** Giving incentives for customers to return gives customers a reason to return to your site:

  - Offer incentives in the form of coupons, daily specials, and free shipping.

  - Send out e-mails that invite customers to return.

  - Offer customers discounts on their next order.

  - Display a pop-up window welcoming return customers and show your appreciation with special offers.

Maintaining Competitiveness

When you design your site, you determine what makes your business distinct in the e-marketplace. You go online with a large flash and a big marketing push, and the orders start rolling in. But to ensure that the flow of orders continues to grow and customers are compelled to return to your site, you must constantly challenge and refine your base assumptions of what makes your site distinctive. Site maintenance must be a part of your e-commerce plan from the beginning.

Keeping your e-dge

When you roll out your first site, you breathe a heavy sigh of relief and kick back. You did it, and now it is time to enjoy the fruit of your labors. Just don't sit too long.

Your initial tricks and gimmicks grow old fast. You need to keep your site changing and growing. Changing your look, adding new features, and developing new conveniences keep customers coming back — if for no other reason than to see what is new. You need to develop a cycle of gathering customer feedback and changing your site to emphasize the good while eliminating the bad. Sites that continually refine themselves are more likely to maintain their customer bases.

Keeping an eye on the competition

Don't think that your competitors are sitting on their hands while you go after their customers. They are watching you like a hawk and adding features to their sites to compete against yours. You need to keep tabs on what your competitors are up to and make certain that your site's attractions meet and exceed theirs. This is electronic warfare, and only the strong survive.

Providing Cross-Market Customer Support

If your organization maintains both bricks-and-mortar locations and an e-commerce operation, you need both sides of the business to help and support one another. Even if your sales force and store managers don't want cross-market support with your Web sales division, your customers demand it. By building bridges between the online and offline universes, you can keep your organization integrated and your customers happy.

Helping online customers in your store

We say it throughout this book, and we'll say it again: The Web is inherently a faceless, anonymous place to do business. No matter how warm and fuzzy your site is, sometimes it just can't compare with the personal touch that your bricks-and-mortar store (and its living, breathing sales staff) can provide. And one way to bring the personal touch to your online business is to tightly integrate it with your *offline* business. Encourage online customers to use your bricks-and-mortar stores, and encourage your traditional customers to go online. Great, you say, but how? Make both sides of the business depend on each other and convince customers that they can't live without the total experience of using everything you have to offer.

Integrating the Internet with toll-free support

Many people enjoy doing business online — until a problem occurs. If customers have to send e-mail messages back and forth to a business to resolve a problem, they can easily be turned off by the experience. Don't get us wrong — we are *not* encouraging you to ban the use of e-mail on your site. We're just saying that sometimes customers want to pick up the phone, dial a toll-free number, explain what they want to a friendly human (not a recording or a grouch), and have the problem taken care of right then and there. (Hey, real time is real time, whether you're online or not.) There's a fine line between supporting your customers and encouraging them to use the tools on your Web site. Here are some tips:

- ✔ **Make sure that customers who have an immediate need can find your toll-free phone number.** For example, customers who have received an order may want to speak to someone about returning an item they don't want. These customers should have easy access to a toll-free personalized assistance — they've paid for it.

- ✔ **Encourage customers who want to place an order, or who have questions about a product, to get answers from the Web site.** Help customers use e-mail or other resources on the Web site to discover product information. Use a different toll-free number than the one you use for customer service calls.

  Don't hide your customer service number, but don't make it the most prominent feature on the page, either. If your site features are easy to use, you should experience reduced call volume.

Finding the kiosk to online sales — when customers are offline

Several major retailers — including Barnes & Noble and Kmart — have started using kiosks to integrate their Web sites with their bricks-and-mortar stores. A *kiosk* is a standalone computer that is available for real-world customers to use. Kiosks are usually encased in attractive housing or placed on a pedestal, and often have a touch screen instead of a mouse. In-store customers can use these kiosks to browse a company's Web site and find products that may be out of stock (or not regularly stocked at all) in the store.

Blurring bricks and clicks:
A medley of success stories

As we mention elsewhere in the book, converting your bricks-and-mortar customers to online customers offers some distinct advantages, such as lowering the cost of doing business, enabling customers to shop 24 hours a day, and so forth. One way to ease your customers into e-commerce is to make the distinction between your physical stores and your online store as indistinct as possible. Think of creative ways you can meld bricks and clicks to provide better customer service.

Gap.com (www.gap.com) purchases can be returned or exchanged at any Gap store. Clothing is especially difficult to sell online because size, color, fit, pattern, and a variety of other variables can be difficult to accurately gauge on a computer screen. By allowing customers to return or exchange online purchases at its physical stores, the Gap makes online purchases safer and more convenient for consumers.

Make sure that your kiosks are suitable for displaying and navigating your Web site. If you use a touch screen kiosk, test to make certain your pages work well when people use their pudgy digits to select things from the screen. If your site looks best at a particular screen resolution, make sure the kiosks use that resolution. You may need to create alternate pages to work with your kiosks — or alternate kiosk hardware that works with your pages.

True kiosks are designed to provide limited access to the computer's operating system, preventing customers from breaking the computer. Use a professionally built and configured kiosk, such as the ones offered by CeroView (www.ceroview.com) or Cybertotems (www.cybertotems.com).

Helping bricks-and-mortar customers online

Your Web site can be more than just a place to buy products and services over the Internet — it can also be a place where your bricks-and-mortar customers can research products, get post-purchase support, and more. Your online business can help your bricks-and-mortar customers by providing convenient self-service features, and can be a great way to cement your business relationship with your customers.

Adding online help desk

Customers who need post-sales support usually return to the store where they occupy a salesperson's valuable time. By providing an *online help desk,* customers can contact support or customer service personnel without creating a distraction for the salespeople in your stores.

Providing products updates and information

Many customers have become accustomed to using the Web to retrieve product updates and information. Whether they need to download a copy of a product manual for something they bought from you, a software update for computer-related products, or recipes to use with their new electric wok, e-commerce Web sites provide a valuable post-sale resource for customers.

What if you're in the reselling business and you don't actually make the products you sell? Customers won't generally expect your site to provide them with information and updates — but you can surprise them and do just that. Provide helpful hints for using new products, links to manufacturers' Web sites where customers can download updates and information, and so forth. Look in Chapter 20 for ideas on building business partnerships and trading data.

Encourage your in-store customers to check out your Web site for this information by including leaflets or other promotional materials with their purchases. Remember, if you can get customers to visit your Web site, you have the opportunity to display promotional messages that can result in future sales.

Giving customers just the FAQs

How do I change the belt in my vacuum cleaner? What's the best oil to use in my deep-fat fryer? How can I get spots out of my blue carpet? These are examples of *FAQs,* or Frequently Asked Questions.

A FAQ is simply a list of questions that customers commonly ask about a product or service, along with helpful, clearly written answers. Until people have asked real questions, you will need to use your imagination. Your customer representatives, service personnel, and technical writers are the best source for these questions — and the answers.

Remind your in-store customers that they can find tips and advice for using their purchases on your Web site, and make sure that you have FAQs to help them out. Encourage your customers to make your online FAQs their first stop for answers to any questions they may have. FAQs provide a satisfying customer experience because customers are able to help themselves. FAQs also help relieve the burden of handling customer service and support calls through a phone center.

You can even use in-store promotional materials, such as shelf cards, to inform customers about the FAQs you have for various products. These promotional materials not only direct customers to the FAQs if they need them, but also help blend your bricks-and-mortar and online businesses in your customers' minds.

Steering them in the right direction — to your URL

You use advertising specialties — magnets, key chains, and pens — to get people to remember your phone number. Use these same devices to give them your URL. Put your Web address on every brochure, invoice, proposal, bag — anything you put into their hands. Such opportunities always produce results.

E-xtra, e-xtra, read all about it!

E-mail newsletters are a great way to keep in touch with all of your customers, whether they shop on your Web site or in your store. Almost every major e-commerce company uses promotional e-mail in some fashion because it's inexpensive, provides instant delivery, and allows the companies to target newsletters to their customers' interests for very little additional cost.

Use your newsletter to help people use the products and services they receive from you. Include new ways to use the product, stories of how people solved real problems with your service, news on new models — even workarounds for common problems in the field. Make your newsletter more than just another brochure. If your customers find it useful, they will find you useful and come back for more.

Encourage your in-store customers to sign up for your e-mail newsletter. You can provide sign-up cards, fliers instructing them how to sign up on your Web site, or even an in-store kiosk that allows customers to access your site and sign up on the spot.

Offering your support through e-mail

Sometimes customers have questions that aren't covered by your FAQs, but don't have the time to pick up the phone and call someone. By offering customers the ability to e-mail your customer service staff, you can address customers' concerns and answer their questions without having to pay for the phone call.

Some customers prefer to ask their questions via e-mail even if a phone number is readily available. After all, they don't have to wait on hold when they send you an e-mail!

If you do provide a customer-service e-mail address, make sure that your staff is able to respond to customer e-mails in a timely fashion. Your Web site should give customers some expectation of a response time — a few hours, a day, a week, whatever — and you should stick to that promise.

Don't make answering customer service e-mails a task for your phone center employees to handle in their so-called spare time; the end result would be that they'd make the e-mails a lower priority than the incoming phone calls, which isn't fair to your customers. Either assign a dedicated staff to handle e-mails or schedule time for your regular customer service staff to focus exclusively on e-mails.

This e-mail is a recording

Automated e-mails are another great way of providing customer service. Although it's common enough to send automated e-mails to customers doing business with you online, think about the ways you can use automated e-mail to provide better customer service to your bricks-and-mortar customers:

✔ US Airways sends electronic account statements to its frequent-flyer members, saving thousands of dollars in paper and postage every year. These statements are sent automatically every month and provide a great convenience to customers.

✔ American Express enables cardholders to opt out of receiving a monthly account statement by regular mail. Instead, the company sends these customers an automated e-mail when their online statement is available for viewing on the company's Web site.

✔ Truck accessory retailer Quadratec sends order and shipping confirmation e-mails to customers who purchase through the company's Web site *and* to customers who make a purchase by calling the company's toll-free phone number. This service cuts down on repeat calls to the phone center to check the status of an order or obtain tracking numbers, and gives customers instant information about their order.

✔ The Good Sam Club, an organization for RV owners, sends automated e-mail reminders to members whose memberships are about to expire. The e-mail is followed up with the traditional paper mailing, but because many customers renew after receiving the e-mail, the company saves money and can eliminate the paper reminder.

You can use automated e-mail in many ways to improve customer service for customers who never even visit your Web site — and save money in the process.

Any time that your company interacts with customers, be sure to remind customers of the electronic customer service tools you offer. Encourage them to provide their e-mail address and to sign up for one or more of these convenient, helpful services.

Using artificial intelligence to automate support

You and your staff can't be everywhere at once. And, although you want to help every one of your customers to the best of your ability, there are a lot more customers than there are of you.

What you need to do is get organized — *really* organized. You need to automatically route customer service requests to the person or people who can handle them the best. You need to fire off automated answers whenever possible to stall for time, if necessary, while your staff catches up. What you need is a super assistant who can do all of this for you — what you need is some *artificial intelligence*.

No, we're not talking about building a computer that can take over the world. You just need to have computer systems that are programmed to analyze incoming customer requests and make some complex decisions to get them to the right place.

Organizing and routing support requests

A key to organizing, of course, is getting incoming customer requests to the right people as quickly as possible. One method is to have your staff screen incoming e-mails and forward them to the appropriate people. Sound crazy? Yes, because you may get thousands of incoming requests a day. But you'd be surprised how many companies actually handle things this way.

You can program your systems to automatically route incoming requests several ways. Here are the major techniques, which you can combine or use individually:

> ✔ **Have customers submit their requests by filling out a form on your Web site.** This allows you to ask customers to indicate what type of request they have — pre-sales information, a service issue, an order status check, and so forth — by selecting it from a drop-down list. Your Web site can then route the request to the appropriate destination based on the customer's selection.

✔ **Have customers send e-mail requests to different e-mail addresses for different types of requests.** For example, you could use `sales@mycompany.com` for pre-sales information, `orderstatus@mycompany.com` for checking the status of an order, and `returns@mycompany.com` for initiating the return of a product. Your e-mail system can route incoming e-mail based on the e-mail addresses that are used.

✔ **Have customers send e-mail requests to one e-mail address, and use an artificial intelligence system to scan the contents of those e-mails and route them appropriately.** For example, if the system finds the phrase *status of my order* in the text of the e-mail, it would route the request to your order status person. If it finds a phrase like *need more information on*, it can route the e-mail to a salesperson. Although these systems can be expensive to program, they're a great way to handle a large volume of incoming mail. Companies such as Right Now technologies provide artificial intelligence systems that improve customer service.

Answering questions automatically

You can create (or purchase) mail-handling systems that automatically respond to certain requests. For example, suppose you establish an e-mail address like `orderstatus@mycompany.com`. Customers can find out the status of their purchase by sending an e-mail to that address and including their order number in the subject line. Your e-mail system can then route the incoming e-mail for that e-mail address to a computer system, which looks up the order number and sends an automated e-mail to the customer with the order's status.

Creating automated mail-handling systems for common requests can save a lot of time and money, freeing up your customer service staff to handle more complex customer requests.

You can combine an automated mail-handling system with an artificial-intelligence response system. The integrated system can scan for phrases like *more information* and the names of products or services that you offer, and then respond by e-mailing the customer with additional product information or links to product information on the Web. The system could then forward the e-mail to a salesperson, who could follow up and make sure the customer received the information he or she was looking for.

Unless they're just handling simple requests, such as order status information, don't rely on automated systems to handle all customer requests. These systems are useful for providing customers with an immediate response, but customer requests should always be forwarded to a person, too, who can follow up to make sure the customer's needs were met.

Servicing What You Sell

Selling is only half the story. After customers purchase products, they are filled with questions and apprehensions, which you can handle by providing them with the information they need in order to use those products.

You can provide this information efficiently and cost effectively by using the technology of your suppliers' sites, and with a little creativity, you can boost your own revenue to boot! By helping customers use and maintain their products, you earn their trust and give them a reason to regularly visit your site (where you can also hit them with promotional messages at the same time).

Part of providing service, of course, is enabling customers to return items that they've purchased online. Returns are always a sensitive situation, and your return policy has a big impact on the success (or failure) of your e-commerce venture, as well as on your customer's opinion of your company.

Let me show you a great way to use that

Customer service doesn't end with handling complaints and returns. In fact, if you provide great, proactive customer service, you can avoid a lot of complaints and returns! Find ways to provide more information to your customers that will help them use the products and services they buy from you. Even if you didn't actually manufacture the products or provide the service, you can still use your Web site to add a lot of value to your business and strengthen your relationship with your customers.

Making the most of the manufacturer's site

Most product manufacturers include valuable information for customers on their Web sites, and you should try to do business with manufacturers who make a point of doing that. You can enhance your relationships with your customers by making this online information available to them. Here are some ways that you can do that:

- ✔ **Provide links to manufacturers' Web sites** so that your customers can hunt down product manuals, software downloads, and other information.

- ✔ **Obtain additional product information** from manufacturers' Web sites to enhance your own site's product descriptions, photos, and so forth. Your partners will usually provide this information freely — just ask before you take.

✔ **Create a directory of product information** that is available on manufacturers' sites and provide links directly to the content. This saves your customers the hassle of hunting through the manufacturers' sites for the information.

✔ **Link to a manufacturer's site** to take customers directly to useful features, such as a troubleshooting tool, or how-to articles for using its products (assuming the manufacturer has these features) — or provide copies of those articles on your site.

One big, happy discussion group

Many online customers love to share their ideas and opinions. To enable your customers to share tips, ideas, and opinions about the products and services you sell, create online discussion groups. Customers may get enough information from these discussion groups that they don't need to bother contacting one of your customer service reps for their questions. This relieves the burden on your customer service staff.

Always make sure that a representative of your company monitors these discussion groups to respond to any questions addressed to your company and to ensure that the discussions stay on topic.

Accessorize!

When customers purchase certain products — such as clothes, computers, video games, cars, and so on — they often come back later to purchase accessories. Making it easy for your customers to find accessories for their earlier purchases is a good business tactic and good customer service.

Make sure that you provide any necessary cross-reference charts so that customers can find, for example, the correct replacement light bulb for their car or the correct memory card for their digital camera. Make the accessories easy to find, perhaps by linking them to the original product's detail page. Look through Chapter 9 for ideas on building your catalog pages.

Time for a checkup

Unfortunately, some of the products that customers buy will, at some point, break down. And although you may not be responsible for providing repair service, your Web site is the first place your customers will look for repair information. If you're committed to providing good customer service, your site must include the information customers will be looking for, and maybe a bit more.

Providing automatic reminders

You have a record of when customers bought their products, and you can easily find out what the manufacturer's recommended maintenance schedule is. Using this information, you can set up an automated e-mail service that reminds customers when service is due. Car dealers commonly use this technique to send reminders using snail mail, but it can easily be applied to any product that requires regular maintenance, including

- ✔ Audio/video equipment that requires regular cleaning (for example, DVD players and VCRs)
- ✔ Bicycles and other sports equipment requiring regular maintenance
- ✔ Computer equipment that benefits from regular cleaning (for example, CD-ROM drives and digital cameras)
- ✔ Cellular phones, which periodically require new rechargeable batteries
- ✔ Office equipment that requires regular maintenance and new supplies (for example, fax machines and copiers)

Offer your customers the opportunity to subscribe to a reminder service when they purchase the product. Also make sure that the e-mail reminders include information on how customers can unsubscribe to this service, if they want.

Giving out maintenance information

Customers will come to your Web site as their first stop for information regarding their purchases. Provide them with the necessary service information, including manufacturer maintenance recommendations, telephone numbers and addresses of repair facilities, and so forth.

You can gather much of this information directly from the manufacturer's site. And, with the manufacturer's permission, you can use the information on your site to better serve your customers.

What, they didn't like it?

Although businesses don't like to deal with returned merchandise, they usually try to put a good face on it because it's a necessary part of doing business. In the world of online commerce, you'll have a much higher return rate than in the bricks-and-mortar world, especially for luxury goods. After customers finally get the products in their hands, those products might not look as nice and shiny as they did on your Web site.

Returns with a virtual smile

Camping World is a mail-order company that sells camping and recreational vehicle supplies and equipment. Although the company has more than 30 bricks-and-mortar stores through the United States, much of its business comes from a thriving mail-order division. It seemed natural to extend that division to include a Web site, www.campingworld.com.

As an established mail-order business, Camping World already had experience in accepting returns through the mail and already had a return policy in place. So Camping World extended that great return policy to include its online business.

Returns are accepted for up to 30 days, no questions asked. Customers are not required to call in and obtain an authorization number; instead, they simply fill out a form on their packing slip and send the unwanted merchandise back. Customers can either receive a full refund, less shipping and handling charges, or they can indicate alternative merchandise they would like to receive instead.

How you handle returns can make or break your customer relationships. With the additional complications involved in returning online purchases, how you handle returns says a lot about what you think of your customers. Make sure that you handle returns promptly, consistently, and in a way that places as little stress — and blame — on the customer as possible.

Developing return policies

The time to let your customers in on your return policy is *before* they purchase something from you. Make your return policies easily available on your site. Be proud of these policies — they show how far you're willing to go to keep your customers happy — and don't hide them in a corner of your site.

If you sell products that have special return policies, post those policies on the products' detail pages so customers know what they're getting into from the start. For example, many online computer retailers will accept returns of unopened products, but computer hardware is often subject to a 10–20 percent restocking fee. Make sure that customers are aware of that policy up front. After all, losing sales because customers don't like your return policy is far better than waiting until they buy something, want to return it, and *then* find out how things work. They'll be angry and may tell their friends not to buy anything from you.

Reiterate your return policies on the customer's packing slip, or include a separate sheet with information about how returns are handled with each shipment.

Here are some tips for developing friendly, realistic return policies for online purchases:

✔ **Give customers enough time to return merchandise.** Allow time for the products to reach customers, for them to examine the products, decide whether they want to keep the products, and make the return, if necessary. Thirty days is typical, and anything shorter than 15 days is impractical.

Of course, you may want to set an outer limit (six months, a year? — it depends on your market).

✔ **Indicate how customers initiate the return process.** Do they have to contact you for an authorization number? If so, think about providing an automated tool on your Web site to handle this request. Or can customers simply fill out a return form, perhaps included on the back of their packing slip, and ship the product back to you? The latter policy is certainly easier on the customer, and you should try to arrange your return process and policies to keep things as easy as possible for customers.

✔ **Clearly indicate how soon customers can expect to receive a refund.** It's unfair for you to take much longer to process the refund than it took you to process the original order, so organize your returns process to quickly handle incoming shipments.

✔ **Indicate who pays return shipping charges.** Generally, shipping and handling charges are not refundable, and customers must pay to ship returned merchandise back to you. You should always refund shipping for returns that were your fault, such as shipments that included the wrong products.

✔ **If you want customers to insure their return shipments, clearly state that in your return policy.** Indicate that you will not accept returns if they arrive in poor condition or never arrive at all. Or just *encourage* customers to insure their shipments.

Developing clear, friendly return policies and making them readily available on your site is a preemptive strike in the customer service war!

Preparing for returns

Does your business have a returns department in place to handle returns of online purchases? If your company already does a lot of mail-order business, then you're probably an old hand at handling these types of returns. If not, you need to create a returns department and have it up and running before you open your online store. Here are some things to think about when creating this department:

✔ **Decide where you will keep the returned merchandise.** You'll need a miniature warehouse just to store the boxes in while they're processed.

✔ **Find out how your vendors handle returns.** Find out whether you're permitted to resell returned merchandise and whether you can return it to your vendor for a refund or credit.

✔ **Decide how you will process returns.** You need some means of returning payments and updating your inventory, which may require additional back-end systems that your programmers will have to create. These systems should also provide e-mail confirmations to customers (as shown in Figure 11-1) indicating that their returns have been received and accepted.

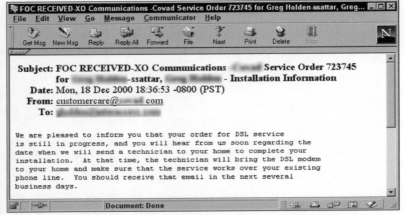

Figure 11-1: Confirmation e-mail messages keep customers informed and ease worries.

✔ **Decide whether you want to resell returned merchandise as "opened box" at a discount price.** If so, make sure that your Web site notifies customers of the availability of this discounted merchandise or make plans to transfer the merchandise to your bricks-and-mortar stores for the next clearance sale.

✔ **Be ready for extra work.** Returns can generate a lot of trash — packing materials, boxes, packing slips, and so forth. Make sure your returns department can handle the boxes — and the paperwork. Read Chapter 5 for clues on keeping systems streamlined and paperwork at a minimum.

Set up your returns department before you start accepting returns. Figure out how you're going to handle returns as part of your basic business plan, get the right people and tools in place, and then hope they won't have much work to do!

Returning to bricks-and-mortar locales

Many online retailers allow customers to return online purchases to their nearest bricks-and-mortar store for a refund or exchange. This is a great idea — it turns the return process into a personal experience, and offers the store's associates the opportunity to turn the return into an exchange or, at the very least, a pleasant customer experience.

Make sure that your stores don't have a reason to hate online returns that come in the door. Your in-store systems should provide some means of separating online returns in your transaction records so that stores' sales and returns figures aren't affected by incoming returns from your online business. Make sure that store employees understand the process for accepting online returns and the importance of making it a pleasant experience for the online customer.

Returns affect your bottom line — in the taxes you pay and even the rent paid to the shopping center where your bricks-and-mortar stores are located. If you use returns from online sales to lower your bricks-and-mortar taxes and lease payments, make sure you play by the rules and keep your accounting straight.

Handling Complaints

No one likes to listen to complaints. But if you want to stay in business, you can't ignore them. You need to provide a way for customers to provide constructive feedback and then let customers know that you're really listening. Use that criticism to unearth weak areas in your organization so that you can improve how you do business and give customers a reason to come back and try you again.

Listening to the bad news

How can you let your customers know you want to hear from them, even if all they want to do is complain? How can you respond to your customers' complaints in a way that will help salvage or improve your business relationship with them? And, most importantly, how can you tell whether your customers really mean all that horrible stuff they said about you, your company, your parents, and your dog in their last e-mail?

Complaints are an unpleasant part of customer service, but they're an important part. Take them seriously. And remember that nine out of ten customers won't even bother to tell you they're upset.

Providing complaint mechanisms

So how can customers give you their opinions? Obviously, they can send you e-mails, and you should encourage them to do so. Set up a special e-mail address just for customer comments, compliments, and complaints, and put your friendliest customer service people in charge of monitoring the incoming messages. You can also provide forms on your Web site that customers can fill out.

Providing an online form enables customers to indicate how they would prefer to be contacted. For example, the form can ask for the customer's phone number, which enables your customer service reps to follow up by phone, for example.

Whatever you do, make sure customers know that you heard them. Enter customers' messages into a database and assign tracking numbers to them. Give those tracking numbers to customers via an automated e-mail, and encourage them to refer to the number if they have any additional comments or questions to add to their original message.

Tracking numbers give customers a sense that their message will be read by *somebody*. Just knowing that they will be heard in the faceless, voiceless world of e-commerce can be a powerful tool toward calming upset customers, giving you and your staff a chance to salvage the relationship.

Providing an appropriate response

After you receive a customer's complaint, you have to do something about it. Start by sending an automated message that confirms your receipt of the customer's message. Give the customer some idea of how long it will be before someone will contact him or her to follow up on the message. You may also want to refer customers to an online survey, if you have one, that they can complete to express their opinion of your company.

From there, of course, your response depends on the message. You can resolve some complaints by offering customers an incentive, such as a coupon, to compensate them for an inconvenience they experienced (make sure your site supports the ability to award these types of incentives). Other responses may require a personal follow-up from a customer support representative.

Try to follow up via phone when possible to add a personal touch. That alone can often help smooth things out.

Taking it all in stride

We tend to take for granted the subtle interactions that make society livable. Customer complaints at bricks-and-mortar stores are a great example of how those interactions keep us all sane. Customers who have a bad experience may get upset and drive angrily to the store, prepared to give somebody a good screaming. On the way, of course, they may calm down a bit and act more politely when they actually arrive.

Online customers, unfortunately, can instantly fire off a flaming-hot e-mail before they have time to cool down. The result is that customer complaints from online customers can be especially vicious.

When your customer service reps read these e-mails, they probably can picture the customers standing in front of them, screaming the words in their e-mail at the top of their lungs, eyes bulging and hands gesticulating wildly. Angry e-mails can make the most hardened customer service representatives defensive, and it's easy for them to respond in kind or to just ignore the e-mail completely.

Ask your customer service reps to think about what the person may have written a few hours later, after his or her initial wave of anger passed. Also remind them that most customers aren't Pulitzer Prize winners, and their writing style or use of language may not accurately convey their feelings — in other words, things may come off a lot worse in the e-mail than they actually are. Remind your customer service representatives that they must be patient and respond as politely to customers as possible. Have them call customers on the phone rather than send an e-mail if they can — people tend to be more polite when they're talking to a real person than they might be to a faceless corporation that they're sending an e-mail to.

Online customers are much more likely to issue complaints than other types of customers. After all, firing off an e-mail is much easier than finding postage for a comment card or driving to the nearest store to complain in person. So don't be overwhelmed by the volume of e-mail complaints your company may receive — that comes with the territory.

Adjusting your site based on complaint patterns

After you start receiving complaints (and hopefully some compliments), you can analyze them to find out where your site — and your business — needs to improve.

Remember, if one customer complains, bunches more are probably thinking the same thing and just not bothering to let you know. So if you get several complaints about a particular subject, assume that you have a pattern that needs to be fixed.

Now that you know what customers are complaining about, you have to fix those problems. If it isn't immediately clear how to fix a problem, try asking your customers.

Conduct an online survey. You can either have your programmers develop your own survey or use a third-party survey firm, such as WebSurveyor (www.websurveyor.com), to conduct the survey. Make sure that you invite the customers who originally complained to participate in the survey, demonstrating that you took their complaints seriously and are doing something about it.

Because the results of this survey will affect the growth and operation of your company, make sure that it's scientific. You don't want a single customer to submit a million survey entries and skew the results. Using a third-party research firm to conduct the survey can help; those folks have the experience and knowledge to keep things on the level.

Keeping customers informed of the changes

After you make changes to your site or business to correct or improve conditions that were causing customer complaints, make sure you let your customers know that you found a situation that was causing some problems and you've taken steps to make things better. Thank your customers for their feedback, which brought the situation to your attention and resulted in the changes.

This type of communication has several benefits:

- ✔ You show customers that you're listening to them.
- ✔ You show customers who may have gone off to your competitors that your site has improved, encouraging them to try you again.
- ✔ You show customers that they can have an impact on your business, giving them a sense of ownership.
- ✔ You keep in touch with your customers outside of normal marketing and promotional contacts.

Making customers feel understood, valuable, and appreciated will keep them coming back for more.

Chapter 12

Cashing In: Processing and Fulfilling Online Transactions

• •

In This Chapter

▶ Enabling customers to make purchases

▶ Understanding online payment systems

▶ Collecting payments online

▶ Avoiding payment pitfalls

• •

Shopping on the Internet is a very different experience than shopping in a store or ordering by phone. Online shoppers hide in anonymity behind their monitors, knowing that they can close their browsers at any time to end a transaction.

Every e-commerce enterprise that sells to consumers faces a universal challenge: making sure that every shopper stays online long enough to select one (or many) of the business' wares. Additionally, shoppers need to go through the entire sales transaction process, which entails completing the order and making payment arrangements (usually by credit card) — all without looking anyone in the eye. Here's a list of the things that you can do to avoid clogging up the purchasing process:

✔ You must handle customers' payments reliably and securely. Even the perception that a business doesn't take security seriously can turn consumers off in the length of time it takes them to click their collective mice. (Uh, mouses? Whatever.)

✔ If you offer customers the option of storing their account and credit card information for future purchases, you need to back up that promise with security measures that can do the job.

✔ Make sure that your business receives payment for orders.

This chapter shows you how to close sales safely and securely, and fulfill customer orders efficiently. You can find out more about buying and selling between business partners in Chapters 17 and 19.

Empowering Your Customers

Most shoppers look for a way to avoid making the final commitment of buying because they are cautious of sending personal information across the Internet. Ironically enough, even the most cautious shoppers use the Internet for the convenience it provides. A well-designed Web site enables customers to make purchases as easily and safely as possible. By providing a variety of payment options and assuring customers that the system is secure, you can empower customers to make the final commitment to buy.

A well-designed site can make buying so easy that consumers don't bother second-guessing themselves. A few short clicks, and the order is on its way.

In order to finalize the sale, you must

> ✔ **Provide as many options for receiving and processing payments as you can.** When you go to a bricks-and-mortar store, you can pay with cash, a debit card, a credit card, a check, or sometimes even with terms. Businesses with Web sites need to be able to offer similar options.

> ✔ **Assure customers that transactions on your Web site are secure.** Transferring checking account or credit card numbers over the Internet (which is about as public a place as you can find besides an airport restroom) poses real security risks. You must take steps to ensure that your customers' data is transmitted securely. You must also assure customers that purchasing through their Web browsers is safe.

> ✔ **Offer multiple delivery options.** Many people who shop online are too busy to go to a bricks-and-mortar store and use the Internet for convenience. But if they have to wait 10 to 15 days for their orders to arrive, much of the convenience of Internet shopping is lost. Moreover, most customers are not willing to pay $14.95 for overnight delivery of a $7.99 book. You can address these issues by providing customers with a range of options so that they can choose an acceptable price/delivery time option.

> ✔ **Make it as easy as possible to check out.** Most people are impatient. Internet shoppers tend to be very impatient. They often will not wait for sites that are slow or require too many steps to finalize a purchase. You can make the checkout process easier by using technologies such as electronic wallets or Microsoft's new Passport services. (See "Accepting digital wallets," later in this chapter, for more on electronic wallets.)

Opening the door for easier commerce

eBay's sales have been as high as $4 billion a year. But until it teamed up with Wells Fargo, the only ways that winning bidders could pay sellers directly was by check or money order. Using plastic wasn't an option. (How many people do you know who have credit card machines in their homes?) To make payments easier and safer for everyone, eBay cut a deal with Wells Fargo Bank. Under the agreement, Wells Fargo accepts credit card and personal information from winning bidders, and then credits the sellers' checking accounts for the same amount.

This relationship helps sellers close more deals (which ensures that eBay gets its cut) and accelerates the process of buying and selling.

eBay bidders can use PayPal to speed up payment. PayPal ensures that the funds are available from the buyer online, and the seller is guaranteed to receive the funds from the bidder. This type of payment technology facilitates _peer-to-peer (P2P)_ commerce. P2P is selling between two parties, facilitated through a Web site, like eBay.

Cashing In with Credit Cards

Most people use credit cards to pay for Internet purchases. And many people avoid making Internet purchases for fear of having their credit card numbers stolen (but, interestingly enough, they will let a stranger leave the room, credit card in hand, and think nothing of it). If you want their patronage, you must allay their fears.

If you limit yourself to accepting only credit cards as payment, you will turn people away at the door. By offering more choices and more options, which we discuss in the next few sections, you remove obstacles and encourage customers to make the final commitment and complete their order.

Accepting credit card payments

Credit cards offer a fast, convenient way to do business over the Web. The credit card company protects the consumer from fraud, and you receive guarantee of timely payment for goods delivered or services rendered. The small transaction fee charged by your financial institution is a small price to pay.

How you process credit card information depends on your business model. Whether you process interactively, in batches, or manually depends on how fast your site needs to react to clients' requests.

Interactive, online processing

If you want to process credit card payments quickly, process them interactively online. Program your site to collect credit card data and immediately send that data to a *service bureau.* Service bureaus deal in secure electronic transactions with banks, collecting individual transactions from a myriad of merchants and sending them in batches for the banks to process. Service bureaus return an approval or rejection of the transaction, and then return an approval code to the site.

Here are some of the advantages and disadvantages of interactive, online processing:

✔ Only orders with approved credit are fully processed.

✔ You don't have to store credit card numbers, which reduces security risks.

✔ An approval or rejection of the credit card is returned interactively, so if the transaction is denied, the customer can immediately correct data entry errors or change to an alternate form of payment.

✔ You have to pay these fees:

- • Monthly maintenance fees

- • Transaction fees, a fixed fee for each transaction processed

- • A discount rate, which is a percentage of the total transaction

These fees vary greatly from one provider to another; so do your homework to find the best deal.

✔ Processing can take time and make the purchase to appear to hang, causing buyers to abandon the transaction.

Batch processing credit card confirmations

You don't have to make your customers wait while a group of computers gets together to decide whether to approve a purchase. You can capture the data and tell the customer that you will send out an order confirmation after you get an approval. Every so often (once every ten minutes, once an hour, once a day — it depends on the volume), a group of transactions are processed together in a batch.

Here are some of the pros and cons to batch processing:

✔ The fees may be lower.

✔ You can avoid paying a service bureau by submitting transactions through your own merchant account.

✔ Because you don't approve credit card transactions online, you don't have to check inventory online.

✔ The customer does not need to wait for the charge request to be processed.

✔ You have to store the credit card data. If the security of that data is compromised, your business will be held liable.

✔ You lose interaction with the customer. You can't correct things such as mistyped credit card data. And if a credit card is rejected, the customer may elect to cancel the order rather than to choose an alternate payment.

Manually processing credit card transactions

As consultants, we dealt with a man in San Francisco who had opened a storefront on the Internet for his wife. She received orders via e-mail and processed the credit card payments manually. She spent four to five hours a day processing orders and preparing shipments. Her business grossed over $250,000 a year. Although manual processing won't get you on the Fortune 500 list, it's not a bad place to begin.

Here are some of the advantages and disadvantages of processing credit card payments manually:

✔ No learning curve — it's how you process credit card orders today.

✔ Freedom from complex, expensive technology.

✔ Integration with your existing business processes.

✔ You have an employee doing a very repetitive, mundane task.

✔ Manual processes are not always performed on time.

✔ You have the possibility of introducing errors as the data is re-keyed.

If your company already has a process in place that handles credit card orders internally, the most efficient solution may be to continue the process. When you get to the point that you're spending too much time manually processing cards, you may be able to justify putting an automated process in place.

Storing credit card data

One of the more critical decisions you must make is whether or not to store credit card information as part of a customer's profile. Storing the data can make shopping much more convenient for repeat customers. After the credit card number is stored initially, your Web site can automatically retrieve it along with the shopper's profile. When items are backordered, you can create distinct transactions for each shipment.

The obvious risk of storing credit card data is the possibility that your security could be breached. Web site security systems are favorite targets for international hackers. They breach the system undetected and download credit card information. For example, in December 2000, Egghead.com's Web site was breached, and over 3 million credit card numbers were stolen. Egghead had to inform those customers that their credit cards were at risk. You need to balance the risk against the convenience of storing that data. As a general rule, we recommend not storing credit card data.

Of course, most companies store credit card data securely. Understanding that you are a target and exercising due diligence to protect your customers' data may well determine your success.

The International Information Systems Security Certification Consortium provides training and certification for professionals who have proven their ability at detecting and preventing cybertheft and intrusion. You can also hire consultants, such as @stake (www.atstake.com), to review your site and make specific recommendations on how to keep your data safe.

Of course, you can also mitigate the risk by not storing credit card data. After a credit card transaction has been approved, all you need is the approval number. Thieves can't steal a credit card number from you if you don't have it.

Preventing credit card fraud

When customers make a purchase at a bricks-and-mortar store, they have to hand their credit card to a human who can look them in the eye, check their signature, and ask for additional identification, if necessary. You don't have that luxury over the Internet. So you need to collect enough information to be confident that person using the credit card is actually the cardholder.

About 1 out of every 100 purchases made with a credit card in the flesh is fraudulent, and estimates on Internet credit card fraud run as high as 10 in every 100 purchases.

One of the most common ways to detect fraud is the address verification system. You require customers to enter their name and address exactly as it appears on the credit card bill. If the information does not match the data stored by the credit card provider, you can reject the order or ask for additional information. The address verification system can help prevent fraud, but it can also annoy shoppers who do not have immediate access to that data (not to mention the ones who, like us, are spelling-challenged). Remember, most merchant accounts hold you 100 percent liable for submitting fraudulent information and may charge you a fee to boot.

You can purchase software that helps verify credit card transactions. This software can check the customer's e-mail address (free e-mail addresses and addresses from suspect domains are often questionable), the size and type of order (large orders for multiple camcorders could be suspicious), and the time of day the order was placed (believe it or not, criminals often order late at night, their local time). eFalcon from HCN Software (www.efalcon.com) or programs from VerifyFraud.com (www.verifyfraud.com) automate the process of verifying the validity of credit cards.

Using credit-card-processing software

A wide variety of commercial off-the-shelf products are available for processing credit card data. To use the software, you need to establish a merchant account with a service bureau. You may use an existing merchant account, if your current bureau handles online payment processing. Then you can choose software that conforms to the specifications of your service bureau.

Credit card processing consists of several steps, as shown in Figure 12-1:

1. The consumer submits his or her credit card number to you.

2. Your credit card software grabs the credit card information, checks to make certain that the card number, expiration date, and, optionally, the billing address, are all there (no sense sending a request for a card that expired two months ago). The software then sends the information to the service bureau.

3. The service bureau looks over the credit card information and then submits the transaction request to the issuing institution over a secure network.

4. The issuing institution forwards either an approval or denial of the transaction back to the service bureau.

5. The service bureau forwards the approval or denial to the your credit card processing software.

6. The software informs the consumer of the success or failure of the transaction.

7. Approved transactions are processed in batches. Payments are forwarded to your bank within 48 to 72 hours of accepting the transaction.

The credit card software that you buy must work with the service bureau you use. Credit card software, such as Payflo Pro from VeriSign (www.verisign.com), has become more flexible and easier to incorporate into your site. Work with your financial folks and your programmers to find the right combination of a service bureau and software to take the risk and the pain out of the credit card approval process.

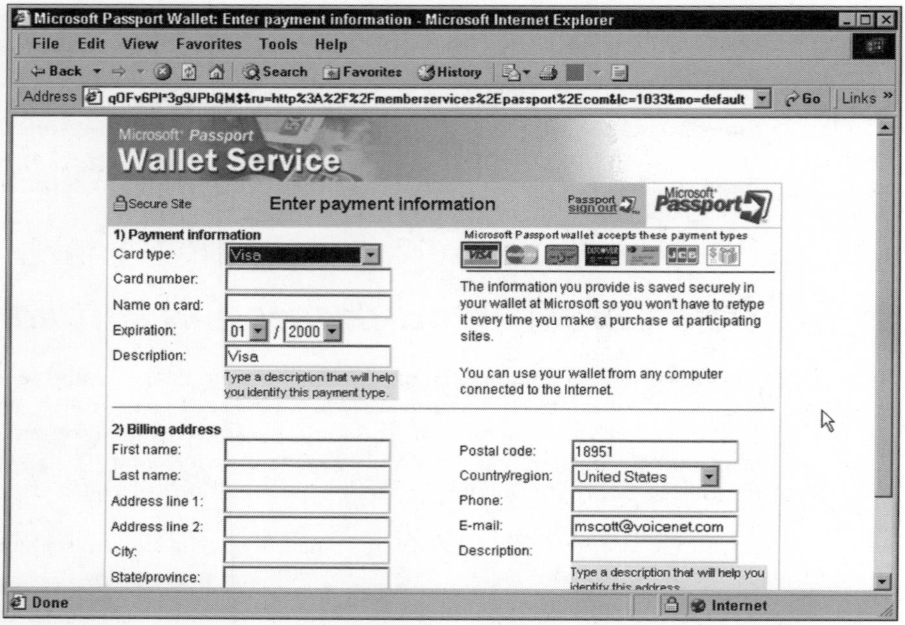

Figure 12-1:
Processing
credit cards
from Web
site.

Try before you buy. Many software vendors will provide sample code that you can try on your site before you commit to purchasing it. You want to make sure that the software collects and formats the data your processor needs and integrates into your site correctly. Do not choose the software until you've decided how you'll process the credit card payment data.

Checking Out with Checks

Yep, you can accept checks over the Internet. Some consumers feel more comfortable paying with a check. Businesses may also feel more comfortable paying with a piece of paper; checks fit most existing business models, leaving neat paper trails behind. Not everybody has a credit card (or one that isn't maxed out). And checks are another option you can add to encourage people to buy over the Internet.

Accepting electronic checks

Some service bureaus process checks by using the routing and account numbers found on the bottom of the check. Customers enter these numbers from the check into a form on your site (they don't even need to mail it in). You forward the check information to the service bureau. The service bureau then processes the payment one of two ways:

✔ **By creating a paper document, similar to a counter check, and depositing it in the traditional manner.** This option provides a paper trail. The check is generic, but it works just the same way as the checks in the customer's checkbook. Customers feel more comfortable because they receive a canceled check with their bank statement.

✔ **By initiating an *electronic funds transfer* (EFT).** Electronic fund transfers are automatic deductions from a checking or savings account. They don't involve checks, but they do appear on the customer's bank statement. Because EFTs can be processed only if sufficient funds are in the account, customers can't incur insufficient fund charges or returned check fees.

Electronic funds transfers are ideally suited for recurring charges, such as monthly subscription fees.

Using the postal service: The check is in the mail

Not everything is instantaneous in the world of e-commerce. You can accept an online order and allow the customer to mail in a check as payment. Some Web sites create an online order form that the customer can print out and return with a check. Although we do not advocate accepting checks by mail as the primary form of payment, this may be a good option for customers who are reluctant to send account information through the Internet.

You do need to consider a few factors before deciding to offer this payment method, however. In a world of automated systems and accelerated delivery cycles, holding orders until you receive the payment by mail may be difficult to accommodate. This option works best for organizations that are accustomed to waiting for payment to fulfill orders, such as mail-order firms or organizations that offer their customers terms.

Accepting Paper Orders

Your site can enable customers to place paper orders. Customers fill out the order form on their computer, and then print it out and mail it in. The computer helps them fill out the order form correctly and can automatically calculate taxes, shipping and handling fees, and order totals. Some people feel more comfortable submitting a paper order than an electronic order.

The downside to accepting paper orders is losing the automation advantages of electronic commerce. But if you're already handling paper-based orders, this shouldn't be a problem for you.

Of course, you can use your technology to make the process simpler for customers. Here's how: Customers go to your Web site and enter the products that they want to purchase. The Web site then automatically generates an order form that includes all the critical model numbers, quantities, prices, and so on, which helps reduce order errors. After customers print out their order form, they can deliver it to you several different ways:

- **By e-mail:** Customers can e-mail the form to your company. If customers e-mail a form that was created on your site, you can automatically process this form by using special software.

- **By fax:** You can create a fax-friendly form. Customers can print the form to the fax software on their computer or print it out on paper and then fax it in conventionally.

- **By mail:** When all else fails, let customers mail in their order forms. They can print out a form from your Web site, fold it up, and stuff it in an envelope. People who are leery of electronic payments may find this a more attractive alternative, even though it's slower and decidedly low-tech.

Taking Advantage of Other Payment Avenues

Don't limit yourself to payment systems used in the bricks-and-mortar world. E-commerce opens the door for alternative payment methods you may never have considered.

Setting up shopping cart transactions

Most e-commerce systems allow customers to build an order with an electronic *shopping cart*. A shopping cart is a list of the items they want to buy. Customers can add items to or delete items from the cart, as well as update quantities. They can even leave the cart and come back to the site later to complete their purchase. The cart keeps track of the order total, and usually calculates taxes, shipping, and handling fees. To complete the transaction, all you need to do is collect the amount of money that the shopping cart requires.

Many ASPs (we cover ours by covering them in Chapter 14) offer shopping cart transactions as part of their service offering, often without charging you additional fees (beyond those of processing the payment). The ASP provides template-based pages that allow you to integrate its online payment system into your site. This arrangement gives you the ability to accept online payments without the hassle of setting up the systems yourself.

Getting down to the nitty-gritty: Micropayments

Micropayments are small (less than $1) payments that subsidize the cost of Web content. At least, that's how they began. Because the cost of processing individual transactions can be very high, a variety of vendors have developed technology that collects a small fee (usually several pennies) each time a person visits the site. The user keeps a prepaid account at the vendor and pays for all visits once a month. The provider then pays your site the fees due monthly. Neither you nor your customer needs to deal with individual transaction fees.

The consumer gets an electronic wallet from the micropayment software vendor in order to establish an account with that vendor (see "Accepting digital wallets," later in this chapter). Micropayment accounts often draw funds automatically from credit cards. CyberCash (www.cybercash.com), a leading online payment software vendor, along with IBM and many others, provide micropayment systems.

Although micropayments are supported by a variety of vendors, the technology has lost much of its momentum. Because so much content on the Internet is free, most consumers resist the concept of paying for access to content. And because each vendor's technology is proprietary, consumers need the correct brand of wallet to be able to use the site.

Using a secure commerce server

When you do business with other businesses, it may be worthwhile to establish more secure systems that allow orders to pass through more quickly. If you are a supplier and provide large-volume orders to other manufacturers, for example, you can establish virtual private networks and extranets with your customers. We cover these private, secure networks in Chapter 13.

Business-to-business (B2B) orders are often much larger than business-to-consumer (B2C) orders. The systems that handle B2B orders must verify that the individuals placing the orders have the proper authorization to do so. Frequently, software must be designed to allow for your customers' custom authorization processes. By helping your customers manage their purchase request systems, you can save money for your customers as well as for your business. Because payments are made through credit, your order-entry systems must integrate with your accounting system.

Using supply chain management and business-to-business integration systems offers tremendous advantages, such as reducing costs, enabling you to respond quickly to customer requests, and reducing or eliminating paperwork errors. To create these types of systems, you and your customers must find a way to get your systems to share information. Unfortunately, no universal system has been created for exchanging this type of information from one system to another. It's not that system vendors haven't tried; they just can't agree on common formats. Several common formats have met with moderate success, but to make this work, you really need to roll up your sleeves and work things out with your customers.

Electronic Data Interchange (EDI) is one of the most successful attempts at this type of systems integration. It is commonly used in transferring financial data and large purchase orders. However, setting up EDI is typically difficult and expensive. Extensible Markup Language (XML) is being promoted as a low(er) cost alternative to EDI. You can find out more about EDI and XML in Chapter 13.

Why Securing Communication Is Essential to Payment Processing

After you establish a relationship with customers, they expect you to protect their privacy. If you violate that trust, the results can be devastating to your business. Companies such as Western Union, which had 16,000 credit card numbers stolen in 1999, have had to learn the hard way how important it is to secure your networks and preserve the privacy of your customers.

Ensuring safe communications

To secure your network, you need to protect the flow of information between you and your customer. You can do that with encryption. *Encryption* is the process of encoding or scrambling data. You set up a secret code with your customer's browser that allows it to scramble the data in a way that only you can decode it. This system is called *public/private key encryption*. A variety of technologies enable you to provide encryption security through networks.

Why do you need to encrypt data on the Internet? Data passed through the public Internet goes from one network to another. The computers on the intermediate networks ignore packets of data that are not addressed to them and simply forward them to their intended destination. But the data is a lot like a postcard in that anyone who wants to can just pick it up and read it. Encryption puts the data in code so that even if someone else reads the data, it doesn't make much sense. You can take security to an even higher level by using virtual private network technology, which places the data in a digital envelope and makes it even more difficult to read.

Getting to know SSL (Secure Sockets Layer)

The technology for the encryption of data is readily available. The most common form is Secure Sockets Layer (SSL). When a customer visits your site, your server sends a public certificate to his or her browser. The certificate contains a method of encrypting data, which is a mathematical formula that converts the data into what appears to be nonsense. After the code is applied, only the data on the server can decode it.

Well, at least that was the theory. After the SSL programs were published, hackers immediately started trying to break them. By using supercomputers or networks of individual PCs, hackers can, by brute force, crack SSL security. But to do so takes a lot of time and energy.

You can make it harder for hackers to break into your system by increasing the size of your *key*. The key is the magic number used to decrypt the coded text. The more bits you have in your key, the harder it is to break. The original key length was 40 bits (due the United States' restrictions on exporting encryption technology). Most current browsers allow you to use keys up to 128 bits. If you are a U.S. company and deal with customers internationally, however, you may need to use smaller keys to comply with U.S. laws.

Of course, encryption isn't free (what is?). Your site's computer will use more CPU cycles and take about 10 percent longer to encrypt and decrypt SSL network packets than unencrypted packets. Because of the added cost, most sites encrypt only sensitive data, such as payment information.

If you've ever been to a Web site that begins with `https`, you have used SSL. The *s* tells savvy shoppers that their payments will travel across the Internet in a secure, encrypted manner.

Understanding server certificates

Any commercial-grade Web server allows you to use SSL. For a public site, you need to obtain an *X.509 certificate*. This digital certificate indicates that a third-party certificate authority, such as VeriSign (`www.verisign.com`), has determined that you are a legitimate business (as opposed to a cyberpunk hacker looking to steal what he or she can). When you pass your public key to the customer, that digital signature goes with it.

X.509 certificates, established by the International Telecommunication Union (ITU), are a standard means of passing public key information to customers. This standard is the basis of encryption for Secure Electronic Transactions, discussed in the next section.

You need a unique certificate for each server. Each certificate uses data that is specific to that server, such as its Internet name and network card address. This information helps prevent hackers from impersonating your site. (When you impersonate one computer to another, you are said to be *spoofing*.)

Setting up Secure Electronic Transactions

Visa, MasterCard, and IBM have teamed together (with Microsoft, VeriSign, and a host of others) to develop an even more secure system. Secure Electronic Transactions (SETs) require consumers to have their own digital certificate. Similar to customers having a credit card in their possession when they make a purchase in a store, this certificate acts as proof that they are who they say they are when they make a purchase online; it's a digital signature.

If you can verify who your customer is, you can do business with that customer more securely. You don't need to worry about verifying his or her identity, because the digital signature does that for you. It provides a basis for non-repudiated transactions, just as if the customer had provided a check. SET even allows you to accept the customer's digital certificate in lieu of his or her actual account information so you don't need to pass his or her sensitive credit card information through the Internet.

SET also protects the consumer. The SET software checks the credentials and certificates of the vendor before it passes the digital certificate. This verification prevents vendors from spoofing consumers into surrendering their account information.

A digital wallet manages the consumer's SET certificate (see "Accepting digital wallets," later in this chapter). To obtain a certificate, consumers must download and install the software. After they register their credit card information, they electronically obtain a certificate from the financial institution that issued the credit card. From that point on, secure credit card transactions require little more than two mouse clicks.

To make this process work, however, customers must obtain digital certificates. And right now, this technology has been slow to catch on. Much of the attraction of the Internet is anonymity, and obtaining a certificate that identifies them has been unattractive to many consumers. SET transactions will offer many advantages when consumer adoption becomes prevalent.

Utilizing private networks

When you link your systems directly to vendors, suppliers, and customers, you may want to use *private networks*. These connections prevent electronic eavesdropping and can provide a much greater level of security. Consider private networks for these areas:

- ✔ Connections to suppliers
- ✔ Connections to financial institutions and credit card processors
- ✔ Connections with other members of your organization (remote warehouses, offices, and so on)

CASE STUDY

Being paranoid is good when it comes to data security

CD Universe (www.cduniverse.com) knows about the dangers of having critical information stolen. In January 2000, a hacker penetrated the security of the online music provider and stole 300,000 credit card numbers. To avoid this type of problem with your online business, you must do these things to protect your sensitive data:

✔ Perform thorough security evaluations of your site. Try to have this done by a third party who has no vested interest in anything other than finding security holes in your site.

✔ Audit access to anything that holds or stores sensitive data.

✔ Prepare a plan to follow if your data is compromised. Moving quickly and decisively can determine how well your organization weathers the storm.

You have several options for setting up private networks, including dial-in connections, leased lines, and virtual private networks that create private encrypted networks within the public Internet (see Chapter 13 for more details). When you choose a network, you must weigh cost versus risk.

Ensuring payment information security

In addition to securing network traffic, you need to secure the data you keep on your servers. You can make the shopping experience more convenient for your customers by storing their credit card and checking account numbers at your site. After the information is initially transmitted, customers do not need to reenter it when they want to make another purchase.

The risk that you take on by offering this convenience is the potential loss of that data to hackers or disgruntled employees. Hackers penetrate commercial sites, sometimes to extort money, sometimes just to prove that they can. Disgruntled employees, who often have access to the data to perform their jobs, can also abscond with this sensitive data. So consider whether the convenience of storing credit card information is worth the risk of losing that data.

TIP

Most industrial-grade databases (Oracle, Microsoft, Sybase, Informix, and so on) are designed to provide high levels of security. Your development staff must use those tools to keep your data safe. All too often, security is added as an afterthought, rather than integrated into the product from the beginning.

If you perform online validation of account payment information, you do not need to store credit card numbers. Think about it; how many stores or restaurants have customers' credit card numbers on file? It is typically safer not to store data if you don't have to.

Delivering the Goods

After you know what your customer wants, you need to deliver the order. It's important to offer a variety delivery options so your customers can decide how quickly they want their order and how much they're willing to pay.

At a minimum, you should provide standard ground and overnight shipping, which assumes your items can be shipped though services such as UPS. Most customers expect to pay for the shipping costs, but deciding how much to charge for shipping presents some interesting challenges and some unique opportunities.

Calculating shipping costs

Shipping costs depend on a complex web of parameters, such as package size, package weight, distance, and speed. It is not always easy to determine in advance what it will cost to ship goods, but here are a variety of methods you can use:

✓ **Standardized shipping costs:** Many Web sites assign a flat charge for shipping. This fee can be based either on the maximum shipping charge or the average shipping charge (if you can reliably determine that figure). Shipping costs add to the customer's overall cost, so setting them at the right level may make the difference between the customer buying your product or going elsewhere.

✓ **Shipping cost per item:** Many sites assign a different shipping cost to each item, based on the size, shape, and weight of the item. The shipping cost can be added to the database and easily retrieved.

Remember, shipping costs change periodically. So make sure that the system you use to calculate shipping charges enables you to make simple adjustments for price changes.

✓ **Dynamic calculation of shipping charges:** Because shipping companies can calculate a different price for each package that you ship, so can you. By placing weight data into your computer system for each package, and using a little software slight of hand, you can determine what the actual shipping price will be. By calculating the shipping costs yourself, you can pass the exact costs on to the customer. This approach requires you to enter a lot of shipping charge data, so be prepared to keep up.

✔ **Ship it now, bill later:** Particularly in business-to-business transactions, you may not need to calculate the shipping charges upfront. You can put together the order, ship it, and just add the shipping to the customer's invoice. If you *drop ship* from your vendors, this may be your only realistic option.

If you drop ship a package, you are asking your supplier to ship the item directly to your client.

✔ **Free shipping:** Depending on how you price your goods, offering free shipping may be a good choice. You can market it as a competitive advantage (as long as your overall price is competitive). Offering free shipping is another good choice if you drop ship goods from your suppliers to your customers.

Don't forget that the United States Postal Service delivers small parcels. It has made great gains in tracking capabilities and offers low shipping costs. The postal service may add effective alternatives to your customer's menu of shipping options.

So where is my order, anyway?

If just putting an order into the hands of a shipping company meant you were done with the order, your life would be sooo much simpler. Unfortunately, you need to track the order until it reaches your customer. And most e-commerce sites provide tracking information to customers.

Your site should track the process of an order from shipping through delivery to the customer. If you ship merchandise from your existing stock, you simply note when the order was shipped. If you build to order or need to use your supply chain to assemble an order, you need to enable your customer to stay in touch with the progress of the order.

After the shipper has the order, both you and your customer will want to know where it is. Fortunately, most of the larger commercial delivery services now offer Web-based shipment tracking. Most of these services automatically assign a tracking number to a shipment as soon as they receive it. You can pass that number on to your customer so that he or she can track the shipment through the delivery service's Web site. Even the United States Postal Service enables you to track deliveries through the Web.

Dealing with backorders

Backorders are a tricky business, both from a billing and shipping standpoint. You can deal with backorders several different ways, so select the one that will best fit your business model:

- ✔ **Always take the order.** You can always find a way to fill it. The advantage is that you don't surrender any potential sales. The risks are that you'll irritate customers when they don't receive their orders fast enough and have to pay extra shipping costs for having two (or more) separate shipments. You can mitigate this charges by holding the entire order until it is complete.

- ✔ **Don't take orders for items you don't have.** You can use your Web site to let customers know what you have in stock and what you don't. If you do not take orders for things you don't have, you don't have to deal with backorders. The advantage is a much-simpler order tracking system. The downside is that you risk losing customers who go to find the product elsewhere. You can help mitigate this risk by offering to notify your customers as soon as you have the items in stock. You also need to keep an accurate inventory online (a daunting technical challenge on its own).

You have to determine your payment policy for backorders as well. Most firms do not charge customers for goods until they are shipped. With this policy, you can incur additional transaction charges, and you must store credit card data until all items are shipped.

Arranging for shipments

As long as you are performing a brisk trade, you will likely have daily shipments. This may mean that you're willing to commit to your customers when you will ship their orders. "Order by noon, and we will ship it today" can help motivate consumers to buy, but if you make that promise, you need to deliver on it.

Some businesses do not have shipments every day. Others may have to make special arrangements with trucking firms for delivery of larger items. Business-to-business sites are more likely to ship larger items and larger quantities.

The dream scenario is to automate this process. Many of the parcel companies provide software to help you track shipping costs and integrate them into your accounting system. And some third-party companies, such as Pitney Bowes, will integrate software with scales and postage metering equipment.

If you have implemented supply-chain enterprise software, you should integrate your shipping process with this software as well. You can eliminate a great deal of time, errors, and paperwork by properly integrating these systems.

You can spend a fortune integrating shipping information and pricing into your system. It makes little sense to spend $100,000 to integrate shipping so that you can avoid hiring a $30,000-a-year shipping clerk. Consider the return on investment when making these decisions.

Order cancellations

If you don't ship an order the minute the customer places it, or even if you do, the customer may want to cancel his or her order. It's important to have clear policies about handling order cancellations so that your staff knows what to do and your customers know what to expect.

Keeping the Checkout Process Simple

When customers finally decide to buy something on the Internet, they have to give up their anonymity. They have to provide personal information such as their home address, phone number, credit card information, and so on. Many people are apprehensive about giving out personal information over the Internet, so a well-designed site will help them through the process.

Collecting customer information

For you to deal with customers, you eventually need to know who they are or gather some minimal data about them (such as where they want the merchandise to go). At one of three points, you will need customers to introduce themselves to your system:

- ✔ **When customers enter your site.** In this scenario, you ask customers to log in as soon as they enter the site. This will scare some people away, but your marketing department will be thrilled to receive the tracking information (see Chapter 15). You can also store the customer's last shopping cart and help him or her check out quickly.

- ✔ **When customers create shopping carts.** This scenario is our personal favorite. You let customers browse through your wares anonymously. You allow your advertising and sales people to entice them into putting together an order. But in order to build that shopping cart, customers need to identify themselves by logging in. Shopping carts are mapped to individual users so that when they log in again, you can ask them if they want their last shopping cart. You separate the process of providing basic user information from the process of purchasing, but you allow customers to do anonymous window-shopping before they start building a cart.

- ✔ **When customers place an order.** In this scenario, you don't need to know any details about your customers until they place an order. They can remain anonymous until they actually want to transact business. You collect all the necessary data — name, address, credit card info, and so on — right at the end of the checkout process. You don't need customers to log in, and you don't need to keep customer profiles. You lose valuable marketing information, but you eliminate running the risk of losing sensitive customer data.

Ensuring a fast response time

When customers check out, they want the process to go quickly. If you are interactively processing their payment information, your site must be responsive because customers will be irritated if they have to wait two or three minutes while you verify their payment information. They may abandon the site and believe they have abandoned their order. You may complete the order processing, not knowing that the customer is gone. The customer thinks that the order was never placed, and you fulfill the order by shipping the products.

To help avoid this problem, always send order confirmations to customers via e-mail. An order confirmation via e-mail is not a replacement for a page that displays an order confirmation immediately. You send out this e-mail after an order has been placed so you can reiterate all the details of the customer's order, such as the total order price, shipping method, and tracking information.

You may want to confirm all orders through e-mail, rather than by processing them online. Although you lose interactivity with the customer, you don't have to worry about leaving the customer waiting. In this scenario, you need to store the customer's payment information, at least temporarily. After the customer places the order, you can put up a page quickly that gives the customer an order number. Then you can check inventory, credit card approval, and other factors in a batch process offline. If you encounter a problem with the order, e-mail the customer and get him or her to come back to the site and answer any questions you may have.

 You should also be monitoring response times. If your servers begin to slow down, it will impact your customer relationships. Online performance monitoring and baseline performance measurements will keep you informed about the condition of your site.

Accepting digital wallets

Digital wallet technology was developed to help facilitate the checkout process. Digital wallets enable consumers to store basic order information, such as their shipping and billing addresses and credit card data, in a small database as part of their Web browser.

You need to configure your checkout page to detect the wallet software. If it is there, the user is prompted to use the data stored in the wallet to answer the most common checkout questions.

Sensitive data, such as credit cards, are password-protected. Most wallets can store multiple addresses and multiple credit card numbers. A simple menu pops up and allows the consumer to send the data with just a click. And SET certificates are stored and administrated through the wallet.

So why doesn't everyone use this technology? Wallet software differs from browser to browser. Your wallet software must match the wallet software on the consumer's browser. The consumer must go through a process of installation and configuration, and many are reluctant to go through the process. The Microsoft wallet was a standard part of Internet Explorer 4.*x,* but Microsoft removed it from Internet Explorer 5.01. You can still get a wallet as of part of Microsoft's Passport services. Netscape also included a wallet in Communicator and Navigator 4.*x.* Other third-party payment-processing software companies, such as CyberCash (www.cybercash.com), also provide wallets.

If you incorporate wallet software in your site, you can automatically download the software to your client. Your site can determine if the consumer has the wallet software installed and offer to download it automatically if they do not. You can easily configure the site to handle payment with or without wallets so that you don't limit yourself to customers who have your wallet software.

Microsoft Passport (www.passport.com) provides client wallet services. Consumers who provide Passport with credit card information (see Figure 12-2) can check out quickly. Passport fills out most of the forms for the customer and communicates with the vendor's site quickly and securely. All you need to do is include the Passport payment software on your site.

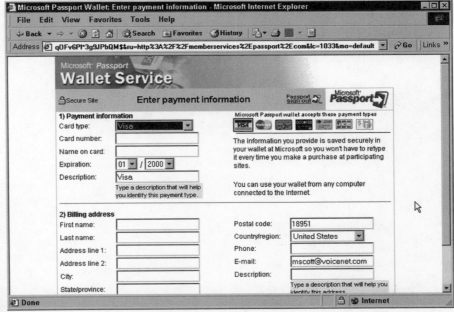

Figure 12-2:
Setting up an electronic wallet with Passport.

Chapter 13

Minding the Farm: Your Hardware and Network Infrastructure

*F*rom the outside, the Internet may appear like a dark, scary jungle filled with longhaired, cola-chugging geeks; greasy, slick consultants; and arcane software vendors. Take a look inside, however, and you discover a set of technologies that work together to deliver your content to customers when they ask for it. If you want to control the delivery of your e-commerce material, you must build a structure to deliver it.

Infrastructure refers to the various technologies that support your e-commerce business. These technologies include

▶ **Servers,** which run the software that makes the whole shebang work. (Servers are the large, expensive computers that lurk in some locked, wire-tangled room in the back of your office.)

▶ **Network connections,** which allow your servers to communicate with one another and with the world.

▶ **Firewalls,** which protect your servers from hackers and other unwanted access.

▶ **Network components** (such as routers and switches), which help make your network connections work properly.

C-3PO, 10-4, TCP/IP . . . hike!!

The Internet is a public network that's made up of millions of private networks. Just as people communicate with languages, the networks interact with each other by using compatible languages: *protocols*. Various protocols have been invented over the years to enable computers to communicate with one another for specific purposes, such as exchanging banking information or transferring files. TCP/IP — the Transmission Control Protocol/Internet Protocol — is one set of protocols designed to allow computers to communicate with one another. TCP/IP won the protocol bake-off for the following reasons:

✔ **Flexibility:** TCP/IP is actually an entire suite of protocols. Each has its own function, and the protocols can be mixed and matched to meet most needs. TCP/IP can handle many different tasks, including transferring files, sending Web pages, and so on.

✔ **Public domain:** Colleges developed TCP/IP for the government, and it is built on public specifications. Anyone can read the specification and write TCP/IP communication software. And everyone has. You can get TCP/IP for almost any computer platform, from mainframes to minicomputers to PC to Macs, and this protocol enables those computers to talk to each other. Sure, other protocols such as IPX/SPX and AppleTalk are easier to set up, but they are *proprietary* (that is, owned by specific companies). Such other protocols don't have the popularity or interoperability of good old TCP/IP.

✔ **No blame game:** TCP/IP is designed to be fault tolerant. If a portion of the global network becomes unavailable, TCP/IP is able to find new ways of reaching computers, thus effectively bypassing the affected portion of the network.

We don't have enough room in this chapter to explain all things Internet-related. But we can at least arm you with the knowledge you need to make an informed choice about the systems that you use for your e-commerce business. With this knowledge, you can customize your plan to keep those systems up and running, as well as determine how to plan for disaster and your company's (and your computer system's) eventual growth. We may not be able to give you all the answers you need (hey, give us a break, we're not perfect), but we can help you ask the right questions — and find the answers.

If your idea of technology is a pair of tin cans connected by a piece of string, or if you just want a speed course on the workings of networks, the Internet, intranets, real-time communication, and other ethereal-but-cool technologies that make e-commerce happen, check out Chapter 2. In Chapter 8, we cover the ins and outs of *domain* and *domain names,* the ethereal places online where businesses and other "spheres of knowledge" (ohhh, fancy) are located. Domain names are just like vanity license plates, only these names refer to a set of network addresses, not whether or not UR2FUNE.

Carving Out Your Own (Internet) Domain

Domains, in the Internet, provide the means for people to locate your computers. As we explain in Chapter 8, domains convert your name (www.mycompany.com) to a TCP/IP address (192.168.1.2). The TCP/IP address number allows information to move to that specific computer.

Founding the domain

InterNIC (www.internic.org), an organization run by Network Solutions, Inc., keeps a database that maps domain names to TCP/IP addresses and TCP/IP addresses back to names. This database keeps a list of Source of Authority (SOA) servers.

Source of Authority servers maintain the addresses for the computers in the domain. To find the support.mycompany.com server, a Web browser asks your DNS server for the address. The *domain name system (DNS)* works like a directory-assistance operator. You provide DNS with the name of a server, and you get back a TCP/IP address. People who set up TCP/IP on their computers have to provide the TCP/IP address for one or two DNS servers to keep the system running.

The DNS server queries the InterNIC servers, "Who is the SOA server for mycompany.com?" The InterNIC servers return a TCP/IP address. Your DNS server uses that address to contact the SOA server and gets the TCP/IP address for support.mycompany.com.

Have a headache yet? Sorry, but this is what you need to know. Someone has to keep a Source of Authority computer for you to maintain your domain. You can do this yourself or have your ISP take care of it. A number of companies allow you to register a domain name and then *park* the name on their domain name server. They act as the Source of Authority until you are ready to move your name. Most ISPs offer some version of domain name parking, often for free.

Be careful how much you pay for registering a domain name. Some companies charge hundreds or thousands of dollars to register a domain with InterNIC and hold it for you. InterNic, as of the time of this publication, charges $35 per year to register your domain. If somebody already owns the domain name you want, you may have to pay to buy the name from that person. But getting and maintaining a domain name from InterNIC costs very little. We discuss domain name registration strategies in Chapter 8.

Ruling the domain

After you secure your domain name, you need to decide who should maintain the SOA server. As we describe in the previous section, you can keep it in-house, or you can let your ISP handle it.

If you keep this maintenance in-house, you will need at least two domain name servers. All major versions of UNIX, Linux, and Microsoft Windows offer DNS server software. This software is often part of the operating system or available as open source software, so licensing is not usually costly (for a change). If you set up your own DNS server, you can add and remove servers at will. You can give servers aliases, or *canonical names*. Thus, the same server can be `mycompany.com` and `widgets.mycompany.com`. Aliases provide the greatest flexibility.

The downside is that if your DNS server goes down, no one can find you or your site. You simply vanish without a trace. That's why we recommend a minimum of two servers — you simply can't afford to disappear.

Alternatively, you can let your ISP handle your DNS. ISPs are in the business of keeping servers up and running. They usually have redundant Internet connections and multiple servers in place. Although you have to pay extra to have your ISP provide the server and you don't have the flexibility you have when your DNS is on your server, you don't have the hassles of maintaining the servers that keep your domain running.

I Know You — I Never Forget a Certificate

When a Web browser prepares to transmit a credit card number to a Web server, it likes to make sure that it knows who it's talking to. Ill-doers can set up a Web server that impersonates another company's Web server, acting as a kind of electronic con artist.

Using certificate technologies prevents this problem. When preparing to transmit private information, a customer's Web browser asks the Web server for a copy of its certificate. The certificate is a specially encoded piece of data that cannot be altered, and it contains the server's name along with information about the company or individual who owns and operates the server. If the information in the certificate matches the identity that the server claims, then everything's kosher. If not, the Web browser shows you a warning message.

Certificates are issued to companies and individuals by public certificate authorities such as VeriSign (`www.verisign.com`). When a browser receives a copy of a certificate, it checks with the authority that issued it to make sure the certificate is valid and that it hasn't expired. Web browsers are pre-configured with a list of several certificate authorities, which enables them to verify a certificate. In Figure 13-1, you can see the certificate authorities that Microsoft Internet Explorer is pre-configured to trust.

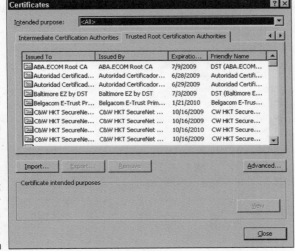

Figure 13-1:
Pre-configured
Internet
Explorer
certificate
authorities.

Certificates are used to verify identities on the Web. In addition to verifying the identify of a server, they can also be used to verify the identity of individuals, software programmers who create programs and place them on the Web, and companies and organizations.

An Oink, Oink Here, and an Oink, Oink There: Creating an E-Commerce Server Farm

Your e-commerce system runs on computers — typically powerful computers called *servers*. Servers are hooked up together, and to the Internet, using communications and networking equipment that allows them to communicate with one another. Most e-commerce companies use anywhere from a few servers to thousands of them. These large groups of servers are collectively referred to as a server farm.

The servers run an *operating system*, which is special software that makes all the pieces of hardware in the server work together efficiently. The operating system allows the computer to run application software, which actually performs some useful task, such as delivering Web pages across the Internet. Of course, the application software has to be written by someone and customized for your specific needs.

Be prepared to make a lot of decisions while you're hammering out the configuration of your farm and its components. Each choice you make affects all the other decisions. Your project architect is responsible for helping you make these decisions — which can be pretty complicated. But because this is *your* business, you should have an understanding of how your architect selects these different technologies.

Of course, if you decide to have some other business use its servers to host your Web site, such as an application service provider (ASP), then you won't have many decisions to make regarding server hardware or software — they'll all be made for you by the ASP. For more discussion on ASPs, see Chapter 10.

Deciding What You Need Your Servers to Do

Servers, the physical hardware that your e-commerce company runs on, are computers just like the desktop or laptop computers you probably already have — only more powerful. Each server has the responsibility of running some part of your e-commerce system — building Web pages, maintaining security, saving and retrieving data, running accounting and inventory applications, and so forth. Some servers can run software to accomplish more than one function. But sometimes, depending on the capability of the server and the volume at your Web site, you may need several servers working together to accomplish just one function. Don't fret — your systems architect and network administrator (as we discuss in Chapter 5) will keep you on top of your server hardware needs.

Although computers are multipurpose devices, capable of running many different pieces of application software at once, they have limitations. Just like when you get bogged down when you have too many things to concentrate on, servers perform best when they have a single application to work with. That's why e-commerce servers tend to be specialized, performing a single task. That task, of course, depends on the application software you install on the server.

Knowing your hardware

In the computer world, *hardware* refers to anything you can physically get your hands on. Servers are considered pieces of hardware. But servers are complex machines, comprising many smaller pieces of hardware all working together. These pieces include

✔ **Microprocessors:** The brains of any computer, the microprocessor — also called a central processing unit (CPU) or sometimes just processor — controls everything that happens in the server. Servers can contain multiple processors, which allows them to perform several tasks at the same time. Processors come in various speeds, with faster obviously being better — and more expensive.

✔ **Memory:** Formally known as random access memory (RAM), memory contains the information that the server is currently working with. Memory is measured in *bytes* — a *kilobyte* (K; about a thousand bytes) is roughly equivalent to a page of typed text. Most servers commonly have several *megabytes* (MB; a million bytes) or even *gigabytes* (GB; a billion bytes) of memory. Again, more is better — and more expensive.

✔ **Drives:** Drives, or disk drives, serve as long-term storage for computers. Unlike memory, which is fairly expensive and empties itself when the computer is turned off, drives are relatively inexpensive and continue to retain their information even when powered off. Drives come in different forms:

  • Compact disc, or CD drives, which can contain about 600MB of data

  • Digital versatile disc, or DVD drives, which can contain several gigabytes of data

  • Floppy disk drives, which can contain a megabyte or so of data

  • Hard drives, which can contain many gigabytes of data

  • Specialty drives, such as Zip drives, which can contain hundreds of megabytes of data

✔ **Network interfaces:** These components connect a server to a network, which in turn allows the server to communicate with other computers attached to the same network. The network interface is responsible for handling all the electrical wizardry necessary to make this communication possible. Some servers may contain multiple network interfaces, allowing them to communicate with several networks at the same time.

Work with your system architect to determine the structure of your farm by weighing the advantages and disadvantages of the different types available, and choosing one that best suits the needs of your business.

Understanding operating systems

A server is controlled by an *operating system,* which coordinates all the different pieces of hardware, making them work together efficiently and effectively.

An operating system (OS) is written to run on specific server hardware. For example, Microsoft Windows (www.microsoft.com) runs on computers built around Intel (www.intel.com) or Intel-compatible microprocessors. This is the hardware used to build most desktop and laptop computers, which is why Windows is so common. Other server operating systems include

- ✔ **OS/400:** This OS runs on IBM AS/400 computers. If you have an IBM AS/400, your choices are extremely limited.

- ✔ **Sun Solaris:** This variant of UNIX primarily runs on Sun Microsystems hardware. If you have Sun's SPARC chips in your server, this is your OS. But Sun has developed a version that you can run on the same Intel computers that run Microsoft Windows.

- ✔ **OS X:** This OS is a merger of UNIX and the Macintosh OS (www.apple.com), running on Apple G3 and G4 computers. If you run Apple hardware, your OS choices are quite limited.

- ✔ **Linux:** This OS is another UNIX variant, which is available in versions that run on several kinds of hardware, including Intel.

- ✔ **Others:** Other variants of UNIX, such as HP-UX for Hewlett-Packard (www.hewlettpackard.com) and AIX from IBM (www.ibm.com) run on specific types of hardware.

Among techies, choosing an OS is often a matter of religion more than getting the most functionality for the dollar. Make certain the choice made is for the good of your bottom line — not the ego of your developer. Have your developer present costs for multiple options — along with the advantages and disadvantages of each OS — before you commit to one.

Choosing an operating system

The hardware you choose narrows down your operating system options a bit because not all operating systems run on all server hardware. Keep these considerations in mind when making this choice:

- ✔ **Go with what you know:** Select an operating system that you feel comfortable working with and that your staff will be able to support. If your team has three year's experience on UNIX servers writing Common Gateway Interface (CGI) scripts, consider getting a UNIX-based solution because that's the technology they know.

✔ **Stick with what you've got:** If you have already purchased servers (an unfortunate but frequent occurrence), you will probably stick with them. And the type of servers you have will have an impact on what OS you use. For example, if you own three IBM RS/6000 servers that you intend to use on this project, then you're likely headed for an AIX solution.

✔ **Plan your support:** If you know you want to use a particular software package or framework, your OS needs to support it. Plan the entire system before you commit to a particular OS and server hardware. For instance, if you are leaning toward Microsoft Commerce Server, you are leaning toward Microsoft Windows servers.

Your server hardware and operating system limit the choices you have for application software. If you plan to build your system on a specific commercial off-the-shelf software application, you need to choose hardware and operating systems that work with it. Be sure that you work with the project architect to plan the entire system before purchasing anything. For more coverage on purchasing an off-the-shelf software application, read through Chapter 10.

Choosing application software

The application software you select will limit your choices of operating systems because application software must be written for a specific operating system and specific server hardware to run properly. An *application* is a piece of software that provides a specific service for the user. For instance, Microsoft Word is a word processing application, Apache is a Web server application, and Oracle 8i is a database application.

We recommend that you plan the project first, choose the application software next, and then get the servers and operating systems that support that application software.

After you order your servers and an operating system is installed on them, rev up the motor and put those babies to use. Most operating systems aren't terribly useful from a business point of view; that is, they don't do anything specific. Think of them as the foundations of a house — not very pretty or flashy, but darned important. Instead, your OS provides a basis on which application software runs, and it's the application software that does all the cool stuff your business needs. Here's a list of the kinds of applications to consider adding:

✔ **Web server software:** Web server software allows a server to receive and fulfill requests from Web browsers. Some Web server software is free, such as the Apache (www.apache.com) Web server software that has become popular for Linux servers, or the Internet Information Services software included with Microsoft Windows Server.

Select Web server software that meets your specific needs. Consider performance as well as features. You need a Web server software package capable of serving Web pages to thousands of customers simultaneously. You also need software that is reliable and easy to manage to prevent your staff spending all its time keeping the servers up and running.

✔ **Database server software:** E-commerce sites use and generate a lot of data — product catalogs, customer lists, orders, payments, advertising campaigns, and more. This data is kept in a database. A *database server* is simply a server — with an operating system — that runs database software. Just like Web servers, the software that you choose depends upon the hardware and operating system you select, the level of performance you want, and the specific features you want.

Database software has to do a lot of work to keep up with your customers. The software has to be fast, and it has to run on powerful server hardware. In fact, the servers running your database software will probably be the most powerful ones in your server farm. Three of the most popular database server packages are Microsoft SQL Server, Oracle 8i (www.oracle.com), and IBM DB2. You may also want to consider database server software from companies like Sybase (www.sybase.com) and open-source packages like MySQL (www.mysql.com).

Open-source software is distributed under licensing terms that make the underlying source code available to a licensee. These licenses typically grant rights to the licensee to modify the software and to distribute the source code to others as long as they extend similar liberties to subsequent recipients of the code. We talk more about open-source software in Chapter 8.

✔ **Application server software:** Your server farm will need a variety of application software packages to perform specific tasks. This includes software that enables systems to talk to one another, software to manage security, software to handle payments securely, software to track and report on site activity — you get the picture. Your systems architect (the key player we talk about in Chapter 7) will figure out the best packages to buy to build your site quickly and reliably.

Choosing e-commerce software

The single most important aspect of your infrastructure (in addition to the servers themselves) is your choice of e-commerce software. This software provides the basis for your Web site, providing the important commerce functions you need, such as catalogs, customer tracking, and order processing.

The e-commerce software you select must not only run on your servers' operating system but must also be compatible with the Web server and database server software you use. Packages include Lotus Domino Server (www.lotus.com), Microsoft Commerce Server, IBM Net Commerce, and many, many others.

Here's what to look for in an e-commerce package:

- **Cost, Part 1:** Some of these packages cost more than the annual budget of some third-world nations, but don't just look at the initial price tag. Get numbers on total cost of ownership, including the cost of the hardware, software licensing and maintenance fees, and labor costs to maintain the software from day to day. Most software vendors have this data. If they don't, you should ask them why not.

- **Ease of maintenance and operations:** You're going to keep this software running for a long time, so make certain it's easy to use.

- **Cost, Part 2:** Did we mention cost? How much will it cost to keep the software up-to-date? How much will it cost to upgrade the operating system to use the latest version of the software? What will ongoing maintenance do to your bottom line?

- **Configuration and programming:** You need to customize this software to make it your own. And that requires time and talent. Get figures from case studies on the time and cost for configuring sites using this software. You may want to talk to customers who currently use the software to see what they learned deploying it.

- **Cost, Part 3:** We didn't want to forget to mention the cost. Software that's less popular and less well known will have fewer people who can update and maintain it, making your resource people scarce commodities. When we took economics, Scarce = Expensive.

- **Stability of the software publisher:** You may be able to find a great deal (dollar-wise) on innovative new Web software. However, if the enterprising company that publishes this software goes out of business two months later, no one on the planet can (or will) maintain it.

- **Cost, Part 4:** Finally, consider the whole cost. For instance, your Web software needs to talk to other systems in your company (if you doubt this, read Chapter 5). If the software doesn't already come with the capability, you need to write that software — and maintain it. Those costs contribute to your final cost figure.

When choosing your e-commerce software, carefully consider all the costs associated with that software.

More than anything, your choice of e-commerce software will help define the features available to your customers, and will also shape the development and growth of your entire e-commerce business. You and your project architect should carefully review your options before settling on a particular package.

Choosing Development Platforms

When you customize your site, you need programmers, who tell your servers what to do with programming languages. Because all programming languages are not created equal, you need to match the programming languages and the ways they communicate with one another into a *development platform*. A development platform balances the operating and network systems and the services available from your servers to get everything to work together in harmony. Your development platform choices include the following.

Microsoft .NET

Microsoft's .NET development platform — including C# (pronounced *cee sharp*), Visual Basic .NET, Visual C++ .NET, and other languages — is designed to work on the Microsoft Windows platform. If you decide to build an e-commerce business based mostly on Windows and other Microsoft products, .NET makes a great development platform choice because it integrates well with Microsoft's other products.

Java

The Sun Microsystems (www.sun.com) Java development platform was designed with platform independence in mind. Your programmers can write code in Java that runs on any server hardware or operating system. Unfortunately, Java programs tend to run somewhat more slowly than programs written in other languages, which is the price you pay for platform independence.

CGI

Common Gateway Interface (CGI) is a standards-based means of allowing Web servers to run program scripts. Programmers write these scripts in Practical Extraction and Report Language (Perl), Python, or other scripting languages. PHP is a script language and interpreter that's freely available and used primarily on Linux Web servers. (PHP was formerly called Personal

Home Page Tools.) PHP uses CGI's foundation to create server-side embedded program scripts in HTML pages (visit `www.php.net` for more information). And PHP is open source (translation: no licensing fees).

Other choices

Custom software can also be written in the C++ programming language and compiled to run on just about any operating system because C++ compilers are available for most of them. A *compiler* is a special program that reads statements written in a particular programming language and translates them into a machine-readable language that a computer processor uses.

Many operating systems also support scripting languages — such as Visual Basic Script, Perl, Python, and more — that can be used to write smaller custom software applications for your site to use.

Making the Right Connection

Your servers have to be connected to one another to do their jobs. This connectivity is provided by a high-speed local area network (LAN), which will generally support 100 megabits per second (Mbps) or more of data to be passed between the servers. The speed of the network is also referred to as its bandwidth.

Your servers' connections to the outside world won't be as fast. These connections are called wide area network (WAN) connections because they connect your local network to the larger worldwide network — the Internet. Unfortunately, WAN connections are more difficult to make than LAN connections, and thus they are slower. The cost of a WAN connection depends on the bandwidth that it offers. Some of your choices are

- ✔ **DSL (the younger whippersnapper):** Digital Subscriber Line (DSL) is actually available in several flavors such as ADSL, SDSL, and more. DSL subscriptions come in a variety of bandwidths, but unfortunately are not available in all areas. DAL may also not be as reliable as other, more mature WAN technologies, but it often costs less.

- ✔ **T1 (the granddaddy):** A T1 line, available from most phone companies, is a high-bandwidth telephone trunk line that provides a bandwidth of about 1.5 Mbps, which is 26 times faster than a modem but 66 times slower than a typical LAN connection.

- ✔ **T3 (the granddaddy's stronger younger brother):** A bigger version of a T1 line, a T3 line provides significantly more bandwidth (44.7 Mpbs) for significantly (10–20 times) more money than a T1.

You pay for Internet access based on the amount of bandwidth you use. To save costs, you may want to buy less bandwidth. And that's where your troubles can begin. You probably know what it's like at rush hour, with 80 bazillion cars all trying to squeeze over to their exits while 80 bazillion other cars try to squeeze into the fast lane. The Internet is often called the Information Superhighway — go figure. Consider the magnitude: The Internet is a whole great big world of networks, with millions of people on computers, all trying to get from one Web site to another. When customers enter your Web address into their browsers, they join a whole host of other users, all of whom are trying to exit the highway to get to their destination. You need full-strength WAN bandwidth to keep your servers working at full capacity.

In fact, the high price of WAN bandwidth is why most e-commerce companies don't keep their servers at their own offices. Instead, they use ASPs, hosted environments, or co-location arrangements (as we discuss in Chapter 2). Co-location allows companies to share the cost of really big-bandwidth WAN connections with a service provider's other customers, making the high-speed connections economically feasible for everyone.

For in-depth coverage of LAN, WAN, and other networking topics, check out *Networking For Dummies,* 5th Edition, by Doug Lowe and published by Hungry Minds, Inc.

Connecting Connectivity Connections

Simply having a LAN or WAN connection isn't enough to put your servers in touch with one another or with the world — you need some additional networking hardware to control all those connections.

Routers are used to connect one or more local area networks to one another, or to connect a local area network to a WAN connection. A router might be configured in a network, as shown in Figure 13-2.

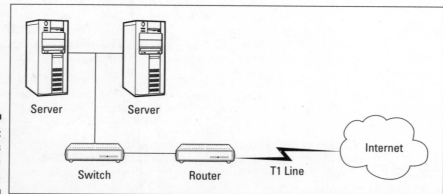

Figure 13-2:
A router's position in a network.

Server   Server

Switch   Router   T1 Line   Internet

The router ensures that communications between your servers stay private — on their side of the router — and that communications destined for the Internet are sent over your WAN connection. Incoming communications from the Internet are accepted from the WAN connection and routed to your servers' local area network.

The other issue in connecting these servers is spreading out the workload. We call this *scaling out,* or getting multiple computers to help with the same task. Such a configuration makes a huge difference in performance and can affect your price. For instance, if you do business in the United States and the Pacific Rim, you can reach the entire area with a single server. Or you follow the path that Canon takes, setting up one group of servers in the U.S. and another group in Japan. This arrangement helps Canon manage more content, gives it back-up capability, and helps provide U.S. customers with English pages and Japanese customers with Japanese pages.

Use routers to connect your server farms together. They still need to work hand-in-hand, and you want to manage them easily from a single point. Your routers let you link your entire network together, regardless of geographic location.

Protecting Those Who Serve: Firewalls

Unfortunately, the Internet can be a scary place. Irresponsible hackers try to crash e-commerce systems for the fun of it, and businesses attempt to retrieve confidential information from one another's servers. You have to protect your servers, and one of the best ways to do that is to use a firewall. A firewall serves as the gate to your business fortress, and fits within your network configuration, as shown in Figure 13-3.

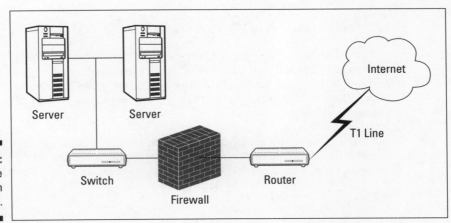

Figure 13-3:
Locking the castle with a firewall.

A firewall ensures that only certain protocols — such as HyperText Transfer Protocol (HTTP) or File Transfer Protocol (FTP) — are allowed into your local area networks. A firewall can also be used to allow only certain computers to communicate with your servers, such as computers owned by business partners or specific customers. Any communications not specifically allowed to pass through the firewall are blocked, thus protecting your network and your servers.

Most ASPs, hosting facilities, and co-location facilities provide firewalls along with the WAN connections that they provide. Take advantage of their expertise when configuring firewalls to provide the best possible protection for your servers.

Maintaining the Plantation

After your servers and software are up and running, you need to keep them functional. Plan for the load you expect your servers to bear and develop a disaster recovery plan so that you can determine how much it will cost to keep your site up and running 24/7/365, and then balance that cost against your revenue stream. You should also ensure that your systems can be brought back from the dead quickly, should the worst occur. Plan ahead for the grief that happens when a disaster strikes — a fire, lightning, riots, or meteors — and takes your servers out of commission.

Also realize the risk you take if you place all your business on one server and that server malfunctions. Think of this as having only one salesperson in a bricks-and-mortar store — what do you do when that employee gets sick or takes a vacation? How much money will you lose, per hour, when customers cannot purchase anything?

Balancing high availability and cost

Today's computer systems can be configured for high availability: They can be configured to survive all kinds of hardware failures and external disasters and keep right on running. They can also be configured to spread out the load of your customer requests, making each server in your farm perform as well as possible.

Of course, this power and flexibility doesn't come for free, or cheaply, or even moderately priced. We're talking tens of thousands to hundreds of thousands of dollars (but don't quote us)! Nonetheless, these technologies can literally save your business, so be prepared to fork over the dough when necessary.

Building redundancy

No one gets any younger; taxes are due on April 15; server hardware fails. Get used to it; it happens. Servers will eventually break down and have to be repaired. The only variable is how much effect this failure has on your online business — after all, your servers are your business, in many ways.

Hardware manufacturers are sensitive to the concerns of online businesses regarding hardware failures. They have responded by creating several technologies to lower — and often eliminate — the impact that a hardware failure has on a business. Four major technologies are

- **Redundant components:** Many hardware failures occur in simple components, such as server power supplies. Manufacturers compensate by including multiple power supplies (and other sensitive components) in each server so that the failure of one doesn't take the entire server offline.

- **Hot-plug replacements:** Manufacturers often combine redundant components with hot-plug capabilities — a failed component can be removed and replaced while the server is up and running. This prevents the downtime usually necessary to perform a repair. Many different components can use hot-plug technology, including power supplies, hard drives, network interfaces, and cooling fans.

- **Clustering:** Sometimes entire servers — or critical components — fail, taking the server down despite redundant components and hot-plug replacement capabilities. In these cases, configuring your system with clustering servers is a good preventative move. A *cluster* comprises two or more complete servers, each with the same task. If one server has a total failure, the others take over until it can be repaired. Sweet!

  Some clusters that require the member computers are located within a short distance of one another — generally right next to one another, in fact. Other clustering technologies permits members to be located far away from one another, allowing you to place them in different rooms, different buildings, or even different states. This helps ensure that some cluster members survive, even if one member is destroyed because of a fire, a flood, or some other catastrophic event.

- **Drive arrays:** Putting all a server's data on a single hard drive is literally putting all your eggs in one basket — if that drive fails, you lose everything. Use drive arrays to configure two or more hard drives in a way that makes them act as one. Formally referred to as a Redundant Array of Inexpensive (or Independent) Disks (RAID), these arrays provide built-in fault tolerance and can generally continue functioning with no data loss if a single drive in the array fails.

Load balancing "Big Brother"

The national TV broadcast network CBS used one extreme example of load balancing in its reality show *Big Brother*. The show offered viewers the opportunity to watch several housemates in a house that was completely wired for video and sound. Although the broadcast show lasted only an hour, viewers could visit the show's Web site to play voyeur at any time.

A handful of Web servers would have been completely unable to handle the load when millions of viewers tried to access the streaming video and audio content of the site. In anticipation of this heavy load, the CBS technical staff created a site that was hosted by more than 200 Web servers. Each incoming visitor was directed to whichever server had the least number of connections at the time, evenly distributing the load across the server farm and making it possible to delivery audio and video content to millions of visitors every day.

How expensive are these technologies? That depends on your hardware manufacturer and the technology you want to implement. Redundant components and hot-plug technologies are standard features in most mid- and high-end servers. Clustering can usually be performed only with specialized high-end server hardware, and is the most expensive because it requires a minimum of two complete servers. RAID arrays are generally considered a requirement for any business; hard drives are too susceptible to failure to take any chances.

Lean on me: Sharing the load

Shop around for Web server hardware, and you'll notice that most Web servers are fairly inexpensive and don't include most of the high-availability options we describe in the previous section. That's because businesses usually take a slightly different approach with Web servers.

Rather than buying one or two big, expensive Web servers, businesses tend to buy a handful (or more) of smaller, inexpensive servers. Each is configured to be identical to the others, and incoming customer requests are evenly distributed amongst them by load-balancing technologies. If one server fails completely, you don't have to panic because several identical servers can pick up the slack. If the Web site's traffic picks up, additional servers can be configured and added to handle the additional load.

Calculating the cost

Is all this redundancy and load balancing worth it? Only you — and your business — can answer that question. Generally, you'll find that at least some of these techniques are worth the cost.

Determine how much money you expect to make per hour when customers start placing orders on your Web site. That will tell you how much money you'll lose every hour if a Web server, application server, or database server experiences a failure. Figure that every server will suffer about four hours of downtime a month. (Not all of that will be attributable to hardware failures — some of that time will be required for regular maintenance and other tasks — but being offline for any reason means a negative impact to your business.)

Now multiply your lost sales per hour by four. Weigh this number against what you'd have to fork over to buy servers with redundancies, a whole cluster, or a couple of extra Web servers.

Most businesses do the math and come up with the following conclusions:

- ✔ Database servers should always include the maximum amount of redundancy, hot-plug technology, and drive arrays that are available.

- ✔ Database servers should usually be configured in clusters of at least two.

- ✔ After you determine how many Web servers will be necessary to handle the customer load you expect, purchase 25 percent more servers for redundancy. For example, if you expect your site to need four servers to handle the load, buy five.

- ✔ Because of the built-in redundancy offered by having multiple servers, Web servers should contain a minimum of redundancy and hot-plug technologies. Eliminating these technologies also makes the servers physically smaller, enabling you to use more of them in a smaller space.

- ✔ Application servers that can be load balanced should be treated as Web servers; application servers that cannot be load balanced should be treated as database servers.

Protecting the plantation through business continuity planning

When a failure eventually does occur — or worse, some catastrophe takes out an entire office or data center — have a plan in place. Just like leaving a list of instructions for the baby-sitter before you go out for the evening, write down your plan so that you have all the techno-repair info and resources in one document. Always include the following information in your plan:

- ✔ Who to call for warranty repairs (or out-of-warranty repairs) on your server hardware

- ✔ Account numbers for your warranty service

- ✔ Who to call to get electricity or wide area network connections restored to your facility if it's damaged

- ✔ Who is responsible for fixing your servers if they encounter software problems

- ✔ Who can restore data from tape backups in the event of a hard drive failure or other data loss

- ✔ How often tape backups are performed, the maximum amount of data that can be lost, and where the backup tapes are kept

- ✔ Whether copies of back-up tapes are kept off-site in case the office or data center suffers damage; how off-site copies are retrieved; and the phone numbers, contact people, and account numbers for the off-site storage service

- ✔ After-hours access instructions for your staff

 Make sure that everyone in your company knows where to find this information if disaster should strike. The answers to these questions, along with related information, should be investigated and documented in a disaster recovery handbook for your company. Copies should be given to key company employees to keep at home in case of emergency.

Geographically distributing processing

Putting all your company's servers in one location is a really bad idea. You're just asking for a disaster to happen. With all the uncertainty in the business world and the world at large, do yourself a huge favor and shield your business from potential destruction by geographically distributing your servers. Such organization gives you two major benefits:

- ✔ A disaster at one location won't take out the servers at other locations.

- ✔ Geographically distributing your servers puts them electronically closer to a wider range of customers, making access to your site faster.

Make no mistake — geographically distributed servers are more difficult to manage and obviously involve additional expenses. For companies relying heavily on their e-commerce business, though, the costs can be worth it.

Cloning: Not just for sheep anymore

If you decide to spread your servers out across the country — or across the world — you'll have a few technical problems to deal with.

The first problem is making sure your customers' access to the servers is distributed across all the servers, not just the ones at a particular location. Round-robin DNS is one technique for handling this properly; this approach randomly sends your customers to different servers for each request. These techniques often require that your server software be programmed to work that way, so your programmers may have to make adjustments to their code.

The second problem involves your servers' content. With servers spread out all over the place, you need to find a way to make sure that they all have exactly the same content. That way, no matter which server your customers connect to, they'll see the same Web site every time. Use replication technologies to solve this problem. For more on replication, read through the following section.

Making clones: Replication

Replication is the process of copying information from one place to another place. Replication exists in any server farm with more than one Web server. On a small scale, replication occurs when Joe Programmer manually copies files to each server when updates are necessary. Larger server farms rely on automated replication processes that copy content from a special staging server to the Web servers.

Most Web development environments include one or more development servers. Programmers and Web designers use these servers to create new content, test it, and fix any bugs. After everything works perfectly, the content is copied to a staging server. Replication systems then copy the content from the staging server to the actual Web servers, ensuring that each Web server receives an identical copy of the content on the staging server. This whole process is shown in Figure 13-4.

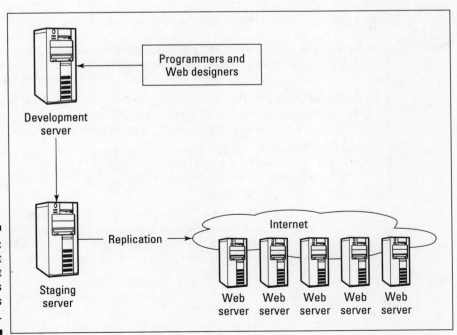

Figure 13-4:
A content deployment process uses replication.

Planning for Growth

Success means you can quickly outgrow your existing systems — what a great problem to have! The bad news is that overburdened systems make things slower for your customers, which can hurt your success. Thus, you need to measure system utilization to ensure that you continue delivering content to your customers despite your growth. Although the techniques for actually doing this are pretty complicated — and best left to those over-caffeinated network engineers you hired — the concepts are important.

When is it okay to start small?

Some areas of your infrastructure will be able to grow more easily than others. For example, you can always add more Web servers to deal with increasing customer demand. Depending on exactly how your Web site is built, adding more application servers can be easy, too. Adding database servers is often difficult because a variety of technical issues make it difficult for many database servers to work together as one in some circumstances. For example, you can only have one copy of a customer's address. You have to determine which server stores that copy and how it gets shared between servers.

Follow these guidelines when designing your site:

- ✔ **Design your site with great potential growth in mind.** Have your project architect create a design that includes multiple tiers of functionality so that each tier can be expanded as necessary to accommodate growth.

- ✔ **Start with as many Web servers as you feel you will need to meet initial customer demand.** Your architecture should allow you to add as many Web servers as are necessary to meet later demand.

- ✔ **Start with enough application servers to meet the demand you anticipate for your first year or so.** You should be able to add additional servers to handle growth, although doing so will be more expensive than simply adding Web servers.

- ✔ **Start with a database server — or a server cluster — big enough to meet your anticipated needs for at least two years.** Make sure that your architect designs your site so that the database can be partitioned, if necessary, and implemented on additional database servers if your growth requires it.

Performance baselines and growth trends

After your site is up and running, you need to immediately start monitoring its performance. A variety of tools can help you do this, including products from WebTrends (www.webtrends.com) and tools that should be provided with your servers' operating systems.

Based on the load created by your initial customers, establish a baseline for your servers' performance. This baseline should tell you how hard your servers are working to meet the demands of a specific number of customers.

Baseline measurements for servers include microprocessor utilization, random access memory utilization, disk access time, network bandwidth utilization, and many others. You network administrator should be well versed in what should be measured and how to measure it. Just keep on top of that person to make certain he or she does it.

As your customer demands grows, monitor the performance of your servers carefully. You should be able to draw a chart that compares specific performance indicators — such as network utilization or microprocessor utilization — with the number of customers accessing your site.

This information will help you project how many customers your current servers will be able to handle — just extend the chart until your servers and network connections are completely utilized and simultaneously extend the number of customers accessing the site.

Playing "I Spy"

As part of your ongoing maintenance plan, have your QA person set up a test script that captures the performance of the system. You can automate these scripts or just have a person go through the shopping process. The point is to measure site the response time. Then, on a scheduled basis, run the script — without warning anyone that you intend to measure the site — and use your results to determine whether site performance is up to snuff.

Vary the time of day that you run this testing script. Try to find times when the site experiences peaks and lulls in activity, measuring the differences in response times. If the response time is three times faster when the site has little activity — and the response time is irritatingly slow when the site is heavily loaded — you may be ready to add some more servers or network bandwidth to speed things up.

Planning for future capacity

After you determine how many customers your current setup can handle, start planning for future growth.

Plan to add capacity — additional servers or network connections — when your existing resources are about 70 percent utilized. Decide how many resources you need to add by projecting your customer growth using whatever business forecasting tools you feel comfortable with. Modify your baseline chart to reflect that anticipated number of customers and then extend the server resources to match. If your projected customer growth will require 300 percent capacity from your current resources, then you will need to triple those resources in order to meet the demand. Actually, we recommend that you quadruple them to provide a little padding.

Chapter 14

Avoiding a Pain in the ASP: Streamlining Business Operations by Outsourcing

In This Chapter

▶ Working with ASPs to get things done faster and more economically

▶ Finding the right ASP for your needs

▶ Upgrading accounting through the Web

*J*ust as you plan to offer products and services through the Web, many other companies can offer you their expertise through the Web. You can use the skills and systems of those companies to build your e-commerce business more quickly.

In this chapter, we look at outsourcing sources called *application service providers* (ASPs) that offer customized software-based solutions online, and consider the advantages and disadvantages of using them.

Understanding the ASP Phenomenon

If you think you need help setting up or maintaining your e-commerce operation, don't feel bad — you're actually acting very e-commerce savvy. The radical speed of change and the high level of technical expertise that's needed to do business online almost necessitate that every business *outsource* some work — or set up a contract with another business to have it do the work for you.

The outsourcing boom is a huge chunk of the B2B economy. You'd better believe that there are more businesses on the Internet than we can count that provide outsourcing services as their primary means of income.

Letting the professionals handle your storefront: ASPs

A good ASP can save you time and money, because where your expertise is making doohickeys, the ASP's focus is to provide cutting-edge technology solutions for e-businesses. You don't have to know how to customize Web-based software, and the ASP doesn't have to know how to build doohickeys.

You're renting expertise (plus hardware and software in many cases) when you choose an ASP to create some aspect of your Web store. No matter how challenging your e-commerce requirement is, a good ASP has done it before. ASPs are focused e-commerce machines, and they can probably get your operation up and running in a fraction of the time that it would take you to do it yourself. ASPs are familiar with pitfalls you don't know about yet, and they've seen — and lived through — some e-commerce mistakes.

Understanding the benefits of using an ASP

Even though we can't quantify how much money you'll save if you use an ASP, we agree with whoever it was who first said, "Time is money." Consider these benefits that ASPs offer:

- ✔ The ASP writes the software and tests it for bugs prior to implementation.

- ✔ The ASP purchases and configures the hardware, such as Web servers, for you.

- ✔ The ASP sets up and configures network connections, in most cases with much more sophistication than a single business might require. That ensures a more dependable site with back-up systems to keep your store open 24 hours a day.

- ✔ The ASP sets up the entire infrastructure, including technical-sounding computer network stuff such as load-balancing, fault-tolerance, routers, and switches (which you can read all about in Chapter 13).

- ✔ The ASP provides the personnel to make all of this come together, and the training to keep those people up to speed with ever-changing technology.

In theory, all you have to do is stand back and watch the bucks start flowing in.

Avoiding the pitfalls of using an ASP

ASPs aren't all happiness and light, or everyone would use them — and not everybody does. Although not all ASPs are alike — they differ significantly — here are some common drawbacks to their way of doing business:

- **The ASP wears the pants.** Sometimes an ASP customizes a solution, such as a shopping cart, and then goes away to let you run it. But if you're going to hand over the ongoing maintenance of your e-commerce site to an ASP, you don't have complete control. If you want to change the site's content several times a day, you have to submit changes to the ASP, and changes can take longer to apply.

- **ASPs can be very laissez-faire.** Not all ASPs are vigilant about proactively monitoring your site's capacity for handling traffic. It may be up to you to tell the ASP when things are slowing down and a new Web server is necessary. Because nobody is as concerned with your business' success as you are, you have to be sure to monitor your own Web store like a very conscious floorwalker to make sure the ASP is doing its job right.

- **ASPs are resistant to change.** Because many ASPs base all their clients' solutions on proprietary software, they may try to keep customers' sites as similar to each other as possible. That means you may not be able to customize your storefront, or if you can, customizing services may cost an arm and a leg. Many of these out-of-the-box solutions are just fine, but if you need special attention, be aware of the costs and choose an ASP that offers the level of customization you need and prices it fairly.

Note that if you build your store on a hosted software solution, and you leave the ASP for another, you may have to start from scratch with somebody else's application. If you have paid for customized software, you should own it, but making a change of hosting vendors who offer their own applications can be problematic. Because choosing an ASP may mean a big investment in upfront design and customization service costs, choose wisely.

- **The markup's where they get ya.** ASPs have to pay for all the same things you would pay for if you built your site on your own — a team of programmers, servers, network connections, managers, software, and so on. Some ASPs divide these costs and make customers share them, but they also mark up these costs, too. (After all, they're businesses, too.) In short, paying for convenience can sometimes wind up being very expensive.

- **You don't own your servers, the software, or anything associated with your site.** If the ASP goes out of business, your store does, too.

Just because you decide to start your site with an ASP doesn't mean you have to continue using that ASP forever. Many companies use ASPs as a way to get online quickly, giving them time to build a customized site from scratch — on their own. If timing is a factor for your business, then using an ASP to jumpstart your online store can be a good idea.

Finding a Reliable ASP Partner

Okay, you're sold on the idea of using an ASP to provide your customer support solution. Where do you find one? Actually, that's not hard — they practically grow on e-trees. Just type **ASP** or **e-commerce provider** (just another way to say ASP) or **CRM** (for customer relationship management) into an Internet search engine and stand back as hundreds of results scroll by. What's hard is picking one you want to do business with.

Examining an ASP's portfolio

The first step in examining an ASP is to check out its work. Ask for the names of its other customers and look at its online stores. Focusing on the services this ASP provided for a customer, what do you think of its solutions? Here's a checklist you can use to examine the sites in an ASP's portfolio:

✔ If the ASP provides hosting services, visit several sites and click links. If the sites (and their links) load quickly and seem to perform smoothly, that's a very good sign that the software programmers and Web designers know what they're doing. If the sites don't work so well, the ASP either has software or infrastructure problems — either of which is a bad sign. (See Chapter 10 to find out about the seven-second rule.)

✔ If the ASP provided site design, take a good look. Tilt your head a little. Get snooty. Do the sites look good? Are they aesthetically pleasing? Do they have a professional appearance? Although customers influence a site design, an ASP providing these services should guide them to a professional look and feel; find out who's behind any ugly sites to be sure yours won't turn out the same way.

✔ Do all the sites in an ASP's portfolio look or function alike? If they do, then the ASP's software may not be very customizable. This isn't a problem if you don't mind your site looking like everybody else's — but remember, distinctiveness is a key ingredient to a successful e-commerce business.

✔ If the ASP provides a shopping cart function, try buying a few small items from the sites in the ASP's portfolio. Were your purchases handled smoothly? Did every site's checkout process look exactly the same? Many ASPs can customize your store, but use a common shopping cart and checkout for all customers. Be sure that the ASP's approach is right for your site before you agree to it. (See Chapter 9 for more on the checkout process.)

Getting a clear picture of an ASP's management and financials

After you've looked at several ASP candidates and zeroed in on one you're interested in, you should talk to the company's management team before making a final decision. Before you sit down with management, visit the company's Web site to find out how long it has been in business. Take a look at what the turnover is like (especially in management), and find out who its investors are. If the company is publicly traded, find out how its stock is doing. How are the company's financials — did the ASP lose money or make money last year? If there's something you feel uncomfortable about, use the upfront meeting with management to ask targeted questions until you feel comfortable — or move on to the next ASP candidate.

Not only do you have the right to ask these questions and receive answers, but you *should* ask these questions if you're a savvy business-person. An ASP is more than a just vendor; it's a business partner of the most intimate kind. Your fate is directly tied to your ASP's performance, so make sure its future looks bright before you jump on board.

Be sure to call some of the businesses whose sites are handled by the ASP. Ask them about the ASP's service record, its responsiveness to problems, and its ability to monitor and manage the site. Ask them if they would do business with the ASP if they were starting a new site.

Remember: Not all ASPs are created equal. What one business regards as a weakness, such as what it considers a too-sophisticated customization process, may be the very thing you're looking for in an ASP. Be sure to ask other customers and the ASP plenty of questions that help you decide if the ASP is right for your business. And be sure to check out the sidebar, "Getting a clear picture of an ASP's management and financials," for more suggestions on how to evaluate an ASP.

Fostering a healthy relationship with an ASP

In bricks-and-mortar commerce, if your store burns down, your business does, too. In the e-commerce world, your ASP (if you use one) is like an extension of your physical store, and if it catches fire (goes out of business), the disaster is likely to spread in ways you don't like to think about.

When you're sure you're interested in working with a business, but you're not quite ready to sign a contract, you're ready to start the courtship process.

Fostering a relationship with an ASP may seem as familiar — and as important — as courting the love of your life. Here are some tips on what you should do when getting to know an ASP:

- **Spend some quality time together.** You may have to spend some money to get an ASP's experts to spend some time with you, but the money is worth it. You may not be buying fancy dinners or flowers, but you're paying for the opportunity to discuss your future and to find out about the projects and plans that the ASP has seen fail, and the things that have worked really well for other clients. You'll get some great ideas, and you may avoid learning some hard lessons on your own.

- **Talk about your feelings.** Discuss your plans with the ASP's experts, outlining what you want out of this important relationship. Talk about what you want your site to do for your business. Get a response from the people you're talking to. They've probably seen similar goals before, and they can tell you how some of their other customers fared. They can also let you know if they think your plans are inherently risky and tell you how you can reduce the risk. And like any good partner, the ASP may be able to suggest alternative (cheaper, faster, and more efficient) ways of accomplishing your goals.

- **Don't be bullied into changing for someone else.** The people who run ASPs know what has worked for other customers, but just because they have experience doesn't mean that they can run the show. They haven't been a part of your business previously, and they don't necessarily know what will work for you. The most important goal of your site is to be distinct. You need to work with your ASP to get exactly what you need — even if it costs a little more.

    If creating a unique site that stands up to, and doesn't mimic, your competition requires extra dinero, don't hesitate to spend to go above and beyond the package price. Of course, we're not paying your bills, so we can say that — free of charge.

- **Make sure the ASP gets around.** The quality of the advice you receive, of course, is as good as the experts who give it. Make sure the ASP has a solid reputation and can give references to satisfied and successful clients.

- **Tell the ASP if you're ready for a shotgun wedding.** One huge advantage to using an ASP is that it can get your store up and running faster than if you did the work yourself. Some ASPs, such as Tiova (www.tiova.com) and Portera (www.portera.com), use *proprietary* storefront software, which is software that the ASP's team of programmers created. Only the ASP's clients can use this software, and for an off-the-shelf solution, it just needs minor customization before clients can go online — which is usually a matter of days.

If you're more interested in taking things slow, you still have options, but it'll cost ya. Higher-end ASPs, such as YellowBrix (`www.yellowbrix.com`), use a mix of off-the-shelf tools and custom software to create a unique storefront for each customer. These ASPs may need several months to get a complex store up and running.

✔ **Don't think that an ASP can change you overnight.** No ASP is a miracle worker. If you're asking for something totally new, a service provider will need some time to create what you want. Even though it may take time, if you're interested in starting from scratch, or if you've got a complex site and need to address integration with your back-end systems, you're still going to get the job done faster with an ASP than if you took the time to buy equipment and hire a staff on your own.

A good ASP can usually help you complete any customization of its software solutions faster, too. Because ASPs are more familiar with the products and tools that they offer, and because they have worked on numerous other e-commerce sites, they know the tricks and shortcuts to getting maximum results in minimum time.

Writing prenuptials

When the time comes to sign a contract with an ASP, don't just sign the first stack of papers the business sends over. Read through the contract carefully and make sure that it contains terms that protect your business. Ask for modifications, if necessary, and be prepared to walk if the ASP can't make some important contractual guarantees, such as

✔ A *service level agreement,* which specifies the maximum amount of time your store may be offline in a year (or month) before the ASP owes you financial compensation.

✔ Guaranteed response times that state exactly how long the ASP will take to respond to problems of varying priorities. Make sure that you also understand what kinds of requests fall into its priority categories, and that its priorities are similar to yours.

✔ A guarantee of when your site will be up and running. This is especially important for custom-developed sites. A good ASP will offer a guarantee, but will also place restrictions on you that prevent you from making changes to your site while it's under development. This is a fair restriction, and it prevents you from affecting the ASP's delivery date.

✔ A determination of who owns your software. You should have a right to any custom-developed software that you paid to have created, along with any internal documentation that accompanies the software.

✔ Minimum notice in the event that the ASP shuts down. The contract should also provide for financial penalties that you can attempt to collect if the ASP fails to provide you with enough notice.

As with any contract, make sure that a competent attorney reviews your agreement with the ASP before you sign.

Discovering Other Outsourcing Solutions

You're probably accustomed to (or at least familiar with the concept of) sending work out to a contractor. Many retailers contract loss-prevention specialists to find out where they are losing money and how to keep losses to a minimum. Any time you send work to another business on a short-term or long-term basis, you're *outsourcing*.

When you outsource to an ASP, you are outsourcing some type of online software-based solution — for example when you hire an ASP to design and customize and run its customer support software product. But you can also outsource to *e-service providers* that simply take advantage of the Internet's features for communication and sharing of data. For example, you might work with an online payroll service: You upload your weekly electronic timesheets to its site, and the payroll service inputs the data back at its office, generates paychecks, and posts a weekly payroll report to your online account for your review.

E-service providers are not so much hosting your software application, as taking on a business function in a way that is made possible by Internet technology. As such, they are in a B2B outsourcing relationship with your company. Other outsourced services in this vein might include

- Human resources functions, such as online headhunting.

- Web-based training.

- E-marketing, for example by hiring a company to conduct a permission-based e-mail campaign.

- Management of your ASP relationships. Yes, in this world of ASP-driven e-commerce, some companies exist just to help you orchestrate all the ASP relationships you may have established.

Consult your attorney before having your bricks-and-mortar business provide services for your online business. Depending on how you set up your business, your e-commerce business may need to pay a fee to your payroll department to keep the two businesses legally distinct.

Using online payroll services

Federal income tax, FICA, state taxes, local taxes, withholdings, W-2 forms, W-4 forms — who can keep track of it all? Obviously, the IRS can, and those folks definitely let you know if you miss something!

Save yourself the headache and the potential legal and financial troubles by contacting a payroll e-services provider. Payroll services have been around for ages, but you had to mail, fax, phone, or courier information to the payroll company, who then cut the checks and mailed them out. Web-based payroll services are much easier to use.

Long-time payroll processor ADP (www.adp.com) offers Web-based payroll services. Its software interfaces with many popular accounting packages, such as Intuit's QuickBooks, and allows you to enter all of your payroll information online. ADP then cuts the checks and mails them out, and can even pay your employees via direct deposit if desired.

QuickBooks users can also check out the QuickBooks Payroll Services (www.quickbooks.com/hiring_employees). Pulling information directly from QuickBooks over the Internet, these payroll services support regular checks as well as direct deposit and, like ADP, provide you with all the necessary year-end tax forms to file your company's return.

Online payroll services charge a monthly fee, but that's usually a pittance compared to the cost of adding a payroll specialist to your staff or handling payroll yourself. Unless your company is in the business of doing payroll (and few are), then it's just another distraction best left to the professionals.

Of course, if you already have an in-house payroll specialist (or staff) for your traditional business, the best solution may be a combination of internal resources interfacing with e-service providers.

Using online accounting tools

If you're trying to keep your online business as lean as possible, you may want to consult a professional accountant for advice and tips on setting up your online business properly, but rely on a lower-paid clerk to handle the day-to-day bookkeeping. Although you can use off-the-shelf accounting software, such as Intuit's popular QuickBooks package, you still have to pay for yearly software updates, extra licenses if you want to have more than one person using the software, and so on.

Online accounting tools are an attractive alternative. They're Web-based, so they don't require any software. They're often inexpensive, and they provide the most commonly used business functions. They're also updated automatically and at no extra charge, so you always have the latest features available. Here are some online accounting services you may want to check out:

- ✔ Peachtree, maker of the off-the-shelf Peachtree Accounting software, offers online accounting services through its Web site at www.peachtree.com.

- ✔ Intuit offers a Web-based version of its popular QuickBooks software at www.quickbooks.com.

Most online accounting services range from $15 to $20 a month and are usually able to interface with online payroll services, giving you a one-stop online solution for your business needs.

Part IV
Dealing with the Back Office

In this part . . .

As if dealing with customers weren't enough, you also have to deal with the processes that make your business function. Lots of people totally ignore this fact when they put together an e-business, but we don't let you down. We show you how to manage customer relationships with customers you've never met, take advantage of the amazing new supply chain models that the e-commerce world offers, and make the most of exciting business-to-business technologies, such as e-procurement, that can save you a bundle of cash. We also talk about ways to keep your traditional back-end business systems running smoothly — even with all the e-commerce business you're about to dump into them. After you read these chapters, your accountant will love you, and your other managers will wonder how you figured it all out!

Chapter 15

Digging for Gold: Using Information to Build Market Share

*Y*ou run your business on information. Key decision makers decide the fate of your organization on the reports and analyses produced by systems and staff. Providing accurate data that can be clearly read — and delivering it in a timely manner — can keep you from making fatal mistakes.

No matter how you do business, information flows faster when fewer people are involved directly in the process. This fact is especially true in e-commerce, which moves faster than the speed of light compared to traditional business. You need effective, high-speed reporting systems that keep everyone in your business (and everyone you do business with) on top of the activities of your entire organization. You also need to integrate information from departments and systems scattered throughout your enterprise to paint that big picture for your top-level executives.

Getting the Lowdown on CRM

How can you do the things that make customers feel comfortable with your organization? *Customer relationship management (CRM)* is a system that helps your enterprise organize and manage relationships with your customers. Use CRM to gather sales, customer service, and accounting information so that you can paint a complete picture of how you deal with your customers. Nothing's more important than love (except money), so use this information to help your customers feel known and loved. But also use CRM to keep your staff loving you — CRM systems are so integrated with each other that you will save money and time. Figure 15-1 shows you LivePerson.com, an ASP eCRM.

Identifying the Functions of a Good CRM System

CRM systems address several areas that deal with customers but that traditionally have individual systems that don't have much (if any) contact with each other. That means that Sales may not share information with Accounts Payable. By integrating these systems and sharing the wealth, everyone in the organization can work together to keep customers loyal and satisfied.

CRM can help your team members sell in several direct areas:

- **Cross-sell related products and services.** If your salespeople or systems know which products or services a customer has already purchased, they can suggest complementary products, accessories, warranties, and supplies.

- **Upsell superior (yes, that's code for more pricey) products and services.** You may consider replacing aging equipment free of charge or for a discounted price, exchanging returned items for better models at no extra charge, or for a real bargain, or enabling customers to upgrade their service agreements, and so on. You know the drill — it's easier to sell a small upcharge than it is to sell an entirely new product. In the bricks-and-mortar world, you see this tactic all the time. Budget Rent a Car (www.budgetrentacar.com) has made a business out of bumping up coupes to sedans. Its Web site is no different. Check out the Deals & Programs link.

- **Keep track of the sales you thought were in the bag.** Record customer interest in products that didn't make it through the checkout process. CRM systems can keep track of abandoned shopping carts on your Web storefront and keep a tally of sales calls that do not yield sales.

- **Above all, hold on tight.** Continue to contact customers (especially the ones that get away) when you change prices, introduce new models, run promotions, and so on. Don't sound desperate, but be diligent.

One of the advantages of your Web store is that you can automatically track the products your customers look at. CRM services enable you to use that data to determine customers' shopping patterns and build a clear profile of their interests.

Figure 15-1:
LivePerson provides live, real-time customer service for businesses.

Sharing and sharing alike: How CRM keeps everyone on task

If customers can fill out a form on the Web site or call a representative of your company to get accurate and reliable information they will feel important and cared for. After all, your customers see your entire organization as a single entity — not a group of disassociated departments. The CRM system allows the data to be updated and share from a single data source.

Your Web site collects data about your customers. (Or, at least it should.) If both your Web site and the salespeople in your bricks-and-mortar store enter and save data in the same database using the same methods, they can reinforce each other's efforts. It works something like this:

1. **Paul Purchaser visits the Web site and checks out one of your Farmblebees.**

2. **He fills out a quick form on the Web site and you send him product information about the Farmblebee line, such as colors, sizes, prices, and features. This product information is stored in your company's CRM system.**

3. **Armed with the information Paul provided when he filled out the online form, Colleen Closer, one of your salespeople, makes a follow-up call.**

   Colleen finds out that Paul wants to purchase a Farmblebee, but he's leery of the cost.

4. **Colleen makes a note and enters it into the CRM system:** `Follow up with Purchaser, Paul, when Farmblebee price falls by 15 percent.`

   She makes another note for herself: "Check Farmblebee price point and talk to Sam M. Sales, (the Sales manager) about whether this price is right for our core customers."

5. **Four weeks later the product goes on sale.**

   The software that handles data about promotions examines the CRM database and flags Paul Purchaser as an interested shopper. The software automatically sends an e-mail message notifying Paul of the price reduction and reminding him that Colleen can answer his questions.

   The email message contains Colleen's e-mail address and phone number.

6. **Paul sends an e-mail to Colleen to say he wants to ask a few more questions about the Farmblebee.**

   They schmooze and Colleen closes the sale over the phone.

7. **Colleen shares her success story when she receives her Top Gun sales award at the international sales meeting.**

   Bob Bumbler, and 14 other salespeople just like him, makes a mental note: "Must remember to enter important information into the CRM system."

8. **Sales closings skyrocket. Profits begin to soar.**

   Life is good.

Using CRM to get customers, customers, and more customers

Most salespeople understand that selling to existing customers is more fruitful than trying to find new customers. Your most productive efforts come from improving your relationships with the customers who already know and trust you. Investing in improving that relationship can quickly produce more business. Of course, finding new customers is a good thing, too.

The point of your CRM system should be to increase your customer base by drawing in new customers, developing stronger relationships with existing customers, and retaining your key, profitable customers.

Your CRM system should help you

✔ **Increase revenue in existing relationships:** Use the knowledge you already have about your customers needs and challenges so that you can create targeted products and services specifically meant to fill those needs, to solve a problem, or to reduce the impact of a challenge.

- ✔ **Discover what sells:** By setting up and recording the results of strategies to convert prospects into customers, you can discover which strategies rule — and which ones drool.

- ✔ **Understand and address customer concerns:** Track customer service and data on which products are returned to figure out what irritates your customers — then fix it.

- ✔ **Present yourself as a single organization to your customers:** Sales, shipping, customer service, accounts receivable — every department in your business can see the same information about your customer at the same time. Everyone shares notes and reads off the same page. Your customer will be delighted by the results.

Using CRM to expand on existing relationships

Your systems need to use a customer-centric view and provide a unified, consistent front. Sharing information across sales channels is the best way to kill two birds with one stone: Simplify life for your staff *and* meet your customers' needs.

Your customers view your organization as a single unit, not several units comprised of traditional sales, Web sales, and so on.

Most of customers' apprehensions vanish by the time they place their first order. The first purchase is always the hardest — unless you do something to irritate a customer, he is much more likely to buy from you again. Use your CRM data to help make the next sale. Address two avenues in this effort:

- ✔ **Say, "Nice to see you again, Ms. Soandso!"** Every time your customers visit your Web site or walk in the door of your shop on Main Street, attempt to identify them. Access their sales history, remember who they are, and let them know that you remember them.

   Note the products or services customers investigate on the site. If you can get a handle on customers' interests, you can use their history of browsing your site to customize pages to meet their interests (as we describe in Chapter 9) and to increase the odds that a sale will be the result.

- ✔ **Mom always said, "Choose spam wisely."** Contact customers based on their interests and buying patterns instead of *spamming* (sending unsolicited e-mail messages). In the old days, you may have sent out mailers to your entire client list telling everyone everything you sold.

   Nowadays, the thing to do is to send targeted promotions and offers tailored to meet the specific interests and needs of smaller groups of people. Remember, Web-savvy shoppers may receive dozens of e-mail messages a day. They get a tad cranky about the spam. Targeted promotions have higher success rates and make customers feel as if you understand them and their needs.

CRM involves more than the Web side of your business. Your systems should be integrated across the board and take hold of your traditional business practices and functions, as well as targeting and developing new online customer and sales channels. That may mean rethinking the way you handle mail promos so that it coincides with your online plan.

Picking and choosing: Using CRM to decide which relationships are going to pay off

You never want to turn down sales, but not all customers are created equally. When customers become demanding, how do you know how much time, money, and energy to expend to satisfy their demands?

For instance, several insurance companies (who will remain nameless) provide excellent service and very low rates to customers who pay their bills on time and file few claims. These insurance companies carefully monitor customer history and quickly drop customers who have proven themselves to be too much of a financial liability (they have too many claims) or too unreliable (they are a little on the flighty side when it comes to paying up). To stay on top of the customer profiles, they need timely, accurate information about their customers.

Your CRM system can rate customers based on their value to your company. The idea is that the senior managers use the systems to establish whether the benefit of closing a sale is worth the cost of having your top salesperson working exclusively on chasing down Customer X (who will also remain nameless) for six long weeks. Maybe six days is more like it. Or maybe six months is appropriate.

Knowing whom to keep

One of the key benefits of a CRM system is knowing which customers are keepers and which can fall by the wayside. At the Cutler-Hammer division of Eaton, Inc. (www.ch.cutler-hammer.com), which services businesses with power and electrical systems and engineering services (not a small thing), managers found that salespeople were striking too many deals with too many customers. Believe it or not, they thought this was a *bad* thing because some of the information about potential customers was a little on the sketchy side. You've heard the expression, "Too much information?" Well, in this case there wasn't enough

information to evaluate the risks. When you're selling expensive machinery and services, there's no such thing as too much information.

So Cutler-Hammer implemented a CRM system to help managers decide which customers they should pursue. The company evaluated several software packages before settling on one that worked well with the company's customized order management system. The CRM system draws transactional data from the order management system and historical data from a data warehouse to provide decision-makers with the right data to formulate the right decisions.

You also need to listen carefully to customers and integrate their suggestions into your business model. The question is which customers should you listen to: the guy who visited your site for the first time two months ago and bought a discounted, closeout doodad for a fraction of its value two months ago — and chose today to slam you for your crummy service? Or the lady who faithfully and exclusively buys 50 doodads a month, every month from you? If she has a bone to pick with you about your annoying logon system, you may want to listen up, and be grateful, because you're making something off last year's doodad. You may want to ignore his e-mail message that says `You're service sux.`

If you weigh customers' input based on their value as a customer, you can give the proper attention and prioritize customer requests.

Using CRM to create targeted marketing campaigns

Analyzing the effectiveness of marketing and advertising campaigns is difficult. Your CRM system can help you develop targeted promotions designed to specific groups, and it even can help record data to discover how effective a campaign has been by letting you know which customers responded and which ones didn't pay attention.

For instance, say you develop a new attachment to the Doohickey Pro. You access your CRM system to find all the owners of the Doohickey Pro, and send them all an e-mail. The e-mail has a link to your Web site where customers can order the attachment at an outstanding 25 percent off. (Of course, this is limited time offer, and some restrictions may apply.)

If you really wanted to be slick, you'd use some of that money you save to print snazzy fliers for the customers who walk into your store — you'll boost sales *and* increase interest in your Web site.

Improving customer service and support with CRM

CRM provides indispensable data to your customer service department. When customers need service they are not usually in a good mood. The CRM system gives your reps the information to quickly earn the trust of your customer and help them rapidly deal with the matter — with a minimal amount of exchanging information that your organization already knows.

What kind of information might customer service expect from the CRM system? You should get the following data:

✔ **The digits:** Customer identification information, such as address, phone number, and any demographic information that has been acquired.

✔ **The big picture:** Purchase history, including which products and services the customer has already purchased (and when). Purchase history can serve as a basis for cross-sells and upsells as well as helping you determine how significant the customer is to your organization.

✔ **The whole sordid story:** You need to know customers' service history if you're really going to meet their needs. If Clint Customer returns repeatedly, the customer service rep needs to know why. Did he manage to get the *only* defective product in the lot, or is Clint's middle name Closet Klutz? If Clint keeps coming back for help, maybe your user's manual reads like Swahili. (May we suggest a good book series with a blindingly yellow and black cover?). Customer service can only do its job if the employees know the facts (as the customer views them).

✔ **The status of the relationship:** Find out the current order status and service status. You need to know what you currently have in process for every customer.

You need to integrate your CRM functions with your storefront design to take advantage of these function. We discuss designing storefronts in Chapter 9.

Automating sales force processes

One of the issues you face when your dealing with your sales staff is figuring out what they are doing and keeping them productive. Sales force automation systems help you plan and track activities for sales professionals to keep them accountable and on track.

Your CRM system needs to keep tabs on the activities of your salespeople and continue to collect data as they make customer contact. You can also support them through your Internet-based systems in the following ways:

✔ Provide e-mail support as follow-ups to sales calls.

✔ Automatic generation of proposals and offers.

✔ Offer access to CRM data through the Internet.

✔ Organize and manage sales activities through Internet browsers, Internet-enabled cell phones, and Personal Digital Assistants (PDAs).

You can also use your Web site to draw and qualify sales leads. These warm leads can automatically be routed to the CRM system for follow-up, either by electronic means or by your staff.

Making a CRM Plan Work

As with any system, you have to overcome resistance from within your organization. You need to circumvent several obstacles to reap the benefits of a comprehensive CRM system.

You knew it was too good to be true, didn't you? Yes, there's another hitch: The cost (in the short view) of implementing a CRM system is high. The good packages are expensive, and they must be integrated into a variety of other enterprise systems to be effective. You often need to hire consultants to get the system running to your satisfaction. In the long run, a good CRM will save your business unspeakable amounts of money and increase sales exponentially. (And if your CRM system is good, you will know just how much money the system is earning you — to the penny.)

The following sections show you what to do.

Picking a CRM package

The first step is to choose a CRM system package that suits your company's particulars. The packages vary greatly in what they do and what they cost. Consider the following when choosing a package:

- ✔ **Integration capabilities:** Your CRM system needs to talk to your existing systems. Make sure that it can extract order history from your order entry system, payment history from your accounting system, sales data from your contact management system, and customer service history from the customer service system. If you've had systems in place for years, you need to determine the time it will take and the expense in getting your existing systems up to par with a CRM system and the time and monetary expense of several CRM manufacturers.

  CRM manufacturers, such as Siebel (www.seibel.com) and I2 (www.i2.com), often provide the flexibility you need to integrate with many common software packages. These integration features help offset the rather steep sticker price.

- ✔ **System interface:** Make sure the software allows as many options as possible. For example, sometimes you may want your computer systems to collect data from the CRM system and send it to your Accounting system. On the other hand, sometimes you may want or need to gather the information and transfer it manually. Make certain that both options work (and are easy to use).

- ✔ **Gathering and reporting capabilities:** Not every CRM system provides the data gathering and reporting capabilities that you want. And many packages provide a lot of data you don't want — or need. Find a system that meets your needs — and then some. You want to have room to grow.

✔ **System cost:** Of course, it all comes down to cash money, and if you don't have the dough, Joe, you need to save up your allowance until you do. You will spend tens of thousands of dollars (Ouch, that does hurt, doesn't it?) on most of these systems. Make sure you know exactly what the CRM system will deliver. At this price, we probably don't need to tell you that you need to get your money's worth.

Tangling with your team

You can't just walk out one day and pick up a CRM system. You need key players to help choose the right package. They can create the same type of project and business justification that we describe in Chapter 3. Here's a list of steps:

1. **The business analyst and project manager determine how the CRM can improve your business.**

   They gather a list of requirements the system must meet.

2. **When the requirements are clear, the project manager and system architect weed out the systems that don't make the grade and take a close look at what's left to choose from.**

   This way, they only have to worry about evaluating packages that pass muster.

3. **The architect and project manager provide the executive sponsor and other key executives with a report that compares the best of the systems, listing individual strengths and weaknesses.**

   The presentation ought to include a recommendation on which product is the best choice. The business analyst should also participate, offering her two cents.

4. **The head honcho makes a decision.**

5. **The project manager and system architect set out looking for the right people to install and configure it.**

   Look for professionals who have experience with the product you've chosen.

You can also train your existing techie staff on installing the system and training the other employees on how to use it. The costs will be lower, but the time to for implementation is longer. Chapter 7 addresses *insourcing* (using your own staff) versus *outsourcing* (hiring outside consultants) to help you do the job. If you're serious about making CRM an integral part of your overall e-commerce strategy (a good idea), you may need to consider outsourcing implementation because the installation and integration stuff is tricky. Translation: You've already invested a lot of money, so what's a little more, big spender? The money may be worth letting someone else handle the headache.

Teaching old dogs new tricks (We mean that in the best possible way)

CRM systems change the way people work. For your CRM system to be of value, folk have to use it. John Sellsalot has to use the new-fangled system to report his sales calls. Victoria Service has to enter the results of each customer service contact. Martin Marquet has to analyze customer demographics to determine who is buying and who is not. Most people resist change and need to be coaxed into embracing new things. If no one uses the system, you wasted a large chunk of change.

Remind your staff that they are already providing status updates to their managers; using a uniform system makes the process, well . . . uniform. And it really helps employees determine which details are important enough to include. (There's no field for personal assessments, like, "Mr. Fat Cat has smelly breath.")

Acknowledge that because of the system's limitations (hey, nothing's perfect) staff will have to change its ways, but also highlight the good changes that come with the package:

- ✔ Bill Booker can get a *ton* of great customer information before he meets with a customer.

- ✔ Fran Chise can calm customers who call in for service by using the CRM system to remember what they bought, when they bought it and the comments they made the last time they called.

- ✔ Rachel Receivables can see payment history on her computer screen so that when she deals with customers who owe money she can be fair. (We're pretty sure she's not as harsh to first-time offenders as she is with habitually lazy payers.)

For more on the political muscle you need from the line-of-business managers and top level executives, see Chapter 3.

Benefiting from CRM systems: A Staples story

Properly used, CRM systems can greatly enhance customer satisfaction. Staples (www. staples.com/) has used its CRM system to upsell online customers and discover ways to improve the site and keep customers coming back. The end result has been quintupling sales through the Web site during fiscal year 2000. With over one-half billion dollars in sales, the Staples site posted the highest levels of traffic of any office supplies retail site. Staples gathers key information to provide more to its customers while containing labor and other costs.

Organizing Corporate Information with Business Intelligence Systems

You have reams of important, useful information about your products, your manufacturing processes, and your inventory. If you could organize this data and distribute it to your employees, business partners — and your customers — everyone could benefit from your acumen.

Business intelligence systems (BI) help you do just that. They coalesce enterprise data into a single data structure. They analyze the data to show historical trends and provide clues as to why those trends occur, when and why they usually occur, how they affect the business, and what, if anything, can be done to turn around a bad trend and create a good one to go in its place.

The goal is to use these systems (and the data they provide) to proactively adjust your business based on trends and adjust to maximize your profits. Consider the possibilities:

✔ **Sites for your eyes only:** Tracy visits your Web site. The Web site's back-end system looks at Tracy's demographic information and the business intelligence system, which is fully integrated with the Web site, spits out a list of your products that Tracy is likely to buy. The BI system says that women 25 to 45 like thingamajigs the most. Lo and behold, the next page Tracy moves to features ads for a whole host of thingamajigs The ad catches Tracy's eye and she buys.

✔ **Just enough widget to go around:** You're nearly out of widgets, which are seasonable items with constant (but lower) sales rates in the summer. Your inventory management system asks your business intelligence system to forecast widget sales for the next three months. The BI uses historical sales data to map trends and forecast demand so that you don't order more than you will sell.

✔ **Variation on the widget theme:** Supplier, Inc. sells whatsits to you. The company accesses your business intelligence system to discover how thingamajig sales have been during its four-month long whatsit extravaganza. Supplier uses the sales data to create a new promotional campaign and to forecast manufacturing needs so that you don't run short of product or end up with more whatsits than you need.

✔ **No more "But nobody told me" excuses:** At the end of each day, the business intelligence system analyzes Web site activity, such as the total traffic and number of visitors, average time visitors spend on the site, and the number of pages within the site the average customer accessed during a visit. Of course, the BI also calculates standard stuff like your total sales and other key indicators. If indicators vary more than 10 percent from plan, the BI sends an alert e-mail to the sales manager with graphs showing the current trends on the site.

- **There's always room for another doohickey:** Arthur Pim, your doohickey product manager, accesses the business intelligence system to discover which factors, such as advertising and marketing plans, price adjustments, sales of complimentary products historically increase doohickey sales. Using this model, Art comes up with a scheme to improve doohickey sales by 16 percent.

- **Ralph can't point the finger at you:** The business intelligence system reviews customer services calls and detects higher than normal call volume concerning the Widget 5000. The BI system automatically alerts the Widget Quality Assurance team through e-mail that something is amiss. QA investigates that matter and discovers a defect in the product, develops a solution, and advises the right people on how to fix it — all months before Ralph Nader gets a whiff of trouble.

Business intelligence systems can produce all these results and more. By correlating and analyzing data generated by systems throughout your enterprise (accounting, sales, marketing, manufacturing, shipping, receiving, and so on), you can track the activities of your organization and proactively guide your firm to meet its financial goals.

Applying business intelligence where it can do the most good

Where can your organization benefit most from business intelligence systems? Anywhere that historical trends can help you do business better. Several areas where business intelligence is clearly beneficial include

- Retail market analysis to predict buying trends among consumers

- Health care claims processing to analyze profitability and model account risks

- Financial analysis and revenue projections

- Forecasting for sales and manufacturing

- Analysis of customer service effectiveness and identification of areas for improvement

- Monitoring of Web traffic and site metrics

The list is truly endless. Work with your management team to reveal areas where trends and forecasts are determined using historical data. Business intelligence systems track history and show what influences these trends.

> # Snagging unformatted data
>
> Much of the data you want in your CRM system resides on paper — letters, faxes, and phone conversations contain vital information and a complete historical record of your contact with a customer.
>
> You need to identify and convert critical data. Converting can be costly, not just financially, but to the poor guy who has to wade through all this existing data and enter it into the new system. The hardest part, though is the painful transition from the old way of doing things to the new way. Make sure no customers slip through the cracks — remember, the system is called customer relations management for a reason.

Anatomy of a business intelligence system

Although there are some knowledge management systems that come fully loaded, BI systems are typically constructed by combining several pieces of software into a cohesive system. Most systems consist of

- ✔ **Data warehouse:** A data storage system that collects historical data from systems throughout your enterprise (accounting, sales, marketing, manufacturing, shipping, receiving, customer service, and so on). The data is organized and correlated to make it easy to access and understand how the different departments of your organization affect one another. To discover more about data warehouses, get *Data Warehousing For Dummies* by Alan R. Simon (published by Hungry Minds, Inc.).

  The data warehouse is built in a database system. Microsoft SQL Server, IBM DB2, Oracle 8i and others are all suitable candidates — and you probably already own one. You can also get systems specifically designed for data warehousing, like Essbase from Hyperion (www.hyperion.com), SAS (www.sas.com), and Red Brick Decision Server from Informix (www.informix.com).

- ✔ **Analytical software:** When the system correlates data, you have to analyze it. OnLine Analytical Processing software (OLAP) summarizes the information to make it palatable for human consumption. OLAP can also look for patterns and trends using mathematical models. This search for patterns is called *data mining*.

  OLAP software comes as part of some database software, such as Microsoft SQL Server and Essbase. Oracle and also IBM provide add-on software. You can also purchase OLAP systems as separate software entities. Business Objects and Cognos provide excellent OLAP tools.

✔ **Reporting software:** When you've analyzed the data, you need to distribute to the right people so that they can do something with the analysis. OLAP data can be distributed through traditional means (good old-fashioned paper reports), but because of the nature of OLAP data you may want to analyze it interactively.

Have your business analyst play with the numbers until she discovers what makes your business tick. Then you can get this information out to everyone who needs it quickly and painlessly. (That new-fangled Internet comes in handy.)

Packages from Brio (www.brio.com) and Seagate Crystal Reports can provide excellent reports from the data. Interactive analysis tools from Cognos (www.cognos.com), ProClarity (www.proclarity.com), and others provide interactive access to the data. And most tools automate the process of placing data on the Web. You can even use good old Microsoft Excel to analyze OLAP data by using its PivotTable functionality.

✔ **Automation:** Much of the advantage you glean from knowledge management software comes from proactively searching for trends and heading trouble off at the pass (or riding the wave of success). Some systems, such as SAP (www.sap.com) and PeopleSoft (www.peoplesoft.com), incorporate analysis of data into their everyday operations. But you will probably need to develop custom software to detect those trends and wave the flag so something gets done.

Getting the players onboard

Who do you need to develop your business intelligence systems? When you purchase any big-time business software, you have to gather a team of key players and make sure you have considered all the important steps, perks, downsides, and possible issues before you do another thing. (Check out Chapter 3 if you're looking for information about who makes up this team.)

How PCS uses its PCs to track data

PCS Health Systems manages prescriptions for the health insurance industry. When patients order new prescriptions, PCS's system checks for drug interactions with other prescriptions currently issued to the patient before releasing the prescription to be filled. PCS then automatically sends transactional and billing data to the appropriate insurance company.

Insurance companies can track the effectiveness of individual health plans and make comparisons between plans. The companies access the data using browser-based tools and reorganize and customize data delivery by health plan, prescription, physician, and patient. Health care organizations use this data to evaluate the effectiveness of prescriptions at healing specific conditions.

You may also write custom software to unearth the treasure hidden in your OLAP systems. The programming is straight forward, but working with multidimensional OLAP data is not. You may want to train your existing programmers in dealing with OLAP data. Or you may settle for a package that does most (if not all) the things you want.

Here are some additional tips:

- ✔ Have the project manager and business analyst take the lead in describing the need and business justification for implementing a BI system. Then these two need some expert help to design the system and determine its costs.

- ✔ Find a lead architect or developer who has expertise in data warehouse design and implementation. Experts in this field are scarce, so you may need to turn to consultants to get the help you need.

- ✔ Hunt down programmers experienced in installing and configuring the software packages you choose. Software vendors can help you identify those people. They may also offer training for your existing staff.

Once the BI systems are up and running, you still need to train people to use them. BI software is not for the masses. (Translation: If you're technophobic, be warned — you can't *pick up* BI by messing around with it the way you might pick up Microsoft Word by fiddling around for a few minutes.) Typically, business analysts, marketers, and product managers — the typical MBA crowd — should know how to use your company's BI software to view historical trends and find the factors that influence those trends.

Delivering Key Data

The Internet enables you to distribute information globally. It connects people anytime, anywhere. Its store and forward messaging structures allow you to send data that will wait until people are ready to receive it. You don't have to wait for an immediate response. Here are just a few of the things you can do with the Internet:

- ✔ E-mail reports and summaries of data.

- ✔ Provide Web sites that collect and display data on demand, whenever it is required.

- ✔ Send alerts to key decision-makers through their cell phones or PDAs.

- ✔ Forward electronic reports to customers through e-mails or file transfer through the Internet.

So simple Simplot can do it

J.R. Simplot Company (www.simplot.com) used business intelligence to get data from IT and into the hands of the people who make decisions. The company deployed a business application through its intranet that allows analysts to access data organized by customer, product line, and supplier logistics. The data can be accessed within the walls of the company, or without, using a Web browser to drill through the data. Getting more people to work with the data has improved the reliability and accuracy of that data. With more accurate information, the executives at J.R. Simplot make better decisions.

You can add interactivity to your reports as well. Employees, partners, and customers can access your reporting Web server and set parameters to control the output of reports. The report recipients can interactively drill through multidimensional layers of data to track down sources of trends. They can instantly integrate current data into future forecasts and adjust purchasing and production through the Internet from anywhere in the world.

Visually modeling data results

Your Web-enabled systems provide the technology to deliver data to wherever you need it. By getting mission-critical information to partners, decision-makers, and customers, you can help your business stay ahead of the curve and running in top form.

Your Web browser can go far beyond the limitations of your printer in presenting data. You can show comparisons, compositions, and trends in terms that people understand almost immediately. Color adds a new dimension to your data, drawing attention to critical areas that require attention.

People respond well to visualizations of complex data. Charts and graphs make numbers clear and easy to understand. Color can add rich dimensions to understanding data.

You can also add animation. Using motion to help people understand how data interacts and unfolds can help you emphasize important revelations. But don't just add graphs, color, and animation for the sake of having them. Use these tools to focus and clarify key information, not just to make things look slick.

Nautilus has its tentacles on the pulse of data access and transfer technology

Nautilus Insurance Group uses the Internet to distribute critical business intelligence information to its independent agents. Nautilus established a back-end Web portal that allows agents to access claims information and data about payment history and policy losses. The agents use the information to determine whether or not to renew policies. The best part is that the independent agents can view all the data related to a claim from a single point without having to pick up a phone.

By sharing critical data with their business partners, Nautilus strengthens relationships. The independent insurance agents use the information to make better decisions and improve their profitability. Nautilus uses software from Brio Technology (`www.brio.com`) to make the real-time exchange possible — and keep data distribution costs low. Everyone wins.

Chapter 16

Managing the Supply Chain

....

....

*E*ver feel like your business is just a spoke in a giant wheel of life? The process of getting even the simplest products from manufacturing to consumers requires a staggering number of people. Fortunately, this is one area where e-commerce can really help your business. By automating processes and communications, you can make your business operate faster, reduce paperwork, eliminate mistakes, and cut costs. At least, the potential is there — e-commerce isn't a magic bullet!

A *supply chain* is the chain that goods follow — from the instant they're manufactured right down to the second customers purchase them. Although there's really no difference in the way the supply chain of yore and the e-commerce supply chain actually work, in e-commerce, even more than in traditional business, managing the supply chain is one of the keys to successfully competing.

In this chapter, you find out how the e-commerce supply chain works, discover how your business can take advantage of supply chain management techniques, and design your systems to cooperate with those of your business partners. All you need to do is some clever planning and forecasting, and the next thing you know, you'll see a significant impact on your bottom line. (Did we mention it will be a *positive* impact?) Of course you really aren't in this for the money, right? Well, good news: An efficient supply chain makes customers really happy.

What Is the Supply Chain?

The supply chain is nothing more — or less — than the process of getting a product from a pile of raw materials to a final consumer. Of course, organizations and individuals (suppliers, shippers, distributors, retail outlets, financial institutions, and anyone else involved in the process of delivering goods) are all a big part of the process. For the supply chain to work smoothly, all of these companies and people need to cooperate and communicate with each other.

What's the big deal? Customers don't care whom they purchase geegaws from; they just know that they want geegaws. Not next week or even tomorrow, but now. The worst way to lose customers is to let your competition beat you and be *first to market*. Additionally, most products are worthless if they don't make it to their final destination on time (if your customers didn't need it until next Wednesday, they wouldn't ask for it until next Wednesday).

How does the e-commerce supply chain differ from the supply chain your traditional business is already accustomed to? It doesn't, really. What's different is your ability to leapfrog links in the chain, making direct connections with partner companies and eliminating middlemen. What's different is e-commerce's ability to make things happen instantaneously and automatically, saving your business time and money.

Finding a Cure for the Warehouse Blues

The perfect warehouse, from a business point of view, consists of a receiving dock and a shipping dock — with no storage space needed. Of course, your business may be striving to meet this goal and having varying levels of success.

If you do a little investigating, you'll discover that most warehouse managers, if they had their druthers, would reorder whatever stock was sold at the end of each day instead and of ordering in bulk. Ordering in bulk involves trying to figure out how long a product takes to get from a supplier to the ware-house, adding a day or two for padding, and using sales department esti-mates of how much of a product can be sold in a set period of time. Here's how automated supply chain management systems can make warehouses smaller and more efficient as well as save you paper and time:

✔ **Tracking systems:** By electronically tracking every sale out of your warehouse, computer systems can generate daily reorders automatically. The computer systems can use past sales information to order enough product to cover you on weekends, holidays, or other days when your business won't receive new stock.

- ✔ **Electronic purchasing:** You can send purchase orders electronically to suppliers, and suppliers' systems can automatically process the orders. With the right supplier partnerships, your restock orders may even be processed the same day they're made.

- ✔ **Electronic invoicing:** Suppliers can invoice you electronically for each restock order. This reduces the suppliers' paperwork, which in turn reduces yours, making daily ordering more feasible.

- ✔ **Scanning systems:** Your warehouse can receive incoming shipments using scanners, which informs your systems that new product has arrived. This automatically updates your inventory systems, helping your computers prepare your next daily order.

Many Enterprise Resource Management (ERM) software packages, such as those from the e-business solutions company SAP (www.sap.com), contain the basic capabilities for improving these transactions. ERM systems like SAP R/3, for example, when coupled with compatible e-commerce systems like mySAP or Microsoft's BizTalk Server, have the power to communicate with an unlimited number of business partners.

Drop shipping and virtual warehousing

If the perfect warehouse has no shelves, then building the right business partnerships can actually go one step further. If your business simply resells products without doing any additional manufacturing to them, why have a warehouse at all?

Ingersoll-Rand uses Web service to get more suppliers into the act

Ingersoll-Rand (www.irco.com), a multibillion-dollar manufacturer of industrial equipment, tackled the problem of building a system that helps its suppliers fulfill its need for parts and materials automatically. It created a separate division, 21st Supplier, to facilitate automated parts delivery.

Working with supply chain management software from SupplyWorks (www.supplyworks.com), Ingersoll-Rand developed a Web site that allows smaller suppliers to look at the needs of manufacturers for parts and supplies. Ingersoll-Rand uses the system to schedule delivery of the parts and eliminate costly and error-prone paperwork. The system is estimated to reduce the cost of placing orders with smaller suppliers by as much as 67 percent.

Sometimes being stuck in the middle is a good thing

CABLExpress (www.cablexpress.com), a reseller of network products and services, receives orders from customers and electronically orders the products from large distributors like Ingram Micro and Tech Data, which drop ship the products directly to customers. CABLExpress never incurs the expense of receiving and holding products from these vendors.

Initially CABLExpress had concerns that distributors would cut the middleman out and sell to customers directly. To avoid this potential problem, CABLExpress worked with its lawyers to create non-disclosure agreements with its suppliers to protect the company's information assets and customers. (See Chapter 8 for more information on hammering out agreements with your business partners.)

When an e-tail customer orders a product from your site, your ERM system sends the order directly to your supplier. The supplier sends the order to the customer. When a partner receives electronic purchase orders, the company electronically invoices your business for the products. This process is called *drop shipping*, and as you can see, it can take a lot of time out of your supply chain because it happens instantly across the Internet (or private network connections).

Virtual warehouses carry a lot of hidden disadvantages, though, and you need to make sure you're comfortable with them before making this technique a part of your e-commerce strategy. Here are some of the major cons:

- ✔ **You often have very little knowledge of inventory levels in the warehouse.** To combat this problem, find suppliers that will link their inventory systems to your order-entry system through the Internet.

- ✔ **You can't make your suppliers ship.** However, you can integrate your suppliers' order-tracking systems with yours so you can take an electronic peek at the status of your open orders and remain proactive if shipping gets sluggish.

- ✔ **Controlling shipping costs can be difficult.** You have less control over split shipments. You cannot control which location they ship from — New York or Oregon, for example — which can affect shipping prices and delivery time.

Drop shipping is referred to as *virtual warehousing* when a business handles *all* its inventory this way.

By establishing relationships with several suppliers and integrating your systems with theirs, you still give your customers the advantage of an all-in-one place to shop, but reduce or eliminate the need to maintain stock (especially bulky, large, and rarely ordered products) in a warehouse.

Replenishing inventory automatically

Many companies have inventory managers who are responsible for analyzing the company's on-hand inventory, production demands, and sales patterns and for ordering inventory to meet demand. Supply chain management systems can take the burden of day-to-day inventory management off these employees' plates, freeing them up for more important work and reducing the errors and turnaround time for inventory management.

With the proper forecasting models in place, your supply chain management system can effectively manage your inventory automatically. In order to do so, your CRM system must be able to do the following:

- ✔ Determine how long it takes suppliers to deliver inventory. Use data provided by your suppliers and verify it against past delivery performance.

- ✔ Determine how much inventory you need to have on hand to keep up with production — including anticipated growth or reduction in production.

- ✔ When inventory levels fall below a certain threshold, automatically place orders with electronic purchase.

- ✔ Constantly monitor production demands and supplier delivery performance so that the system can adjust itself (and your inventory) to precisely meet your demands and supplier availability.

Replacing warehouse space with the Internet

Canadian Tire (www.canadiantire.ca) is one of Canada's largest retailers, with revenues exceeding $3.3 billion (USD) in 2000. As a matter of fact, business was so good that the company had trouble managing its inventory. It just couldn't store all the products and get them to its bricks-and-mortar locations fast enough.

The company partnered with Stockholm-based Industri-Matematik to deploy a Web-based supply chain system. The system makes the movement of inventory smoother and reduces the amount of physical warehouse space the company must maintain. The system supplies product forecasts to Canadian Tire's suppliers through the Web. The suppliers use that information to schedule the delivery of goods where they are needed, just before they are needed.

Speeding up manufacturing processes

If you can't avoid maintaining a warehouse because you manufacture products yourself and have to keep them *somewhere*, or because you combine products from several suppliers into a finished product, your supply chain management software can fine-tune your delivery. By increasing inventory turns from 6 or 7 per year to 20 or 30, you save money — and that savings gets added directly to your corporate bottom line.

Use electronic systems to develop accurate forecasting models so that you can plan your manufacturing schedules to produce finished products just in time to meet the anticipated demand.

If you link your systems with your suppliers' systems, you can automate the process further. After you get product forecasts from your customers, you can set a production schedule and schedule delivery of goods and materials with your suppliers.

The world's major shipping carriers are e-commerce ready, just waiting for your systems to integrate with theirs. UPS, Federal Express, Airborne Express, and others — provide these services for free through the Web.

Applying Just-in-Time Manufacturing Strategies

Many products in today's marketplace are available with a wide range of options. Everything from cars to computers is custom-built on a regular basis, and with great success. If you're dealing with products that customers can customize, you can save time and money by using *just-in-time* strategies. Believe it or not, selling customized products no longer requires massive amounts of inventory and manual labor. You need to figure out how to efficiently build products to order and distribute them to customers on demand. This process requires some serious forecasting and demand planning:

✔ *Forecasting* is the process of analyzing your company's past performance and predicting future orders. You use the forecasts to plan your business activities. For example, if customer orders for a particular product have been slowing down over the past few months, forecasting can help you predict when carrying that product will become unprofitable. Forecasting also can tell you how many doohickies you need to build for the Christmas rush. Products from Ariba (www.ariba.com), i2 (www.i2.com), Commerce One (www.commerceone.com), and others help you model the factors that affect your sales and predict what you need when. Chapter 15 explains forecasting in more detail.

✔ *Demand planning* is the process of determining what kinds of orders you expect your customers to place, and arranging your inventory and production schedules accordingly. It's a difficult task, because customers' needs are just as fluid as your own. To properly plan your long-term demand, you need to carefully analyze the entire supply chain that you're a part of. Every week, use the new data from your forecasting system and reevaluate demand.

Opening Your Systems to B2B Customers

If you want to take advantage of supply chain management software, you need to share information. If you can open your systems to your vendors and customers, and provide them with accurate information, they can work better with you and for you.

When you decide to share the data in your systems with other individuals and organizations, many difficult issues come up. How will you protect the data? How will you format your data so that your partners can understand it, and how will you format their data so your systems can work with it? Here's a peek at the important issues:

✔ **Compromise:** Sharing data means making decisions and compromises. You need to decide exactly how your data will be shared with business partners and how much information you're willing to part with.

✔ **Follow their rules:** Ideally, you should offer information to your business customers in *their* format, not yours. They'll be able to browse your information using their own tools, making them more comfortable and more likely to make a purchase.

✔ **Don't go overboard:** Your business owns a lot of confidential data, and there's a fine line between sharing enough information to improve business processes, and sharing too much information — which can damage your business. See Chapter 8 and seek legal counsel before entering into partnerships.

✔ **Find out what you're going to get:** Work with business customers to find out what data they supply. Integrate that data into your data warehouse so you can integrate it into your business intelligence systems (those systems are explained in Chapter 15).

✔ **Integrate, integrate, integrate:** If you're going to automate the supply chain, you have to integrate your accounting, inventory, and production scheduling systems with your suppliers and customers.

✔ **Find the right system:** World-class Enterprise Resource Planning (ERP) software from companies like SAP, Oracle, PeopleSoft, and Baan enables you to manage your business and share information, collect and share data, transmit data directly to partners, and work with EDI and other information-sharing technologies.

✔ **Keep partners informed:** You can keep customers up to speed with e-commerce technologies (such as e-mail), which are reliable, efficient, and inexpensive.

✔ **Don't fudge:** If you know your production output isn't going to meet the demand, you may consider bumping your numbers a bit — after all, it'll keep your customers from going to other suppliers. In the long run, though, you'll lose customers' trust and sales.

Westwave Communications (www.westwave. com) works with third-party manufacturers to assemble and sell circuit boards. It needs software to share bills of materials to keep production flowing (a bill of materials lists the individual parts used to build a particular product). But Westwave couldn't justify the software's $100,000-plus price tag. Instead, it formed a business partnership with bom.com (www.bom.com). bom.com enables suppliers to access Westwave's bills of material through the Internet for just $100/month per user.

Chapter 17

Saving Time and Money with E-Procurement

Your business runs on more than the supplies you buy. You need office supplies, janitorial supplies, light bulbs — you get the drift. Supplies that keep your organization running are called *maintenance, repair, and operating* (MRO) supplies. These supplies can consume a considerable portion of your budget, and most organizations struggle to control their procurement.

You can use the same technology that helps you sell over the Internet to gain control of MRO purchases. These systems can empower your employees to get the things they need and help you control the purchases. Whether you keep control of the system or go to your suppliers for help, e-procurement can pay off for you in a big way.

This chapter addresses procuring MRO goods and services. If you want to know how to sell use e-procurement systems, see Chapter 19, which covers B2C and B2B e-marketplaces. To find out about purchasing materials directly related to the product and services you sell, see Chapter 16.

What Is E-Procurement?

E-procurement uses Internet technologies to buy and sell goods between businesses. E-procurement systems empower employees to work with vendors to order and schedule the products and services they need — right from their desktops. Oh yeah, and you save money, too. MRO is estimated to be a $500-billion market in 2000. And most of that gets spent without proper management.

If you want to keep total control of your e-procurement system, you need to deploy a *buy-side* e-procurement system. Buy-side systems are e-procurement systems that you build to replace your current purchase requisition system. Employees can order and schedule the supplies they need — even book travel — conveniently from their own computers. Many vendors, seeking to help their customers and add value to their organizations build systems that enable business customers to procure products through the Internet. When sellers build and maintain the system, we call them *sell-side systems*.

Your buy-side e-procurement system lives inside your intranet. A variety of commercial-off-the-shelf products from firms, such as Ariba (www.ariba.com) and I2 Technologies (www.i2.com), can give you a leg up. You can also develop your own systems. Just remember that you can spend a lot of money on these systems. Carefully determine the benefits you receive, quantified in dollars and cents, and justify the cost to implement your e-procurement system.

Advantages of buy-side e-procurement systems

You can get vendors to supply e-procurement to your employees. Many marketplaces provide management controls and reporting to enhance value. Investing in building a custom system to deploy e-procurement within your organization is a good idea because

- ✔ **My way:** If it's your system, you set the rules. You can implement any set of rules that you can imagine and that your programmers can code.

- ✔ **Safe!:** You can keep your systems — and your purchasing — safe inside your firewall. Use the internal security and authentication systems of your intranet to control what each individual user can do.

- ✔ **Choices:** You can sometimes choose vendors and products independently. For example, you place a product into your catalog but change its source vendor. This switch from one vendor to another won't affect your end-users — they won't need to learn new software.

- ✔ **Ease:** You can more easily integrate the purchases with your back-end systems. You control the data formats and work flows of information.

- ✔ **Slicing:** You get the exact information that you need out of the system. Because you have control of the data, you can transform and format it to meet the needs of your management team.

Money spent on MRO comes directly off the bottom line. Saving $10 on MRO averages $130 in revenue. A typical firm could improve earnings by 5% by reducing MRO a mere 2%. Imagine what improving your corporate earnings by 5% could do for your firm.

Cutting paperwork and saving time

Here's a good score card for an e-procurement system:

- ✔ **Power to the people:** Employees can requisition or purchase items and services directly from their computers.

- ✔ **No more paper:** Computers handle purchase requisitions, purchase orders, requests for quotation, and invoices and acknowledgements electronically.

- ✔ **The disappearing middle man:** For routine, inexpensive purchases, no one should have to manually approve anything. When purchases need to be approved, do it on computer screens, quickly and cleanly.

- ✔ **Money in your pocket:** E-procurement extends the cost-lowering, service-enhancing powers of your purchase department to the small, frequent purchases that they really don't have time to manage.

- ✔ **Report this:** Everything gets put in reports automatically, without anyone staying three hours after closing to throw them together. The reports can be distributed electronically or distributed through the e-mail system.

- ✔ **Save time and money:** You've probably filled out a purchase requisition and then waited for days to get it approved before you could order something. Then you had to wait even longer for the purchase requisition to be processed into a purchase order. This is a tedious, mechanical process that is annoyingly delayed because the approvers and processors are rightfully engaged in more important tasks. Your order doesn't get attention until its stops people from doing work.

   You can set up the system to automatically notify a supervisor if a purchase seems unusually large (50,000 pencils instead of 500) or expensive ($500 dollars for 50 pencils). And because supervisors only have to approve the big stuff, they have time to give the important, costly, or big orders the attention they deserve.

- ✔ **Automate, automate:** Place orders over the Web to automate paperwork. By integrating the procurement system with the back-end systems, payment approval can be automated, which saves time, paper, and confusion.

Understanding How E-Procurement Systems Work

Take a view of your organization from 40,000 feet. You have employees who need all types of MRO supplies — from paper and pens to bathroom supplies to light bulbs to tools and replacement parts for your machinery. The goal of e-procurement is to enable employees to order what they need from their computers. Here's how it works:

1. **Eric Employee fires up the old Web browser and accesses your chosen e-procurement site, orders a case of copier paper, and goes on about his business.**

   With the security parameters you set, your system knows who has permission to do what. In most networks, employees may already be logged into the network, so they don't need to log into the e-procurement system separately — they just need to find it.

2. **The system shows Eric what he can order.**

   Through their browsers, purchasers search through catalogs of goods and services. These items can come from a variety of vendors.

   No paperwork, no delay, no hassle.

3. **Behind the scenes, your business' e-procurement system displays only the supplies that Eric has authorization to order.**

   When he completes his order, the system checks to make certain Eric hasn't exceeded his budget and can order the amount of paper he requested.

   If an order is over a certain limit (say $200), the system may route an electronic purchase request to Eric's supervisor for approval. Otherwise, the system automatically approves the request.

4. **The system may coalesce several orders from around the company and sends a consolidated order to the vendor.**

   The vendor appreciates the larger orders and cuts your company a break on the price.

5. **The system tracks orders so that employees know the status of open purchases.**

   The data collected provides the basis of management reports and historical performance measurements for vendors.

6. **Because your company's e-procurement system is integrated with your accounting system, payment authorization is made the instant the order is received.**

The system can submit orders directly to vendors when they are placed, or it can coalesce orders and submit larger, single orders on a daily or weekly basis. Look for vendors that will work with you in handling orders and shipments that simplify your internal processes.

Microsoft Market fits the bill

Because the Microsoft employee base grew to thousands, Microsoft wanted to exploit the volume of its purchases to reduce costs. Microsoft (MS) Market, an intranet application built on the MS Commerce Server product, was born from this need.

Microsoft employees use MS Market to purchase MRO goods, such as office supplies, catering, and computer equipment. The system tracks the budget allocated to each employee and automates order processing. Purchases are integrated into Microsoft's SAP enterprise resource planning system to streamline payment to vendors. The system handles an estimated 3 billion dollars in transactions and over 1,000 orders daily and cuts time to get the goods by 60 percent.

Most employees want to prove that they are trustworthy and capable. Giving them a personal budget to manage allows them to prove their worth. As a bonus to you, you can use fiscal performance as a good way of determining who's ready for additional responsibility. Here's another bonus: Morale improves when employees feel trusted.

By reducing the time to procure products and placing responsibility in the hands of the people who use them, you improve productivity and reduce errors. Suppliers get to work directly with those who actually use their wares. Everyone wins.

Positioning Sell-Side Systems and Working with B2B Exchanges

You may not be able to justify the expense of building and maintaining buy-side systems in your organization. You can find vendors who build and maintain systems that you can use. Systems maintained by sellers are called *sell-side systems*. B2B e-marketplaces, or exchanges are communities of vendors. Exchanges are usually sponsored by consortiums of suppliers in a particular industry, and they help customers by enabling them to enjoy many of the advantages of e-procurement with none of the hassle and ownership.

E-marketplaces represent large business opportunities throughout the world. Exceeding 2 billion dollars in 2000, sell-side system sales are projected to exceed 80 billion dollars by 2005.

Setting up shop on employee desktops

Allowing employees to order from e-marketplaces gives them browser access to the wares of a wide variety of vendors. A single site can offer products from literally hundreds of vendors and represent thousands of products.

Employees can obtain products in a variety of forms:

✔ **Wish books:** Standard catalog sales enable employees select items from the marketplace catalog. These products can come from multiple vendors.

✔ **Sold!:** Auctions present an opportunity for suppliers to offer goods and commodities. Businesses can bid for goods or services, such as transportation.

✔ **Quote me:** Public requests are great opportunities to solicit quotes for requested goods. Suppliers can bid to meet the requirements of consumers.

Most of e-marketplace portal sites (at least the ones that should interest you the most) also provide management reports. Instead of dealing with a large number of different vendors, all transactions funnel through a single source, thus reducing paperwork and keeping your accounting department happy. Many supply management reports track spending, simplifying the process of controlling where corporate dollars are spent.

Identifying successful sell-side systems

Successful supply-side systems share common characteristics. When choosing a trading community for your employees, look for these key characteristics:

✔ **Value-added services:** These help you manage purchasing and integrate with your existing systems.

✔ **Seamless integration:** You should not be able to distinguish between vendors within the site.

✔ **Accurate product information:** Suppliers must work relentlessly to keep catalogs up-to-date and to keep accurate data on product availability and delivery information.

✔ **Browser-based:** Community servers must be browser-based to simplify deployment into your enterprise. Their system must provide sufficient scalability to handle customer load and product changes.

Carefully examine the financials and backers of trading communities before rolling out an e-marketplace to your staff.

CASE STUDY

Customized sell-side systems

To wrest negotiated contracts and item control, you need sell-side marketplaces that customize to meet your needs. For example, SciQuest (www.sciquest.com) provides e-marketplace services for science corporations. Going beyond simple e-marketplace services to help customers better manage their purchases, its SelectSite services enable customers to choose specific products and vendors from SciQuests partners. Integration software works with a wide variety of accounting and Enterprise Resource Planning (ERP) systems. SciQuest can customize the site presented to your employees, and can also provide integrated cost controls and management tools to help companies control their spending.

Controlling Travel Expenses

Even with the advent of e-commerce systems, real-time conferencing, and electronic communications, you may need to move (transport) people for business functions. Sometimes you can't avoid attending a meeting in person, traveling between manufacturing and production facilities, or visiting vendors and customers. Handling travel arrangements and processing expense reports is costly and time consuming.

Anytime money is spent is also an opportunity to save money. Take advantage of the e-revolution that has struck the travel industry. Portal sites, such as Expedia (www.expedia.com) and Travelocity (www.travelocity.com), make it simple for consumers to book their own flights and hotels. Similarly, you can provide Web-based travel reservation systems for your employees. Products, such as mySAP (www.sap.com), allow employees to book travel within the limitation and business rules your organization implements.

You can also save money by using electronic submissions of expense reports. Set up systems that enable employees to download electronic versions of the reports to their laptops or personal digital assistants (PDAs) — that way they can fill the forms out while they're on the road. Or make the expense reports a Web application that they can access from home, a hotel, or their office. Configure this program to check for administrative stuff (that columns are added properly, that no maximum limits were exceeded, and so forth) and to provide a well-formatted reimbursement request for approval.

TIP

You can also integrate expense reports with your accounting and other back-end systems to make certain the travel expenses are duly noted, reported and, when appropriate, billed.

CASE STUDY

Watchin' those travelin' dollars

Biztravel.com, the online subsidiary of Rosenbluth International, provides Internet self-service travel through its www.biztravel@mycompany services. This service, offering 24/7 access to live travel agents, works with companies to control which employees can book travel and how billing is arranged. Accessible through e-mail and online chats, its high volume helps negotiate reduced ticket prices and travel guarantees. The service also offers a wide range of management reports to keep tabs on travel dollars, and an unplugged version of the service to allow travel plans to be downloaded and accessible when travelers on are on the road (and without remote server accessibility). When travel arrangements are handled like this through the Internet, cost savings are passed to the customer.

Sounds a bit like a commercial. Our point is, Biztravel. Com (along with expedia.com, travelocity.com and others) go through a great deal of trouble and expense to help your people get where they need to go — and back again — safely and easily.

Procuring a Plan for Your New E-Procurement System

Any e-procurement system is a blend of technology, relationships, and business processes that target specific goals. Planning an e-procurement system is a microcosm of developing any e-commerce system. The steps we list in Chapter 3 can be applied to this system as well.

Following six simple steps helps you organize your efforts:

1. **Define the ultimate business goals of the system.**

   Evaluate what you have to gain and what is at risk if you fail; make certain that your system makes good business sense.

2. **Figure out and write down how you currently make your purchases.**

   You will be amazed at how your system actually works. Then outline how you would make this process more efficient and cost effective. Don't worry right now about how to implement it — just concentrate on making the system right.

3. **Design a system that implements your plan.**

   Choose technologies that achieve the business goals and get the system to work as planned. When you're not certain which way to go, create proof-of-concepts that demonstrate the viability of different technologies and options. (For more on proof-of-concepts, see the upcoming section "Creating a proof of your cool new concept.")

4. **Build the system you design.**

   You may need to purchase software, develop systems, or cooperate with e-marketplace vendors to deploy their sites within your organization.

5. **Plan to test your systems to make certain they deliver as promised.**

   Go back to your original vision to confirm that the features you required are present. Also, make certain that employees can use the system effectively.

6. **Deploy the system throughout the enterprise.**

   Train your employees to use your new system, and monitor it to find its strengths and weakness and to plan the next round of improvements.

Usually, the best method for setting up an e-procurement system (or any other big system) is to hatch a plan (using business analysis), design an architecture that uses it, choose the technology that works best with your design, and build the system.

Defining the vision for your e-procurement system

You can start with several fairly universal goals for your system.

- ✓ Use the combined buying power of your entire organization to obtain better pricing and service.
- ✓ Reduce cycle times and costs through automation.
- ✓ Accurately track and report purchases to apply better control.
- ✓ Control unauthorized purchasing.

After you define your goals, list the benefits of those goals. Try to quantify the cost savings objectives. For example, calculate how much money you save if cycle times are reduced from six days to three. Or how much manpower you can save by eliminating the existing purchase requisition/purchase order paper system. These money amounts will help define the value of the system.

After you know what you can save, figure out how much you think an e-procurement system will cost. (See the following section "Finding areas for improvement.") If the system will only save $75,000 a year and you know it will cost at least $150,000 to build, you have to determine whether a two-year return on investment (ROI) makes sense.

Consider other risks as well. If employees won't use the system, it's wasted money. If you don't have the manpower (or financial resources) to develop and maintain it, then such a system is little more than a pipe dream. As you list risks, brainstorm ways to eliminate them.

You can win a great deal of support for the system by including all the parties involved in producing your vision. Top-level management support will give you the impetus you need to get the project across the finish line.

Finding areas for improvement

After you determine the parameters of your e-procurement system, get your business analyst involved in investigating your existing systems to determine what needs improvement. Be brutally honest when mapping out how your existing purchasing systems work. You can approach it this way:

1. **Diagram/delineate how your system currently works.**

   Accomplish this with narrative text (time flow in nature) or schematic flow chart diagrams. You may need to use both. Include all the ways a purchase gets recorded.

2. **Determine how long the process takes.**

   By assigning average times for each step in the purchasing process, you can determine your current cycle times.

3. **Think through your systems.**

   Identify systematic changes that could improve the way you make purchases, such as reducing paperwork and minimizing approval time.

4. **Create clear specifications of what you would like the system to do.**

   Functional specification for your system should clearly list, in detail, what you expect and require from your system.

5. **Estimate the time and money saved through less paperwork and bureaucracy by comparing the existing and the proposed systems.**

   This is the foundation of your economic justification.

6. **Estimate the cost of developing and deploying the systems you suggested by comparing the cost of implementing a new system with the projected savings.**

   You may discover that the cost savings don't justify the system that you'd like to employ. Maybe you should stick with what you have. You may need to choose less costly technology, or find other means for justifying the project, such as integrating a new business after a merger or expanding to additional remote facilities.

For help preparing your analysis, consider hiring a consulting firm and experienced software developers. These professionals know how to perform this type of analysis and can help you discover and organize the critical data to paint a clear picture of your plan.

Making custom-designed improvements

If you decide that your system needs tweaking, or you want to improve an off-the-shelf product you're considering using, this is the point where you start refining your system. You can

- **Purchase and configure off-the-shelf software.** Just-add-water software may not be custom-designed, but it may be an improvement over what you're currently using.

- **Write your own buy-side systems.** You can use a combination of off-the-shelf products and custom software, or an entire project you implement from scratch.

- **Deploy a sell-side system within your organization.** Find an e-marketplace or private consortium that has the products, pricing, and service that meet your needs. Configure it with the suppliers and make it available to your employees.

Designing the pieces to create the whole

After you settle on the technology, you need to design the system. Like any complex system, you need to design it in pieces and then fit the pieces together. Look at your e-procurement system from these angles.

- **Consider the physical architecture, especially servers.** Sell-side systems rely on the servers of the vendors, whereas buy-side systems require that you host the application software. Your fact-finding mission should include the following questions:

  - Which servers host the system?

  - Can you place the purchasing systems on existing servers, or do you need to acquire servers just for purchasing?

  - Can your employees connect to the servers through your firewalls?

- **Lay out your software.** You need to choose operating systems and security software. You need to decide whether you write custom software or configure commercial off-the-shelf packages. For sell-side systems, you need to provide desktop access to the Web site and configure the customization features of the site.

- **Calculate the way your system will scale (expand).** Make certain that your system can grow to meet future needs.

- **Secure your system.** Your e-procurement system gain velocity by automating approval, so you need to assure that only authenticated users can place orders. You can usually count on network subsystems to protect access, and you can count on the vendors in sell-side systems to authenticate.

Preparing to connect with suppliers

When you've chosen your vendor(s), you have to exchange a great deal of information. You need to fill out electronic catalogs with their products, develop secure reliable communications, and develop a work flow and process that keeps your company and your suppliers in sync.

To protect this information exchange, you need secure channels of communication with your suppliers. With a variety of technologies available, each with its own problems and price tag,

you and your suppliers need to agree on a common communication channel. Realize that this is a decision that is not entirely yours to make.

You also need to agree on how you authenticate data transfers. You may build an extranet or encrypt data flowing between you and your suppliers. Read Chapters 2, 11, and 13 for more on technology used to connect your business to others.

System Construction

After you settle on a system design, it's time to build it. Diligent management of the construction phase is critical as you battle scope creep. *Scope creep* is adding features to a system as you develop it — features not included in the initial design. Scope creep keeps systems from being completed on time — and you from keeping your original budget.

As your programmers and designers work on your system, encourage them to incubate creative ideas that make your site interesting and functional. As your users test and examine your system, they too will come up with interesting ideas to make this system better, or at least more fun.

Setting up a sell-side system may not require the services of programmers or designers. The most technical process is typically configuring security so that the system can traverse your firewall to the desktops of your users.

Invest in training your employees to use the sell-side system. You can spend a lot of time and effort supporting your vendors' application if the users cannot figure out how to use it.

Collecting catalog data

Your suppliers will want to provide you with the latest item and pricing data. Work with your vendors to establish common data formats for receiving catalog information. You can use this data to electronically update your catalogs and keep item data current, but you certainly don't want to spend your time and money preparing (translating, if you will) their data for your system.

CASE STUDY

Coming up rosettas

RosettaNet (www.rosettanet.org), a non-profit consortium formed to promote common Internet commerce standards, works to create common processes to facilitate e-procurement. This group has developed over 100 XML-based business processes, or Partner Interface Processes (PIPs). The PIPs provide a mechanism for creating, canceling, and exchanging purchase orders. Intel uses PIPs to exchange data with its business partners and to keep their back-end systems up-to-date. RosettaNet's technology offers a 2–10 percent savings in purchases — all bottom line dollars for the customers.

Using these common processes and data formats helps companies integrate their systems. By finding standards to simplify sharing data, you can include more companies in your collaboration and write less custom code.

We recommend that you find vendors that transmit data that adheres to common standards; this standardization helps get item data quickly and accurately to your employees. When you base your systems on public standards adhered to by many vendors, you have the freedom to choose from a wider range of vendors that provide you with the data you need.

TIP

Biztalk.org (www.biztalk.org) is a site sponsored by Microsoft to help establish public standards for formatting standard data, such as catalog data, in eXtensible Markup Language (XML) for Enterprise Application Integration (EAI) and B2B document exchanges. Integrating existing data models, solutions, and application infrastructure, and then adapting them for e-commerce, is the emphasis.

Synchronizing processes with partners and vendors

You and your vendors need more than the compatible exchange of data. Your systems and their systems must share an understanding of the workflow of purchasing and delivering products. You need to coordinate processes and ensure that they work hand in hand.

Setting up buy-side commercial off-the-shelf software

What a wonderful world it would be if setting up software packages for e-procurement packages comprised simply popping a CD in the drive on the server and letting it run. Unfortunately, you need to roll up your sleeves and get to work to whip an off-the-shelf software package into shape.

The complexity level of configuring off-the-shelf software can vary from a couple of hours to hiring a consultant for several weeks. The more you invest in customization, the more you can tailor your system to meet your exact requirements and get the precise results you desire.

An important consideration for choosing a commercial off-the-shelf package is its integration capabilities. ERP systems, such as SAP (www.sap.com) and PeopleSoft (www.peoplesoft.com), offer e-procurement modules that integrate seamlessly into their enterprise software.

Writing custom buy-side systems

Writing a custom buy-side system definitely gives you the greatest flexibility but often exposes the greatest risks. With a custom designed buy-side system, you can

- ✔ Capture the precise business rules and processes of your organization.
- ✔ Control the exact options presented to your employees.
- ✔ Integrate custom business rules into your organization at level you choose.

By writing custom software, however, you assume all responsibility for the outcome. If you take on this task yourself, you reap what you sow.

Mitigate costs and risks by reusing the software and processes that you develop for your e-commerce selling systems in your e-procurement purchasing systems. You can even use the e-procurement development as a test bed for your e-commerce systems.

Standardization is key

Ariba was one of the first software firms to provide buy-side e-procurement systems. This company quickly realized that to be effective, standards for providing catalog data were critical. To achieve this, Ariba (www.ariba.com) published standards for formatting catalog data and enlisted partners among business suppliers to provide data in the published formats. When you choose e-procurement software, or when you write your own, the standards for exchanging data between you and your suppliers should be one of the first issues you address.

Chapter 18

Setting Up Distribution and Fulfillment Systems

Anyone who has ever been to the post office at Christmas knows what it's like to be swamped. As the Internet opens new avenues for selling your products, you need the means to handle the increased flow. That means having systems in place that automate taking and fulfilling orders. All the bells and whistles on your Web site won't mean a thing if you don't have the systems in place to manufacture or procure a product, pull it off the warehouse shelf, and send it on its way to your customers.

By analyzing your existing workflow, you can find areas where you can cut time, paperwork, and errors. You can get your shippers online with you to get your goods out the door more quickly, and you can receive incoming goods faster and with less hassle. You can implement just-in-time manufacturing and distribution to reduce the high cost of warehousing materials and products. For some products or services, you can even use the Internet itself as a delivery mechanism. With good e-fulfillment systems, you can also reduce the hassle and confusion associated with back orders and returns.

Handling Order Flow

The amount of paperwork and bureaucracy associated with filling a single order can be crushing. The number of people who must sign, approve, touch, and see paper just to get a single product out the door can increase your business costs quickly. Don't forget the hassle of keeping everyone and everything up-to-date on an order's status, storing all that paper for future reference, and so on.

Your electronic systems must automate many of these processes if you want your business to be competitive. By receiving orders electronically, either from individual consumers loading goodies into a shopping cart over your Web server or through a sophisticated electronic form order system with larger corporate customers, you can virtually eliminate data-entry errors (at least on your end) and get the fulfillment process moving more quickly. As orders are staged to ship, inventory records can update automatically and coordinate with sales systems that reserve items when they're ordered. You can even automatically place orders to replenish the inventory you sell, without tying up valuable personnel. With fewer hands and more accuracy, you'll get things done more quickly and keep employees and customers happy.

Receiving B2C customers' electronic orders

Most modern inventory-management systems involve computers at some level. The best systems are completely computerized, using clever electronic systems to instruct warehouse personnel to fill orders with the required items from inventory. Of course, orders have to be entered into the system in any order fulfillment process. It's at this point in the process when most errors occur — which is one reason why electronic orders can save you so much time and money.

Receiving orders from consumers is the easiest scenario to handle because they will be shopping on your Web site. Your site handles their orders, simply moving them from the site's database into your fulfillment system's database. A variety of commercial tools, such as Microsoft BizTalk Server (`www.biztalk.com`), can help move information from the site's database into your fulfillment system. You can also create your own software to handle this task, if you prefer.

Receiving B2B customers' electronic orders

If you sell products primarily to other businesses, you may find that your Web site doesn't meet their needs for placing orders. Encourage your business customers to submit their orders electronically through other means, such as Electronic Data Interchange (EDI) or similar electronic-document technologies. Such an approach enables your business customers to automate their ordering process, and places their orders directly into your fulfillment systems without the need for manual intervention.

Fulfillment systems: Your weakest link

Even the most powerful, automated order systems rely on a fulfillment system to actually complete a customer's order. If your business is using a manual order fulfillment process — warehouse employees running around trying to remember which bin holds which products and counting on their own memory to be sure the order gets filled correctly — then an automated order system (like your Web site) will still be slow, inefficient, and error-prone.

To increase your efficiency, look into using an automated fulfillment system. Choose from a variety of systems, such as a light pick system.

Light pick systems consist of rows of product bins linked to a computer system. When orders are received, the corresponding product bin lights up, indicating that the product in the bin is required to fill that order. This visual cue directs employees' attention to the correct products, thus improving efficiency and accuracy.

Automated fulfillment systems are generally custom designed and built by their manufacturers for specific applications to handle the types of products that you sell in the most efficient way possible.

You can provide a variety of ways to meet your business customers' needs for electronic ordering:

- ✔ Set up a special Web site dedicated to the specific needs of your business customers.

- ✔ Use products like Microsoft BizTalk Server so that you can accept XML-based order data from customers via the Internet. (XML stands for Extensible Markup Language, one of the languages that makes the exchange of data over the Internet possible.)

- ✔ Employ EDI software to accept electronic orders from customers via a Value-Added Network (VAN) carrier.

- ✔ Investigate other electronic systems so that you can accept orders via phone or fax directly into your order fulfillment systems.

Tracking Your Goods: Inventory-Management Systems

Use inventory-management systems to keep close tabs on the products you have on hand. In addition to helping you better manage your own business processes, accurate inventory information can also help your customers do business with you more easily and more efficiently by providing them with accurate inventory-availability information and anticipated delivery times for backordered items.

Sharing inventory levels with your partners

Many consumer-based Web sites provide indicators of whether products are in stock. This helps the businesses accurately set customer expectations for the products' delivery times and gives customers the choice of ordering an alternative product for one that's out of stock.

Business customers also appreciate this type of feedback, particularly when they rely on receiving product from you to make their customers happy. Your business customers can benefit from updated inventory information, letting them know what you have in stock. You can feed this information to them via XML data feeds, EDI, or text files, or through a common data hub like Commerce One (www.commerceone.com). These hubs provide a hosted location for the sharing of data between companies, companies and employees, or companies and customers.

The ability to share inventory information with your business customers is especially important if you act as the virtual warehouse for them. In essence, they're selling your products. Because in effect they promise their customers that you have those products in stock, they can do a better job of satisfying their customers if they have some insight into your actual inventory levels.

You may be tempted to withhold inventory information or even to fudge the numbers a little bit. After all, if you tell people that you're out of stock on a particular item, they may turn to a different supplier. Losing a sale is better, however, than logging a sale that you can't fulfill — your customers will lose confidence in you if you can't deliver the goods, and you will possibly lose future sales.

Keeping inventory up-to-date

For your inventory information to be useful, it has to be up-to-date. Your inventory-management system has to keep track of the various fluctuations in product supply, and you have to provide ways to tell your system that inventory has changed.

Decreasing inventory when products are sold and increasing it when new shipments arrive is easy enough to track. But don't overlook other things that can change your inventory, such as

✔ Items lost because of damage or theft

✔ Items sent back to the manufacturer

✔ Items returned from customers

✔ Items given away in promotions or as samples

The fine line between enough and too much

Suppose you sell garden rakes, which you order from a supplier. You sell about five rakes a week, and it takes about a week for the supplier to ship new ones after you place an order. You need to have five rakes on hand at the beginning of each week. Therefore, you establish a MIL (minimum) of one and an ERQ (reorder quantity) of five. When your on-hand inventory of rakes reaches one, your inventory-management system automatically places an order for five more rakes.

Managing this level of inventory control may sound complicated, but don't drown in the lingo! If it didn't sound complicated, everyone would do it.

You should also consider tracking committed inventory. A *committed inventory item* is one that has been ordered but not yet shipped to a customer. You remove the item from your active inventory (from which orders are fulfilled), yet still keep the item on the books until it physically leaves your warehouse.

Ordering from Your Suppliers: It's a B2B Thang

A major part of inventory management is replenishing your supplies when they run low. Although ordering new stock is obviously critical to the success of your business, sharing this information with your customers can help them understand your inventory flow and establish realistic expectations when they place orders with you.

Automating replenishment orders

Your inventory-management system should be designed to automatically order new items when your on-hand inventory becomes low. You can use electronic systems such as EDI or XML to place orders with your suppliers, in much the same way that your business customers can place electronic orders with you. Try to work with suppliers that can accept electronic orders because their fulfillment of your orders will be more efficient and easier for you to automate on your end than manual ordering would be.

You also need to determine the quantities you will have your inventory-management system order. A common technique for determining quantities is to establish Minimum Inventory Level (MIL) and Economic Reorder Quantity (ERQ) levels. *MIL* is the lowest level your inventory should go to before an order for new stock is placed by your inventory-management system. *ERQ* is the number of items that will be ordered when an order is placed.

Tracking scheduled deliveries

Automating your inventory replenishment helps you maintain adequate stock for your customers to buy. But occasionally, because of fluctuating demand, you will run out of some inventory item, or a customer will want to order more than you have on hand. Tracking shipments — and providing this information to your customers — can help them do business with you more efficiently.

If your suppliers can provide you with electronic order confirmations that include shipment tracking numbers, you can use shipping carriers' systems — like those offered by UPS (www.ups.com) and FedEx (www.fedex.com) — to get accurate delivery schedules for your orders, which you can provide to your customers.

Keeping Products on the Move: Shipping

Shipping has come a long way. Companies such as FedEx, UPS, and Airborne Express (www.airborneexpress.com) provide technology to automate shipping, calculate shipping charges, and simplify tracking of orders. Even the United States Postal Service (www.usps.com) has gotten into the act, providing package tracking and delivery confirmation services. Check out the iRail.com Web site (www.irail.com) to choose from competing suppliers of rail transport. The list goes on — shipping has truly entered the Information Age.

By using the technology provided by these and other carriers, you gain better control of shipping than you ever could before e-commerce came about. Automated processes provide electronic data for keeping your back-end systems informed about what the shipping dock is doing. And you can even use the Internet as a delivery vehicle for soft goods such as software, bypassing traditional shipping methods entirely.

Automating product shipments

When it's time to ship customers' orders from your warehouse or distribution center, automated systems can save you time and money, and improve the efficiency and accuracy of your shipping operations.

Rakish behavior

Suppose the local gardening club wants to buy five rakes from you, but you only have one on hand at the time. Even if your inventory-management system has already placed an order for five more rakes, the customer won't know that . . . unless, of course, your system can also provide delivery information. When you post accurate inventory information, customers can see that more rakes are on order and when you expect them to arrive.

Use automated, integrated solutions to

- ✔ Weigh your shipments
- ✔ Confirm the accuracy of the customer's shipping address
- ✔ Calculate the most efficient and cost-effective means of shipping the package
- ✔ Print and apply a shipping label
- ✔ Roll the package down a conveyor to a waiting shipping truck

These systems can also provide shipping information — such as the shipping time and tracking numbers — to your back-end systems. This information can be used to send shipping confirmation e-mails to your customers, and to update your e-commerce systems, allowing customers to log on and check the status of their shipments using your Web site.

Improving the efficiency and reliability of your shipping process will make your customers happier. E-commerce technologies that help automate your shipping processes are inexpensive and easy to implement.

Receiving the goods

An automated inventory-management system can be even more useful if you automate the receipt of incoming shipments as well.

- ✔ Incoming shipments can be scanned, telling the inventory-management system that the inventory has arrived.
- ✔ Individual items in the shipment can be scanned, automatically incrementing on-hand inventory levels.
- ✔ Outstanding back orders for received items can be immediately filled by *cross docking*. Cross docking is moving received goods from the receiving dock directly to the shipping dock (without placing them into the warehouse system first). Cross docking is an efficient way to manage inventory flow.

✔ Suppliers' invoices can be matched to the received goods and automatically cleared for electronic payment.

Automating the receipt of shipments can make all your inventory systems more efficient, saving you time and money and keeping your customers happy.

Keeping Righteous Records

Even the most efficient systems are useless without detailed record keeping. Accurate, up-to-the-minute information is required to maintain inventory data, shipping data, order status data, and pretty much all the other data your e-business uses. Although keeping this information updated by hand can definitely be a pain, using technology to keep it all straight can make it a piece of cake.

Data in, data out — capturing what comes and goes

The first trick to maintaining accurate data is to update it whenever a change of state occurs. Changes of state occur all the time regarding the products in your warehouse — when products are received, when they're placed into the warehouse, when they're sold to a customer, when they're pulled from the warehouse, when they're shipped to the customer, and so forth.

You need to implement systems that capture these changes of state so that your data can be updated. For example, you can implement bar-code scanners at your receiving dock, wireless scanners in your warehouse, and scanners at your shipping dock to track the physical movements of products in your warehouse by using your computer systems.

You also have to implement policies to make sure products' physical movements are captured into your computer systems. All of your scanners are useless if nobody's using them!

Letting everyone know wazzup — back-end systems integration

After you configure your computers to track your products' physical movements, you have to get that data into your back-end systems. Accountants need to be aware of the status of your inventory so that inventory taxes and supplier invoices can be paid. Warehouse managers need to know how much inventory space to allocate for particular product categories. Salespeople need to know what inventory is in stock and what's on back order, as well as when new shipments are expected to arrive.

Making this information available means tightly integrating the various computer systems that run your business. You can write your own software applications to move data from one system to another, or you can use platforms such as Microsoft SQL Server or Microsoft BizTalk Server to help move data around within your organization.

Electronic Delivery

Many businesses sell products that don't need to be physically shipped, such as e-books, business research reports, and computer software. These businesses are able to take advantage of electronic delivery: Customers can download their products to a computer as soon as the purchase is complete. Electronic delivery offers instant gratification for customers because they receive their purchases without having to wait. A layer of complexity is also removed for the business because shipping charges, carriers, tracking numbers, and other logistics are eliminated.

Providing electronic goods in electronic formats

Goods that can be delivered electronically need to be made available in a downloadable format. Choose from many types of media to best suit your downloadable product. Some of the major categories are

- **Books:** Often downloaded in an electronic book, or *e-book,* format. These formats include document reader technology such as Microsoft Reader (www.microsoft.com/reader) and Adobe Acrobat (www.adobe.com), as well as e-book display devices such as eBooks' Gemstar eBook devices (www.ebook-gemstar.com), and others.

- **Documents:** Often downloaded in more traditional formats, such as Microsoft Word (www.microsoft.com/office/word) or Corel WordPerfect (www.corel.com).

- **Computer software:** Immediately downloadable, allowing users to install and begin using it right away.

- **Music:** Available in several different formats, including WAV files, the now-ubiquitous MP3 format, and Microsoft's Media Player (windowsmedia.com/download) format.

> ✔ **Movies and other video material:** Distributed in different formats, including Apple QuickTime (www.apple.com), Microsoft Media Player, and Motion Picture Experts Group (MPEG).

With some creative planning, many different types of products can be packaged for electronic delivery. However, be practical about your delivery methods and don't rely exclusively on electronic delivery. Some customers don't have the connection speed or patience to download some products. Simply shipping those products — for example those with a long download time — may be the best option. Or you may just want to let customers decide how they want to receive the product. For example, a customer wanting to purchase a feature-length movie could spend several days (seriously) downloading an MPEG file when the movie could have been physically shipped faster in a traditional format (such as a DVD or videocassette).

Informing the masses — distribution of news and information

News and information were two of the first things to be delivered electronically across the Internet. Publishers such as *The New York Times* and *The Wall Street Journal* allow online subscribers to access information across the Web, bypassing the traditional delivery of a physical newspaper to their office or home. No special electronic formats are required because the information is delivered via the customer's Web browser.

Many other companies also electronically deliver news and information for free, including portal sites such as Yahoo! (www.yahoo.com), Excite (www.excite.com), and MSN (www.msn.com). Although news and information on these sites is freely available, they are still products — that is, what customers come to see. Electronic delivery makes it economically feasible for these companies to offer free information — if they had to physically print that information, they would no doubt have to charge a subscription fee.

Companies that provide information to businesses for a fee, such as IDC (www.idc.com), make published reports on business and technology trends available for a fee or through a subscription model.

Keeping 'em happy — streaming media

Delivery of audio and video content can be especially problematic for two reasons. First, high-quality audio and video files can be huge, requiring several hours or more to download on slow modem connections. Second, after customers receive the content, they can copy it to their heart's content and give it away to their friends for free — a quick way to put the company they purchased it from out of business.

Streaming media offers some solutions to these problems: improved playability and piracy prevention. Envision streaming media as a car factory. There's a huge difference between having one person do every single process to build one car, and having several workers work on various stages of the product simultaneously in an assembly line. Handling small pieces of the process keeps the work moving along efficiently. The instant gratification of streaming media allows customers to begin watching a movie or listening to a song immediately because their computer can download a small piece and begin playing right away. The computer continues to download more in the background, keeping just ahead of the customer's viewing or listening like an electronic assembly line. Streaming media can also be used to prevent customers from copying audio or video. Because their computer never gets all the content at once, they don't have anything to copy!

Many different companies provide streaming media technologies, including Microsoft (`www.microsoft.com`), Real (`www.real.com`), and Vivo (`www.real.com/vivo`).

Order Fulfillment

After customers place an order, they want to know where it is at every moment — and you should, too. Use Internet and electronic tracking software to keep order status tracking current. You can often employ the technology of your shipping vendors to help keep track of order status.

You can also use the Internet to keep customers informed about back orders, and even automate systems that help guide customers to alternative choices. From shipping to receiving to returns, orders can be handled with a minimum of fuss and muss.

Tracking orders

The Internet is all about instant gratification — you click something, and you get it. Purchasing (non-downloadable) products, of course, is anything but instant — you don't receive your purchase for several days or more. Because customers — especially business customers — need to know exactly where their purchases are, you need to be able to provide them and yourself with a means to track exactly when a shipment will arrive. Consider this a professional courtesy: Your customers need to be able to properly time their own business processes, which may depend on your shipment.

Tracking electronically

Obtaining tracking information for packages you ship — or those items packaged and shipped on your behalf — is pretty easy with most of the major shipping carriers, such FedEx, Airborne Express, and UPS. Even the U.S. Postal Service offers shipping options that include package status tracking.

Program your systems to query the latest tracking information from the carriers' systems. Your systems must have the tracking number available, which is easily handled if you automate your shipping process to store that information when a package is shipped.

Keeping customers in the know

After you configure tracking information within your systems, then you can share this order status information with your customers. You can set this up in several different ways:

- ✔ Retail customers can check your Web site, where they log in and view the tracking information associated with their orders.

- ✔ Some customers may prefer to receive an e-mail from you when the status of their shipment changes. You can send update e-mails several times each day, if necessary.

- ✔ Business customers may prefer to receive their tracking information electronically, via EDI or some other sort of data feed. This tracking information can easily be entered into their computer systems, allowing them to make planning decisions based on current delivery status.

Dealing with back orders

Back orders are the inevitable thorn in your side when it comes to fulfilling product orders. Sometimes you just can't get what you want right away — you have to wait. Whether it involves sitting on a plane for two hours awaiting takeoff, or placing an order for widgets, everybody feels better knowing why they're being kept waiting. You can help minimize the customer concerns associated with back orders by providing clear and timely information.

Backordered inventory can be out of your control because you have to rely on your suppliers to provide you with new stock. Sometimes even your own orders are backordered, which can make it difficult to tell your customers when you expect the products to arrive.

We recommend that you be honest with your customers. Give them the best information that you have, and be clear about what that information means. For example, you might send out a status e-mail that reads, Your item has been placed on back order. An order has been placed with our supplier for this item, and the last time we ordered it, we received it in six days.

Make sure your systems are programmed to track the time it takes for back orders to be fulfilled by your various vendors. That way you can provide your customers with some expectations based on historical data when you send the confirmation e-mail. Be sure to let them know that your estimate is just that — an estimate based on historical data.

If a product stays on back order for any length of time, your systems should automatically send out an update such as the following: We're sorry, but the item you have on back order has not yet arrived. Our supplier is unable to give us an expected date of arrival. If possible, offer an alternative product to meet the customer's needs right away. The key is to give your customers every bit of information you have so that they feel updated and kept in the loop.

Suggesting alternatives

Back orders are a prime way for you to lose business. If it takes a long time for you to get the item that a customer wants, chances are that someone else (your competitor) can. If your customer's need is immediate, then that customer will only wait so long before he takes his money elsewhere.

One way to salvage a potentially lost sale is to suggest an alternative product. For example, when an item is placed on back order, you might send out a status e-mail that reads,

> Your item has been placed on back order. We usually receive new stock in ten days, at which time we will ship your item to you. However, if you are in a hurry, you may wish to consider a similar item that we currently have in stock. The details for this alternative item are listed below.

Your goal is to retain the customer's business, and suggesting an alternative can be a great way to do that. Even if the customer elects to stick with the originally ordered item, continue suggesting alternatives in future status updates. That way you continue to provide your customers with options, choices, and alternative solutions. But any customer will eventually get sick of waiting. In the worst-case scenario when you just can't provide what the customer needs, she will appreciate you offering an easy process for canceling the order. This allows her to look elsewhere for now and perhaps come back to you for future orders because your company was so considerate of her needs.

Handling Returns

Like back orders, returns are a fact of business life. Customers will inevitably return a purchase for some reason — perhaps they changed their mind, the order was filled incorrectly, or the product was damaged in transit. Your goal should be to make the returns process as painless as possible for your customers so that you can retain their confidence for future orders. You also want to reduce the cost of handling returns as much as possible.

The electric RMA

Most companies like to have customers obtain a Return Merchandise Authorization (RMA) before shipping merchandise back. Businesses use RMAs to make sure that the return meets their standards and that the customer has a legitimate reason to return the item. Businesses also use RMAs to begin planning for the product's return, and to initiate any processes to return the product to the supplier, if necessary.

We recommend that you set up your e-commerce storefront so that customers can request an RMA via your Web site or other electronic means (such as fax or e-mail). Using RMAs reduces the size of the customer service staff you have to maintain to handle returns. Additionally, you give your customers instant gratification if you set up your site to allow customers to view their past orders, indicate which items they want to return, and print out a return shipping label on their own printers. Use RMAs to enable your site to track whether the return is being made within the allowed return time frame; to ensure that you have tracking information on the incoming package; and to allow your computer systems to begin determining how the return will be processed when it arrives.

Managing the cost of returns

Reduce the cost of returns by automating their handling upon receipt. When the returned package arrives, use a scanner to match the package with the RMA information in your computer systems. The systems can then provide receiving personnel with instructions for handling the package, including a warehouse location that the product should be taken to. Your systems can then help you group returns that are headed back to particular suppliers, allowing you to ship several returned products at once rather than sending them back one at a time (which can cost much more).

Keeping all the information associated with returns can allow you to reduce future returns. For example, if a particular product has an unusually high return rate, or if the cost of handling a product's returns are reducing the overall profit margin on that product, consider dropping the product from your catalog. Using your computer systems to analyze and manage returns can help you reduce returns and maintain profit margins in the long run.

Chapter 19

Building Market Reach with E-Marketplaces

. . . .

In This Chapter

▶ Finding the right e-marketplace

▶ Picking the right style of B2C e-marketplace

▶ Tapping into big money with B2B e-marketplaces

. . . .

Most communities have a marketplace. In the United States, people flock to shopping malls to purchase the goods they need — well, at least the goods they *want*. Shoppers like the convenience of having all their favorite shops together in one place. You can take advantage of this mindset on the Internet. In fact, many businesses already are.

E-marketplaces are sites shared by a variety of vendor businesses so that customers can shop and compare goods and services from many vendors at one place. By selling goods from a single, unified Web store enables customers to make the right choices, simply and easily.

Some e-marketplaces, such as Yahoo! Shopping and Skymall, target consumers. But most studies indicate the largest amount of revenue rests in B2B e-marketplaces — that is businesses buying, competing, and selling to other businesses.

E-marketplaces are still in their technological infancy, and terminology changes quickly (like, while the ink was drying on this book) as new solutions and ideas come together. To make things easier for you, dear reader, we made up our own definitions. Don't worry, we've got good reasons for describing things the way we do. For example, throughout this chapter, we refer loosely to *joining communities*. We're just trying to spice things up — we mean e-marketplaces. If someone uses the term differently than we do — well, it's a free country.

We Don't Need No Stinking Partnerships (Or Do We?): B2B Communities

Maybe you don't need to work with other businesses to get the results you need. But then again, maybe sharing expenses and workloads with another business sounds like welcome help. Consider using the B2B partnerships you find in e-marketplaces to help your company grow in several ways:

✔ **Get vertical:** If you sell dictation equipment, there is a myriad of *vertical markets*, including lawyers, doctors, accountants, and executives of all types that could use your products. But you can't afford to advertise to each of those markets individually. By participating in e-marketplaces targeted at different vertical markets (doctors, lawyers, Indian chiefs, and anyone else) you can reach them at minimal cost — and open new markets for direct sales.

A vertical market is an e-marketplace structure composed of businesses in an industry that buy and sell complementary products and services. Here's an example: A business that supplies doohickeys, a business that makes gas caps, and a business that creates seat belts are all in the same vertical e-marketplace as the manufacturer, which puts the pieces together and makes a car out of them, and the car dealer, who sells cars to consumers. You can find several industries with vertical markets, such as insurance, real estate, banking, retail, hospitals, and government.

✔ **Get a rep:** When you break into a new market, no one knows you. No one trusts you. But if you put your stuff on the same page as well known industry leaders, you get credibility by association.

✔ **Get back to work:** It's not easy setting up a Web store, automating online payment processing, and building fully integrated and secure systems. Many e-marketplace providers, such as VerticalNet (www.verticalnet. com), shown in Figure 19-1 and described in the sidebar, "Hands across the world — and to the moon: VerticalNet," handle technical challenges for you so that you can concentrate on other aspects of your business.

✔ **Get noticed:** E-marketplaces draw lots of visitors (at least good ones do). This exposure gives you opportunities to reach customers and potential partners with ads, press releases, and case studies.

The cyberworld can be a dark, lonely place. Making friends with the other businesses in your 'hood can help you get into the swing of things and make the most of your comfy new Web address.

All e-marketplaces are not created equal

Before you jump into an e-marketplace, you should check it out. Create a shopping list of features and services you'd like to see in the perfect online community, and start looking for those qualities in the communities that are out there. Here are some ideas to think about, whether you're thinking of participating in a B2B trading community or joining a consumer-oriented B2C portal:

- ✔ **Membership has its privileges — and its costs:** The whole point of an e-marketplace is for participating members to share costs, so joining is rarely free. Determine how much you can spend to participate in the marketplaces as a seller, and make sure those costs fit within your business plan and profit model.

- ✔ **It's not a party if you don't have guests:** An e-marketplace with no customers is like a back porch with no barbecue grill — it's not much fun and not very useful. Ask e-marketplace providers for data on customer traffic, dollar volume in sales, growth of new customers, customer retention — any of the metrics they keep to show how effective they are. Their success will be yours, if you join.

- ✔ **Don't sell bikinis in an Eskimo-only e-marketplace:** Before you even consider joining up, take a look at a community's demographics. A good e-marketplace service provider should have the data tucked away somewhere — make sure those demographics will help your business.

- ✔ **Get more bang for your buck:** A good community offers more than just access to customers. It offers *value-added services* to customers, such as providing useful resources to your business and to others in the community. One value-added service to be on the look out for is the opportunity to interact with other like-minded businesses. Hey, where mutually beneficial partnerships are concerned, we say, "Go for it."

- ✔ **Look for a cornerstone business:** Communities that have a good anchor business — or a few of them — to give the community some name recognition with customers are likely to improve your sales. Make sure that any community you plan to join has some major players to keep the traffic coming. If you sell garblegroks, though, make sure the anchor business isn't called GarblegroksBeWe.

- ✔ **Stay away from the competition:** Don't join a community where the competition has already fully entrenched itself. Make sure you'll stand out within the community, and plan how to leverage your company's distinctive attributes to draw customers to your corner.

Understanding vertical e-marketplaces

Vertical e-marketplaces, or portals, are used in business-to-business e-procurement. They focus on meeting the needs of a narrow range of buyers. Instead of passing buyers to another site, they handle transactions directly to provide consistent levels of service. The consistency makes obtaining products and services quick and accurately easy for users.

Figure 19-1:
Not only
does
VerticalNet
have an e-
marketplace
for just
about every
industry, but
it also
supports its
member
businesses
technologi-
cally.

Vertical portals attract the attention of smaller vendors with products specific to that industry. They help vendors market to specific industries, and help customers find what they need. Some specialty products span vertical industries, and portals help companies target their sales and marketing into these specific industries.

Taking a Look at B2C E-Marketplaces

The concept grew naturally. Some sites drew a lot of traffic. Yahoo!, MSN, Netscape, and other Web sites served as home pages for millions of Internet users and became *portals*.

Sites that serve as a starting point for many browsers are called *portals*. They often offer news, Internet search capabilities, weather reports, stock market reports, and a wide variety of services that keep people coming back.

Well, as you can guess, it was a no-brainer for portals to start selling advertising to generate income. These businesses are smart, and it doesn't take much imagination to figure out that if you have lots of traffic (willing shoppers), you're in a position to sell.

CASE STUDY

Hands across the world — and to the moon: VerticalNet

VerticalNet (www.verticalnet.com) makes its living by pulling together companies and technologies to build e-marketplaces. The company has formed strategic alliances with a wide range of software vendors in addition to over 50 electronic marketplaces, and helps industry alliances take their vision of integrated services to the Web. Companies like VerticalNet can help you find, or even build, the right e-marketplace for your organization. Now, that's B2B!

That concept grew, and businesses like Yahoo! figured that they could make more money if they used their portal power to link traffic (willing shoppers) to sellers (seeking profit) and establish themselves right in the middle, having the best of both worlds. You can find a couple of styles of consumer e-marketplaces — the key ingredient in all of them is that portals bring about traffic (yeah, yeah, willing shoppers).

Let's call the mall thing off

The most basic form of Internet mall is organized, well, like a mall. The portal has a listing of vendors. When Sally Shopper clicks the JewelryRoundup link from XYZPortal.com, she automatically jumps to JewelryRoundupPlace.com, where she can shop until she drops — and she never even puts on her makeup. MSN shopping and Netscape NetShops use this model.

PROS AND CONS

Ms. Shopper gets what she wants (mascara and some lip gloss), and so are the businesses:

✔ The portal site wins by selling advertising to vendors. The portal site may place banner ads on participating companies' sites for listing the companies in the portal's shopping area. Or the portal may get paid a flat rate or a commission on sales.

✔ The seller wins by using the traffic of the portal to collect shoppers. An instant and massive audience does sound nice, doesn't it?

REMEMBER

Of course, the deal would be sweeter if there was no one involved but customers and you. Who needs a portal to suck up some of your profits when you could build relationships directly with customers. Get to work making your customers sticking to your site.

Building virtual department stores

Some portals (called *virtual department stores* because their Web sites take shoppers to a cornucopia of Web vendors) take responsibility for handling financial transactions between businesses and their customers. The portal takes orders, and you fulfill them. These portals provide storefront technology like online catalogs, shopping cart systems, shipping and payment pages — all the stuff we tell you you need in Chapter 9. They exercise their expertise — building and maintaining Web sites and computer technology. You are free to do business your way without the hassle of developing your own Web site. Yahoo! Shopping uses this model.

Here's the lowdown on the pros and cons of this kind of arrangement:

✔ **Pro:** A department store e-marketplace model keeps your initial costs down. You can use the portal's technology to roll out a site much more quickly than if you developed one of your own. Costs associated with the portal are usually a percentage of sales (after the initial setup costs) so you minimize risk. If you don't make a lot of money, you don't have to pay the portal a lot of money.

You also have the option to join a virtual department store and build your own site on the side. All you have to do is maintain parallel Internet channels between your Web site and the portal site so that you can garner sales.

✔ **Con:** The portal site wants to keep a uniform look and feel, so it makes all the products it sells — from computers to clothing to coffee to DVDs — fit into one type of catalog page. One. Depending on the portal, you may not be allowed to develop independent branding, so your products are just some among many.

Many portals that use the department store model let you advertise your individual business for a fee.

You can share the strength of your brand with another firm. Amazon.com works with vendors through zShops. The shops allow vendors to create their own unique store, but leverage the technology, traffic, and name of Amazon.

Would You Buy That for a Dollar? Understanding Internet Consumer Pricing Models

When you join your business with a B2C portal you should consider how paying the middleman affects your pricing model. Most companies want to set a price and let the cash roll in. But research from IDC indicates that unless online prices beat prices from bricks-and-mortar stores, consumers aren't buying. Bummer. A Catch-22.

Ah, but there is a solution: *Dynamic pricing* models. In these models, your business negotiates a price with consumers to attract their interest — and their credit card numbers. Four of the most prevalent dynamic pricing models include the following:

- **B2C auctions:** You've probably heard of the auctions held by eBay. Well, now businesses are in on the act. B2C auction portals like eAuctions.com, created by PacFusion.com, enable businesses to join up. The portal sets up an online auction and turns consumers loose to start bidding on your entire inventory of yinyins. The product sells to the highest bidder. Auctions are great way to move overstocked items, last year's models, and other excess inventory.

- **Name-your-own-price:** Made famous by Priceline.com (and those wacky commercials with Captain Kirk), consumers name the top price they're willing to pay for a product or service. Participating sellers determine if they will accept their offers.

- **Group buying:** Businesses offer large numbers of products and offer specific price breaks to consumers and businesses based on the quantity requested. As more and more consumers agree to buy, the price drops incrementally. Businesses can afford to lower prices if they know that a sale is guaranteed. Companies like MobShop (www.mobshop.com) sell programs that enable businesses to buy (and sell) en masse.

- **Declining price:** Businesses offer goobledies at reduced prices for a period of time. After a week or two, the business lowers prices again and sells some more goobledies. The business continues this process until the inventory is sold. The longer consumers wait, the smaller the selection they have to choose from. Land's End has used this model to sell excess inventory and discontinued items.

IDC's research shows that 45 percent of consumers are interested in online auctions, and over 60 percent would consider name-your-own pricing. These schemes can help draw customers. And you don't have to sell everything this way. It's a great way to introduce customers to your organization.

There are some down sides to each of these models. For one thing, they assume that vendors already have several hundred goobledies or yinsyins in stock. If you're into maintaining a virtual warehouse, drop-shipping products to customers, or creating products on demand, this probably isn't your gig. See Chapters 16 and 18 for more information.

We have some tips on using dynamic pricing:

- Make your dynamic pricing simple to use and easy to understand. If consumers don't understand what they are supposed to do or how your pricing works, FUD (fear, uncertainty, and doubt) will send them packing — without buying anything.

- Dynamic pricing isn't for everything you sell. It's best suited for inventory you need to move — discontinued items, overstocks, and so on.

- You may need to develop separate channels for your dynamically priced items than for your regularly priced items — probably at a unique Web site.

- You many need to buy or develop software tools for managing sales at multiple sites.

Selling to Businesses with B2B E-Marketplaces

Although B2C e-marketplaces were the first successes in the e-marketplace revolution, market research over the last few years consistently reaches the same conclusion — B2B e-marketplaces offer the big money for businesses. IDC research indicates that B2B spending is increasing, despite the economic slowdown in the first quarter of 2001. Analysts project that online B2B sales, which reach 282 billion in 2000, will climb to 516 billion in 2001 and top 4 trillion by 2005.

EnviroOne (www.enviroone.com), shown in Figure 19-2, is a unique exchange that provides information and resources to both customers and businesses. Claiming to be *the* place to go if you're looking for anything environmental, the business is creating a separate e-commerce center, which it calls a *vortal* (vertical integrated industrial portal). What will they think of next?

Buyers enjoy one-stop shopping. They get a single bill. They can often compare products side-by-side to make decisions.

uBid, U win: uBid and B2C auctions

uBid (www.ubid.com) works with companies to provide B2C auctions. The company auctions off a little bit of everything, but it's best known for its consumer electronics auctions. uBid handles financial transactions — and accepts financial risks for payment processing. All vendors need to do is upload product info to uBid and ship products to the winners. By partnering with sites like uBid, you can take advantage of dynamic pricing to move inventory — without spending a fortune on new technology and software.

Reaching the masses with public exchanges and targeting key customers with private exchanges

Public exchanges, also called B2B portals, are pretty similar to popular B2C e-marketplaces: Businesses gather together and offer their services jointly at one site. A *private exchange* is just like a *public* exchange, only they're not open to the public. But you knew that.

One significant difference between B2B exchanges and B2C portals is that in B2B exchanges, the various businesses are typically organized around the type of product (for instance, office supplies) or by the market they intend to reach (say, products directed to the pharmaceuticals or furniture industry). This statement is true of B2B exchanges whether the general public has access to the portal or not.

Understanding the advantages and disadvantages of using private and public exchanges

In a public exchange, sellers share the expenses of building a Web store, advertising the site, and maintaining relationships. Smaller businesses can band together and create a site that compares to — and competes with — much larger competitors. And, for little expense, a company can simultaneously participate in multiple marketplaces.

The big bonus in private exchanges is that they become fully integrated into the buyers' internal systems. By providing advanced systems that make doing business less costly and easier for the buyers, private exchanges ease the buyers into a dependence on the sellers in the marketplace — right where we want 'em.

Buyers get faster and more economical transactions with fewer errors. Linking systems with suppliers who reliably meet your organization's needs can reduce costs, minimize errors, and reduce labor made correcting and expediting orders. Of course, you don't want to become too dependent on your suppliers — just enough to get all the advantages you can for your firm.

Although public exchanges offer many advantages by marketing to other businesses, they lack some key features that really enable businesses to take full advantage of the power of the Internet. Enter the private exchange. Table 19-1 offers a side-by-side look at the differences between the two kinds of exchanges.

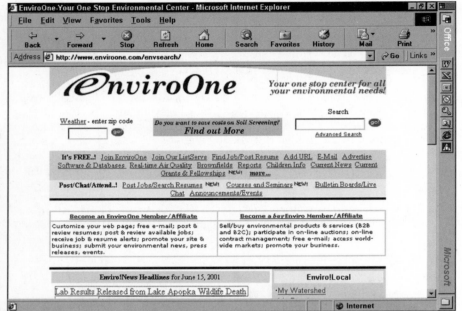

Figure 19-2:
EnviroOne is
one-stop-
shopping if
you're
looking for
pesticides,
smog, and
hazardous
waste. It's a
good thing.

CASE STUDY

The little engines that could consolidate: A horizontal story

Rail lines compete with one another, but moving freight by rail often requires coordinating the efforts of several lines. In January 2001, five of the largest North American rail lines — Burlington Northern Sante Fe, Canadian National, Canadian Pacific Railway, Norfolk Southern, and Union Pacific — announced an alliance. Working with iRail.com and GE Global eXchange Services, they developed RailMarketplace.com. Railmarketplace is a *horizontal* e-marketplace, designed to help companies from a wide range of industries schedule rail transportation services.

At www.railmarketplace.com, customers can obtain rail services at lower costs. The service helps manage transportation services and can accept several currencies.

The site uses technology and services from Global eXchange (www.globalexchange.com), one of the largest B2B e-commerce networks in the world. GE also leverages transportation software developed by iRail, a provider of electronic transportation management systems. By working together, the rail transport companies built a site that consolidates critical information and market access for their customers.

Table 19-1	B2B: Public exchanges versus private exchanges	
Public	*Private*
Businesses have a difficult time standing out or adding value to the products they sell because they are marketed and sold exactly the same way by the exchange as competitors' products are.	Private exchanges offer value to business' existing distributors and middle market customers.
Lack customization options and flexibility.	Offer easy integration between businesses so that they can exchange data and establish partnerships.
Usually have no choice but to remain generic and non-invasive.	Build direct relationships between buyers, suppliers, and distributors so that they all act collectively — a distinct advantage over companies that fly solo.

Going beyond buying and selling: Going private

Private exchanges are expensive to build, so they need to provide services that go far beyond just buying and selling to justify their existence. Advanced services that provide benefit to the entire organization make the commitment to the exchange worthwhile. Examples of components that add value include the following:

✔ Customized catalogs that dynamically adjust pricing and selection based on the customers' sales volume, location, and pre-negotiated contracts.

✔ Dynamic pricing models (see "Finding the Right Price: B2B Pricing Models," later in this chapter) that help liquidate excess and discontinued inventory.

Make dynamic pricing models available only to select customers.

✔ Logistics systems that handle allocation of inventory and combine shipments to lower costs.

✔ Financial systems that reward use of the automation features and penalize firms for bypassing automation systems.

✔ Collaboration systems that help design and develop new products and improve existing products. By enabling buyers to utilize the skills and expertise of suppliers, businesses can often improve quality and reduce design cycles.

Most collaborative systems help companies collaborate with their top 10 to 40 suppliers. Private exchanges provide standards that allow companies to work intimately with the top 100 to 1000 suppliers.

Finding the Right Price: B2B Pricing Models

The growth of dynamic pricing models in B2B e-marketplaces indicates their increasing importance. Many businesses spend money on bells and whistles (using streaming media, creating newsgroups, and so on) when they should be investing in new technologies that show real potential from growth. Here are some options:

- ✔ **Static pricing:** Widgets cost $99.95 — unless you buy 500 or more, in which case they go for $89.95. The features of the product are fixed, along with the price. Most sites sell with a static pricing model. Easy enough to computerize, and by far the most popular pricing model.

- ✔ **Negotiated pricing:** Business A and Business B sit together and discuss prices and product features until the prices are mutually acceptable. Works well face-to-face, but computers don't negotiate well together. You can use this model to establish your price and let your e-commerce system handle getting orders shipped on time — with little or no paperwork.

- ✔ **Dynamic pricing:** Yup, we mean B2B auctions. Businesses put widgets up for auction and see how much other businesses are willing to pay for them. While this method doesn't work for all products and all businesses, it's a great way to move items you don't want — excess inventory and discontinued products, even equipment and office furniture you no longer use — to free space and capital.

Any pricing scheme (or, for that matter *every* pricing scheme) can find a place in the e-marketplace. Just make certain your internal systems can handle the pricing scheme you use.

Integrating Your Business with the B2B Community

Trading communities have technical requirements (data sharing formats, VPNs, and so on) for your participation — make sure you understand those requirements before you join, as well as how much it will cost to integrate your business with the community. Some specific areas you should ask about include the following:

✔ If the community is an online mall, auction, or barter site, how will your products be added to their catalogs? Ideally, you should be able to create an automated process to upload products and changes to the community.

✔ If customers place orders on the community's site — as they do in malls and auctions — how will those orders make it into your systems for processing? Ideally, some form of automated feed should allow you to pick up orders and insert them directly into your business systems.

✔ What kind of management systems are available to help you maximize your use of the community? You want as much flexibility as possible.

✔ Can you tell how many customers visited your corner of the community, saw your ads on the community's site, and so on? Can you see how many total customers came to the site so you can judge the percentage of community customers that see your business? Make sure this info is readily available.

✔ If you're paying for your participation in the community based on the number of visitors directed to your Web site, does the community include robust enough reporting tools for you to monitor the effectiveness of the community in delivering customers to your site?

Developing the back-end systems to support community participation can be difficult and time-consuming. We discuss many of these technical issues in Chapter 20.

Putting it down on paper

PaperExchange (www.paperexchange.com) capitalizes on a common need shared by most companies: the need for paper. It provides a common forum for businesses to negotiate directly with one another. A single point of contact allows buyers to reach a wide range of paper suppliers. This B2B exchange seeks to provide one-stop shopping for paper-related purchases for customers large and small.

PaperExchange has an impressive range of services. In addition to paper manufacturers, such as International Paper (www.internationalpaper.com), Asia Pulp and Paper (www.asiapulppaper.com), Bowater (www.bowater.com), and Port Townsend Paper Corporation (www.ptpc.com), the company integrates transportation services from Schenker (www.schenkerusa.com) and C.H. Robinson (www.chrobinson.com).

Chapter 20

Integrating Your Internal Systems with Business Partners

*W*hen you agree to partner with other businesses and share data, you have the greatest potential for saving money — and the greatest risk for getting burned. Choosing your partners carefully can mitigate these risks and allow you and your partners to save money and get orders out the door like never before. By carefully choosing the right mix of technologies and policies and procedures, you can safely share critical data and accelerate your business processes to the fullest extent.

First Things First: Identifying What Data You Want to Share — and Why

You may think that it's risky to put accounting, inventory, and sales information out into the ether for partners to view. And there is some risk — if you don't take the necessary precautions of evaluating potential partners and integrating systems so that they function securely and well. So why do it? Here's what sharing data enables your business to do:

✔ **Make money:** When you collect targeted information about customers, sales trends, market share, return rates, response to marketing projects, and demographics, among other things, you have to do something with that information. You can share it, of course. Are you kidding? You *have* to share it. In Chapter 15, you find out how to collect data and make sure that Joe in accounts receivable knows what Barbara in sales knows about Customer X.

If you're going to buy technology to improve the collection of data and enable various departments to access that data and tweak it, then you may as well make sure that these data systems enable you to work with partners, as well. Keep reading this chapter — that's exactly what we show you how to do.

✔ **Make money:** By reducing the number of people handling products and materials, you can manage the supply chain and get products to customers fast. On the Internet, which thrives on real time, the faster anything is done the better your bottom line looks. You can't manage the supply chain without sharing some information with your partners, particularly your suppliers and B2B business customers. (See Chapter 16 for more on the supply chain.)

✔ **Make money:** Improve all of your internal processes, reduce paperwork, empower employees, and reduce your operating budget. Where do you sign up? Chapter 17 shows you how to take advantage of data-sharing technology to improve e-procurement processes.

✔ **Make money:** You can fix the supply chain 'til the cows come home, but if you don't make good on promises and expand your company's value, you're not going to have any business to supply. You can't speed up processing and fulfilling orders (see Chapter 18) without sharing data with your business partners. And you can't get into a trading community without doing some serious B2B integration. (Jump to Chapter 19 for the skinny on trading communities.)

As you can see, there's a lot you can achieve (money) by integrating your back office with your partners (money). In the following sections, we tell you what you need to know about creating (money) and integrating (money) all your internal systems so that you can meet your e-commerce financial (money, money, money) expectations.

Deciding Whether Your Business Can Work and Play Well with Partners

Sharing data is complex and costly. Developing systems that share data takes time, and even after they're developed, they require ongoing maintenance. So before you get into a business relationship that requires you to share data, you need to know that you're partnering with the right company. You have to communicate with potential partners, and make sure that you have the same goals and that your systems are compatible enough to make data sharing a possibility. You'd be amazed at how many companies think they have one type of data when, in reality, their data is scattered through a wide variety of systems and stored in many disparate formats.

You can hire a consulting firm to help handle your data-sharing needs — just make sure the consulting group is a good partner, too. You may also consider consortiums, which are groups of organizations that establish common systems and formats for sharing data. Consortiums, such as Covisint (www.covisint.com), integrate suppliers, manufacturers, logistics, and technology firms to help organizations work together.

Deciding what you want to share with partners — and what they have to share with you

So what do your potential data partners have to offer you? In addition to agreeing on the technical issues of data that you and your systems can easily work with, the data partnership has to be useful to you somehow. If you have an e-procurement system, you'll want to receive catalog data and send purchase orders. If you have a supply chain management system, you'll want to provide inventory data and receive scheduling and logistics information. If you are part of an e-marketplace (details in Chapter 19), you'll want to deliver your catalog and pricing information and receive orders.

Read the following examples for details on the information you'll need from partners:

- **From marketing:** Demographics, promotions.
- **From sales:** Trends, regional sales comparisons, pricing information, product discounts.
- **From the warehouse:** Inventory levels, logistics data.
- **From manufacturing:** Production schedules, spoilage.
- **From quality control:** Product testing results, defect statistics.
- **From customer service:** Returns, repair data, common problems.
- **From accounting:** Face it, you're trading orders and money.
- **To suppliers:** In a virtual warehousing arrangement, you need to feed order data to the companies who will fulfill your orders. The easiest way to do this is through an automated exchange of business data, making those companies new data partners.

> ✔ **To retailers of your goods:** You may want to feed your online-catalog data to other online stores, allowing them to carry your products and pass orders on to you. This two-way exchange of data benefits both of your companies.
>
> ✔ **To suppliers, retailers, e-procurement partners, and your own employees:** You may need to accept or provide data for internal business functions, too, such as electronic purchase orders or invoices for your stock, business supplies, equipment, and other transactions.

Every data partnership has costs associated with it. First, you have to consider the startup cost of creating and integrating the data exchange systems, and then you have to deal with the ongoing costs of maintaining and monitoring the data exchange. And sometimes your partner makes changes and upgrades that force you to change and upgrade. Understanding what the data partnership offers you will help you determine if the costs outweigh those benefits. Remember, standards for sharing data (such as EDI documents and common XML data formats) can help keep everyone on the same page — and help you spread the cost of sharing data across many partners.

Finding and evaluating potential partners

Your partners come in two varieties — businesses you purchase goods and services from and businesses you sell goods and services to. Virtually everyone buys stuff, but not everyone sells to business partners.

These are the types of businesses with whom you may want to partner:

✔ Suppliers of goods that you sell.

✔ Technology companies who help you connect with other companies

✔ Shipping companies that get material to and from your organization's bricks-and-mortar locations — and your customers.

✔ Financial institutions.

✔ Purveyors of complementary goods. By partnering with companies that provide products that complement yours (for instance, a manufacturer of electrical wiring devices partnering with a tool manufacturing firm or a seed supplier partnering with a fertilizer processing company), you can provide customers with more complete offerings, and both companies can flourish.

When you evaluate a business data partner, you should consider a variety of factors:

✔ **How viable is it as an organization?** Setting up shared data systems is not simple, and sharing data with a partner that goes out of business in a few months is a great waste of effort and cash.

✔ **What is the long-term future in your relationship?** You need a clear business plan that shows how your firms can help one another over the long haul.

✔ **Is the partnership balanced?** If you provide invaluable marketing research and customer service data, and all that your partner provides you with is more product, the partnership is going nowhere. Share and share alike to keep the relationship valuable.

✔ **What is the potential partner's reputation in the marketplace?** Investigate the company's reputation with customers and suppliers. Companies are known by the company they keep (pun intended), so choose your partners carefully.

✔ **What is the quality of the data the partner has to offer?** Is the data it is offering worth the trouble? Is the data accurate, timely, and useful? For example, two-week-old inventory data will not tell you whether merchandise is available right now.

✔ **What will it take to share data?** If the partner's data is in a format that is too difficult to use, it may not be worth the expense and the effort.

Discovering the beauty of multiple-partner data exchanges

Of course, the challenge of finding the right business partners is shared by everyone. Here are a few of the ways you can share data:

✔ **Common data formats:** Electronic Data Interchange documents and Extensible Markup Language (XML) documents can take a lot of the sting out of trading data. By using common, published formats, you'll find that more people will want to trade data with you.

✔ **Common software platforms:** Many accounting and Enterprise Resource Planning software packages include modules that help you share data. It's easy to share data with partners who use the same software as you do.

✔ **Integration packages:** Software designed to build collaborative systems, such as supply chain management systems (see Chapter 16), support many software packages. Ariba (www.ariba.com), Commerce One (www.commerceone.com), and others market collaborative software to help build bridges between organizations.

✔ **Private exchanges:** A consortium of businesses combine to create a common technology solution for sharing data. These exchanges broker information between suppliers and buyers and facilitate the sharing of information by setting common standards.

Determining System Compatibility and Evaluating Technical Risks

In an ideal world, your data partners would accept the data that comes right out of your systems and provide you with data that can be put right into your systems — no fuss, no muss. In their ideal world, of course, the same applies! So you have to negotiate and settle on a data format that both sides can use.

You need to evaluate the risks of housing some of your business partners' data in your systems and having them house some of your data in their systems. If you house their data, you must protect it from hackers and disgruntled employees. If you share your data, you run the risk that your partners will lose it — or abuse it. An unscrupulous partner could end up with your customer list or bill of materials and give it to your competition — or use it to become your competition. See Chapter 8 for information on cutting legal agreements with your partners.

If you properly manage these risks, you can automate your systems and leverage one another's technology infrastructures to maximize the efficiency of your business processes.

We love phrases like "leverage one another's technology infrastructures to maximize the efficiency of your business processes." They sound so cool. Translated into English, they mean, "Let one hand wash the other, increasing productivity and profits for both businesses."

Multitasking your partnerships

The auto industry spends billions of dollars developing new models of cars and finding suppliers to provide the parts for those cars. To speed up the process and reduce the cost of developing new cars, DaimlerChrysler, Ford, General Motors, Nissan, and Renault partnered with Commerce One and Oracle to create a private exchange for integrating car manufacturer and part supplier data.

Covisint (www.covisint.com), the resulting exchange, seeks to reduce the cycle time to introduce new cars, reduce the time from order to delivery of parts, integrate supply chain planning, and improve the utilization of computer technology for all partners. By working together, the partners were able to share the cost of developing the exchange. The size of the exchange and the participating manufacturers attract vendors to ensure its viability. The data exchange provides all the ingredients for saving everyone involved time and money, which is the point of data integration.

Many of your new partners may be old hands at swapping information. They may even try to convince you of how easy it is to exchange data with them, even if they have had trouble with other companies. They're lying! Don't believe anyone who says data sharing and system integration is easy. Exchanging data doesn't have to be hard, but it always requires careful planning.

Understanding and answering logistical questions

Whether you'll be receiving data or sending it, think about what your company requires. You need to resolve some basic issues with your partners:

- **Got Hieroglyphics, Version 1.0?** What format is your data currently in? If you're going to be sending that data, a big concern is what format your partners use and how hard it will be to make your data fit their format. If you're going to be receiving data, think about how difficult it will be to translate that data into something your systems can accept.

  The burning question is who's going to translate the data — your partners or your business?

- **All decked out and nowhere to go?** Actually, the where isn't the problem, the how is. How do you transfer information from one system to another? If your systems currently require you to manually crunch out data files, exchanging data will also be a manual (which means time-consuming) process unless you can automate things.

- **Can't get a camel through the eye of a needle?** How much data do you have to share, how many partners do you have to share it with, and how often? If you're talking about a whole lot of stats and bar codes, then you run the risk of overburdening your servers or other infrastructure components (not to mention your partners' servers and infrastructure). Make sure your systems are up to the task!

  The same goes for data you're getting from partners. Determine how much you plan to pull into your systems, from how many partners, and how often.

- **Will you be graded on this?** Yes. You have to verify that incoming data is complete, correct, and clean. You don't want to put bad data into your clean systems. You need to check the incoming data to make certain it is properly formatted and makes sense (for example, if 1,400 different products all have the same UPC code, something is wrong). Of course, this goes both ways — you need to make certain that the data you send out is of the same quality as the data you hope to receive. You should establish a channel (e-mail address, person to contact, and so on) that you can use to resole data issues with your partners.

Dealing with data-exchange dramas

Exchanging data never works out as easily as it should — or as easily as the brochure on the software you bought said it would be. It seems that no two businesses keeps their data in the same format as each other — we know that they must, but those two businesses never seem to want to share their data. Here are a few of the common issues that come up when businesses swap information:

✔ Some businesses might store country names as two-letter abbreviations, whereas other businesses spell out country names. Swapping data means that these businesses have to translate from one way to the other. For example, does IN stand for India or Indonesia? It's never as simple as it should be.

✔ Information might be stored in your systems in one language (for example, French), but your partners might require it to be in a different language (for example, Korean). Translation and transformation are necessary to ensure that the data is in the right form for its intended audience.

✔ Business' data may overlap. Say you're sharing catalog information (including prices, discounts, order information, and the number of items being sold to the distributor). Your product ID number for gizmos is 1234321. Your distributor already stocks gizmos, and its product ID is 4321234. So now you have two IDS — one for the manufacturer and one for the distributor.

If the manufacturer, wholesaler, distributor, and retailer all have different product numbers for the same item, you need to store four different IDs — and know when to use each. You need to work with your partners so that they can use your information and their information without anything overlapping, which is what you'll be looking for when they start feeding you orders.

How can you cope with these problems? *Data transformation* enables your tech teams to translate data between different formats. Data transformation software converts data from one form to another. Data transformation can make all countries two-letter abbreviations, convert all currency to euros, and make certain that the weights of products are expressed in kilograms. Many databases include data transformation software, and products, such as Data Junction (www.datajunction.com), can simplify the process and make it automatic and easy to monitor. Of course, you still have to tell the software what to convert and how to convert it. (What is the exchange rate between yen and euros today?)

Abracadabra! Introducing data transformation

Data transformation is a complete set of techniques and technologies in and of itself, with a full range of tools and services to help technical folks mold data to fit your systems' needs. Data transformation encompasses many tasks, including

- **Translating character data:** Data, such as country names or other abbreviations, can be made consistent across systems.

- **Mapping data fields:** Some businesses store customer names in a single data field, whereas others use separate fields, one for the first name and another for the last name.

- **Transforming numeric data:** Some systems store dollar amounts as whole numbers with an implied decimal point, so that 4499 means $44.99. Other systems include the decimal point. You need to know what you're getting in order to transform it properly.

- **Transforming date information:** Some systems use a four-digit year (or at least we hope they do after the whole Y2K thing), whereas others use a two-digit year and (we hope) a century code to cover the first two digits of the year. In the United States, 2-12-01 means February 12, 2001, but in England, it means December 2, 2001. You want to be consistent, so pick a single format and convert the data to comply with the common standard.

- **Validating information:** Not all data makes sense. If you receive a phone number that reads JOH-N S-MITH, you probably have a problem with the data you received. Data transformation can protect you from bad data by performing simple checks — as long as you program it to do so.

Transformation solutions don't solve all your problems: Transferring data

When you have your data — and your partner's data — in the right format, you have to share that data with one another. You have a few options for doing so:

- **E-mail** is a convenient way to send information, but it is difficult to automate. E-mail is best suited for trial runs or infrequent data exchanges. After all, if you try to e-mail inventory data for 2,700 products, your mail server may be overwhelmed. But e-mail is a good means of exchanging confirmations, consolidated reports, and small pieces of data.

✔ **FTP** (File Transfer Protocol) is a common way of transferring data files across the Internet. FTP exchanges can be easily automated and work with almost any computer system that uses TCP/IP (we talk about sharing data between computers in Chapter 13).

✔ **Transfers using special Web pages** are also becoming popular. For instance, you can create a Web page that asks your database server for data and returns it as XML data. The XML data can be read by other computer systems and converted easily to other formats. The data leaves your network through HTTP, the same protocol used by other Web pages, which simplifies security.

Unless special steps are taken, e-mail transfers are unencrypted. However, you can encrypt data before it is attached to the e-mail. FTP transfers are never encrypted, although the files can be encrypted using separate software before the transfer takes place. Web-page-based transfers can be protected using standard SSL encryption. Unencrypted data can be captured and read by almost anyone with simple, inexpensive computer hardware and software. Make sure that you understand the risks of transferring data across the public Internet without encrypting it. Read tips on how to keep your data safe.

Keeping Private Business Data in Safe Hands

Think about the Internet for a moment. It's accessible to the public, nobody controls it, nobody's responsible for it, and people are sending credit card numbers and other confidential information across it all the time! Isn't anyone worried?

Well sure, but some people worry about everything. A long time ago, the people who worried about protecting their private information on the Internet stopped worrying. Instead, they did something about it. They invented technologies to protect information, create secure communication channels across the Internet, and verify the identity of servers, companies, and individuals in this otherwise anonymous cyber-world.

Exchanging business data can place a heavy burden on you. Your company's data — which may include confidential data — is in someone else's hands. Keep in mind that some of your company's data is actually your customers' data, and you (and your partners) have to abide by your privacy policy and protect the data on your customers' behalf.

You have to be careful to protect confidential data from partners. You could open yourself up to legal action if data is compromised.

Use a legally binding contract to specify exactly how your company's data and your partner's data can and should be handled by one another. This contract should specify the remedies available if one partner fails to uphold his or her end of the bargain. Consult an attorney before making final decisions.

Encrypting communications

One of the most important technologies in e-commerce is *encryption.* Just like the Navaho code talkers in World War II, encryption changes data around so that bad people can't understand it if they intercept it. Only the intended recipient can *decrypt,* or unscramble the information and read it successfully.

The Internet's most popular encryption technology is the *Secure Sockets Layer,* or SSL, protocol. This protocol makes e-commerce possible by protecting customers' personal information, including credit card numbers. Web servers and Web browsers use SSL to encrypt and decrypt the information they exchange, protecting it from anyone on the Internet who manages to intercept their communications.

SSL works because anyone connecting to an SSL-enabled Web server can use it — the server doesn't need to know the customer's identity in advance, and the Web server and Web browser handle all the complicated technical tasks of encrypting and decrypting the information.

Hiding in plain site — private networks

For the very best in security, you can't beat a private connection. Short of physically splicing into your wiring (which does happen, just ask the CIA), there's not much a would-be intruder (or *hacker,* someone who breaks into computer systems for the sole purpose of wreaking all kinds of havoc) can do to access your connections.

So if you're in Cleveland, Ohio, and every day you exchange data with a business partner in Japan, you may want to consider creating a private network that links you to your partners without taking you (or the data) into the very public Internet.

You pay for private connections — one way or another. Getting them up and running can be time-consuming and difficult, and maintaining them requires constant vigilance.

The most popular form of private networks are nonpublic connections, such as the ones offered by your local phone company. These connections are carried over wires that run from your office to the provider's central station, and they're pretty much the best you can get in privacy (unless you're a major government, perhaps).

Private dial-up connections

The most common and popular form of private connections is Plain Old Telephone Service. In fact, the dial-up connection is so popular that it has an acronym: POTS. A more formal-sounding acronym you may hear is PSTN, which stands for Public Switched Telephone Network.

The big disadvantage of a phone line, of course, is that it can't carry very much data at once. The best modems out there can only manage 60 pages of text a minute. Your online product catalog could easily contain *millions* of pages of text and take hours to transfer across a phone line.

Using leased lines

The next step up from phone lines are the variety of leased lines available from phone companies and other communications providers. Leased lines consist of wires that run from your location to the provider's central station. From there, they enter the provider's main network and must be paired with a leased line of the same type going to your business partner's location. Leased lines can cost anywhere from a few hundred dollars a month to several thousand, depending on how fast the connection is and how far away your business partner is.

Leased lines have one big advantage: speed. They're faster — potentially hundreds of times faster than a phone line. Unfortunately, they have disadvantages, too:

- ✔ Leased lines — even ones using frame relay — cost a lot more than a phone line.

- ✔ Leased lines can go to only one location, unlike phone lines, which can connect to as many business partners as you want.

- ✔ Leased lines require special equipment to operate, which you must rent or purchase from your provider.

- ✔ Leased lines are generally harder to set up and maintain than regular phone lines.

One step beyond: Virtual private networks

Keep in mind that your business probably already has one leased line in place: the one connecting you to your Internet service provider (ISP) and the Internet. Virtual private network (VPN) technologies enable you to connect to other business partners, using your Internet connection (and theirs) as if it were a private link between you.

Finding high-tech alternatives to old-fashioned private networking solutions

Although phone lines and leased lines have handled almost all of the world's business communications for many years, new alternatives are becoming available that promise to make business communications faster, more flexible, and less expensive. These include

✔ **Cellular technologies.** Based on the same technology that runs your mobile phone, the speed and cost of these connections gets better every day. Cellular connections have the advantage of being very mobile.

✔ **Satellite technologies.** Satellite communications are becoming less expensive and faster every day. Although most installations require a fixed location, some new satellite technologies allow mobile connections as well.

✔ **Wireless technologies.** Primarily useful only for short-range applications, wireless technologies — including microwave — can allow you to establish private connections with businesses in your immediate area.

Of course, many of these technologies are still being developed, so they can be expensive and are difficult to set up and maintain. But as these technologies mature, they will offer new options for creating private business connections without turning to the traditional vendors: phone companies and telecommunications providers.

The idea is simple. Both you and your business partner install VPN software. When you communicate, the software encrypts the data. It's a lot like SSL (see "Encrypting communications," earlier in this chapter), but the encryption is harder to crack. If someone captures a copy of your data packets, that person will have a very tough time breaking your code and reading the data.

VPNs require that the user's identity be known in advance. (Usually, part of creating the VPN connection involves entering a user name and password.)

If you're dying to find out more about VPNs, check out *Virtual Private Networks For Dummies* by Mark S. Merkow (Hungry Minds, Inc.).

PPTP: Fast, easy, and mostly secure

The Point-to-Point Tunneling Protocol, or PPTP, was developed by Microsoft as one of the first VPN solutions available to users of the Windows operating system. PPTP is supported by all recent releases of Windows and offers some great features:

✔ PPTP is easy to set up and requires almost no other computer software, servers, or other components to operate.

✔ PPTP uses industry-standard encryption, making it extremely difficult to decrypt (without the decryption key, of course).

If you're using a version of Windows earlier than Windows 2000, PPTP may be the only built-in VPN protocol available to you.

PPTP has one disadvantage. Rather than encrypting all of the information passed across the Internet, the protocol encrypts only the *payload,* or the data you are passing to your partner. This encrypted payload is surrounded by unencrypted data that defines the information as having been encrypted using PPTP. Although this doesn't actually make your data more vulnerable, it does give potential hackers a starting point for cracking the payload data.

L2TP: Super-secure, super-compatible, super-complicated

L2TP, the Layer 2 Tunneling Protocol, offers two major improvements over PPTP. Of course, both of these advantages are offset by accompanying disadvantages.

L2TP VPNs are completely encrypted. Only enough information is left unencrypted to get data across the Internet. Unlike PPTP, in L2TP, there's no way for hackers to know if a packet is being transferred at any given time. Because hackers don't even know what protocol was used to encrypt the data, let alone what the decryption key is, they'll have a harder time breaking into the payload.

The result of L2TP's ability to completely encrypt all data is that L2TP tunnels cannot be created through firewalls that perform *Network Address Translation* (NAT) (a protocol some companies and many ISPs use to conserve TCP/IP addresses on the Internet). Because tunnels can't pass through some firewalls, you may find complications in your VPN connection if your ISP uses a firewall that performs Network Address Translation.

L2TP: A hacker's nightmare

L2TP is an authentication god. By default, L2TP tunnels are created using certificates. Not only does this make their encryption capabilities a bit more robust than PPTP's, it also helps ensure that the computers and users involved in the VPN are, in fact, who they say they are. Certificates add a layer of complexity, though, and you will have to maintain a certificate server (or use a commercial certificate authority) to obtain the necessary digital certificates.

L2TP tunnels can be created without certificates, using *shared secrets*, which are essentially really long passwords. This pretty much eliminates the advantages of certificates, of course, and brings L2TP one step closer to PPTP in terms of features.

L2TP was created by several major Internet companies, whereas PPTP was created by Microsoft (and subsequently submitted as a public standard). This means that just about everybody supports L2TP (including Microsoft, as of Windows 2000 and later), but PPTP is primarily available in Microsoft products.

Halt! Who goes there?: Authentication and extranets

The best way to protect data is to limit who has access to it. That means keeping data off servers that are accessible from the public Internet.

You can use a variety of authentication mechanisms in your business. Choose the ones that make the most sense and provide the best security for each particular application.

You can ensure that data is only accessible to authorized personnel by using authentication services and extranet technology, both of which can be used together for maximum flexibility in sharing data, with maximum protection for that data:

✔ **Authentication:** This is the process of verifying someone's identity electronically. You can use a variety of different authentication mechanisms, some of which can be used on your internal network to ensure that employees are authorized to access information. Most authentication programs can also be used on an extranet to ensure that business partners logging in to exchange information are legitimate. Some of the most common authentication mechanisms include

• **User names and passwords:** User names and passwords — the oldest forms of authentication — can be easily compromised and intercepted as they are transmitted across a network; user names and password are also very easy to forget. You can improve the odds of safe transfer by ensuring that passwords are long and difficult to guess and by frequently changing passwords.

• **Digital certificates:** A digital certificate is an elaborate code number used to encrypt and decrypt data. You can use digital certificates to create a signature (a special ID number that guarantees the identity of the computer that sends the message) or to encrypt network traffic.

Digital certificates are unique numbers built from the components on users' computers. The system uses a special mathematical formula to convert the numbers from the components in computers to a special code. Your business can use Microsoft's Certificate services to create digital certificates on Microsoft Windows 2000 computers.

- If you use SSL or other public encryption technologies, you may need to have a certificate created and installed. But if your business uses certificates publicly, you should register the certificate with a public certificate authority, such as VeriSign (www.verisign.com). Public certificates allow Internet users to verify their certificates so that they are even more difficult to counterfeit.

- **Smart cards:** These physical devices contain a digital certificate, which cannot easily be stolen. Smart card users identify themselves by providing something they know (a personal identification number, or PIN) and something they have (a card), making it virtually impossible for others to pretend to be them. Users just plug the smart card into their computer, and the computer knows who they are (or at least who the card is).

- **Biometric authentication:** New methods of authentication, including retinal scans and fingerprint scans, are becoming more popular everyday. These mechanisms promise to offer the best authentication ever, because they are based on unchanging physical characteristics, rather than knowledge or possession of a physical key. Although they aren't currently popular for e-commerce, their popularity may change in the future.

✔ **Extranets:** An *extranet* is a TCP/IP-based network that can be accessed from the Internet — but only by authorized individuals or organizations. Extranets provide a safe zone on the Internet where you and your business partners can exchange data without fear of the data being compromised. Here are some tips to remember when building an extranet:

- Although the extranet may be private, it is reached by crossing the public Internet, which means that data can be intercepted while moving between computers and compromised. Ensure that any data transmitted to or from the extranet is encrypted, preferably by using a virtual private network (see "One step beyond: Virtual private networks," earlier in this chapter).

- Ensure that the extranet is accessible only to authorized individuals. Use strong authentication mechanisms, such as smart cards or digital certificates, to ensure visitors are who they say they are.

- If you allow visitors to access your extranet with a user name and password, make sure you encrypt that information, either by using SSL or a virtual private network.

- Because many different partners may log in to your extranet, make sure the extranet is programmed to allow them to access only the data they need — partners should not be able to access data intended for other partners.

Building a secure extranet enables you to leverage the flexibility of the Internet, while still providing a safe, secure place to share information with partners.

Protecting your company's data

Here are some tips for protecting your company's data:

- ✔ Don't share any data unless it's absolutely necessary. Examine what your data partner plans to do with the data, and give your partner the minimum amount necessary to do it.

- ✔ Always encrypt your data when it's being transmitted across the public Internet.

- ✔ Change your passwords on a regular, mandatory basis. Set minimum lengths of passwords (eight characters or more) and make users mix letters and numbers. Don't let users use the same password again for at least six months. This policy slows down hackers and keeps disgruntled employees from slipping back into the system when you aren't looking.

- ✔ Audit your data partners to make sure they're treating your data with respect. Ask to see the systems they use to store your data and have someone on your technical staff talk to their staff to find out how they secure your data against theft or compromise. Spell this out in your contracts with partners.

Most of these tips are procedural — the safety of the data you give your partner is in your partner's hands. Choose your partners carefully and make sure they understand and agree to the terms of your data-sharing contract.

Protecting your partners' data

Your technical staff also has to take steps to protect your partner's data while it's in your hands:

- ✔ Make sure your partner encrypts everything sent across the Internet, either by using a virtual private network or a third-party encryption utility.

- ✔ Make sure received data is promptly processed and placed into your database (or other appropriate) system. The original files should either be deleted or stored offline, such as on a CD-ROM or backup tape. Offline backups enable you to retrieve the data if necessary but make it difficult for electronic intruders to do so.

- ✔ Make sure your partner's data is protected by the same security as your own: firewalls, difficult-to-guess passwords that change frequently, and so forth. No copy of the data should be easily accessible from the Internet or other outside networks after you receive it.

Invite your partners to audit your systems to verify their security. After all, you'll expect them to extend you the same courtesy.

Part V
The Part of Tens

The 5th Wave   By Rich Tennant

SCREEEEEK

"Is this really the best use of Flash 5 animation on our e-commerce Web site? A bad wheel on the shopping cart icon that squeaks, wobbles, and pulls to the left?"

In this part . . .

But wait, there's more! This part is our opportunity to summarize the most important things we discuss throughout the book, including strategies and techniques. It's also a chance for us to quickly put to rest some nasty e-commerce rumors that have been floating around and to keep you from falling into the traps of those myths and lies.

Chapter 21

Ten Winning
E-Commerce Strategies

*W*hen it gets right down to it, what you really want to know is how you can make sure your business succeeds at e-commerce. We'll be the first to admit that getting the e-commerce end of your business off the ground isn't a walk in the park, but it's also not as difficult as you may think — as long as you're using your head. You and the other key players in your business need to be cunning, occasionally ruthless, and well-read. That's why the best strategy is to start memorizing *E-Commerce For Dummies* — and, of course, reading the following ten tips.

Do E-Commerce Like You Mean to Succeed

The news is full of dot-com horror stories, and tech companies are crashing left and right. What the news doesn't cover is the *real reason* why those guys are going out of business. Would you consider throwing a two-million-dollar office party if *your* company hadn't even turned a profit yet? All too many dot coms have done just that, presumably because they weren't taking their businesses as seriously as they could have. Or they were focusing on the wrong aspects of their businesses. Whatever you plan to do with e-commerce, plan it like a business. Make sure

- ✔ That you're convinced that every decision you make is the right one, and make sure that you can explain to yourself why you think you're doing the right thing
- ✔ That you believe in your business plan
- ✔ That your partners and employees are behind you
- ✔ That you stick to your plan and manage it to success

Test for Success

Internet customers are fickle critters. If they get a glimpse of your site before it's totally ready for prime time, they may decide that you don't know what you're doing and never come back. Don't put new pages, new features, new navigation tools — new *anything* — live on your site until you've tested it again and again. Test it yourself and get your mom and your sister to test it. You'll still find problems, of course, when the general public gets its hands on it, but hopefully those problems will be few and far between.

QA can help you get the testing process right (see Chapter 6 for the lowdown on QA). QA should also perform *regression tests* that make certain that the entire site works after you make changes, not just the parts you changed. That process protects you from unexpected side effects from site changes.

Hook 'em

Did you ever wonder how those little boutiques in shopping malls stay in business? Usually, people don't go to the mall just to pick up a new pair of hoop earrings from the accessories shop, or a single magazine from the bookstore. And yet the majority of a mall's square footage is devoted to these tiny stores. How do they attract enough customers to stay in business?

The answer, of course, is they benefit from the traffic that the mall's anchor stores generate. Those stores — mega department stores like Sears and Macy's — are why people go to the mall, and most of the rest of the mall's stores are just along for the ride.

So why does an e-commerce businessperson care? Because no anchor store is generating traffic for you on the Internet (unless you are in an e-marketplace, as described in Chapter 19). If you want your e-commerce business to become a success, your site has to become a *destination,* a virtual place where people come for specific reasons. You have to hook your customers; give them reasons to keep coming back to your site over and over.

Use advertising, loyalty programs, value-added material (such as an online magazine), and other tricks to reel 'em in and keep 'em. If you come up with a strong value proposition and flaunt it with your marketing, you will attract and retain customers.

Making Your Business a Household Name

Businesses need a lot of care and feeding when they're young, and e-commerce businesses are no exception (even new e-commerce ventures created by 100-year old companies). You need to build an engaging site that customers want to shop at again and again. Most importantly, you need to build a name that customers recognize. Only a handful of Internet companies — such as Yahoo!, Amazon.com, Buy.com, and AOL — have managed to build name recognition.

To build a name, you have to create a strategic marketing plan, which means you have to spend money. But a marketing plan doesn't mean a whole lot if you put yourself out of business in the process of creating it.

It's pretty easy to spend a little dough here and a little dinero there until suddenly the business' books look like the national debt. Make sure you're getting value for every dollar you spend, and if you're in doubt, hire a good marketing firm to help you.

Be Careful — People May Like You!

The most common tale of the e-commerce industry is the story about a small, bright group of people who put together a winning business plan. They build an e-commerce site and go live. The site gets featured on *Oprah,* and the next day, 50 trillion people access the site. The site crashes in a ball of flame, and no one hears from that small, bright group of people again.

Make sure that you build your business — and that's the *whole* business, not just your Web site — to handle your success. Not only do you need to buy servers and software, but you also may need to develop your shipping department, your accounting systems, and your order processes.

We recommend that you work in phases. Plan to reach the moon, but only implement what you can handle. Here are some tips to help you grow incrementally:

- Lease and don't buy until you can afford it.

- Use e-service providers' inventory and Internet services until you can build your own.

- Promise only what you can deliver and deliver everything you promise.

- Buy what you can now and build the business so that you can easily add more to it later. And be prepared to add it quickly.

- Make sure that your distributors and other business partners know how successful you plan to be, and make sure that their businesses can handle the load you plan to dump on them.

Calculate Internet Time

Get used to thinking in Internet time. If something goes wrong, calculate how much time you think it will take to fix it. Okay, now divide that number by five to see how much *Internet time* you have. Because things can change so rapidly on the Internet, you need to keep ahead of the curve in a wide variety of areas:

- Keep ahead of what your competitors are doing and how they use the Internet to challenge your market position.

- Stay on top of new technologies that can help your Web site work more effectively or that can give your organization a market edge.

- Continuously look for new areas of process improvement and ways to use your Internet investment to lower costs and increase profits (for example, read Chapter 17 for more on e-procurement).

- Watch for emerging standards that can help you connect to and cooperate with new customers or improve relationships with existing customers in your supply chain (we discuss the supply chain in Chapter 16).

- Keep the site fresh and interesting so customers keep coming back (get some clues on how to do this in Chapter 9).

Sometimes the Numbers Lie

Most e-commerce businesspeople check in on their business' growth and health by relying on site statistics. Your Web server logs compile these numbers and tell you interesting tidbits, such as how many visitors came to your site today. The problem with these site statistics is that they are unreliable.

Internet technologies contain inherent problems that make tracking data, such as the number of visitors to your site, difficult. Programs from companies like WebTrends (www.webtrends.com) gather site statistics and use mathematical stuff to turn hard-and-fast numbers (such as the number of page views) into the kind of information that managers like to see (the number of *people* who visited the site). You can customize almost all the available Web utilization applications to work according to the different rules and assumptions that best suit your needs.

Rely on traditional business indicators, such as the number of sales you're making, the dollar value of each sale, the number of returns you process, and so forth. These numbers tell you how your business is *really* doing.

Get to Know Your Neighbors (And Their Neighbors, Too)

Your neighbors, of course, are the other businesses in the supply chain. You buy your stuff from somebody, who buys the stuff from somebody else, and so on, and so on. It's not enough to just check with your distributor to make sure that he can ship fast enough to keep you supplied with enough products to meet your anticipated sales volume. You should find out about the company he buys from, too. Can his supplier meet your demands? What about the supplier's supplier? And the manufacturer?

Here are some simple indicators:

- ✔ Look at lead times. If things are stretching out, a reason exists, and you need to know what it is.

- ✔ If prices plummet, find out why. No one has a fire sale without a fire.

- ✔ If one of your partners is missing scheduled deliveries, or if its customers are looking for new vendors, you found smoke. Ask for references from several existing customers and discover if they are satisfied customers.

- ✔ Find out how long partners' employees have been with the company, especially senior management. Unstable workforces usually translate into unstable businesses.

Bend Over Backward for Your Employees

One of the biggest challenges facing e-commerce businesses today is the alarming lack of skilled technical labor available. E-commerce is definitely a labor-intensive business. After all, the Web site, the system configurations, the software, and the Internet connectivity are all the fruits of some technical professionals' labor. Finding skilled people who can pull off miracles with computers is tough — and trust us, *keeping* those folks (and keeping them happy) is even harder.

Here are some tips:

- ✔ Get creative in your hiring policies.
- ✔ Offer relocation packages and signing bonuses.
- ✔ Cut your employees in on the action by offering stock options.

Make sure you have *retention* policies, too, because the real battle — keeping employees — begins after you've hired them. Offer flex time, telecommuting, casual dress, free sodas, and any other little perks you can. These perks may cost you and may challenge your dearly-held views on managing employees, but those employees *are* your business.

Use the Internet to Save Money, Too

At its heart, e-commerce is about using the Internet to make money. But don't forget about the ways e-commerce technologies can save your business cash, too. After all, saving money is almost the same thing as actually earning it. Here are some ideas to make the Internet work for your *whole* business:

- ✔ Use Internet-based e-mail systems, such as Yahoo! or Hotmail, to reduce or eliminate the need to maintain your own e-mail system.
- ✔ Reduce travel costs with videoconferencing.
- ✔ Reduce HR costs by replacing paper forms with HTML forms that talk right to your databases.
- ✔ Get into B2B (business-to-business) e-commerce to procure business supplies.
- ✔ Use online auctions to purchase office furniture for lots less than retail.

Chapter 22

Ten E-Commerce Myths Revealed

With all the excitement about e-commerce floating around the news and the Internet, it's easy to think that e-commerce enables you to do anything. But before you start reorganizing your company to focus totally on e-commerce, read through these ten helpful reality checks to make sure that you have your feet firmly on the ground.

If You Build It, They Will Come

A pervasive myth is floating around that you just have to throw your Web site up, buy a few banner ads, and watch the world beat an electronic path to your virtual door. This myth may have rung true during e-commerce's earliest days, when so few online businesses were around that competition was nonexistent and customers flocked instantly to the new kid on the block. Nowadays, that isn't the way things work — and even if it were, that just makes your business a fad (for awhile).

In the modern e-commerce world, you have to drag customers kicking and screaming to your site, just like you have to drag them into your bricks-and-mortar business. And you have the same tools to do the dragging with: advertising, marketing, incentives, and other promotions.

The First Company to Sell a Product Online Wins

Even in the early days of the Internet, beating out the competition to get the new improved superwidget out of the warehouse and into customers' hot little hands never meant automatic success. This just isn't reality (even though it seemed to be). Many of the earliest companies to sell products on the Internet are no longer the big businesses on the block. Many of them aren't even in business any more.

Just because another business is online selling the same product or service you sell doesn't mean there's no room for your business to play. Likewise, if you're the first in your industry to make it online, your seniority alone won't guarantee you squat.

Selling Online Is Inexpensive

If it really were cheap to sell online, it wouldn't take most Web initiatives more than two years to turn any kind of a profit. Selling online certainly *can* be more economical than selling in the real world — in the long run.

If you're smart you'll spend the money you save on renting and leasing bricks-and-mortar properties on advertising and marketing, shipping expenses — and you'll spend more in these areas than you ever did before.

Skimping on Web design, scalable backbone technology, and finding the best people in the business to do the work can certainly make online business cheap, but at the same time it makes it . . . well, *cheap*.

If You Have a Web Site — Poof, You've Gone International

Many corporate types think that the worldwide reach of the Web means that simply having a Web site — which is, of course, accessible from across the globe — makes that business an international concern.

Hardly! There's a lot more to doing business across the border than just being accessible to international customers. First, there's the fact that you can be available until you're blue in the face, but none of that matters if global customers don't know about your business. The answer here is a global marketing strategy, of course:

> ✔ **Be prepared for the language differences you'll face.** You may need customer support representatives to be able to answer calls in Spanish, French, Russian, Chinese, and Klingon. (Hey, we didn't make the rules — it just so happens that *Star Trek* is known around the world.)

Make sure your site uses colors, symbols, and languages that are internationally understood.

✔ **Be equipped to do business in any of the dozen or so popular currencies of the world.** You can demand payment in your local currency (and lose some sales), demand payment in credit cards that handle currency conversions (and lose some sales), or work out a deal with your bank to handle foreign currencies (and lose some sleep as the currency markets fluctuate).

✔ **Know your legalese.** If you don't understand (or have someone in the organization who understands) the complex legal issues surrounding importing and exporting, you're in for a heap of trouble.

Who Needs Profits? We're Winning

How many dot-com companies have crashed since the big stock market correction in mid-2000? We've certainly lost count. Sure, some of those dot bombs just didn't have a good business model, but some of them went out of business at the height of their popularity.

As you put your e-commerce business plan together, launch your site, and begin building a successful online presence, never lose sight of one simple fact: No matter how great the public thinks you are, it's the bottom line that makes you a success. Only numbers in black count, so you don't win brownie points for pleasing your customers but not making any money at it. You're doing something wrong, and you need to fix it.

On the Internet, Being Like Everyone Else Can't Hurt You

Although fewer business are making this mistake now that the Internet economy is beginning to mature, it's still tempting to take a look at what your competitors are doing and copy them. Big mistake! That trick rarely works in the traditional business world, and in the rare cases that it does, it works only when geography separates you and your competition. On the Internet, what incentive does a customer have to do business with you if you look, act, feel, and respond just like your competition? You need a compelling value proposition that makes customers come to you on purpose and return because they like the way you do business.

You have to go out of your way to make sure that your online business is unique and distinctive, and that all your customers know it. Don't let your competition catch up. Add customer convenience features, unique products, distinctive customer support, and patented technologies — whatever it takes to win the loyalty of your customers.

Protect your creative innovations, intellectual property, and brand identification. Register trademarks, service marks, patents, and copyrights whenever appropriate to protect your distinctive business.

You're Losing Valuable Time! Hurry Up and Get on the Web!

Are you in a panic state because your business isn't online yet? Take a deep breath and relax a little. Unless you sell software or other technology, you're not going to go out of business just because you're not online. (There are probably a bunch of other factors affecting your bottom line that you don't need us to nag you about.) And just because you're not online first doesn't mean you can't be successful when you finally get there. If you don't believe us, read the other myths we dispel in this chapter.

The truth is that rushing to get online can do much more damage than waiting until you have your ducks in a row. Many businesses have spent hundreds of thousands of dollars to develop e-initiatives that they eventually threw away. (Of course, they didn't have this book to guide them.)

Do you need to be aggressive in getting your business online? Probably. The Internet can certainly help you grow your business, and it can help you level the playing field between you and your competitors (especially if they're already online). But do you need to rush to the Internet just to get your foot in the door? Nah, take your time and do it right.

Who Needs Salaries When You're Offering Stock Options?

We can't remember how many employers we've talked to who think they can offer valuable, highly-skilled technical employees a pittance salary and make up the difference with generous stock options. Stock options are a great part of an overall compensation package, and they can certainly enable you to offer *somewhat* smaller salaries, if your stock is performing well or at least looks promising. But many of the most skilled Internet gurus have already made and lost paper fortunes with stock options. Once burned, twice careful. If you want the best people, you need to be prepared to pay them.

Stock options? Not unless you're doing *really* well

Microsoft certainly uses the approach of paying salaries that are notably (and notoriously) lower than national averages while compensating with what was — until mid-2000 — phenomenal stock options. And even so, as Microsoft stock fell below $50 per share and started the slow climb back up, Microsoft began suffering a brain drain as skilled technical professionals left for greener — and better paying — pastures.

Quick action by Microsoft execs in early 2001 resulted in salary increases across the company to attempt to stem the tide. Microsoft capitalized on its unparalleled success. Can you compete with Microsoft's reputation? If Microsoft can't buy top-notch talent with its stock option promises, you need to ask yourself how alluring your offering would be.

Offer your technical employees a fair, competitive compensation package. But don't offer a package you wouldn't take if you were a candidate for the position.

Bricks-and-Mortar Business Is Dead

The so-called old way of doing business is still very much alive and kicking. Although it doesn't get nearly the media coverage that e-commerce does, traditional businesses still make up the majority of the United States' commerce, not to mention the world's.

Before you give the ten count on bricks-and-mortar business, think about the purchases that you make every day. In the last week, you probably walked, wheeled, or hopped into a store, thumped a cantaloupe to see if it was ripe, tried on that *fabulous* new shirt, or talked to a salesperson about the warranty package that comes with some big ticket item you have your eye on. Although you could buy your next car, your groceries, food for the dog, the kids' school clothes, or a new VCR online, the fact is that you (and millions of other people) probably won't.

Consumers still purchase most commodities in stores because they like to touch and feel things before they buy them, to ask questions of a real live person, and to carry their products home immediately so that they can start using them. Online shopping invariably means total self-service, paying shipping charges, and waiting for packages to arrive (we show you how to get around these hurdles to building a Web storefront in Chapter 9). Although more and more consumers research their purchases online before buying, there will probably always be a place for bricks-and-mortar business, simply because we humans like it better sometimes.

Appearance Is Everything

Hey, as long as your Web site looks really slick, you're in business, right? Not exactly. Although a professional-looking online presence definitely makes customers more likely to do business with you, customers still want the same things they've *always* wanted: good service, good products, good prices, and fulfillment of the promises you make.

Spend the time and money to make your Web site look as good and work as well as it can. And then spend the necessary time and money to make sure that the business behind that site can fulfill your customers' needs and expectations. It's the *package* of good looks, good technology, and good business practices that keeps customers coming back for more.

Index

• *C* •

Notes

Notes

Notes

Take the Risk out of Your Decision Making

We have the insight you need to ground your business decisions in reality and send your market share soaring.

Being well-informed is the best way to ensure your decisions are sound. IDC, the world's leading global market intelligence and advisory firm, has all the information you need to take the risk out of your technology and ebusiness decision making. Our 700+ industry-leading analysts are scattered throughout 43 countries worldwide and cover a broad range of topics from PCs, printers, and storage to xSPs, emarketing, and erecruiting. We have the insight you need to ground your business decisions in reality and send your market share soaring.

Find out more at www.idc.com.

While you're there, register for our free online newsletter, **eBusiness Trends.**

IDC
Analyze the Future

5 Speen Street
Framingham, MA 01701

FOR DUMMIES
BOOK REGISTRATION

Register This Book and Win!

We want to hear from you!

Visit **dummies.com** to register this book and tell us how you liked it!

- Get entered in our monthly prize giveaway.

- Give us feedback about this book — tell us what you like best, what you like least, or maybe what you'd like to ask the author and us to change!

- Let us know any other *For Dummies* topics that interest you.

Your feedback helps us determine what books to publish, tells us what coverage to add as we revise our books, and lets us know whether we're meeting your needs as a *For Dummies* reader. You're our most valuable resource, and what you have to say is important to us!

Not on the Web yet? It's easy to get started with *Dummies 101: The Internet For Windows 98* or *The Internet For Dummies* at local retailers everywhere.

Or let us know what you think by sending us a letter at the following address:

For Dummies Book Registration
Dummies Press
10475 Crosspoint Blvd.
Indianapolis, IN 46256

FOR DUMMIES™
BESTSELLING BOOK SERIES